Disasters and Politics:
Materials, Experiments, Preparedness

The Sociological Review Monographs

Since 1958, *The Sociological Review* has established a tradition of publishing one or two Monographs a year on issues of general sociological interest. The Monograph is an edited book length collection of refereed research papers which is published and distributed in association with Wiley Blackwell. We are keen to receive innovative collections of work in sociology and related disciplines with a particular emphasis on exploring empirical materials and theoretical frameworks which are currently under-developed.

If you wish to discuss ideas for a Monograph then please contact the Monographs Editor, Chris Shilling, School of Social Policy, Sociology and Social Research, Cornwallis North East, University of Kent, Canterbury, Kent CT2 7NF, C.Shilling@kent.ac.uk

Our latest Monographs include:

Sociologies of Moderation: problems of democracy, expertise and the media (edited by Alexander Smith and John Holmwood)
Urban Rhythms: Mobilities, Space and Interation in the Contemporary City (edited by Robin James Smith and Kevin Hetherington)
Waste Matters (edited by David Evans, Hugh Campbell and Anne Murcott)
Live Methods (edited by Les Back and Nirmal Puwar)
Measure and Value (edited by Lisa Adkins and Celia Lury)
Norbert Elias and Figurational Research: Processual Thinking in Sociology (edited by Norman Gabriel and Stephen Mennell)
Sociological Routes and Political Roots (edited by Michaela Benson and Rolland Munro)
Nature, Society and Environmental Crisis (edited by Bob Carter and Nickie Charles)
Space Travel & Culture: From Apollo to Space Tourism (edited by David Bell and Martin Parker)
Un/Knowing Bodies (edited by Joanna Latimer and Michael Schillmeier)
Remembering Elites (edited by Mike Savage and Karel Williams)
Market Devices (edited by Michel Callon, Yuval Millo and Fabian Muniesa)
Embodying Sociology: Retrospect, Progress and Prospects (edited by Chris Shilling)
Sports Mega-Events: Social Scientific Analyses of a Global Phenomenon (edited by John Horne and Wolfram Manzenreiter)
Against Automobility (edited by Steffen Böhm, Campbell Jones, Chris Land and Matthew Paterson)
A New Sociology of Work (edited by Lynne Pettinger, Jane Parry, Rebecca Taylor and Miriam Glucksmann)

Other Monographs have been published on consumption; museums; culture and computing; death; gender and bureaucracy; sport plus many other areas. For further information about the Monograph Series, please visit: www .sociologicalreviewmonographs.com

Disasters and Politics:
Materials, Experiments, Preparedness

Edited by Manuel Tironi, Israel Rodríguez-Giralt and Michael Guggenheim

Wiley Blackwell/The Sociological Review

This edition first published 2014
© 2014 The Editorial Board of the Sociological Review
Chapters © 2014 by the chapter author

ISBN 9781118531396 and The Sociological Review, 62:S1.

All articles published within this monograph are included within
the ISI Journal Citation Reports® Social Science Citation Index.
Please quote the article DOI when citing monograph content.

Registered Office
John Wiley & Sons Ltd, The Atrium, Southern Gate, Chichester, West Sussex, PO19 8SQ, UK

Editorial Offices
350 Main Street, Malden, MA 02148-5020, USA
9600 Garsington Road, Oxford, OX4 2DQ, UK
The Atrium, Southern Gate, Chichester, West Sussex, PO19 8SQ, UK

For details of our global editorial offices, for customer services, and for information about how
to apply for permission to reuse the copyright material in this book please see our website at
www.wiley.com/wiley-blackwell.

First published in 2014 by John Wiley & Sons

Library of Congress Cataloging-in-Publication Data is available for this book

A catalogue record for this title is available from the British Library

Set in TimesNRMT 10/12pt by Toppan Best-set Premedia Limited

Printed and bound in the United Kingdom

1   2014

Contents

Section 3: Preparedness: Anticipation

Acknowledgements

As with any project, this book has a history. Its origins can be traced to a grant proposal that the three editors, together with Mike Michael, put together in March of 2011. The proposal was unsuccessful, but it incubated what became an open panel chaired by Israel Rodríguez-Giralt and Manuel Tironi in the annual conference of the Society for Social Studies of Science held in Cleveland in November 2011 ('The Politics of Uncertainty: Disasters and STS'). The call for papers was a tremendous success. We received more than 15 abstracts and the organization gave us three session slots in which 12 papers were presented. We want to thank all the participants for their contribution to the debate around which the idea of putting together a book sparkled. In fact, the backbone of this volume comes from that panel: Ryan Ellis's, Rodríguez-Giralt et al.'s, Manuel Tironi's, Deville et al.'s and Katrina Petersen's papers were presented and debated in Cleveland.

When the project of editing a book took shape, and the possibility of submitting a proposal to *The Sociological Review*'s Monograph Series was on the horizon, we invited people working at the intersection between disasters and politics. We also thank Nigel Clark, Ignacio Farías, Lucy Easthope, Maggie Mort and Gisa Weszkalnys, for joining this project and contributing with extraordinary papers.

We are also grateful for the participants of the open panel 'Disasters: redesigning collective orders', organized by Zuzana Hrdličková, Manuel Tironi and Israel Rodríguez-Giralt at the Society for Social Studies of Science and European Association for the Study of Science and Technology joint conference held at the Copenhagen Business School in October 2012. Apart from confirming an increasing interest in disasters, the sessions also provided an excellent opportunity to discuss earlier versions of the work presented in this edited volume.

Two additional elements of the book's genealogy have to be accounted for. First, in November 2012 Manuel Tironi organized the seminar 'Disasters, catastrophes, calamities: radical controversies and democratic theory' at Universidad Católica de Chile. Although peripheral to the book (Israel Rodríguez-Giralt was the only contributor attending the seminar) the event confirmed a sense of momentum for the study of disasters from the perspective of Science and Technology Studies. And secondly, Goldsmiths College's CSISP, the Centre for the Study of Innovation and Social Process, has been, unwittingly and almost ghostly, the *place* of the book. Michael Guggenheim is senior lecturer at Goldsmiths and both Israel Rodríguez-Giralt and Manuel Tironi visited CSISP, although separately, during the making of the volume. Somehow then, the book was seasoned, stirred and cooked in the upper floors of the Warmington Tower in South London.

Series editor's note

The Sociological Review Monograph series publishes special supplements of the journal in collections of original refereed papers that are included within the ISI Journal Citation Reports and the Social Science Citation Index.

In existence for over fifty years, the series has developed a reputation for publishing innovative projects that reflect the work of senior but also emerging academic figures from around the globe.

These collections could not continue without the considerable goodwill, advice and guidance of members of the Board of *The Sociological Review*, and of those anonymous referees who assess and report on the papers submitted for consideration for these collections. I would like to thank all of those involved in this process, especially Linsey J. McGoey for her very considerable input into the collection as a whole, all of the referees, and also the editors of *Disasters and Politics* for having produced such an interesting and timely volume.

Chris Shilling, SSPSSR, University of Kent, UK.

Introduction: disasters as politics – politics as disasters

Michael Guggenheim

Sociology discovers disasters

Suddenly, disasters are everywhere. The social sciences have recently increased their output in disaster writing massively. The world is one big disaster. Crisis looms. The end is near. One way to diagnose this state is by pointing to an actual increase in disasters. This could be called a naturalization of the problem. Another diagnosis is to point to a general catastrophic cultural mood, a Zeitgeist, what we could call a culturalization.

The first diagnosis, naturalization, is problematic for two reasons: disaster statistics tell a complex story: roughly speaking, throughout the twentieth century, the number of people killed by disasters has decreased, while the number of disasters and the damages reported has increased.[1] In short, society protects people better, but disasters have become more frequent because people build and live in increasingly disaster prone areas. Moreover, sociologically speaking, discourses need not be in sync with events, as every student of anti-Semitism or racism knows. Just because there are more disasters, there need not be more attention to them. Conversely, an increase in perceiving disasters does not necessarily mean that there are more disasters. There can be other reasons, as the forecasting of the now-forgotten 'millennium bug' showed.

The second, the general Zeitgeist argument may be true, but it is unlikely: Why should it hold for many societies on very different paths? Why would we assume its continuity, after the end time scare of the millennium bug faded? Also, a preliminary bibliographical analysis with Google Ngram (Figure 1) shows that the general thematizing of disasters did not really increase, while the sociology of disasters increased remarkably since the mid-1990s.[2] The question then is: Why can we observe such an increase in dealing with disasters in sociology and its neighbouring fields, an increase that is way out of proportion compared to the general increase in disaster literature and the actual amount of disasters?

I will thus attempt a third answer, which we could call politicization, much more pertinent to this volume. The answer proposed here is that disasters emerge because our theoretical apparatus makes us more sensitive to them. They allow social science to test various theories and interests that have come to the

The Sociological Review, 62:S1, pp. 1–16 (2014), DOI: 10.1111/1467-954X.12121
© 2014 The Author. Editorial organisation © 2014 The Editorial Board of the Sociological Review. Published by John Wiley & Sons Ltd, 9600 Garsington Road, Oxford OX4 2DQ, UK and 350 Main Street, Malden, MA 02148, USA

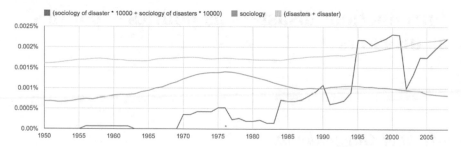

Figure 1: *Google Ngram of books containing the words sociology of disaster, sociology, disaster (relative total amount of books).*

fore in the last ten or twenty years. This third answer does not necessarily contradict the other two. It sits beside them. This volume contributes to a further calibration of our conceptions of disasters, focusing on how accounts of disasters are produced and the effects they have in the world. This calibration of disasters also allows us to move the sociology of disasters from the applied margins of the discipline, as an ancillary science to the practical concerns of disaster management, to the central concerns of general sociology (Tierney, 2007).

The problem of both naturalization and culturalization is that they both conceptualize disasters without recourse to politics. In both options, disasters increase, or discourses increase, but how this relates to politics remains unclear. In contrast, the various articles in this volume attempt to understand disasters as politics, and politics as disasters. In short, they analyse both the notion of disaster and the notion of politics.

Two movements to conceptualize disasters

This new relationship between politics and disasters can be understood by combining two important movements within the social sciences. The first relates to an interest in breaks and ruptures, rather than continuity and structure. This is closely linked to an attendant idea of politics as problematization of the composition of the world. Disasters as ruptures produce new compositions of the world and they are the former's explication. The second movement relates to an interest in reconceptualizing nature or the non-human as actors. Disasters, like accidents, are, sociologically speaking, the result of the combination of these two: they radically question the composition of the world, in all its technical, natural and social forms. Before discussing these two movements in detail, it is important to stress that conversely, there are other sociological ways to understand disasters, which eradicate either of the two. To start with, it is possible to understand disasters not as ruptures but as exaggerated continuations of the normal (Woodhouse, 2011). From such a perspective, there are no disasters as

The Sociological Review, 62:S1, pp. 1–16 (2014), DOI: 10.1111/1467-954X.12121

ontologically different events from other events in the world. To believe that disasters are exceptional is to misunderstand disasters. Disasters are nothing but what happens in the world anyway, just with a different *intensity*. From such a perspective, there is no need for a different way of analysing and reacting to disasters. There is neither a need for a different methodology, nor for a specific theory, and there is indeed nothing inherently interesting that sociology can learn from disasters. Whatever society is, disasters are part of it. To further elaborate this argument, one could say that to insist on the ontological specificity of disasters implies buying into an ideology of disasters, that uses disasters to legitimate certain political goals (more on this below when discussing the state of exception).

Furthermore, in this argument it is possible to understand disasters as purely social events. Indeed, the original sociological attempts to understand disasters first needed to establish disasters as sociological issues, claiming them from the monopoly of the natural sciences. Sociologists introduced the term disaster to differentiate from hazards, understood as physical events (Perry, 2007). According to this definition, a hazard turns into a disaster by its *social effects*. An earthquake happening in a region where no humans live is not a disaster, it is just a trembling of the earth. This definition, then, is not about separating the human from the non-human but instead about trying to account for the fact that some natural events relevant for natural scientists – earthquakes where nobody is harmed – are not relevant for a sociology of disasters. This argument is, so to speak, premised on a negative definition of disaster: a disaster is a rupturing event, specifically one that ruptures human society. Such a definition was needed to create space for sociology within disaster studies, a field still dominated by the natural sciences. But for disaster studies *within* sociology such a definition is tautological: once they are thematized by sociology, what else would disasters be if not social events? Rather, the problem for sociology, once it has identified disasters as a proper theme, is how to conceive of disasters without understanding them as purely social events. Or, in other words: the problem for sociology is how to understand something that has its *origins* (at least in the case of natural and technical disasters) so obviously *not* within society.

Thus both of these negative answers of a sociology of disasters become framed, visible and problematic through the development of two separate trends within the social sciences. The first trend is to conceptualize disasters as ruptures and thus inherently *political* and second to conceive of them as *not* within society but still an object of sociology. Taken together these trends demand certain theoretical changes within the general apparatus of sociology. Only once such a general re-orientation of sociology is in place, do disasters start to make sense as relevant objects for a general sociology as opposed to their being simply another object for the expansion of sociology. Disasters, as non-social ruptures, are ideal test cases for these new strands of sociology, precisely because they highlight and enable the discussion of these new orientations.

To understand the first movement, it is important to see how disasters are at odds with most sociological theories and the foundational assumptions of social theory. Since Hobbes' Leviathan, the problem for social theory was the problem of order and the explanation of stability: in short, to look at what connects one social instance with another over time, rather than looking at events that punctuate continuity and disassemble one instance from another.[3] In this tradition of social theory man is disaster – and politics (or society in general) is what saves men from killing each other. Whether it is the state, or values and the social system (Parsons), fields (Bourdieu), imitation (Tarde) or technology (Latour), the arrow of explanation is always towards explaining what holds society together, what produces stability and predictability, assuming that society has a 'natural' tendency to fall apart.

This is why early disaster studies needed to legitimate this unusual derivation. When Erikson did his pioneering study of the Buffalo Creek flood, he thus felt compelled to defend his decision to focus on one 'unique human event', 'a task normally performed by dramatists or historians' (Erikson, 1976: 246). The predilection to explain stability also explains why many studies of post-disaster communities can make the seemingly counter-intuitive claim that after disasters communities do not necessarily fall apart, but readjust (Carr, 1932), are inventive or even hold together better (Jencson, 2001; Kendra and Wachtendorf, 2007).

Breaching experiments in ethnomethodology were probably the first attempt to put rupture at the expense of continuity at the heart of social theory and to use rupture to learn about the composition to the world (Garfinkel, 1967). The study of controversies has borrowed this insight by understanding that calling into question, critiquing and disagreeing are sociologically productive processes. These perspectives together have informed studies of accidents, breakdown and repair (Heath *et al.*, 2000). As intellectual precursors of disaster studies (as understood here), studies of accidents showed in small scale how the world falls apart and needs to be put together. Disasters considered as ruptures expand these insights and methodologies to a much larger scale and even to the world (see Clark, in this volume).[4] By shifting the focus to large-scale events and the problem of the contingency of the *world* they allow us to see how the world is composed. Disasters, then, become inherently political events because they pose questions about who should be allowed to re-compose the world and how (see Farías and Tironi). The shift from accidents to disasters is, then, not merely one of scale but of focus: if a disaster cannot be contained within one location, one machine or one organization, issues of politics, distribution and justice come to the fore. Who should be responsible for action (Farías)? How does society distribute preparedness (Easthope and Mort, and Deville *et al.*)? How should collectives make decisions regarding risks (Weszkalnys and Ellis)? How should the world be rebuilt (Tironi)?

To understand the second movement, it is important to understand that the concepts of disasters and of preparedness measures are both at odds with a purely *social* sociology. If sociology is the analysis of the social world, actual disasters (and not only their aftermath) become difficult to describe for sociology. How to describe a disaster, if not by describing the movement of earth, the

The Sociological Review, 62:S1, pp. 1–16 (2014), DOI: 10.1111/1467-954X.12121
© 2014 The Author. Editorial organisation © 2014 The Editorial Board of the Sociological Review

masses of water, the falling trees, levees and houses, the rubble and dust, the birds (Rodríguez-Giralt and Tirado) and contaminated letters (Ellis)? How to explain preparedness and recovery without recourse to bulldozers, dams and bunkers (Deville *et al.*)?

This new sociological interest in materiality has its roots in the laboratory and in new technologies. It emerged from attempts to understand how scientists construct facts and invent new technologies. From these initial questions, it has spread to all kinds of fields, but it is important to keep its origins in mind since, as Clark has argued, the materialism of Actor-Network Theory (ANT) and its allies is a materialism of divide and control over technological artefacts (Clark, 2010). It usually assumes scientists and engineers construct things in order to control other things or people.

In disasters, however, the situation is very often quite different. Disasters are situations when matter is out of control and, compared with studies of accidents, out of control on a massive scale. In fact, if there were a need to tell accidents apart from disasters, it would be the remaining amount of control over actor networks. Accidents are contained and control lapses momentarily and spatially on a relatively small scale – a space ship explodes, a car crashes, a train derails – but the larger network continues to work (it is no coincidence that the examples here most relate to traffic). Repair, as a counter strategy can focus on the technology that stopped working (Graham and Thrift, 2007). In an earthquake, nuclear disaster or flood, there is no such possible focus. Disasters then, would be defined as networks or cosmograms themselves that collapse, which radically poses the question of the composition of the world as a whole. Power and intelligibility ceases not just for one particular part, but for all parts involved. Disasters, even more than accidents, are test cases to understand a world in which the material and the natural are not only an object of concern and control, but the very origin of radical change.

But this very wholeness also poses a problem for Actor-Network Theory because the vocabulary of ANT is geared towards disentangling big concepts into micro-processes. But, one might argue, disasters are precisely those events that cannot be disentangled and that act and are experienced as one big entity. As suggested in the articles of this book, it might be argued that the analytical tools of ANT, and sociology in general, are not very well equipped to deal with such things. It is no coincidence then that the articles assembled here do not give an account of disasters as wholes but of what follows before and after. Temporalization of punctual events is the analytical strategy of choice, but we can legitimately ask whether this does not miss the very object of analysis. In that sense, a true sociology of disasters still remains to be written.

Based on the two central movements in the sociology of disasters, described above, the articles in this volume adopt different angles in analysing disasters. The articles collected here are attempts to look at how disasters reconceptualize politics and how politics reconceptualizes disasters. Thereby they engage in various kinds of symmetry (Law, 2003). By symmetry it is implied that the articles shy away from settling too quickly for one side of any hot or strong dichotomy: whether it is truth or falsehood, political or scientific explanations, the attempt at explanation or the attribution of blame (Potthast, 2007). Symmetrical approaches rather take as their starting point to inquire how attributions to one side of various distinctions are empirically accomplished: why and when are people blamed or systems explained? When are scientific or political accounts preferred? When are situations explained with symbols and meaning and when with materiality?

However, independently of such symmetries, the authors in this collection begin from different starting points and it is therefore worthwhile to point out how these starting points relate to disasters and politics. The following pages thus try to analytically grasp what it means to start with politics or disasters as the vantage point of analysis. This also allows us to situate the contributions in this book within a wider literature on these issues, including some vantage points not covered. Starting from either disasters or politics produces different accounts of both of these concepts with quite different political solutions, even if these remain often implicit. To sketch these options then allows us to also better understand the underlying conceptions of disasters and politics, through a comparison with some alternatives not taken and not covered in this book.

Disasters and politics may be conceived in the two following analytical ways: first, as 'disasters producing politics' and second, as 'politics producing disasters'. In the former case, disasters are relevant because they are productive. The disaster itself is noteworthy for its capacity to produce a particular kind of politics. The latter focuses on the problematic role of politics to produce disasters. From this point of view, it is politics itself, as a mode of ordering the world that produces disasters for its own purposes and according to its own rules.

Apart from asking how these approaches conceptualize the relationship of disasters and politics, further questions follow: What are their aims of explaining or changing the world? How do they distribute power and blame in the world among actors? Do they seek to distribute it among many actors, or attribute it to one? How do they take into account 'non-traditional' actors, such as lay people or nature? How do they distribute an empirical focus between these various actors?

Disasters as producing politics

There are at least three versions of 'disasters as producing politics' with changing levels of force attributed to disasters. First, there is an approach, which could be termed *disasters as prime empirical sites to understand about politics*. This approach is not particularly attentive to disasters as ontological events, but rather starts from empirical practicalities: disasters, it turns out, are particularly good empirical sites for understanding politics. This approach does not necessarily depart from established sociological research. It also does not necessarily

The Sociological Review, 62:S1, pp. 1–16 (2014), DOI: 10.1111/1467-954X.12121

theorize disasters, but takes them for granted as *events*. What this strand does understand, and historically, has been early to grasp, is that disasters are prime events for understanding politics, simply because, empirically, all kinds of sociologically interesting things happen, in the same way as ethnomethodology understood that in the collapse of interaction sociologically interesting things happen. In the words of Hoffmann and Oliver-Smith: disasters 'unmask the nature of society's social structure' (Oliver-Smith and Hoffman, 2002: 9), echoed by Petersen in this volume when she writes that disasters 'are messy times when norms . . . fail' and 'make it possible to analytically denaturalize and examine these practices that create norms'. This insight is paralleled by the idea in technology studies to study accidents and breakdown to understand technology in use (Wynne, 1988).

According to this view, disasters change not society, but the work of the sociologist: they decompose what is usually difficult to analyse. Disasters are primarily a welcome methodological tool.

Considering disasters as *material events* is different from the first perspective, as it takes its guidance from Science and Technology Studies (STS) and ANT to analyse disasters as events in themselves. This approach focuses on disasters as events, but unlike the first approach, does not leave disasters intact, instead disassembles them into their constituent parts. A disaster, as a rupturing event, then, does not rupture a social system, but is produced as an event (also see the conclusion by Michael). Historically, this research strand follows the shift from religious to scientific explanations of disasters. If disasters are not punishments by the gods, but natural events, then the naturalness of the events can be analysed. Measuring the location, strength, likelihood and damage of possible or previous floods, earthquakes or nuclear strikes is a scientific problem, for which different solutions with different answers exist (for some examples see Lane *et al.*, 2011; Bijker, 2007; Demeritt *et al.*, 2013 and Farías, Petersen, Weszkalnys, and Rodríguez-Giralt *et al.* in this volume). It may depend on who does the calculation, what is included in the calculation, and which objects are seen as intervening in the composition of disasters.

This approach takes a different route to the first with regard to the way in which the empirical focus is distributed. The first attempt accepts disasters as big, single events that pose a problem for society and politics. The focus of analysis becomes the political response, its actors and organizations and the decisions they take to answer to the event. The latter breaks the disaster apart: the question becomes rather when and how[5] a disaster as a unitary event comes into being. The standard STS answer is that disasters are a result of techno-scientific processes, rather than natural or political. The focus of this approach is to disassemble a disaster and turn it into a problem: there are not hurricanes as disasters in themselves, but techno-scientific processes that produce hurricanes, floods, or nuclear accidents – both as events themselves and as accounts of these events. The naturalness of (natural) disasters gets bracketed, not just because political processes are guilty of producing disasters in the first place, but because science and technology in themselves are not taken as simply recording the occurrence of disasters, but producing them. This is not to blame science and technology in an anti-modernist impulse, as the environmental movement is prone to do, but to accept both that the very materiality of social disruption is co-produced by science and technology and that there is no way to account for such material disruption without the help of science and technology.

For such an analysis there are thus two levels. First, to study how modern science and technology produces disasters as material events. This may include a study of the building technologies of dams, cars, space shuttles or buildings, or – on a broader scale – of ecological change and how such technological advances in themselves create disasters. Second, it is about studying how scientists account for risks and for existing disasters. What are the scientific assumptions, theories and descriptions for distributing blame between levees, engineers and political decision makers in practice?

Disaster as cosmopolitics is a combination of the two former approaches. Disaster as cosmopolitics uses disasters to understand how the world is reorganized on multiple levels through and after disasters. From the viewpoint of cosmopolitics a disaster recomposes the world on every level. Cosmopolitics asks what the world is composed of, who is recognized as a legitimate actor (Farías) and what capacities these actors have (Tironi). The 'who' implies not only distributions of decisions among scientific experts and policy-makers, but also among different entities, such as tsunamis, birds and measurements, or actants in ANT terminology. Cosmopolitics then ideally does not disassemble politics or disasters but observes the assembly of worlds, with politics and disasters both constituting events within this world. Disasters are particularly amenable to cosmopolitics, as they unravel the foundations and processes of composing the world, and may therefore offer a place 'in which the cry of fright or the murmur of the idiot' can be heard (Stengers, 2005). One may remember here the movie 'Train de Vie' by Radu Mihaileanu, in which a village of Romanian Jews, hearing of the oncoming holocaust, entrusts itself to the idea of the village idiot: they charter a train, half of the village dresses as Nazis and 'deports' the other half and they all drive west, through enemy lines into freedom, duping the real Nazis into believing they are fellow Nazis. The looming disaster, and the hopelessness of the situation literally puts the world at stake, making the proposition of the village idiot one worth taking into consideration.

The analytical difficulty of a cosmopolitical approach, then, is how to juggle the assembly and disassembly of worlds. While the two former approaches can each drill in a single direction and probe the composition of either disasters or political processes, the problem of cosmopolitical approaches is that their field of inquiry and analytical focus is potentially unlimited: who or what should be included in the analysis, and to what extent? This becomes a particular problem if cosmopolitics is conceived as a 'positive' form of analysis, that looks into the composition of worlds, and not just the decomposition, into an attempt to ask for new forms of disaster planning (Latour, 2007; and see Farías, this volume).

Politics as producing disasters

The first, and probably most prominent, version of politics producing disasters is the notion of the state of exception or state of emergency. The state of exception is primarily a legal and technical concept that was originally given political prominence by Carl Schmitt (2005), and more recently through the writings of Giorgio Agamben (2005). While none of the articles in this volume are concerned with a state of emergency directly, it is a crucial concept to think about the relationship between disasters and politics, because it highlights the political decisions behind what counts as a disaster from the viewpoint of a state. For Schmitt, to proclaim a state of exception is a sign of sovereignty. But the argument can be turned around. Through the lens of the state of exception – but also 'smaller' decisions of the state to act in cases of disasters – it becomes apparent that a disaster, for politics, is not an event out there, but a decision to be taken with repercussions for state action and the state's relation to the population. A disaster in this version is an event *outside* the state, considered as an organization, but (usually) within its territory,[6] and which the state uses to do something it could not do without a disaster: change laws, make experts produce reports, send recovery organizations (see Easthope and Mort), and control the movements of people and things (Ellis).

The neo-Foucauldian outlook of Agamben and his followers have pointed out in a critical mode the ways that states use the state of emergency to impose new forms of politics on the population. The argument implies that the state of emergency is usually a trick to enforce stricter control of the population, a new biopolitics that would not be possible in normal circumstances. But different to Agamben's focus, what matters here more is not the problem of these extensions of state control, but the way disasters are used to produce these extensions. In a state of emergency, what matters is that disasters become a resource to justify whatever the state of emergency proclaims. This is a different take from the Foucauldian route Agamben and others take. It focuses not so much on the fact that a state of emergency creates an exception to the law within the law, but rather how the state relates to disasters through a state of emergency. For politics the problem then is to show and prove that its solutions follow from, and are connected to, this external event. While the disaster itself is of no great interest in this perspective, the legal and political processes to connect to the events are. How is it that democratic governments use democratic powers to strip the population or individuals of the very rights that democracy grants them? What is the (discursive) power of a terrorist attack or an earthquake in these strategies?

Where the state of exception takes disasters as a starting point, the second version of politics as producing disasters shifts to focus on the risk of the disaster, prior to its occurrence. It is one of the most notable features of modern states that they develop all kinds of theories and practices to imagine, calculate and protect against future disasters. The terms 'risk' and 'preparedness' have come to embody these practices (Anderson, 2011; Lakoff and Collier, 2010).

The Sociological Review, 62:S1, pp. 1–16 (2014), DOI: 10.1111/1467-954X.12121
© 2014 The Author. Editorial organisation © 2014 The Editorial Board of the Sociological Review

To focus on risk and preparedness implies to shift the focus away from actual disasters: risk and preparedness are both concepts that try to deal with disasters before they happen. It is constitutive of both of these terms that they deal with the unknown. They express the fact that various actors, as in the case of a state of exception, use disasters to act in the here and now, assuming that these actions will change the course of eventual disasters. Studies that analyse risk and preparedness, then, are not so much studies of disasters as material events, but studies of how disasters produce effects before they even happen. In the case of risks, such effects are mostly of the calculative sort, in the case of preparedness it ranges from exercises, to food larders (Collet, 2010) and bunkers (see Deville *et al.*). Studies of risk and preparedness are very much studies of dealing with the time of disasters. Like the precautionary principle (Dupuy and Grinbaum, 2005) or prevention (Ewald, 1986), risk and preparedness move the time of action *before* the event, and since they are aimed at undoing or at least alleviating the event itself, and nobody knows when an event will happen, they decouple it from the event. The centre of analysis becomes the *imagination* of the disaster and the *consequences* various actors derive from these imaginations. Politics becomes a mediator between the imagination and the practices derived from it. As in the cosmopolitical approach, such an analysis is very much an analysis of how we want to live, how we want to compose the world and what we imagine the world is and should be composed of. But rather than looking at how actual disasters recompose the world, this is about how the expectations of disasters recompose the world. Politically speaking, the problem of risk and preparedness is more difficult and worrisome than post-disaster intervention since the historical basis for action is unknown. While disaster as cosmopolitics builds on some known events and seeks to rebuild a community out of it, preparedness needs to imagine these very events (Weszkalnys).[7]

The final approach analyses politics itself as (producing) a disaster. While the former two approaches take politics as answering actual or eventual disasters, politics as disaster assumes that the disaster is an effect of political decisions.[8] As with Foucauldian studies of the state of emergency, such studies assume that disasters are not events beyond political control, but instead are produced by politics in the first place. Underpinning these studies is very much a distrust of the notion of 'natural' or 'technical' disaster. Rather than taking the disasters as the starting point of analysis, they take the political as the starting point in the production of disasters. They operate from a critical perspective, which seeks to reorient the blame question and deneutralize it through sociological analysis. By putting political processes centre stage, and very often concentrating on a particular range of political actors (such as elected politicians and government office holders), disasters become thoroughly politicized. These studies become primarily about actions of political actors, and very often, from a critical angle, about their failure to act before, during and after disasters. Such research is deliberately asymmetrical, since it attempts to point to the fact that it was political decisions that caused a disaster and its subsequent effects. This research is the mirror image of the account given of 'politics as producing disasters

The Sociological Review, 62:S1, pp. 1–16 (2014), DOI: 10.1111/1467-954X.12121

as risk' since it is about the failure to have created, and prepared for the right risks. 'Politics as producing disasters' research points either to the failure of producing the right risks, or, having prepared for the right risks, to have failed to act adequately to address these risks. For example, a large part of the discussion on Hurricane Katrina has focused on the question of whether national and local government assessed the risk of a hurricane adequately, whether the material forms of preparedness, the levees, were adequately designed, and whether Federal Emergency Management Agency and other government agencies acted adequately after the hurricane. Politics as disaster research also points to the fact that the state and its disaster organizations use disasters for a militarization of response and for taking responsibility out of citizens' hands (Tierney and Bevc, 2007). Historically, it follows a trajectory of arguing for a demilitarization of disasters and for preferring the improvisational skills of the population over the organized, bureaucratized and militarized work of state organizations (see Easthope and Mort).

Overview

The book is organized in three sections. Each section focuses on a different problem of the relationship between disasters and politics. It starts with a section 'Materials: Ontologies' that circles around the issue of how to conceive of disasters once we take seriously the non-human and material nature of disasters. First, Nigel Clark sets out to clarify how the notion of the anthropocene challenges our understanding of politics and disasters. Clark radically seeks to shift agency not simply to the non-human as a general category, but to the earth's climate and its long-term human induced changes. For Clark, the main question is how we can politically understand temporal and spatial processes that far exceed normal sociological concepts of human agency and nation state. In the second article, questions of the redistribution of agency are taken from the biggest scale of the anthropocene to the smallest scale of birds. Israel Rodríguez-Giralt, Francisco Tirado and Manuel Tironi look at a toxic spill in the Doñana National Park in Spain to question the notion of disaster: Rather than being circumscribed in time and space, they show that disasters should be understood as 'meshworks'. As the authors show, it is the ringing of the birds, and the possibility to trace how they spread toxic spill, that turns the disaster into a meshwork, with birds as moveable and traceable distributors of what was initially a local event. Drawing on the work of Tim Ingold, they argue that disasters are dynamic realities, difficult to localize and always distributed along disparate scales and actors. In their view, disasters have a dual reality, unfolding actually and virtually at once.

In the next article, Ignacio Farías uses the example of the failing of the Chilean tsunami warning systems to argue that we should analyse disasters not as instances of accidents but as instances of inquiry. For Farías, what is at stake in the case of cosmopolitics is a generalized problem of recognition, as it has been phrased in critical theory: Who recognizes whom as legitimate and irreducible actor? For Farías, the failure of the warning system must be discussed as a failure to recognize tsunamis as actors and based on this first failure, a failure to openly explore the world.

In the second part entitled 'experiments: governance' we focus on collective political experiments: these articles deal with different ways of deploying heterogeneous technologies for managing disasters, technologies that are in each case contested, challenged and mutable. Hence the section title: disasters enhance uncertainty, yet the technologies aim to stabilize them, but become matters of conflict and experiment.

Katrina Petersen in her article 'Producing space, tracing authority: mapping the 2007 San Diego wildfires' takes a look at how technologies of representation produce different kinds of disasters. In the case under discussion, two different kinds of maps produced completely different disasters with different repercussions for how to deal with the fires. The county produced maps, which ended at the borders of the county, whereas those produced by a group of local media and local academic organizations with Google My Map tracked the actual fires. The former aligned with the responsibilities of the state organizations responsible for dealing with the fire, whereas the latter followed those of the population affected by the fires. Petersen's main point here is to highlight that the groups that produce the maps are actually overlapping and have similar interests, but it is the different forms of map production that result in different forms of disasters and how to deal with them. In the fifth article Manuel Tironi asks to what extent disasters, as radical moments of vital indeterminacy, create extended and iterative forms of political experimentalism. Tironi grounds his argument in the case of Talca, Chile. After the 2010 earthquake, two competing participatory experiments coalesced in Talca. On one side stood the idea that the disaster only unveiled the previous deterioration of the city. This endemic problem should be overcome with a masterplan and the role of the Talquinos would be to evaluate proposals. Against this stand the ideas of Talca con Tod@s, whereby the problem of Talca was not its decay, but its rich history of citizen groups, and its social capital: citizens in this view were engaged, and they were experts. These experiments publicly contested each other's assumptions and principles. The result was what Tironi calls an atmosphere of indagation, an amplified exploratory setting in which the experiments themselves became objects of political inquiry – thus creating a much messier and topological modality of governance.

The sixth article by Lucy Easthope and Maggie Mort looks at recovery work after the floods in Toll Bar, UK. They engage with a detailed comparison of how the regulated recovery work clashes with the contingent world of post-disaster recovery and how what they call 'technologies of recovery' shape and become shaped by these local situations. They show that recovery work has to balance the adaptation to these local circumstances with keeping to its standardized practices, but they also show how local residents remake the technologies of recovery themselves.

12

The third and last section entitled 'preparedness: anticipation' focuses on the fact that disasters exist and create political (re)arrangements *without* even happening. Disasters are politically powerful and generative even when absent, looming or simply being invoked. The section starts with Ryan Ellis on 'Creating a secure network: the 2001 anthrax attacks and the transformation of postal security'. Ellis looks at how the anthrax attacks led to a reconfiguration of the postal network, which eventually favoured large commercial mailers. For Ellis, the anthrax attacks were just spikes in a story which experts had seen coming. The attacks were not so much a disaster, as the events which led to a political reorganization of infrastructure: re-enforcing problematic power asymmetries by distributing costs unequally across different categories of users, and engaging in the policing of labour in an effort to aid the shift toward temporary labour.

Next, Joe Deville, Michael Guggenheim and Zuzana Hrdličková look at shelters as materialized forms of preparedness. Drawing on the notion of concrete governmentality, they highlight how shelters, as particularly stubborn and stable forms of preparedness, produce a number of surprising effects. First, they compose preparedness by changing the relationship between citizens and the state. They also decompose preparedness by falling out of use. Lastly, they recompose preparedness because they remain, while disaster experts need to find new disasters to justify their existence. In Deville *et al.*'s view, it is not so much the disaster itself, but particular kinds of preparedness that create different relationships between citizens and the state. In the last article entitled 'Anticipating oil: the temporal politics of disaster-yet-to-come', Gisa Weszkalnys looks at an extreme case of preparedness and what disasters could be. She looks at how the prospect of oil in São Tomé and Príncipe is dealt with as a disaster yet to come. Her interpretation closes a circle by linking back to the problem of anthropocene in Clark's opening article. Weszkalnys asks when a disaster starts and she presents a sliding scale, from the timescales of geology to theories of resource curse and ethnographic observation of how the people in São Tomé and Príncipe react to the expectation of oil and their attendant ontological conversions, from crude oil to commodity into money. Finally, in the afterword, Mike Michael complements this introduction by looking at the relationship of disasters and politics through the lens of temporality. For Michael, what the diverse articles do is that they tie disasters into knots: they turn past experiences into preparations for the future and they turn these preparations into actual events.

These articles draw in various ways on the notion of disasters as politics and politics as disasters. As the section titles make clear, some focus on temporal aspects, some on material and others on those of governance. Where they all converge is to turn the relationship between disasters and politics into a problem. The problem we face is not how to react to existing disasters. The problem we face is how to live in this world knowing that we produce innumerable disasters, which ones we want to prepare for, and how we want to live together in the wake of acknowledging these disasters. These articles are but a first step to answering these questions.

The Sociological Review, 62:S1, pp. 1–16 (2014), DOI: 10.1111/1467-954X.12121

Acknowledgments

This article was written with generous funding from an European Research Council starting grant (GA 263731 OD). Many thanks to Joe Deville, Zuzana Hrdličková, Monika Krause, Linsey McGoey, Jörg Potthast, Israel Rodrìguez-Giralt, Chris Shilling, Manuel Tironi and Alexis Waller for their constructive criticism and comments.

Notes

1 The number of people killed by natural disasters has decreased from an average of a million or so per year in the first half of the twentieth century to a few hundred thousand per year in the last decades, but the number of disasters reported, the number of people affected, and the reported damage measured in dollars has increased by several orders of magnitude since the 1960s. For technological disasters, the same holds, except that the number of disasters reported has decreased since ca. 2000. All data are taken from the International Disaster database EM-DAT: www.emdat.be/natural-disasters-trends (accessed 2 May 2013).

2 Google Ngrams shows the *percentage* of books containing certain words relative to all books on Google books. It is a relative, not an absolute measure. I have used the Ngrams for 'sociology of disaster' and 'sociology of disasters', because these are a small amount of texts. The Ngram presented here has 'sociology of disaster' multiplied by 10,000 to make them comparable with the other two Ngrams. In other words, unsurprisingly the word 'disaster' occurs approximately 10,000 times more often than 'sociology of disaster(s)'. The Ngram for sociology is included to show that the increase of 'sociology of disaster' is not a function of a general increase in literature containing the words 'sociology' (which actually decreases after a peak in the mid-1970s).

3 Note that this is quite opposed to the general procedure of history (at least before the advent of social history) that looks at relevant events and how they create historical islands of importance.

4 From here onwards, author names without dates refer to articles in this volume.

5 See the section below on 'Politics as producing disasters as risks', for a discussion of temporality, and particularly how disasters have effects *before* they happen, qua risk analysis and preparedness.

6 However, this does not need to be so. After Chernobyl and Fukushima, various pandemics, and also after 9/11 many states embarked on various paths of disaster preparedness, even if their territory was not directly affected.

7 For a new method of how to imagine these events, see Guggenheim *et al.* (forthcoming).

8 This view has been popularized by Naomi Klein in her bestseller *The Shock Doctrine* (2007).

References

Agamben, G., (2005), *State of Exception*, Chicago: University of Chicago Press.
Anderson, B., (2011), 'Preemption, precaution, preparedness: anticipatory action and future geographies', *Progress in Human Geography*, 34 (6): 777–798.
Bijker, W. E., (2007), 'American and Dutch coastal engineering', *Social Studies of Science*, 37 (1): 143–151.
Carr, L. J., (1932), 'Disaster and the sequence-pattern concept of social change', *The American Journal of Sociology*, 38 (2): 207–218.

Clark, N., (2010), *Inhuman Nature: Sociable Life on a Dynamic Planet*, London: Sage Publications.

Collet, D., (2010), 'Storage and starvation: public granaries as agents of food security in early modern Europe', *Historical Social Research*, 35 (4): 234–252.

Demeritt, D., Nobert, S., Cloke, H. L. and Pappenberger, F., (2013), 'The European Flood Alert System and the communication, perception, and use of ensemble predictions for operational flood risk management', *Hydrological Processes*, 27 (1): 147–157.

Dupuy, J.-P. and Grinbaum, A., (2005), 'Living with uncertainty: from the precautionary principle to the methodology of ongoing normative assessment', *Comptes Rendus Geosciences*, 337 (4): 457–474.

Erikson, K. T., (1976), *Everything in its Path: Destruction of Community in the Buffalo Creek Flood*, New York: Simon and Schuster.

Ewald, F., (1986), *L'Etat providence*, Paris: B. Grasset.

Garfinkel, H., (1967), 'Studies of the routine grounds of everyday activities', in H. Garfinkel (ed.), *Studies in Ethnomethodology*, 35–75, Englewood Cliffs, NJ: Prentice-Hall.

Graham, S. and Thrift, N., (2007), 'Out of order: understanding repair and maintenance', *Theory, Culture and Society*, 24 (3): 1–25.

Guggenheim, M., Kräftner, B. and Kröll, J., (forthcoming), ' "I don't know whether I need a further level of disaster": challenging the media of sociology in the sandbox', *Distinktion, Scandinavian Journal of Social Theory*. DOI: 10.1080/1600910X.2013.838977.

Heath, C., Knoblauch, H. and Luff, P., (2000), 'Technology and social interaction: the emergence of "workplace studies" ', *British Journal of Sociology*, 51 (2): 299–320.

Jencson, L., (2001), 'Disastrous rites: liminality and communitas in a flood crisis', *Anthropology and Humanism*, 26 (1): 46–58.

Kendra, J. M. and Wachtendorf, T., (2007), 'Community innovation and disasters', in H. Rodríguez, E. L. Quarantelli and R. C. Dynes (eds), *Handbook of Disaster Research*, 316–334, New York: Springer.

Klein, N., (2007), *The Shock Doctrine: The Rise of Disaster Capitalism*, New York: Metropolitan Books/Henry Holt.

Lakoff, A. and Collier, S. J., (2010), 'Infrastructure and event: the political technology of preparedness', in B. Braun and S. Whatmore (eds), *Political Matter: Technoscience, Democracy, and Public Life*, 243–265, Minneapolis: University of Minnesota Press.

Lane, S. N., Landström, C. and Whatmore, S. J., (2011), 'Imagining flood futures: risk assessment and management in practice', *Philosophical Transactions of the Royal Society A: Mathematical, Physical and Engineering Sciences*, 369 (1942): 1784–1806.

Law, J., (2003), 'Disasters, a/symmetries and interferences', available at: www.lancs.ac.uk/fass/sociology/papers/law-disaster-asymmetries-and-interferences.pdf.

Oliver-Smith, A. and Hoffman, S., (2002), 'Introduction. Why Anthropologists should study disasters', in A. Oliver-Smith and S. L. Hoffman (eds), *Catastrophe and Culture: The Anthropology of Disaster*, Santa Fe: School of American Research Press.

Perry, R. W., (2007), 'What is a disaster?', in H. Rodríguez, E. L. Quarantelli and R. C. Dynes (eds), *Handbook of Disaster Research*, 1–15, New York: Springer.

Potthast, J., (2007), *Die Bodenhaftung der Netzwerkgesellschaft. Eine Ethnografie von Pannen an Grossflughäfen*, Bielefeld: Transcript.

Schmitt, C., (2005), *Political Theology: Four Chapters on the Concept of Sovereignty*, Chicago: University of Chicago Press.

Stengers, I., (2005), 'The cosmopolitical proposal', in B. Latour and P. Weibel (eds), *Making Things Public: Atmospheres of Democracy*, 994–1003, Cambridge, MA: MIT Press.

Tierney, K. J., (2007), 'From the margins to the mainstream? Disaster research at the crossroads', 33: 503–525 (accessed 29 January 2010).

Tierney, K. and Bevc, C., (2007), 'Disaster as war: militarism and the social construction of disaster in New Orleans', in D. Brunsma, D. Overfelt and S. J. Picou (eds), *The Sociology of Katrina: Perspectives on a Modern Catastrophe*, 35–49, Lanham, MD: Rowman & Littlefield.

Woodhouse, E., (2011), 'Conceptualizing disasters as extreme versions of everyday life', in R. Dowty and B. L. Allen (eds), *Dynamics of Disaster: Lessons on Risk, Response and Recovery*, London: Earthscan.

Wynne, B., (1988), 'Unruly technology: practical rules, impractical discourses and public understanding', *Social Studies of Science*, 18 (1): 147–167.

Section 1
Materials: Ontologies

Geo-politics and the disaster of the Anthropocene

Nigel Clark

Abstract: Recently, earth scientists have been discussing the idea of the 'Anthropocene' – a new geologic epoch defined by human geological agency. In its concern with the crossing of thresholds in Earth systems and the shift into whole new systemic states, the Anthropocene thesis might be viewed as the positing of a disaster to end all disasters. As well as looking at some of the motivations behind the Anthropocene concept, this article explores possible responses to the idea from critical social thought. It is suggested that the current problematization of planetary 'boundary conditions' might be taken as indicative of the emergence of a new kind of 'geologic politics' that is as concerned with the temporal dynamics and changes of state in Earth systems as it is with more conventional political issues revolving around territories and nation state boundaries: a geo-politics that also raises questions about practical experimentation with Earth processes.

Keywords: disaster, Anthropocene, climate change, Earth systems, politics of emergency, geologic politics

Introduction: live fast, die young, leave a good-looking fossil

In recent years, the question of what residues the human species will leave behind once we have gone has emerged as a theme in academic and popular science (see Weisman, 2007; Zalasiewicz, 2008; Zalasiewicz *et al.*, 2011). Palae-ontologist and stratigrapher Jan Zalasiewicz notes that a situation in which discernibly similar fossilized remains are found in many different places across the planet while also being clustered in the same geologic stratum assists researchers in identifying the species in question and placing it in relation to the geologic events that laid down the stratum in which it is found. 'Early brilliant success, a worldwide reach, and then a sudden death' is his recipe for a service-ably conspicuous fossilization (2008: 102). Our own species, Zalasiewicz notes, is looking increasingly likely to meet these criteria.

Amongst other more ambiguous or insidious remainders, our urban centres – or what philosopher Michel Serres once described as 'enormous and dense tectonic plates of humanity' (1995: 16) – have a fair chance of leaving a recog-

The Sociological Review, 62:S1, pp. 19–37 (2014), DOI: 10.1111/1467-954X.12122

nizable trace in the stratigraphic record. But only if cities go down quickly. If sea levels rise gradually, buildings and infrastructure will be pummelled into pebbly insignificance by the force of tides and storms. Should sea levels rise rapidly, however, which is likely to be the case if runaway climate change triggers the break-up of the Greenland ice cap, many coastal cities would quickly sink beneath the rising ocean, beyond the reach of scouring waves and currents. There, '[o]ur drowned cities . . . would begin to be covered by sand, silt, and mud, and take the first steps towards becoming geology. The process of fossilization will begin' (Zalasiewicz, 2008: 84–85).

An obvious question is, leave a fossil for whom or what to find? At an earlier moment in our modernity, philosopher Immanuel Kant considered the possibility that 'revolutions of the Earth' would one day annihilate human life, as they had done to those long-lost creatures that populate the fossil record (1993: 66–67). Such events, he pondered, would leave the universe bereft of its one and only thinking being. Not only would one of nature's creations vanish, but the very existence of thought would be extinguished for all time, leaving the cosmos cold, barren and unable to reflect upon itself: 'all of creation would be a mere wasteland, gratuitous and without final purpose' (Kant, cited in Grant, 2000: 50). Kant's agonizing was prompted by the novel sense of deep geological time that he and fellow eighteenth-century savants were then taking to heart. But it may also have had a more immediate and substantial referent. The destruction of the city of Lisbon by earthquake, fire and tsunami in 1755 had a profound impact on Kant, as it did on many literate Europeans (see Kant, 1994; Chester, 2001). Lisbon, before it became the precursor of a definitively modern form of urban renewal, stood for the exposure of humankind to the forces of the Earth. At the time when faith in an omnipotent and orchestrating deity was waning, Lisbon's fate gestured not only at the vulnerability of one urban centre, but to the frailty of humankind in general in the face of a not-necessarily accommodating cosmos (Ray, 2004; Neiman, 2002).

Kant's answer to the threat of eventual human extinction was to turn away from the weakness of the flesh and affirm that part of man capable of rising above the blind forcefulness of nature: the human faculty of self-willing and super-sensible reason. This solution is itself now frequently charged with fomenting new problems, not least the backfiring of nature's mastery into environmental upheaval and uncertainty (see Colebrook, 2012: 205). But the problem Kant had the audacity to confront never really went away. From time to time, the convulsions of the Earth continued to play havoc with human achievements great and small. And now, after several centuries of differing priorities and multiple distractions, Kant's greatest fear is back on the agenda.

Today it is the coming of 'the Anthropocene' – a term popularized by atmospheric chemist Paul Crutzen in the early 2000s – which most clearly expresses the reinvigorated concern with human species-threatening upheavals of the Earth (see also Crutzen and Stoermer, 2000; Weszkalnys, this volume). The concept of the Anthropocene designates a move beyond the geologic conditions characteristic of the 10,000 to 12,000 years since the end of the last glacial epoch, and the

The Sociological Review, 62:S1, pp. 19–37 (2014), DOI: 10.1111/1467-954X.12122

shift into a novel epoch whose signature is irreversible human impact on earth and life processes (Crutzen, 2002; Zalasiewicz *et al*., 2008; Davis, 2008). In 2008, the Stratigraphy Commission of the Geological Society of London passed a motion to consider the possible formalization of the term Anthropocene. An Anthropocene Working Group was set up, tasked with gathering evidence about the latest contender for a permanent place in the Geological Time Scale (Zalasiewicz *et al*., 2010).

It is anthropogenic climate change, and especially the prospect of passing over thresholds or tipping points in the Earth's climate system, that is helping drive forward claims for a geological transition at the planetary scale. Other human impacts, however, such as the triggering of a mass extinction event, the depositing of nuclear and chemical wastes, and the large-scale geomorphic transformations of the Earth's surface are also taken into account. In each case, what is under consideration by the commission is not the experience of living through upheavals in Earth systems, but what these changes will mean for the geological stratification of the planet. As sociologist Bronislaw Szerszynski sums up: 'it is important to realise that the truth of the Anthropocene is less about what humanity is doing, than the *traces* that humanity will leave behind' (2012: 169).

We might imagine the Anthropocene, then, as the disaster to end all disasters. Here I set out at once from disaster studies – the interdisciplinary field which seeks to inform practical measures to help keep people out of the path of hazardous events – and from the thought of the philosopher Maurice Blanchot (1995) for whom the disaster is a crisis of such severity that it undermines our very capacity to make sense of the world. The figure of the Anthropocene announces the prospect of multiple, interconnected and cascading transformations in Earth systems whose current state human beings and other species have come to rely upon. This presents an immense challenge to those tasked with managing environmental change, but at the same time underscores a human embedding in dynamical physical processes which, as Earth scientists would have it, ensures that we 'cannot be in a position to manage the Earth System in any objective fashion' (Steffen *et al*., 2004: 286). In other words, the Earth sciences disclose material conditions that not only defy prediction, but reveal the precarious existence of those beings who are asking questions of it. With the coming of the Anthropocene, literary theorist Timothy Morton argues, geoscience finds itself confronting 'an abyss whose reality becomes increasingly uncanny, not less, the more scientific instruments are able to probe it' (2012: 233). And yet, scientists continue to go to the ends of the Earth, literally, in search of evidence about the past, present and future operation of Earth systems.

Such an entanglement of the known and the unknowable, the tryst between that which adds to knowledge and that what radically undoes this knowledge, is not a world away from the paradoxes of the disaster in which Blanchot (1995) immersed himself. For Blanchot and his heirs, the disaster is an event that we cannot simply turn into an object of knowledge – for such is its force and shock that it dismantles the very platforms from which we apprehend reality. And yet, even as the disaster overwhelms our taken-for-granted senses and sensibilities, it also challenges us to try and begin sensing, thinking, acting in new ways. It ends the world, and begins it turning anew.

Is there more we could do with our renewed sense of implication in 'revolutions of the Earth'? What might it mean 'geo-politically', I ask, to think of the Anthropocene as a disaster – and to think disaster at the spatial and temporal scale of the planet in its entirety? In the light of the failure of all attempts thus far at global governance of climate and other Earth systems – the summit by summit drift of compromise and deferral – what are the political potentialities that might yet be drawn out of the geological conditions of human existence?

I want to first review the emergence of the concept of the Anthropocene and look at the meaning and implications of the changes assembled under its name. I will then address political risks that have, with some justification, been seen to accompany declarations of a global 'state of emergency', before moving on to consider what else might be done with a dawning sense of geophysical disaster. There is, setting out from this predicament, no clear-cut or obvious passage from the countenance of planetary disaster to a novel sense of geo-politics – the fate of Kant's answer to geologically induced trauma being an object lesson here. But Kant was right about one thing: the disaster is a moment that calls for an audacious response. If it is not to be a prelude to despair, the disaster must be an incitement to risk-taking, improvisation and experiment. Though none of this should distract us from an understanding that this is also a time for mourning – for dwelling on the experience of loss.

Constructing the Anthropocene

'The Anthropocene, on current evidence, seems to show global change consistent with the suggestion that an epoch-scale boundary has been crossed within the last two centuries' observes Zalasiewicz and his colleagues (2011: 840). This shift would take us out of the Holocene, the brief civilization-friendly span of exceptionally clement and stable climate that has reigned on this planet ever since the violent climatic vacillations of the Pleistocene eased off. A more extreme but quite feasible possibility is that the effects of the current human-induced climate change coupled with a major extinction event will bring to a close the 2.5 million plus years of the Quaternary period (consisting of the Holocene and the much longer Pleistocene epoch) – taking the Earth back to temperatures and sea levels approximating those of the mid-Pliocene epoch located some three million years ago (see Zalasiewicz *et al.*, 2008: 6).

Speculations about a novel human-induced geological period go back at least as far as Italian geologist Antonio Stoppani's coining of the term the 'Anthropozoic era' in the 1870s, and took a further turn in Russian mineralogist Vladimir Vernadsky's reflections on the place of humankind in what he referred to as the 'biosphere' (Crutzen, 2002; Zalasiewicz *et al.*, 2011; Vernadsky, 1998

[1926]). If not exactly new, what is remarkable about the recent incarnation of an anthropogenic geologic epoch is its rapid ascendance since Crutzen and marine scientist Eugene Stoermer first introduced the term in 2000. Understandably, stratigraphers resist snap decisions: historian Dipesh Chakrabarty (2008) notes that it took the International Geological Congress over 50 years to warm to the idea of the Holocene. Or as Zalasiewicz and his colleagues remind us: 'The Geological Time Scale is held dear by geologists and it is not amended lightly' (2010: 2228).

If the Anthropocene's elevation from passing remark to dedicated working group in eight years seems positively fast-track, it is important to keep in mind how dramatically the geosciences themselves have developed over the last six or seven decades. As Kant's musings remind us, a sense that the deep time of the Earth is punctuated by major convulsion has a long history (see Rudwick, 2005). However, it is only since the confirmation of the theory of plate tectonics in the early 1960s that a unified schema has emerged, in which volcanoes, earthquakes and other geologic upheavals are viewed as ordinary and ongoing manifestations of the planet's crustal dynamics (Davis, 1996; Clark, 2011). Intervening decades have seen rapid advances in the understanding of the Earth as a single integrated and dynamical system – through a series of major research projects that have tracked the dynamics of the planet's hydrosphere, atmosphere and lithosphere (the distributions of water, gases and rocks that make up the outermost layers of the Earth), identified the cycles and reservoirs of its main chemical components, and begun to decipher the complex external influences (or 'forcings') and internal feedback effects that orchestrate periodic shifts in the state of major Earth systems (Westbroek, 1992; Wood, 2004; Davis, 1996).

It is this integrative perspective that provides the basis for understanding the variability of the planet's climate over time and the influence of human activity on the dynamics of climate and other Earth systems. Rather than simply measuring the human imprint on the Earth in terms of brute geomorphic transformations – shifting soil and water or the building of substantial structures – it is now possible to gauge anthropogenic impact on Earth systems in terms of changes in the trace components of the atmosphere and other relatively imperceptible chemical and biological signals (see Zalasiewicz *et al.*, 2010). At the same time, extensive investigation of ice cores and other proxies of past environmental conditions have enabled geoscientists to make confident comparisons between present and previous Earth system states. The resultant evidence of human-induced global climate change, although it is only one of a number of 'anthropogenic' or human-triggered transformations, is generally presented as a key to identifying the onset of the Anthropocene (see Crutzen, 2002).

While the take-off of fossil-fuelled industrialization is currently the preferred transition point in claims for epochal shift, the pivotal significance of climate change also suggests that we may have yet to witness the Anthropocene's full unfurling. In particular, it is the as-yet unrealized possibility of passing over a threshold into abrupt and runaway climate change that brings the sobriety of most stratigraphic discourse up against the increasingly alarmist pronouncements of climate science. It is when he is focusing on climate that Crutzen makes clear his view that the more extreme manifestations of the new epoch may lie in the near future. As he observes: 'studies . . . indicate that global average climate warming during this century may even surpass the highest values in the projected IPCC global warming range of 1.4–5.8 °C' (Crutzen, 2006: 211). In the conclusion to one of the first major studies of Earth systems to operationalize the concept of the Anthropocene, climatologist Will Steffen and his colleagues likewise suggest that the most threatening transitions are still to come: 'The human-driven changes to the global environment . . . may drive the Earth itself into a different state that may be much less hospitable to humans and other forms of life' (Steffen *et al.*, 2004: 299).

Recent evidence points not simply to a failure to stabilize anthropogenic emissions of carbon dioxide, but indicate that CO_2 levels in the atmosphere are actually increasing – *at an accelerating rate* (Robock *et al.*, 2009; see also Crutzen, 2006), with the result that many climate scientists are beginning to view 'dangerous' – or even 'extremely dangerous' – climate change as a serious possibility (see Anderson and Bows, 2011). Journalist Ross Gelbspan reports of his encounters with climate scientists: 'On the record, they use very conservative scientific language; they speak in terms of estimates and trends and probabilities. Off the record, they told me this stuff is scary as hell' (2006: unpag.). But a growing number of scientists feel obliged to express their full concerns publically. Gaia-theorist James Lovelock, for example, puts it like this: 'Whatever we do is likely to lead to death on a scale that makes all previous wars, famines and disasters small. To continue business as usual will probably kill most of us during the century (2008: 3889).

In this way, what is 'catastrophic' in the technical sense of a threshold transition between states or regimes of a physical system (see Scheffer *et al.*, 2001) looks likely to visit the experience of catastrophe or disaster upon social worlds. In response, critical social thinkers characteristically focus on the profoundly uneven distribution of the impacts of climate change and other catastrophes – a predicament rendered still more unconscionable by a consideration of the inverse unevenness of the enjoyment of the benefits of the Earth's material-energetic resources (Roberts and Parks, 2007). However urgent and necessary this approach is, it should not eclipse other possibilities – such as a more speculative 'outward' gaze that looks beyond the orbit of humankind to impacts on other-than-human life, and even beyond the terrestrial biosphere itself. Pondering the significance of human-induced mass extinction, Jan Zalasiewicz works on the same grand scale as Kant. Only this time, the human subject is far from centre stage. As Zalasiewicz ruminates:

> . . . conserving living organisms is far more important than conserving fossils (and here one speaks as a life-long palaeontologist). The Earth, in sustaining and harbouring these organisms, is by far the most complex and valuable object in space for many, many billions of miles in any direction. It would be not merely an Earthly disaster if its surface was converted to the kind of wasteland that appeared after the Permian-Triassic or Cretaceous-Tertiary boundary extinction events. It would be a cosmic

The Sociological Review, 62:S1, pp. 19–37 (2014), DOI: 10.1111/1467-954X.12122

tragedy, one in which the injuries sustained would not heal for millions of years. (2008: 240)

Humanizing geology?

The relationship of social, cultural and philosophical thought to the nascent science of the Anthropocene is already complicated, and likely to become more so. A decade or so ago, many social scientists would have recognized in the concept an echo – or even a vindication – of their own pronouncements of the 'end of nature' and the rise of an irrecuperably socialized or humanized natural order. Others might still be drawn to the apparent resonance of a sense of human-geologic interactions with notions of hybridity, of co-constitutive culture-natures or cyborg planetary orders. But contemporary critical thinkers are as likely to rail against the apparent recentring of planetary dynamics – however bleakly this is articulated – on the agency of our own species. In the words of literary theorist Tom Cohen, the very idea of the Anthropocene 'seems the epitome of *anthropomorphism* itself – irradiating with a secret pride invoking comments on our god-like powers and ownership of the planet' (2012: 240).

While there is indeed a discernible whiff of dark grandeur to certain framings of the new geologic epoch, critical engagements of all hues need to be careful not to take the elevation of 'the anthropic' – the role and place of humans – at face value. It is important to remember that any ratcheting up of the influence of our own species relative to conventional geological forces plays to the disciplinary interests and political desires of social thinkers at least as much as it does to the affective and empirical dispositions of natural scientists. However ominous it may be, the idea of the Anthropocene – at least at first glimpse – offers many of the same temptations to expand the domain of the collective social agency as any previous depiction of human impact on the environment. This is one way we might read Slavoj Žižek's claim, which follows on from a spirited engagement with the notion of the Anthropocene:

> There is . . . something deceptively reassuring in our readiness to assume guilt for the threats to our environment: we like to be guilty since, if we are guilty, then it all depends on us, we pull the strings of the catastrophe, and so in principle we can all save ourselves simply by changing our lives. (2011: 423).

But even Žižek – following Dipesh Chakrabarty's (2008) path-breaking engagement with the idea of human geologic agency – seems to see the Anthropocene predominantly in terms of what it says about *our species*. What is vital for critical thinkers in the humanities and social sciences to recognize, however, is that the scientific thematization of the Anthropocene is as much about the *decentring* of humankind as it is about our rising geological signifi-cance. At the heart of the developments in Earth sciences in the latter twentieth and early twenty-first centuries is the keen sense that Earth systems are inher-ently changeable, *with or without human influence*. As Steffen and his colleagues sum up: 'detailed paleo-records show that the Earth is never static and it is almost impossible to define an equilibrium state; variability abounds at nearly all spatial and temporal scales' (Steffen *et al.*, 2004: 295). It is this intrinsic variability that explains why climate and other Earth systems are susceptible to human impacts or 'forcings'. As climatologist Richard Alley explains, in relation to global climate: 'Sometimes a small push has caused the climate to change a little, but other times, a small push has knocked Earth's climate system into a different mode of operation' (2000: 13; see also Broecker, 1987).

The trouble is that, even after all the interrogations of the nature-culture binary of recent decades, researchers in the social science and humanities still tend to treat natural and social agency as sliding points on a linear scale, analogous to a tug of war in which one side gains as the other loses. Similar imagery does arise in the natural sciences, but in general the relatively novel acknowledgement of humans as a 'global forcing agent' does not seem to imply any corresponding diminution of the universe's more established forces (see Zalasiewicz *et al.*, 2010: 2228). A human-triggered mass extinction event might well be considered a tragedy of cosmological proportions, but as Zalasiewicz's musings suggest, a catastrophe of this magnitude ought to be viewed in the context of a series of similarly momentous 'boundary events' which have had nothing remotely to do with humans. Through its own dynamics and interactions with the solar system, the Earth is quite capable of generating upheavals, geoscientists remind us, which is precisely why it is possible to identify a sequence of transitions in the Geological Time Scale.

There is ample evidence indicating that the idea of a transition from the Holocene to the Anthropocene is implicated in the deepening ethical-political entanglements of scientific research that are associated with the era of global environmental change (see Frodeman, 2000). Already the concept of the Anthropocene has been marshalled to make a case for identifying a range of 'planetary boundaries' that designate 'the safe operating space for humanity' (Rockström *et al.*, 2009). This is a move – controversial in some quarters – with clear policy implications. As Zalasiewicz *et al.* note, in relation to this operationalization of the Anthropocene concept in the framing of planetary boundaries: 'formalization may represent "official" acknowledgment that the world has changed, substantially and irreversibly, through human activity – an acknowledgment akin to the IPCC consensus statements on climate change' (2010: 2230). They go on to gesture to the wider political ramifications, including the risks, of foregrounding human geological agency:

> The concept of the Anthropocene might . . . become exploited, to a variety of ends. Some of these may be beneficial, some less so. The Anthropocene might be used as encouragement to slow carbon emissions and biodiversity loss, for instance; perhaps as evidence in legislation on conservation measures; or, in the assessment of compensation claims for environmental damage. It has the capacity to become the most politicized unit, by far, of the Geological Time Scales and therefore to take formal geological classification into uncharted waters. (Zalasiewicz *et al.*, 2010: 2231)

The Sociological Review, 62:S1, pp. 19–37 (2014), DOI: 10.1111/1467-954X.12122

While Zalasiewicz and his colleagues fall short of suggesting that the proclamation of the Anthropocene epoch is primarily politically or ethically motivated, this is clearly science that has come some distance from principles of disinterestedness or affective neutrality. This in turn raises interesting questions for the political and the ontological commitments of critical social and humanistic thought (see Mackenzie and Murphie, 2008; Clark, 2011). Perhaps, rather than excoriating physical scientists for conjuring up concepts which bolster their 'god-like powers', we might deign to see the idea of the Anthropocene as an overture towards the world of social thought and action: something in the nature of a rift-bridging offering or gift.

In an influential formulation, sociologist of science Bruno Latour (1993) has argued that the 'modern constitution' has involved parallel manoeuvres in which the natural sciences have evacuated the presence of human agency and ordering from the realities they describe while social thinkers have ignored the manifold non-humans which help compose the social (see Farías, this volume). If there is any substance to this claim, then the rapid uptake of the idea of humans as global geologic agents represents a significant transformation in the operation of the natural sciences – a shift that raises questions about what might figure as a corresponding gesture on the part of the social sciences or humanities. Not an exchange, perhaps, but a counter-gift, with something of the excess or exorbitance that sets the gift apart from an 'economic' transaction.

It is not nearly enough, I would argue, that social or cultural thinkers simply take hold of the idea of a fully humanized geology and use it to extend our own disciplinary dominions. Or even choose the predictable and non-excessive option of meeting in a middle ground. What we need to attend to is the way in which the very issue of geological boundary-transition that underpins the figuring of the Anthropocene puts social thought into contact with other epochs and eras.

While a case might be made that natural scientists ought to take the 'stratifications' or hierarchies discernible in human society more seriously, the onus is also on us to consider geological strata and planetary upheavals other than those in which humankind is now implicated. Whereas much recent social theoretical work around questions of society-nature relations assumes some kind of symmetry between social and natural processes (see Clark, 2011), one of the most profound (if initially counter-intuitive) effects of Anthropocene discourse is to disclose the radical asymmetry of human and non-human forces. By encouraging us to imagine worlds both before and after us, the idea of the Anthropocene offers a bold depiction of an Earth that has no need of humankind, a planet that will one day quite rapidly – in geological terms – scour most of the traces of human existence from its surface. It prompts us to consider the extent to which all human life remains utterly dependent on geologic and biological conditions bequeathed to us by Earth and cosmic systems. And reminds us that our existence is reliant on certain states or regimes of Earth systems that in many cases represent only a narrow range of their potential operating spaces.

A generous – and apposite – response to Anthropocene inquiry, then, might be a new willingness in critical social, cultural and philosophical thought to embrace the fully *inhuman*, in all its variability and volatility. This means putting thought and questions of practical action into sustained contact with times and spaces that radically exceed any conceivable human presence – with all the risks and the paradoxes this entails. It would require us to connect up the question of political possibility with the dynamics and the intransigence of vast domains that are themselves recalcitrant to the purchase of politics. In this way, the Anthropocene – viewed in all its disastrousness – confronts 'the political' with forces and events that have the capacity to undo the political, along with every other human achievement, by removing the very grounds on which we might convene and strategize – to the extent of annihilating political beings themselves. It puts politics – the realm of what we can and might do differently – head to head with what philosopher Claire Colebrook refers to as the 'monstrously impolitic' (2011: 11, see also 2012; Clark, 2012). Or to put it another way, it dramatically raises the stakes on the familiar question of 'how to find freedom in relation to a past we are stuck with and did not author' (Honig, 2009: 28).

Planetary crisis and the politics of emergency

But is this a good time to evoke realities that exceed the political? Is it wise to be pumping up 'the impolitic' at a juncture when the threat or the visitation of disaster seems to have become a justification for rolling back the achievements of political struggle? One of the most commanding themes in contemporary political thought – popular and academic – is the idea that states of emergency are being wielded by powerful actors to advance their own interests at the expense of less-resourced and more vulnerable groups (see Honig, 2009; Clark, 2013). Disastrous events or threats of impending disaster, it is argued, are being presented as the rationale for stringent and far-reaching regulatory practices that have profoundly 'antipolitical' connotations. This mode of critique, I want to suggest, offers a well-tuned framework for addressing some of the key proposals for responding to the upheavals of a humanized geology, even before the idea of Anthropocene has been fully absorbed into critical social and political thought.

In a world in which it is widely accepted that significant hazards and risks accompany intensifying globalization – a mood exacerbated by the events of 9/11 – it has been noted that authorities at every scale are taking it upon themselves to render the spaces under their jurisdiction more 'secure'. Along with rogue human collectives, physico-material agencies such as biological life or climatic processes are also being addressed as elements with the potential to act unpredictably at a global level – and thus to threaten the security of cities, regions or nation states (Dillon, 2007; Cooper, 2006). What concerns critical commentators is not so much the acknowledgement of these risks, as the way they are being mobilized to make it appear as though securitization measures are the only viable response (Braun, 2007: 15). Drawing variously on the work of Walter Benjamin, Carl Schmitt, Michel Foucault, and especially Giorgio

The Sociological Review, 62:S1, pp. 19–37 (2014), DOI: 10.1111/1467-954X.12122

Agamben, progressive thinkers have sought to expose the ways in which the exceptional conditions of the emergency or disaster are being invoked with such frequency that they risk being normalized (Aradau and van Munster, 2011). A generalized condition where potentially catastrophic events might suddenly irrupt in any form, at any moment, anywhere in the world, they argue, is being invoked to justify sweeping new measures of surveillance, ordering and regulation, to the point of undoing hard-won political freedoms. But perhaps most relevant to the event horizon of the Anthropocene, is the claim that active pre-emption – getting in first and changing the conditions which might precipitate a crisis – is a vital tactic of forces of securitization (see Dillon, 2007).

'Pre-emption', observes sociologist Melinda Cooper, 'transforms our generalized alertness into a real mobilizing force, compelling us to become the uncertain future we're most in thrall to' (2006: 125). The trouble with pre-emptive measures, she cautions, is that they can be just as unpredictable and irruptive as the hazards they would defuse (2010: 184). It is precisely this logic that Cooper recognizes in a 2003 report on the consequences of abrupt climate change for the US which proposes 'geoengineering' the Earth's climate to stave off dangerous climate change:

> The paradox of this argument is that it calls for a strategic intervention into the atmosphere in order to pre-empt the worst effects of climate change, while acknowledging that such an intervention may itself be indistinguishable from the process of climate change – that is to say, equally unpredictable, incalculable and turbulent in its unfolding. (2010: 184)

Over the last decade or so, the possibility of technological intervention into Earth systems on a planetary scale has been on the ascendant in some scientific communities as an emergency measure that might be attempted if global climate looks likely to pass into a 'dangerous' or 'extremely dangerous' phase. Several key thinkers associated with the Anthropocene idea, including Paul Crutzen, have speculated that some form of intentional large-scale climate modification – or 'geoengineering' – might be considered, in the light of the failure of global climate governance to reverse or even slow greenhouse gas emissions (Crutzen, 2006: 214). Nearly all proponents of geoengineering research, however, stipulate that this would be an emergency measure, just as they stress that collective political action to abate greenhouse gas emission would be greatly preferable to technical interventions to alleviate or counterbalance the effects of changing atmospheric composition.

For Cooper, the possibility of a geotechnological pre-empting of dangerous climate change not only comes with profound risks and uncertainties: the mindset of a permanent state of emergency to which it belongs shores up existing imperial power – the power of global or planetary capitalism – at the expense of alternative, more progressive possibilities (2010: 184). If not quite in these terms, many other commentators, including a number who are involved in research in the geoengineering field, have voiced strong concerns about a commitment to technical fixes taking on a life of its own at the expense of pursuing socio-political transformation (Hamilton, 2011; Keith, 2000; cf. Heartland Institute, 2007).

As it becomes clearer that it is not simply climate, but a range of interconnected Earth systems that are currently under profound stress (see Steffen *et al.*, 2004), geotechnical responses are taking into their purview more than just climate stabilization.[1] Geo-engineering, in this sense, might best be viewed as a response to *all* the entangled and mutually reinforcing geologic transformations that are gathered under the rubric of the Anthropocene. Debates about geoengineering, in other words, could be seen as a nascent expression of the much bigger issue of governing the Anthropocene – as a vehicle by which the question of the political implications of the experience of wholesale planetary emergency is being broached.

Whether or not 'apocalyptic' imagery serves to promote or incapacitate politicization has long been debated in environmentalist circles and in critical social thought (see Swyngedouw, 2007; cf. Yusoff and Gabrys, 2011). In another register and another field, the question of whether 'actual' disasters provide opportunities for political transformation, or whether they are primarily occasions for the entrenchment of pre-existing power relations, has also been a matter of lively discussion (Cuny, 1983; Pelling and Dill, 2010; Kelman, 2012; Tironi, this volume). Whereas Naomi Klein's (2008) bestselling inquiry into the machinations of 'disaster capitalism' comes down firmly on the side of the latter, geographer Mark Pelling and anthropologist Kathleen Dill sift through a range of case studies to arrive, cautiously, at a more hopeful prognosis. 'Disaster shocks', they propose 'open political space for the contestation or concentration of political power and the underlying distributions of rights between citizens and citizens and the state' (2010: 34).

Engaging in a more general sense with the political potential of the crisis or emergency, political theorist Bonnie Honig comes to a similar conclusion. Taking issue with the rush of recent critical work that characteristically equates the state of emergency with the suspension of civil liberties and the closure of political possibility, Honig argues for the fundamental ambivalence of invoking emergency, observing that no declaration of emergency can dictate how it will be received, interpreted and acted upon. In contrast to claims that the 'emergency brings an end to real politics', she seeks out and discovers new possibilities for political renewal and change: 'hidden resources and alternative angles of vision that might motivate action in concert in emergency settings' (2009: xv; see also Aradau and van Munster, 2011).

But what might these political possibilities be? What is demanded of the political in the face of the threats and challenges designated by the Anthropocene? In the final section, I want to sketch out some of the ways that responses to the current geologic predicament of humankind are awakening to Michel Serres' call for a 'geopolitics in the sense of the real Earth' (1995: 44; see also Dalby, 2007). More than a matter of confronting the consequences of our own actions, I want to suggest, a growing conception of the inherent instability of the Earth is beginning to impact upon our understanding of the composition

The Sociological Review, 62:S1, pp. 19–37 (2014), DOI: 10.1111/1467-954X.12122
© 2014 The Author. Editorial organisation © 2014 The Editorial Board of the Sociological Review

of the political; our sense of what it is we work with – or against – when we mobilize collectively.

Towards an Anthropocene geopolitics

Resonating with other researchers in the field of science and technology studies, Sheila Jasanoff writes of 'the indeterminacy and complexity of many novel risks, and their refusal to stay within neatly drawn geopolitical lines' (2010: 19; see also Petersen, this volume). It is timely, however, to ask what exactly the 'geo' in 'geopolitical' is doing in this scenario, and what claims about the coming of an Anthropocene epoch might mean for such an understanding of 'geopolitical lines'. Perhaps the most crucial lesson of the Anthropocene is that the Earth itself must be understood as much more than a mere surface or stage on which political contests take place: it must acquire a volumetric or vertical dimension (Dalby, 2013; see also Elden, 2013). That is to say, the 'geopolitical' can no longer simply refer to a horizontal and synchronous globality.

But this requires something more than extending the conventional concerns of geopolitical discourse and practice upwards into the atmosphere or downwards into the depths of the ocean or Earth. It requires us to bring politics into an intensive engagement with the planet's own dynamics: its processes of sedimentation and mobilization, its layering and folding, its periodicities and singularities. This means that the crucial borders or thresholds on the political agenda are not only those which divide nations or other socially inscribed territorial divisions of the Earth's surface, but also the spatio-temporal junctures at which one state or regime of an Earth system passes into another (Clark, 2011, see Weszkalnys, this volume on the Cenomanian Turonian extinction or boundary event). Or to put it another way, politics must expand its concerns with the shaping and reshaping of territory to embrace processes of stratification and destratification (see Deleuze and Guattari, 1987).

When it comes to the threat of crossing boundaries or thresholds in Earth systems, as Johan Rockström and his interdisciplinary team observes: '[c]urrent governance and management paradigms are often oblivious to or lack a mandate to act upon these planetary risks' (2009: unpag.).While the repeated failure of climate summits to achieve the binding commitments necessary to ward off 'dangerous' or 'extremely dangerous' climate change is the most conspicuous manifestation of this shortfall, the relative paucity of attention to other imminent or already-transgressed 'planetary boundaries' is no less revealing (Anderson and Bows, 2011; Rockström et al., 2009). Recent calls for what has been variously termed 'planetary stewardship' (Steffen et al., 2011); 'Earth System governmentality' (Lövbrand et al., 2009); and 'global earth system governance' (Dryzek and Stevenson, 2011: 1873) express a growing recognition of the need for new or greatly strengthened frameworks to meet the political challenge of maintaining Earth systems in socially desirable states.

Needless to say, normative reasoning is far from enough to conjure such architectures into existence. Any conceivable success, political theorists John Dryzek and Hayley Stevenson remind us, must work through and from existing experience (2011: 1873).

But what kinds of experience might be relevant here? We have seen that critical social thinkers can be as apprehensive about the successful operationalizing of strategies to 'manage' Earth systems as they are about inadequate planetary governance. While radical critics tend to champion a generalized advancement of democratic or deliberative political processes, they are often less than forthcoming about their own preferences for responding practically to the challenges posed by dynamic Earth or life processes. There are, of course, no easy answers to the question of how to gain experience of 'governing' the forces of the Earth. As Latour argues, novel situations configured by messy admixtures of social and material ingredients present a new imperative to improvise or experiment (see Farías, this volume). When it comes to situations with the scale and complexity of global climate change, however, he suggests we are way out of our depth: 'The problem is that while we know how to conduct a scientific experiment in the narrow confines of a laboratory, we have no idea how to pursue collective experiments in the confusing atmosphere of a whole culture' (Latour, 2003: 31).

But who exactly the 'we' is in this statement raises questions of its own – inviting us to consider the historical and geographical depth of the human experience of living through environmental extremes. One of the motivations for thinking through geological durations, after all, is to contextualize the events of the present in a much broader framework. As philosopher-geologist Robert Frodeman explains, '[e]arthquakes, floods, hurricanes, and droughts are places where deep time erupts into more familiar temporal rhythms' (2003: 125). If such threshold transitions or destratifications might be seen as ways in which the Earth experiments with its human (and non-human) inhabitants, they are equally occasions which oblige human populations to respond with experiments of their own. Many of those peoples who still live in relatively close proximity to the rhythms and upheavals of the Earth have learned how best to shelter from extreme events, when to move to safer ground, how to channel excess energies, what to cache or stockpile, and when to fight fire with fire (Clark, 2008; 2011). The shaping of such practices and the decisions out of which they are forged might well be seen as a form of geologic politics – though this is not necessarily 'politics' which is played out in the patient, deliberative manner that social theorists such as Latour or Ulrich Beck (1995) prefer (see Michael, this volume).

As philosophers Gilles Deleuze and Felix Guattari (1987) suggest, our engagement with the organizational layerings and dynamics of our material worlds can be more than reactive or defensive. There is always the possibility of constructive traversals of compositional strata, of intercession in the flows of matter and energy, with no purpose other than the joy of experimentation and the pleasure of creating new forms and structures. At the same time, Deleuze and Guattari counsel about the dangers of 'a too-sudden destratification',

The Sociological Review, 62:S1, pp. 19–37 (2014), DOI: 10.1111/1467-954X.12122

warning that this 'will sometimes end in chaos, the void and destruction, and sometimes lock us back into the strata' (1987: 503). If this cautionary note applies in a general sense to the planetary predicament that results from unrestricted consumption of fossil fuels, so too is it apposite with regard to strategies for deliberate geotechnical interventions into Earth systems – not least the kind of unauthorized geoengineering experiment that recently took place off the Canadian coast (Geere, 2012).

While geoengineering proposals have justifiably attracted critical scrutiny, they have in the process helped put practical experimentation with dynamic Earth processes more explicitly on the academic and the political agenda (see Galarraga and Szerszynski, 2012). Today, alongside speculative planet-scaled 'smoke and mirrors' geoengineering schemes (Humphreys, 2011), a host of more moderately scaled and easily reversible strategies for intervening in Earth systems are currently under experiment and review. These include localized alterations of the planet's albedo involving brightening of water and transformations of vegetative cover or the built environment, a range of forms of biological and geological carbon capture such as soil enhancement using charred organic matter, and a whole raft of proposals to protect and enhance ecosystems (Olson, 2012; see also Chris, 2013). Such strategies are of interest not because they promise quick solutions to climate change and other Earth system threshold problems, but because they give an idea of the possible mix of techno-physical and socio-political issues that may characterize emergent 'geo-political' agendas. They direct our attention not only to the kind of material interventions over which collective decisions must be made, but to the need for political constituencies to consider their own everyday practical or material implication in the dynamics of Earth systems – to ask how they themselves might take matter-energy flows into their own hands. And this implies that, just as critical social thinkers increasingly demand political awareness on the part of Earth systems scientists and engineers, so too must we require of ourselves a willingness to commit to some form of experimental intervention in Earth processes – with all the risks this inevitably entails.

Arguably the most audacious proposal on the contemporary geo-political agenda – one that also seeks to legitimate itself through rhetorics of planetary emergency – is to leave fossil fuels in the ground (see Temper *et al.*, 2013). If industrialism – or more precisely, industrial capitalism – has established itself as a geologic force primarily through growing reliance on fossilized hydrocarbons, then the imposition of any significant restriction on fossil fuel extraction and usage would itself constitute an experimental geologic intervention. It would be at once a mode of geotechnics and an object of geo-politics. But any mass reduction of reliance upon oil, gas and coal would also withdraw the primary means by which a large proportion of the planet's human population currently modulates many of the effects of the variability of the Earth systems – both directly and indirectly. To decrease reliance on the buried solar energy of past geologic eras, in other words, is not simply to turn to a more benign and dispersed solar through-flow. It is to renew, after a geologically infinitesimal interval, our characteristic exposure to the volatile forces of the Earth and the cosmos.

Not that human susceptibility to dynamic physical processes ever really withdrew, as the incessant and escalating impact of natural disasters on human populations makes clear. What the emergent geo-politics of the Anthropocene is beginning to look like, I have been suggesting, is a complex blend of socio-political and physico-material negotiations, in which either side of the conflu-ence is as experimental or improvisational as the other. As is the message of disasters in general, and the ascending mega-disaster of the Anthropocene in particular, this is more or other than a matter of expanding the realm of effective political-material deliberation until it becomes coextensive with nature or the Earth. It is about fronting up to the inescapable – though shifting and non-objectifiable – limits of the political; about recognizing the crucial importance of the juncture where the effective range of collective intervention comes up against the 'monstrously impolitic' reaches of the Earth and cosmos.

Acknowledging that material existence vastly exceeds the measure of the human – an undercurrent of the Anthropocene idea – drives home the fact that all interventions in Earth systems are matters of trial and error. At whatever scale they are attempted, experiments with flows of matter and energy have a fair chance of failing, falling short, or having unintended consequences. Efforts to deflect or modulate disaster, in this sense, can be expected to precipitate new disasters. The geo-political or cosmo-political challenge of the Anthropocene then, may be as much about how we choose to engage with others whose experiments have fallen short or been overwhelmed, as it is about how we make decisions about our own strategic interventions. And ethical relating too, as the most searching theorists of the disaster have long observed, is a matter of risky experimentation and urgent improvisation.

Note

1 See, for example, Crutzen's (2006) consideration of geoengineering proposals not only with regard to anthropogenic greenhouse gas emissions, but also in relation to the role played by atmospheric aerosols in contributing to 'global dimming'.

References

Alley, R. B., (2000), *The Two-Mile Time Machine: Ice Cores, Abrupt Climate Change, and Our Future*, Princeton, NJ: Princeton University Press.

Anderson, K. and Bows, A., (2011), 'Beyond "dangerous" climate change: emission scenarios for a new world', *Philosophical Transactions of the Royal Society A*, 369: 20–44.

Aradau, C. and van Munster, R., (2011), *Politics of Catastrophe: Genealogies of the Unknown*, London: Routledge.

Beck, U., (1995), *Ecological Politics in an Age of Risk*, Cambridge: Polity Press.

Blanchot, M., (1995), *The Writing of the Disaster*, Lincoln, NE: University of Nebraska Press.

The Sociological Review, 62:S1, pp. 19–37 (2014), DOI: 10.1111/1467-954X.12122

Braun, B., (2007), 'Biopolitics and the molecularization of life', *Cultural Geographies*, 14: 6–28.

Broecker, W. S., (1987), 'Unpleasant surprises in the greenhouse', *Nature*, 328 (9 July): 123–126.

Chakrabarty, D., (2008), 'The climate of history: four theses', *Critical Inquiry*, 35: 197–222.

Chester, D., (2001), 'The 1755 Lisbon Earthquake', *Progress in Physical Geography*, 25 (3): 363–383.

Chris, R., (2013), 'Geoengineering, climate change and future generations: the emergence of systems thinking in response to complexity and uncertainty', PhD thesis, Department of Geography, The Open University, Milton Keynes.

Clark, N., (2008), 'Aboriginal cosmopolitanism', *International Journal of Urban and Regional Studies*, 32 (3): 737–744.

Clark, N., (2011), *Inhuman Nature: Sociable Life on a Dynamic Planet*, London: Sage.

Clark, N., (2012), 'Rock, life, fire: speculative geophysics and the Anthropocene', *Oxford Literary Review*, 34 (2): 259–276.

Clark, N., (2013), 'Mobile life: biosecurity practices and insect globalization', *Science as Culture*, 22 (1): 16–37.

Cohen, T., (2012), 'Polemos: "I am at war with myself" or, Deconstruction™ in the Anthropocene?' *The Oxford Literary Review*, 34 (2): 239–257.

Colebrook, C., (2011), 'Matter without bodies', *Derrida Today*, 4: 1–20.

Colebrook, C., (2012), 'Not symbiosis, not now: why anthropogenic change is not really human', *The Oxford Literary Review*, 34 (2): 185–209.

Cooper, M., (2006), 'Pre-empting emergence: the biological turn in the war on terror', *Theory Culture and Society*, 23 (4): 113–135.

Cooper, M., (2010), 'Turbulent worlds: financial markets and environmental crisis', *Theory, Culture and Society*, 27: 167–190.

Crutzen, P. J., (2002), 'Geology of mankind', *Nature*, 415 (6867): 3–23.

Crutzen, P. J., (2006), 'Albedo enhancement by stratospheric sulphur injections: a contribution to resolve a policy dilemma?', *Climatic Change*, 77: 211–219.

Crutzen, P. J. and Stoermer, E. F., (2000), 'The "Anthropocene" ', *IGBP Newsletter*, 41: 17–18.

Cuny, F., (1983), *Disasters and Development*, Oxford: Oxford University Press.

Dalby, S., (2007), 'Anthropocene geopolitics: globalisation, empire, environment and critique', *Geography Compass*, 1: 103–118.

Dalby, S., (2013), 'The geopolitics of climate change', *Political Geography*, in press.

Davis, M., (1996), 'Cosmic dancers on history's stage? The permanent revolution in the earth sciences', *New Left Review*, 217: 48–84.

Davis, M., (2008), 'Living on the ice shelf: humanity's meltdown', *TomDispatch.com* 26 June, available at: www.tomdispatch.com/post/174949 (accessed 20 November 2009).

Deleuze, G. and Guattari, F., (1987), *A Thousand Plateaus: Capitalism and Schizophrenia*, Minneapolis: University of Minnesota Press.

Dillon, M., (2007), 'Governing terror: the state of emergency of biopolitical emergence', *International Political Sociology*, 1: 7–28.

Dryzek, J. and Stevenson, H., (2011), 'Global democracy and earth system governance', *Ecological Economics*, 70: 1865–1874.

Elden, S., (2013), 'Secure the volume: vertical geopolitics and the depth of power', *Political Geography*, 34: 35–51.

Frodeman, R., (2000), 'Preface: shifting plates: the new earth sciences', in R. Frodeman (ed.), *Earth Matters: The Earth Sciences, Philosophy, and the Clams of Community*, Upper Saddle River, NJ: Prentice-Hall.

Frodeman, R., (2003), *Geo-logic: Breaking Ground between Philosophy and the Earth Sciences*, Albany, NY: University of New York Press.

Galarraga, M. and Szerszynski, B., (2012), 'Making climates: solar radiation management and the ethics of fabrication', in C. Preston (ed.), *Engineering the Climate: The Ethics of Solar Radiation Management*, Lexington, MA: Lexington Books.

Geere, D., (2012), 'Rogue geoengineer creates massive Pacific plankton bloom', *Wired*, 20 October, available at: www.wired.co.uk/news/archive/2012-10/20/plankton-bloom (accessed November 2013).

Gelbspan, R., (2006), 'Scepticism, disinformation and obstruction in U.S climate circles', *Tipping Point Conference*, Environmental Change Institute, Oxford University, available at: www .capefarewell.com/climate-science/comment-opinion/scepticism.html (accessed 16 March 2013).

Grant, I., (2000), 'Kant after geophilosophy: the physics of analogy and the metaphysics of nature', in A. Rehberg and R. Jones (eds), *The Matter of Critique: Readings in Kant's Philosophy*, Manchester: Clinamen Press.

Hamilton, C., (2011), 'Ethical anxieties about geoengineering: moral hazard, slippery slope and playing God', available at: www.clivehamilton.net.au/cms/media/ethical_anxieties_about _geoengineering.pdf (accessed 16 March 2013)

Heartland Institute, (2007), 'Geo-engineering seen as a practical, cost-effective global warming Strategy', *Heartlander*, available at: http://news.heartland.org/newspaper-article/2007/12/01/geo -engineering-seen-practical-cost-effective-global-warming-strategy

Honig, B., (2009), *Emergency Politics: Paradox, Law, Democracy*, Princeton, NJ: Princeton University Press.

Humphreys, D., (2011), 'Smoke and mirrors: some reflections on the science and politics of geoengineering', *Journal of Environment and Development*, 20: 99–120.

Jasanoff, S., (2010), 'Beyond calculation: a democratic response to risk', in A. Lakoff (ed.), *Disaster and the Politics of Intervention*, New York: Columbia University Press.

Kant, I., (1993 [1938]), *Opus Postumum*, Cambridge: Cambridge University Press.

Kant, I., (1994 [1756]), 'History and physiography of the most remarkable cases of the earthquake which towards the end of the year 1755 shook a great part of the earth', in *Four Neglected Essays*, Hong Kong: Philopschy Press.

Keith, D., (2000), 'Geoengineering the climate: history and prospect', *Annual Review of Energy and the Environment*, 25: 245–284.

Kelman, I., (2012), *Disaster Diplomacy: How Disasters Affect Peace and Conflict*, Abingdon: Routlege.

Klein, N., (2008), *The Shock Doctrine: The Rise of Disaster Capitalism*, London: Penguin.

Latour, B., (1993), *We Have Never Been Modern*, Cambridge, MA: Harvard University Press.

Latour, B., (2003), 'Atmosphère, Atmosphère', in S. May (ed.), *Olafur Eliasson: The Weather Project*, London: Tate Publishing.

Lövbrand, E., Stripple, J. and Wiman, B., (2009), 'Earth system governmentality: reflections on science in the Anthropocene', *Global Environmental Change*, 19: 7–13.

Lovelock, J., (2008), 'A geophysiologist's thoughts on geoengineering', *Philosophical Transactions of the Royal Society A*, 366: 3883–3890.

Mackenzie, A. and Murphie, A., (2008), 'The two cultures become multiple? Sciences, humanities and everyday experimentation', *Australian Feminist Studies*, 23 (55): 87–100.

Morton, T., (2012), 'Ecology without the present', *The Oxford Literary Review*, 34 (2): 229–238.

Neiman, S., (2002), *Evil in Modern Thought: An Alternative History of Philosophy*, Princeton, NJ: Princeton University Press.

Olson, R., (2012), 'Soft geoengineering: a gentler approach to addressing climate change', *Environment: Science and Policy for Sustainable Development*, 54 (5): 29–39.

Pelling, M. and Dill, K., (2010), 'Disaster politics: tipping points for change in the adaptation of sociopolitical regimes', *Progress in Human Geography*, 34 (1): 21–37.

Ray, G., (2004), 'Reading the Lisbon Earthquake: Adorno, Lyotard, and the contemporary sublime', *Yale Journal of Criticism*, 17 (1): 1–18.

Roberts, J. T. and Parks, B. C., (2007), *A Climate of Injustice: Global Inequality, North-South Politics, and Climate Policy*, Cambridge, MA: MIT Press.

Robock, A., Marquardt, A., Kravitz, B. and Stenchikov, G., (2009), 'Benefits, risks, and costs of stratospheric geoengineering', *Geophysical Research Letters*, 36: 1–9.

The Sociological Review, 62:S1, pp. 19–37 (2014), DOI: 10.1111/1467-954X.12122

Rockström, J., Steffen, W., Noone, K., Chapin, F. S. III., Lambin, E., Lenton, T., Scheffer, M., Folke, C., Schellnhuber, H., Nykvist, B., De Wit, C., Hughes, T., van der Leeuw, S., Rodhe, H., Sörlin, S., Snyder, P., Costanza, R., Svedin, U., Falkenmark, M., Karlberg, L., Corell, R., Fabry, V., Hansen, J., Walker, B., Liverman, D., Richardson, K., Crutzen, P. and Foley, J., (2009), 'Planetary boundaries: exploring the safe operating space for humanity', *Ecology and Society*, 14 (2): 32, available at: www.ecologyandsociety.org/vol14/iss2/art32/ (accessed 16 March 2013).

Rudwick, M., (2005), *Bursting the Limits of Time: The Reconstruction of Geohistory in the Age of Revolution*, Chicago: University of Chicago Press.

Scheffer, M., Carpenter, S., Foley, J. A., Folkes,, C. and Walker, B., (2001), 'Catastrophic Shifts in Ecosystems', *Nature*, 413 (11 October): 591–596.

Serres, M., (1995), *The Natural Contract*, Ann Arbor, MI: University of Michigan Press.

Steffen, W., Sanderson, A., Tyson, P., Jäger, J., Matson, P., Moore, B. III., Oldfield, F., Richardson, K., Schellnhuber, H., Turner, B. and Wasson, R., (2004), *Global Change and the Earth System: A Planet under Pressure*, Berlin: Springer-Verlag.

Steffen, W., Persson, A., Deutsch, L., Zalasiewicz, J., Williams, M., Richardson, K., Crumley, C., Crutzen, P., Folke, C., Gordon, L., Molina, M., Ramanathan, V., Rockström, J., Scheffer, M., Schellnhuber, H.J. and Svedin, U., (2011), 'The Anthropocene: from global change to planetary stewardship', *Ambio*, 40 (7): 739–761.

Swyngedouw, E., (2007), 'Impossible "sustainability" and the post-political condition', in R. Krueger and D. Gibbs (eds), *The Sustainable Development Paradox*, 13–40, New York: Guilford Press.

Szerszynski, B., (2012), 'The end of the end of nature: the Anthropocene and the fate of the human', *The Oxford Literary Review*, 34 (2): 165–184.

Temper, L., Yánez, I., Sharife, K., Ojo, G., Martinez-Alier, J., CANA, Combes, M., Cornelissen, K., Lerkelund, H., Louw, M., Martínez, E., Minnaar, J., Molina, P., Murcia, D., Oriola, T., Osuoka, A., Pérez, M.M., Roa Avendaño, T., Urkidi, L., Valdés, M., Wadzah, N. and Wykes, S., (2013), *Towards a Post-Oil Civilization: Yasunization and Other Initiatives to Leave Fossil Fuels in the Soil*, EJOLT Report No. 6.

Vernadsky, V., (1998 [1926]), *The Biosphere*, New York: Copernicus.

Westbroek, P., (1992), *Life as a Geological Force: Dynamics of the Earth*, New York: W. W. Norton.

Weisman , A., (2007), *The World without Us*, New York: Virgin.

Wood, D., (2004), *Five Billion Years of Global Change: A History of the Land*, New York: Guilford Press.

Yusoff, K. and Gabrys, J., (2011), 'Climate change and the imagination', *WIREs Climate Change*, 2: 516–534.

Zalasiewicz, J., (2008), *The Earth after Us*, Oxford: Oxford University Press.

Zalasiewicz, J., Williams, M., Steffen, W. and Crutzen, P., (2010), 'The New World of the Anthropocene', *Environmental Science and Technology*, 44: 2228–2231.

Zalasiewicz, J., Williams, M., Smith, A., Barry, T., Coe, A., Bown, P., Brenchley, P., Cantrill, D., Gale, A., Gibbard, P., Gregory, F., Hounslow, M., Kerr, A., Pearson, P., Knox, R., Powell, J., Waters, C., Marshall, J., Oates, M., Rawson, P. and Stone, P., (2008), 'Are we now living in the Anthropocene?' *GSA Today*, 18: 4–8.

Zalasiewicz, J., Williams, M., Fortey, R., Smith, A., Barry, T., Coe, A., Bown, P., Rawson, P., Gale, A., Gibbard, P., Gregory, J., Hounslow, M., Kerr, A., Pearson, P., Knox, R., Powell, J., Water, C., Marshall, J., Oates, M. and Stone, P., (2011), 'Stratigraphy of the Anthropocene', *Philosophical Transactions of the Royal Society A*, 369 (1938): 1036–1055.

Žižek, S., (2011), *Living in the End Times*, London: Verso.

37

Disasters as meshworks: migratory birds and the enlivening of Doñana's toxic spill

Israel Rodríguez-Giralt, Francisco Tirado and Manuel Tironi

Abstract: The aim of this article is to revisit disasters as materially enlivened events. The sociology of disasters has usually rested upon two assumptions. First, that disasters are phenomena circumscribed in time and space. They are geographically situated and time-specific, thus their effects can be controlled and compared. And second, that the main actors involved in disasters are humans and institutions, the basic units of sociological research and theory. These principles, taken together, help in converting disaster into objects for cultural inquiry, but at the expense of diluting their material surplus. Based on the work of Tim Ingold, and drawing on the case of the Aznalcóllar ecological disaster in Doñana, one of the most damaging environmental disasters in the history of Spain, we propose to define disasters as meshworks in order to fully grasp the vibrant ontology of disasters. More specifically, by focusing on the role played by migratory birds in the enacting of the disaster, we argue that disasters are dynamic realities, difficult to localize and always distributed along disparate scales and actors. Moreover, disasters have a dual reality, unfolding actually and virtually at once – and therefore comprising a form of cosmopolitics rather than conforming to classical political imaginations. Finally, our larger point is to take disasters as opportunities to rethink our ways of living together.

Keywords: environmental disasters, Doñana's toxic spill, non-humans, ontology, meshwork, cosmopolitics

Introduction

On 25 April 1998, more than 40 metres of the retaining wall of a tailings lagoon in the Aznalcóllar mine, in the south of Spain, collapsed. Up to two billion litres of tailings with a high metal content from the pyrite flotation process, together with another four billion litres of acidic water filled with dissolved heavy metals, spilled out over an area measuring 62 kilometres long. The spill affected inhabited zones (about 10 municipalities, 46,000 inhabitants), enormous extensions of cultivated agricultural fields (mainly fruits and vegetables, cotton fields, olive orchards and cattle pastures), river-fishing areas and hundreds of potable water

The Sociological Review, 62:S1, pp. 38–60 (2014), DOI: 10.1111/1467-954X.12123

wells (Bartolomé and Vega, 2002). But it also seriously threatened the watershed and the fauna of Doñana's National Park, one of the premier wildlife reserves in all of Europe and a crucial actor in the economy of the region.

Disasters, as the one in Doñana, have gained momentum in sociology. After decades of intense work, they have been rescued from the dungeons of the earth sciences and positioned as valid objects of social inquiry. Indeed, the so-called sociology of disasters has convincingly argued that, as represented by the toxic spill in Doñana, disasters function as breaching experiments in which the social, shaken by an external force, emerges unveiled. Disasters are, in this sense, excuses to fully comprehend the social: a methodological shortcut into behaviors, cosmologies and structures. Although conceptual adjustments have been made, Charles Fritz's (1961) original definition of disasters still represent the general framework with which disasters are assessed. For him, disasters are:

> actual or threatened, accidental or uncontrollable events that are concentrated in time and space, in which a society, or a relatively self-sufficient subdivision of a society undergoes severe danger, and incurs such losses to its members and physical appurtenances that the social structure is disrupted and the fulfillment of all or some of the essential functions of the society, or its subdivision, is prevented. (Fritz, 1961: 655)

In this definition at least two important assumptions are made in relation to a sociological configuration of disasters. First, disasters are thought of as a phenomenon circumscribed in time and space. They are geographically situated and time-specific, thus their effects can be controlled and compared. Second, the main actors involved in disasters are humans and institutions, the basic units of sociological research and theory. The disastrousness of disasters resides in their power to distress the 'fulfillment of all or some essential functions of society'. The internal dynamic of disasters (the movement of winds, the logics of tides, the geological conducts) are outside the social sciences. The sociological bearing of a disaster lies in the possibilities of social change brought about by disaster itself.

From this perspective the toxics of Doñana are not relevant in themselves but in their capacity to reveal the complex social, political and cultural arrangements causing the disaster or explaining its unfolding. The sludge polluting the basin is significant only insofar as its damaging effect allows for a better understanding of how state and municipal institutions reacted to the emergency, what type of power relations are entangled in the shaping of the event, or to what extent eco-movements have gained presence in the Spanish political arena. Thus while disasters are always extremely (even excessively) material and affective events, sociologists have usually neglected this worldliness and have looked *beyond* it in their search for the social.

However, recent social research has compelled us to rethink the role of materiality and non-humans in our social explanations. These vindications come from Science and Technology Studies (Callon, 1986; Latour, 1993; Michael, 2000; Mol and Law, 1994; Law and Mol, 2008), the new cultural geography (Murdoch, 1997; Whatmore, 2002; Braun, 2008; Bear and Eden, 2011; Castree, 2003; Hailwood, 2000; Hinchliffe *et al.*, 2005; Holloway, 2003)

The Sociological Review, 62:S1, pp. 38–60 (2014), DOI: 10.1111/1467-954X.12123   39

and 'speculative realism' (Harman, 2009, 2010). Put bluntly, these approaches converge, first, in understanding the functions and attributes of materiality as being neither singular nor stable. Materials are singular and recalcitrant (Bennett, 2010; Connolly, 2010; Stengers, 2010; Braun and Whatmore, 2010). Second, the recognition of materials and objects as an integral part of social life implies reshuffling the classical modern dichotomies (society/nature, human/ non-human, technology/culture). And third, materials not only redistribute existing categories; they also create new ones: objects unearth more-than-human political arenas in which conventional notions of representation, democracy and participation have to be expanded (Barry, 2001; Latour and Weibel, 2005; Marres, 2012).

The aim of this article is to enrich our understanding of disasters by connecting these insights with the already existent conversation driven by disaster scholars. Environmental disasters, we claim, are privileged laboratories in which to analyse how humans and non-humans interchange their capacities and attributes, and to rethink what counts as an actor when establishing *a priori* differences between the agency of human beings, the activity of materials and the intervention of institutions becomes difficult. We are not alone in this task. Clark (2011), Schillmeier (2011) and Harada (2000) have already proposed a material-oriented understanding of disasters. With them, we will claim that disasters need to be embodied, materialized and cosmo-politicized in order to fully apprehend their mutable, dynamic and uncertain nature.

We also aim, however, to expand further this material-oriented argument. While the objectual and affective condition of disasters has been emphasized, there is still a sense of generality: materiality is mobilized as an anonymous and generic condition, and not as a situation-specific and entangled way of being-in-the-world with its particular engagement and affordances. In order to shed light upon these points we utilize the concept of *meshwork* recently proposed by Tim Ingold (2007, 2008a, 2008b). For Ingold, materials (he explicitly refuses to use the notion of materiality) are better viewed as improvised and constantly 'moving-forward' meshes that entangle different kinds of lines and different types of matters with varied and variable properties (Ingold, 2008b: 211–212). Conceptualizing disasters as meshworks helps us to understand how a general and exclusive definition of their delimitation is highly problematic, and how a fixed delineation between the material and the non-material, or between different scales of action, is unproductive: only the trajectories bounding the formation and development of lines prevail. Therefore the meshwork should not be identified with a static network that connects and defines entities based on such connections. Its operation is much more complex and sophisticated. The lines that constitute a meshwork signal a flow of activity, a source of difference and, therefore, generation of an ever-changing reality. We use the case of the Aznalcóllar ecological disaster in Doñana, one of the most damaging environmental disasters in the history of Spain, to explore disasters as meshworks, and how this exploration allows for a richer accounting of the materiality of disasters.

The Sociological Review, 62:S1, pp. 38–60 (2014), DOI: 10.1111/1467-954X.12123
© 2014 The Authors. Editorial organisation © 2014 The Editorial Board of the Sociological Review

Conceptualizing disasters

Disasters have been present in the research agenda of the social sciences for almost a century.[1] Sociologists, anthropologists and social psychologists have turned to disasters, traditionally secluded in the field of engineering and earth sciences, as a way to understand the premises of social structures and behaviours. During this time, how disasters have been defined and to what end they have been included into social research has changed significantly. Between World War II and the early 1960s,[2] sociologists were interested in disasters as exceptional events that provoke particular types of behaviour – from panic to solidarity (Gilbert, 1998; Perry, 1998, 2007). In the 1970s disasters are, on the contrary, redefined as the consequence of sociostructural risks – for instance the social vulnerability preceding and facilitating disruption (García-Acosta, 2002). And later in the 1980s (Perry, 2007), disasters are seen not only as the effects of pre-existent sociocultural vulnerabilities but as objects socially constructed themselves (Spector and Kitsuse, 1977); the effect of the mediation of discourses and representations shaping its meaning, extension and intensity (Stallings, 1997).

However, despite the differences, the sociology of disasters shares a kind of Durkhemian drive. Generally speaking, the different approaches tend to see disasters as a phenomenon that can be studied in purely *social* terms. As Michael Guggenheim points out in the introduction to this volume, this socialization of disasters can be partly explained due to the need of social science to rescue disasters from the monopoly of earth sciences and engineering. But the cost of this boundary-work has been to neglect the materially recalcitrant nature of disasters (Farías in this volume), its objectual surplus, its thing-power (Bennett, 2010). Indeed, the sociology of disasters has mobilized a highly dematerialized definition of its object of inquiry. It has assumed an ontology in which the material liveliness of disasters appears as a passive and out-worldly feature – as a residual characteristic whose only function is to trigger or unveil relevant social processes. Or as Perry (1998: 204) puts it, 'disasters are socially defined events in social time' and 'create disruption of social intercourse and, in that regard, are a context for social action, *but the disaster agent itself is not a key component of the definitional task*' (emphasis added).

As a result of this, the disaster as a material and vital object is either relegated to a dark and primary place outside the social world (hence its capabilities to shock the world from the outside) or invited to participate in the collective realm of social relations as a symbol, a mediation, a cultural artifact. Or to put it differently, the objectual, sensitive and affective nature of disasters – the furious winds, the untamed tectonic plates, the excessive water bodies, the ubiquitous toxics – are acknowledged, but only insofar as they allow for the social to happen *elsewhere*. In either case its tangible worldliness is discarded.

Drawing on STS' materialist view of the social, several authors have recently compelled social scientists to recognize disaster and nature at large in their full excessiveness. Nigel Clark (2011), for instance, claims that disasters are configured by atmospheric, chemical or geological forces that are outside the control – both politically and ontologically – of humans and their institutions. There is a surplus that cannot be assumed as being already given for assemblages to enroll. Therefore, Clark asserts, politics have to be geologized: any account of disasters have to recognize tectonic plates, incandescent bodies and water masses as entities of their own. So, a major upheaval of earth, the author argues, not only takes the ground out from beneath our feet, but reveals that there's a world beyond us:

> Whether we are dealing with the cyclicality of cyclones, the rhythms of wildfire, the emergence of novel pathogens, the availability of mineral or energy resources [. . .] we find ourselves parting company with any significant human presence. (Clark, 2011: xvi)

This is not an isolated argument. Authors like Schillmeier (2011) and Harada (2000) have also stressed that if we want to understand the dimensions of a disaster we need to pay (more) attention to the role and dynamic of material heterogeneous networks in the production of new orders, scales, relations and organizations. The former, for instance, has shown how the outbreak of severe acute respiratory syndrome (SARS) in China 2003 disrupted societal organizations on a trans-continental level, establishing new and unexpected local, regional, national and global relations. In the opinion of this author, the SARS outbreak was an important actor in redefining a new cosmo-politics reassembling the poles of nature-culture, local-global and private-public regarding new global risk practices. In a similar vein, Harada analysed how materials and spaces in the 1995 earthquake in Japan were able to (re)create both a new social order and new individual relations. Our article recovers this new way of thinking disasters and tries to develop further the aforementioned argument regarding material heterogeneity.

In the last decade, indeed, several authors have also compelled us to be (even) more judicious in the way we think about, arrange or incorporate these other-than-human worlds. Inspired by the so-called speculative realism, as elaborated by Graham Harman (2009, 2010), and other object-oriented ontologies (for a discussion see Bennett, 2010), several authors have pushed the inter-mixity argument through more asymmetrical zones (Braun, 2008; Hird and Roberts, 2011; Bennett, 2010; Connolly, 2010). Although differently articulated, the aspiration of these authors converge in the need to better articulate the *vibrant materiality* of the world and explore how social theory changes if we give this force of things more due (Stengers, 2010). Things, these authors tell us, are not only that which connects us and makes society more durable (Latour, 1991). Things also affect us, bind us together and force us to think. This vitality and affective capacity of things is what forces us to talk about them, to think about their relationships with other things, entities, practices, ideas and institutions (Braun and Whatmore, 2010). It does not make sense, therefore, to see them as the opposite of human. They are much more than that. It is rather for them,

The Sociological Review, 62:S1, pp. 38–60 (2014), DOI: 10.1111/1467-954X.12123

through them and around them (as Stengers reminds us) that we become human (Stengers, 2010).

This shift, from an epistemological understanding, of which we cannot know, to a more ontological understanding of a thing's own agentic capacity is particularly interesting for the study of disasters. As Clark (2011) reminds us, it is now not enough just to think of a disaster in terms of mere negotiation, as a process or as a product of a chain of associations that bring together and articulate an infinite number of humans and non-humans. On the contrary, problems like ozone holes, global warming and pathogen outbreaks, show that there is a multitude of things (other-than-human things) that do not simply do our bidding, but have agency or forcefulness of their 'own'. Studying a disaster, therefore, involves analysing a complex entanglement in which we find social, cultural, political, but also complex and recalcitrant material dimensions (Clark in this volume).

This simplification of the material to just being the effect and result of a negotiation, a mere association between humans and non-humans, is also what Ingold criticizes with his concept of a meshwork. As we will see in the next section, an insistence on the idea of a network that associates and mixes humans and non-humans equally may be unsatisfactory, even risky, to explain disasters. The concept of a meshwork in this context will help serve to explore more deeply this concern through the vibrant materiality of disasters.

Meshworks

As we have seen in the last section, the new proposals about the role of materiality in our social explanations have led several authors to view disasters as networks. These structures link different types of actors (humans and non-humans, individuals and collectives etc.), diverse kind of actions and several dynamics and effects. Nevertheless, the idea of network has an important handicap. In order to clarify this problem, we have to imagine the following situation.

Two lines, A and B, intersect. Their intersection defines a point, P. But what if A and B were points and P a line that connects them? In the first case, we have an intersection, in the second a connection. Apparently, the difference is purely mathematical or formal. Reaching an understanding of the phenomenon does not seem to differ much since in both cases we are giving meaning to a relationship. However, if we apply the first schema to reach an understanding about how living entities establish relationships, differences start to appear everywhere. Indeed, as Tim Ingold (2011) points out, it is not enough to consider the inevitably intricate destination of humans and non-humans (a concern he shares with Actor-Network Theory) as a network connecting localities, or more-or-less defined entities. The world for him is much more than a world 'merely shared', much more than a 'network of interconnected heterogeneous elements'. This image, he argues, reduces rather than resolves the complexity, development and vitality of a world full of differences and lines of force that spread out and intersect unabated.

The question of the vitality of the world is key to understanding Ingold's critique (2011). In his view, the question of life, of ways of living, should be the key question for social sciences. However, it is not difficult to see that this question has been progressively expunged or displaced – life is spoken of as a mere context or scenario. Or it becomes consequential and derivative. A product of codes, structures or cultural or social systems (natural or genetic). The reason for this neglect, in his view, must be sought in the assumption of an essential relationship where on one side there is matter and on the other form, on one side the inert and on the other the living, on one side structure and on the other attributes. This essential distinction, with Aristotelian roots, is what ultimately prevents us from understanding how the world is made and how it is constantly bustling with activity. According to this structure, humans and non-humans are not only separated but also ontologically different. Some have life and agency, others constitute an abstract and inert world of materiality.

But, as he reminds us, we never interact with an external, substantive and passive materiality full of self-defined objects. For Ingold, life is neither external nor is it handed to us. It is not a task or outcome that is predictable. Nor is it something that goes from one point to another, nor has it a clear origin or end. To live is to develop, to open oneself to the world. We enmesh with the world in an open process that goes beyond any finalist or telenomic conception (Ingold, 2006). Hence Ingold's concern with the use of the network metaphor when thinking about the web of relationships between the human and non-human. In the opinion of this author, reality is much more than these kinds of networks. While a network generates an image of static relations between stations or elements, Ingold suggests we think of the set of relationships created in this reality as groups of lines that grow, develop and intersect, creating new lines and ultimately giving birth to dynamic and processual worlds. While a network generates an image of clearly defined and self-contained elements that relate to each other in a clear, defined and specific manner, lines offer a depiction in which no entity is clearly specified. Their definition is confused with their trajectory, their boundaries with those of their neighbors and in this permanent becoming the human-materiality distinction is erased and reconstructed in a process in which one cannot mark an obvious start or end point.

Ingold's proposal draws on Heidegger's (1971) distinction between objects and things. For the German philosopher, objectivity, rather than a state previous and external to being human, is a dimension reached when any object of the many that are around us becomes useful. This occurs when the object is inserted into our projects. At that moment they rightfully become objects. But that characterization is not the final end of the Hedeggerian ontology. There are, also, what he calls things. These are not to be confused with objects but neither are they something autonomous. How, then, does Heidegger define the *thingness* of a thing? To illustrate this difficult idea Heidegger (1971) uses the example of

The Sociological Review, 62:S1, pp. 38–60 (2014), DOI: 10.1111/1467-954X.12123

a jug. We can take the jug as an object, assimilate it to its function as a vessel and think that its fate is its appearance. However, this idea hardly captures the thingness of the jug. 'The jug's thingness', he remarks, 'resides in it being *qua* vessel' (1971: 169). That is, it resides in the vessel's quality of holding. This means that the vessel thingness does not lie at all in the material of which it consists, nor in what it contains, but 'in the void that holds' (1971: 169). It is by containing and pouring that the jug exceeds itself, showing that it is an empty space, a holding vessel.

So, thingness is found in the nothingness of the void. This is what marks a presence. What brings the jug into another realm of being where the gift of water, the rock, the spring, the cloud and the thirsty dwell together at once. So, in contrast to objects, talking about things is to talk about things-in-the-world, things that enmesh and become entwined with the world, generating and opening complex totalities (Heidegger, 1971). In this context, Ingold brings Heidegger's notion of thing back as a way to speak of these 'ever-extending trajectories' that 'spill out into the world'. Forces, flows, paths, strings, or even better, *lines* that constantly flow, mingle and progress. Indeed, this is for Ingold the ontology of the world. Rather than facing a world of enclosed 'objects', of differentiated and reified ontologies, we constantly engage with a world made of, and animated by, the entwined trajectories of 'things'.

To illustrate this he presents the example of a stone. Despite being the almost quintessential representative of the supposed inert external world, a stone never presents itself as an enclosed and unchanging object. You only need to watch one carefully to realize that its properties are constantly changing depending on the light, shade, moisture, posture and motion of the observer. Of course, this does not mean that the stone is alive, or that it has agency on its own. But it makes evident that the stone is a 'hive of activity'. That is, that the stone is a line constantly enmeshing with the world.

The concept he uses to represent these animated meshes in constant formation and reconstitution is the notion of meshwork. Originally coined by Henri Lefebvre (1991), this concept defines for Ingold the texture of those knots, tissues composed by different interwoven lines or threads. Importantly, the meshwork cannot be identified with a sort of field or network of interconnected points or entities, but of interwoven lines (Ingold, 2007). The result, then, is never a mere association[3] but a lively entanglement, a complex and transitory involvement in games of constant intersection, friction, growth and movement. In a meshwork there are no entities but trajectories, improvisatory movements of opening continually surpassing themselves. There are no self-contained objects but moving-forward lines (things) that live *along* (not between) other lines of growth and movement (Ingold, 2008b). So, in a world of meshworks, as Ingold reminds us, the action is never symmetrically distributed. It flows as a result of the interplay of forces and differences accompanying the becoming of its component lines. Thus, in a meshwork each entity acquires a mode of existence within these meshes of different lines that, in turn, organize and redefine other actors' (things') modes of existence.

So, in contrast to the more static and well-bounded representations of disasters, including the very concept of network, the concept of meshwork offers a far more dynamic figuration and opens up the possibility to disasters as messy processes permanently enacting new actors, actions and scales. We will illustrate this argument in the next section with the empirical case of Doñana.

Doñana's environmental disaster

On 25 April 1998 the downstream dam of a tailings lagoon owned by the Boliden-Apirsa mining company collapsed. This residue tank was responsible for storing pyrite tailings from mining activities. The rupture led to 5.5 Mm^3 of acid and metal-rich[4] water cascading into the Guadiamar River, together with a thick sludge of toxic tailings (estimated to be between 1.3 and 1.9 Mton). The spill, the equivalent of 500 Exxon-Valdez tankers, flooded the riverbanks along the Agrio and Guadiamar Rivers down to the Entremuros marshes, 40 km south of the mine, at the border of the Doñana National Park (see Figure 1).

According to the estimates from the Regional Government of Andalusia, approximately 4,600 hectares of arable and wild land were immediately affected by the toxic flood.[5] The spill also affected inhabited zones (10 municipalities, 46,000 inhabitants), enormous extensions of cultivated fields (mainly fruits and vegetables, cotton fields and olive orchards, cattle pastures, river-fishing areas and hundreds of potable water-wells (Bartolomé and Vega, 2002). In the days following the spill, nearly 30 tons of fish and 170 kg of crabs, frogs and eels were also found dead.

Under any circumstances, then, the spill was a major disaster (Simón *et al.*, 1999). But it was especially so due to the proximity of the Doñana[6] National Park. This is considered a 'pearl' of nature conservation in southern Europe, as it is the place where some of the most protected species live, such as the lynx and the imperial eagle. Additionally, it is an important resting site for wintering and migrating birds (up to 6,000,000 individuals), as well as a habitat for 875 different plant species.

Actually, apart from being highly protected for its exceptional ecological qualities,[7] the Park was (and still is) a crucial actor in the economy of the region. Apart from the mine, which was one of the main employers in the area at the time of the accident, the region of Doñana had traditionally been strongly dependent on agriculture and tourism. Both activities had been positively influenced by the proximity of the Park. This might explain why, since the very beginning of the disaster, the protection of the Park was a major concern. This was so for the Spanish Authorities, mainly the Spanish Government and the Autonomous Government of Andalusia; the media ('Environmental disaster in Doñana!', 'Nature is in danger!', 'World disaster'); environmentalist groups, historically very active in the area[8]; as well as the many scientists working daily in the Park.[9]

To coordinate the response, the authorities, including the Park director and civil protection services, agreed on sending heavy machinery (bulldozers, exca-

The Sociological Review, 62:S1, pp. 38–60 (2014), DOI: 10.1111/1467-954X.12123

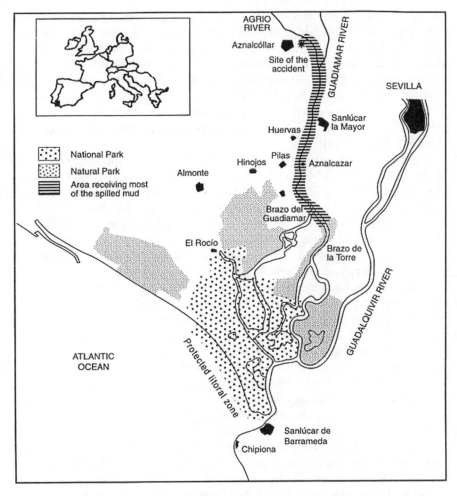

Figure 1: *Map of the Doñana Park and its surrounding area, including the location of the Aznalcóllar mine (see Grimalt et al., 1999).*

vators and trucks) to Entremuros, a hydraulic barrier that runs along the border with the Park. They planned to build improvised containment walls to stop the toxic wave from flowing into the Park (Junta de Andalucía, 1998). Additionally, they also agreed to establish a group of experts, mainly scientists from CSIC (the Spanish National Research Council), to help monitor the accident and prevent further possible negative effects.

After those initial measures, though, consensus among the various parties quickly broke down. The different actors, either those directly affected or those involved in the management of the aftermath of the spill (from scientists to farmers, neighbours, politicians, technicians and environmentalists) became entangled in manifold disputes. For instance, environmentalists and scientists disagreed with the authorities on what to do with the significant volume of toxic water that had been retained in Entremuros. The initial plan of the Spanish authorities was to release that water into the Guadalquivir, a major river flowing into the Atlantic Ocean. However, environmentalists and scientists strongly opposed such measures. They believed that this could seriously damage the river and its wildlife, especially the estuaries on which many fishermen depended to make their living. This was also the concern of many fishermen associations (Junta de Andalucía, 1999b).

Another issue of concern was the passivity with which the authorities were acting (Greenpeace, 1999). The mine, the environmentalists denounced, was only partially closed and the dam that caused the toxic wave wasn't sealed yet (with the subsequent risk of new collapses and further spills due to rainfalls). Equally important for them was the banning, as quickly as possible, of all forms of land use, as well as the prohibition of hunting, fishing and using wells for irrigation in the entire area. These measures would help to prevent further damages to the people and fauna living in the polluted area.

However, farmers were strongly opposed to these suggestions. To them, the accident might result in the expropriation of their land, the vetoing of cultivation or the loss of temporary employment related to harvesting activities. Even worse, it could foster consumers' distrust towards local products, like strawberries, citrus fruit and rice. For them, as well as for the authorities, the most urgent action was to undertake a rapid removal of the sludge and the material left by the toxic flood. The affected area had to be restored before the arrival of the rainfalls in autumn. Heavy machinery, mainly excavators and trucks, would be sent to the area to speed up those operations.

For scientists and environmentalists, however, this could be dangerous (Aparicio *et al.*, 1998). The use of heavy machinery could foster severe soil and ground-water contamination, as well as atmospheric pollution. Although slower, the best way to carry out the clean-up operation was by using manual methods.

But probably the main debate in the aftermath of the spill was the one related to the very reach of the spill. From the beginning the main concern was whether the toxic wave had penetrated the Park. If this was so, according to the environmentalists, the spill would be a catastrophe of *'untold magnitude'* (Greenpeace, 1999; Vega and Bartolomé, 1998). For the administrations, however, these claims were considered rather *'alarmist'* (*El Mundo*, 1998a). While the situation was far from being solved, there was nothing to be worried about. The first emergency measures had been a success and the 'heart of Doñana' had been saved (García-Novo, 1998). In a few months Doñana would be completely restored and the tragedy would be just *'a sad memory'* (Bravo, 1999). A point of view also shared by local farmers and neighbours, who felt they had more immediate problems than worrying about wildlife.

For environmentalist groups, though, these were attempts at undermining what had happened. In contrast to the authorities, they considered it crucial to find out whether the spill was affecting areas, species or ecosystems that were

The Sociological Review, 62:S1, pp. 38–60 (2014), DOI: 10.1111/1467-954X.12123

beyond the 'instant' and 'visible' dimensions (Bartolomé and Vega, 2002). Indeed, Greenpeace went a step further and sent one of its most equipped boats to the area, the MV Greenpeace, to evaluate for themselves the damages of the spill (Greenpeace, 1999). Following the same principle, SEO/Birdlife (1998) also decided to pick up dead birds and samples of sludge and waters along the affected area. Most of these samples were sent to an independent laboratory in Barcelona, which months later published a report the findings of which caused quite a stir.

According to this report, the affected area was twice the size of the official estimation (both in terms of acres of land and kilometres travelled by the sludge). The study also showed that a significant number of wells and aquifers had also been affected (Grimalt *et al.*, 1999; *El Mundo*, 1998b). This was important information as the authorities had been repeatedly denying that the contamination had penetrated the Park. The report also found evidence of heavy metals dissolved in the water, an important point as it proved such material could travel by water rather than remaining in the sludge in solid form. These 'mobile pollutants' could easily reach the deepest parts of the aquifers, seriously damaging these crucial hydrological unities, which in turn would damage the whole underground water cycle that connects the interior and the exterior of the Park (*El Mundo*, 1998b). The Park, the Greenpeace-sponsored study concluded (1999), was anything but *out of danger*.

Without a doubt, the Doñana disaster can be conceptualized using the toolbox of the sociology of disasters outlined previously. This disaster demonstrates how relations between different actors are activated, and how debates originate and re-signify the causes and consequences of a disaster. It also shows how unexpected relationships are generated, ones which would not be discovered in a more traditional analysis (Guerrero *et al.*, 2007; Sauri *et al.*, 2003). For example, we see the important role of pollutants, or of the aquifers, and how these non-human elements mediate and attract the attention of environmentalists and the press. However, neither the most sociological nor the most symmetrical approaches are capable of accounting for the role played by some very unique actors. We are referring to the birds nesting in Doñana at the time of the incident.

Disasters as meshworks

If some actors stood out in the aftermath of the disaster, as we will see below, these were the birds. The migratory birds nesting in the Park at the time of the accident were key in the development and transformation of the disaster itself. Ringed and monitored by environmentalists groups active in the affected area, these birds passed from being secondary and passive victims of the disaster to being 'the catastrophe itself', that is, they became uncontainable vectors of contamination capable of spreading the disaster to other species, environments and contexts of action.

Birds as lines

As we have said, Doñana was famous for being a strategic location for birds. Many bird species use the park annually (designated Reserve of the Biosphere in 1981) as breeding and wintering sites. ADENA/WWF and SEO/Birdlife were the first organizations to raise concerns in this matter (Schmidt *et al.*, 2002; SEO/Birdlife, 1998). They feared that toxic metals could easily be absorbed by these birds and quickly enter into the food chain. Even worse, they were worried about the possibility that birds, searching for food and water, could move toward Entremuros where the toxic spill was being contained. However, the authorities did not seem to share the same degree of concern. Although they were aware that the spill had affected protected species, birds included, in their opinion there was no reason to be alarmed (Benito *et al.*, 1999). First, because the risk to them was certainly *not lethal*. Secondly, because if certain zones that served as drinking sites were dried out, and if the movement of particular species of birds was restricted, the matter would not take on any further importance.

In spite of these arguments, environmentalists decided (again) to undertake studies and monitor for themselves the long-term effects of the contamination of birds (particularly SEO/Birdlife, Greenpeace and WWF). According to WWF (Bartolomé and Vega, 2002) about 19,000 birds had contaminants in their system. SEO/Birdlife, some months later, also noticed important malformations in the chicks of the species most exposed to the contaminants. Similarly, Greenpeace revealed white stork beak deformities never seen before in Andalusia. Most of these figures were progressively confirmed by the group of CSIC experts in later reports, which also revealed that 11 per cent of the birds were affected, rising to approximately 30 per cent in the case of geese, stork and herons (Junta de Andalucía, 1999a; CSIC, 1999).

This cascade of studies put birds into the centre of the debate. As some scientists confirmed, the spill was a dominant source of contamination for birds (Meharg *et al.*, 2002). Even more, this contamination was actually entering into the Park *through* birds. So, it was not just a matter of the danger posed by the contamination for the birds' colonies themselves, but also the risk that this pollution could entail for other species living alongside the birds. This was specially so in the case of white stork and the black kite (Pastor *et al.*, 2004). White storks and black kites are long-lived species that occupy a high position, respectively, in the terrestrial and aquatic trophic webs. So, from that moment on they turned into 'sentinel organisms' for evaluating the long-term polluting effects of heavy metals (Hernández *et al.*, 1999; Pastor *et al.*, 2001).

Indeed, they insisted that there were reasons to think that birds could even be spreading the contamination far beyond Doñana (ABC, 1998). As we already said, at the time of the accident, Doñana was crowded with migratory birds, first from Africa, and when those left it began to fill up with birds from northern Europe. All these birds had spent long periods of time after the spill gorging on poisoned fish, vegetables or even soils. Weakened by pollution, environmentalists alerted, they could easily pass toxic substances accumulated in their

The Sociological Review, 62:S1, pp. 38–60 (2014), DOI: 10.1111/1467-954X.12123

bodies to other animals higher up in the food chain when they would return to northern or southern countries. This likely 'globalisation of the disaster' rapidly drew the attention of the international media (*The Guardian*, 1999) and alerted the authorities of several countries, mainly Holland, Britain, Germany and the Scandinavian countries. They all feared that birds, now global 'toxic-bombs', were passing toxic substances to fauna living in their countries.

Here it is important to highlight the important contribution made by networks of banded birds that had been in operation for years in the area. Bird banding (also known as bird ringing) is a well-known monitoring and data collection method that enables tracing of migratory birds' flight paths, and hence monitors the development of different species and colonies. This recording work usually involves the participation of a wide range of scientists, activists and volunteers from different countries. Now it was this infrastructure, in which environmental groups like SEO had been involved[10] for some time in the area of Doñana, which enabled ecologists to exhaustively monitor the most distant and deferred effects of the spill.

In actuality, this concern about birds definitely forced the involvement of the European Union. Although EU bureaucrats had refused to intervene in what they considered was a national issue, now they were explicitly called into action against what was considered a potentially global natural disaster. Environmentalists reminded that the contamination of birds was appealing to the Community's obligation, under the UN Contention on Biological Diversity, to protect the biodiversity and to ensure a sustainable management, ecologically but also economically, of Europe's most valuable and threatened habitats. This was so for Doñana but also for other valuable and protected sites (now threatened by the flight of birds) included in the network Natura 2000.

So, this growing concern around birds was also seen by environmentalists as an opportunity to put into action a global campaign to reclaim international instruments (political and legal) against corporate crimes (Greenpeace, 2002). The episode, they argued, discredited the main Spanish environmental authorities (Ministry of the Environment and Consejería de Medio Ambiente), the mining authorities (Consejería de Industria) and the water authorities (Confederación Hidrográfica del Guadalquivir). Although the mining company was responsible for the incident, these agencies were considered partly responsible for the disaster, for failing to monitor safety standards at the mine, for lacking an emergency plan and for their uncoordinated response (Schmidt *et al.*, 2002; WWF/ADENA, 2004). It was not an isolated case, they argued. Many other cases all over the world gave evidence of similar deficiences in the laws protecting the environment from the mining industry (Greenpeace, 2002).

But environmentalists also raised other concerns thanks to birds. For decades, they argued, Doñana's National Park had been thought of as an 'island' isolated from its surroundings, 'as if the bureaucratic boundaries once established would also limit the water, soil, living things . . . or 5 million cubic meters of toxic sludge' (Departamento Confederal de Medio Ambiente de

CC.OO, 1998: 1). So the disaster was also seen as an opportunity to publicly display the problems of the existing administration. Doñana's National Park, like many other natural reserves, needed to open up to the outside as a way to safeguard its future (Díaz Pinedo, 1998). Actually, as a result of this debate, the Spanish authorities finally launched (pressured by the communitarian authorities) two important restoration programmes: the Guadiamar Green Corridor and the Doñana 2005 Plan (Garrido, 2008). Both projects addressed some of the environmentalists' concerns over a more 'comprehensive' and 'horizontal' management of Doñana (WWF, 2010).

So, as we see, thanks to the birds the disaster acquired new dimensions and enrolled new actors. Rephrasing Ingold's argument, we can say that what our case shows is how in the aftermath of the disaster birds turn into complex lines of becoming that constantly 'spill out into the world'. When this occurs, the disaster transforms itself. Rather than being an easily localized tragedy, a black piece of land stained by the sludge, the disaster turns into a far more global and uncertain kind of concern. It is important to underline that this is an empirical transformation, not the expression of a hidden or quintessential capacity of birds. As we have seen, it is in the process of exploring and recomposing *what the disaster is* that birds eventually turn into a matter of public concern. That is, they turn into a matter of explicit intervention by environmentalists. A key practice in this regard, although not unique, is the ringing of birds. It is through this scientific practice that environmentalists associate birds to networks of expertise, conservationism and European bureaucracy. It is through ringing that these groups unite and breach the limits between signs and things, between humans and non-humans, and establish bonds and regimes of interdependence between them. As a result, birds take part in the shaping of a given order. They bring together different actors and enable the coordination of a global protest against Doñana.

However, the pivotal argument is not only that in these operations around and for the birds that the birds themselves are converted into a mere hybrid, the effect of a chain of relations and associations that equally distribute agency among the various components (Brown and Middleton, 2005). The power of the birds cannot be explained in terms of a network or the aggregate sum and order of associations (technology + experts in ornithology + heavy metals + protection agreements for natural habitats + public opinion, etc.). To account for the power of the birds in the aftermath of the disaster we also need to account for how they mark, in Heideggerian terms (1971), a presence in the dispute. In other words, how they became a constant source of differentiation. It is important to note at this point that we are not hereby suggesting that we should return to the birds-in-themselves to explain the effects of the birds' politics. It is not this kind of materialism that we want to reinforce. On the contrary, we think that this transformation of the birds involves a much more complex and dynamic process that is in turn semiotic, political and also material.

The key issue here has to do with the vitality of these birds, with the fact of being manifested, in large part thanks to the banding, as forces, as lines or

The Sociological Review, 62:S1, pp. 38–60 (2014), DOI: 10.1111/1467-954X.12123

trajectories that represent the disaster. It is in this moment that the birds cease to be a self-contained and reified entity, mere animals 'out there', minor victims of what happened, to being far more uncertain and indeterminate.

Doñana as a meshwork

The banded birds in Doñana became ever-extending lines constantly surpassing themselves and enmeshing with other species and ecosystems. This transformation fuelled and dragged the disaster itself into a kind of holism where entities, bounds and limits were constantly blurred and enmeshed. The boundaries between inside and outside the park were erased, but so also were national and international borders. Other species, ecosystems, actors and contexts that were in principle distanced from the accident took on increasing relevance, to the extent that other European governments began to complain and European institutions took up the matter. Therefore, the ringed birds, now turned into lines, transformed the very definition of the disaster. They turned it into something that overflowed its technical-geographical location. They converted the Doñana disaster into a meshwork. Undoubtedly, other elements could be added to this analysis. For example, the contamination of the aquifers or some land animals could have been subject to similar scrutiny. However, the birds serve to illustrate our purpose here: understanding disasters as a meshwork.

This understanding suggests several important consequences for disaster sociology. First, it becomes evident that a disaster is not a phenomenon that can be defined clearly in scope, extent or location. Clearly, a disaster occurs in a geographic transformation, it has biological and physical effects on the environment, it alters the lives of certain communities and brings into question the activity of human institutions. But it is much more than all of this. It is a set of relationships between actors with different qualities and the composition of different scales of activity that interact with each other. However, again, it is much more than all of this. It is all of this plus an inherent and immanent activity that constitutes something dynamic and changing. In the words of Deleuze and Guattari (1988), it is pure becoming. As we have noted in previous sections, defining a disaster means tracing this becoming through the air, water, land, through hydrological cycles and food chains . . . It means to understand both that all these elements are processes and that they are the immanent parameters of the disaster evolution. Therefore it is no exaggeration to say that a disaster is a mode of existence tout court (Latour, 2013). That is, it is an event that produces a piece of reality, of new reality; this is deployed following immanent causes and vectors of activity, it establishes its ways of opening and closing action, evolving in multiple pathways and enrolling new and unexpected actors and dimensions. Simply put, disasters are existences per se: modes of reality only apprehensible attending to their own idiosyncrasies.

The second important consequence of this approach to the phenomenon of disasters has to do with a question: Who should analyse disasters and how should they be analysed? What elements are central to their examination and which should be discarded? The answer is both simple and highly complex. The single answer lies in understanding that disasters are not the exclusive realm of political institutions or technicians directly affected as a result of their work. Given their changing and dynamic nature, disasters become an object of analysis that can be of interest to all kinds of scientists, and specialists, but also to laypeople affected or groups or movements simply concerned with how public policies affect human groups. And the more complex answer lies in recognizing that any element, actor or dimension related to the disaster can be a good item to start with in an analysis. The disaster-as-meshwork provides the possibility that any of its lines is a good starting point for analysis. Actually, we are affirming that disasters, like other dimensions (historical, political or cultural) are susceptible to being analysed from the point of view of their genealogy (Foucault, 1998). That is, any thread we choose will lead us to a set of intertwined practices that show the transforming nature of the disaster, the constitution of the different limits and dimensions and the interconnection with other actors and phenomena. And as indicated by the genealogical method, time and space are not parameters that externally mark a delineation of the disaster but are variables defined from within these practices.

The third consequence has to do with the dual feature manifested by the reality of the disaster. It is something actual but also virtual. That is, it is a reality with a dimension that is defined and measured at a given moment – it is photographed, acted upon etc. But it also differentiates and actualizes itself in another way thanks to the many courses of action that are opened up by the lines that compose it (Brown and Middleton, 2005). This almost constitutive indeterminacy, this ability to constantly surpass itself, is what makes the disaster into a powerful political reality. For one, because it becomes a focal point, that is, something that increasingly attracts the attention of other actors, from the media to other political actors, and contexts of action. On the other hand, it also transforms Doñana into a centre of constant difference and connection with other realities and actors. The disaster moves and is constantly changing. It enrols new entities and redefines them. This makes it difficult to quantify and define who or what it integrates.

The fourth consequence is directly linked to the previous one. Conceiving the disaster as a meshwork presupposes an approach to political action in disasters that is different to previous approaches. The dynamics of continuous transformation, generation of different topologies, diverse realities and at times unexpected interconnections with actors, leads one to think that in the case of disasters it is more appropriate to speak of cosmopolitics than politics. This concept has been recently defended in Social Sciences by Latour (2007) in accordance with the proposals of Isabel Stengers (1991). According to this philosopher, politics becomes 'cosmopolitics' when we assume that political action consists precisely in the arrangements and orderings stabilized between non-humans and humans (although Stengers speaks of things as a way to include a much more recalcitrant and vibrant world). Arrangements that can become a common-world to live in. That is, politics is always a matter of producing a cosmos, a daily universe composed of relations between humans and those things that eventually *force* us to think, feel and hesitate.

For example, as we saw above, once the controversy surrounding the disaster had been stoked, environmentalists seized the occasion to put into play a whole series of measures to problematize the disaster and the politics of dealing with it. For these groups this was not to get back to normality or find immediate solutions as fast as possible (as was demanded by the Spanish authorities). Neither did it mean leaving the disaster to the specialists, the containment dams and the heavy machinery. Quite the contrary. The ecologists wanted, thanks to the opportunity handed to them by the disaster in Doñana, to criticize the Spanish administration for its precarious environmental policies and indifference to the environment. They wanted, in short, to change environmental legislation and management of the Park itself according to more horizontal and comprehensive criteria. They wanted to take what happened, this virtuality that was being actualized at different levels, as an opportunity to articulate another (cosmo)politics in the region, one that was able to integrate more and better ecological policies and also economic, social and cultural processes to articulate and foster an identity for the region.

Finally, we are left to evaluate a consequence linked to the question of how to define disasters. As is clear from the above, a disaster has the initial quality of an event (Whitehead, 1985). Suddenly, something new breaks into our reality, it tears it and converts it into something different. From there, nothing can ever be as it was. The disaster unfolds from its own lines of self-transformation and rewrites and recontextualizes the reality in which it unfolds. The disaster is comprised of multiple actors, diverse dimensions, scales and topologies. It involves many institutions and undergoes qualitative changes. All this is important but also quite obvious. What is relevant in relation to the question of the disastrousness of a disaster is that, understood as a meshwork, every disaster becomes a valuable opportunity to rethink our living-together.

Concluding remarks

This article has explored the role played by birds in the Doñana disaster. This was one of the worst ecological crises in Spanish history. The spill at Doñana generated a heated debate in Spanish society and a political conflict between different public administrations. Its echo reached Europe and its institutions. Our analysis has moved away from usual approaches that focus on a geographical-technical description of disasters, their effect on human behaviour and the role played by the institutions concerned. Our analysis has sought to go beyond the current characterizations that make a disaster a negotiated or socially constructed reality, or a reality composed of a network of actors with different characteristics and qualities. We have proposed, instead, that disasters should be analysed as dynamic realities.

To do so we analysed how birds in Doñana operated as more than just animals threatened by the pollution. The intervention performed on them by some environmental groups, using banding to measure how the contaminants were being spread, converted them into dynamic lines of action that were able to redefine the scale of the disaster, connect with global dimensions that went beyond Doñana Park's location and relate it with actors that a priori seemed not to be involved in the spill. Using the theoretical proposals of Tim Ingold, we have argued that these practices caused birds to change from being non-humans involved in the disaster to a process or thing whose activity was capable of producing a new reality.

The birds have enabled us to postulate that disasters are parliaments of lines, sets that are referred to as meshworks. This concept comes from the philosophy of Lefebvre and has recently been utilized by Tim Ingold (2011) to question the metaphor of the network we use to explain virtually any phenomenon in our daily lives. The meshwork concept indicates that the relationships we build in our daily lives have dynamic characteristics, a kind of vitality that escapes the network metaphor. The meshwork implies that any relationship between entities can have an unintended effect, generate another unexpected relationship or conflict not previously outlined. Living means relating, and there is always a nested opening or a level of uncertainty that vanishes in the static and metric representations of the network concept.

The concept of meshwork reconceptualizes the idea of disaster and has the following consequences. First, it helps us to understand that a disaster is a dynamic reality, difficult to locate in space and time and often distributed among different scales and diverse actors. Second, the analysis of disasters comes close to the methodology offered by Foucault's genealogy. Anything becomes a good line to analyse the sets of practices that arise from the self-transformative power of the disaster. Third, the disaster appears with a dual reality, it is an actual and virtual phenomenon. Indeed, its capacity for differentiation thanks to this second feature makes it an unpredictable phenomenon with powerful political effects. Fourth, we should assume that the politics of disasters is a cosmopolitics. Disasters produce a cosmos that reconstructs the relationships between different actors and dimensions. Finally, all of this leads us to believe that disasters are an opportunity to re-evaluate our ways of living together.

Acknowledgements

We would like to thank Daniel López, Brian McCarthy and three anonymous reviewers for their comments, criticisms and suggestions. This article has been possible thanks to the support of the Commission for Universities and Research of the Ministry of Innovation, Universities and Enterprise of the Autonomous Government of Catalonia and the Cofund programme of the Marie Curie Actions of the 7th R&D Framework Programme of the European Union (BP-A 107, 2009).

Notes

1 Samuel Prince's (1920) research on the Halifax explosion is usually considered the first systematic study of disaster in the social sciences.

2 There is a broad consensus that there are at least three key paradigms or phases that can be identified in the articulation of disasters as a matter of inquiry for the social sciences (García-Acosta, 2002; Gilbert, 1998; Perry, 2007).

3 Actually, the notion of meshwork is quite critical to the notion of network suggested by Actor-Network Theory (for a discussion see Ingold, 2008b).

4 The waste contained a high concentration of heavy metals such as cadmium, lead, zinc and copper.

5 According to mapping of the tailings carried out by the Spanish GeoMining Institute (IGME), at the beginning of May 1998, the spill left 62 per cent of tailings in the first 13 km downstream from the broken dam. The thickness of the tailings layers was also varied from approximately 2 metres near the mine to a few centimeters in the furthest away areas.

6 The Doñana National Park is located in the western part of the Andalusia region, in the south of Spain. It was created in the 1960s by the conservation efforts of environmentalist organizations. It spans 54,250 hectares and is bordered on the north with the Natural Park of Doñana. Together they are commonly referred to as the Doñana Park, which is the terminology we use in this paper. Together, they both have significant natural diversity: 40,000 hectares of marshland, more than 5,000 hectares of conifers and 24,000 hectares of undergrowth.

7 The National Park was declared a marshland of extraordinary ecological importance through the Ramsar Convention, Biosphere Reservation (1980) and a World Heritage Site (1994) by UNESCO. It was also part of the Natura 2000 network and was given status as a Protected Area by the Council of Europe (see De Lucio, 1997).

8 The National Park of Doñana is a historic place for Environmentalism in Spain, as it was for and around the Park, its constitution and protection, that conservationist organizations initiated their activities in Spain. Greenpeace, WWF/ADENA, the Coordinadora de Organizaciones de Defensa Ambiental (CODA), SEO/Birdlife, AEDENAT and CEPA (Coordinadora de Ecologistas y Pacifistas de Andalucía, a pacifist and environmentalist network) were the organizations that most actively participated in this mobilization.

9 The Integral Biological Reserve of Doñana is an area owned by ADENA/WWF that comprises 3,214 hectares and that is managed scientifically and administratively by the Spanish Research Council (CSIC), a research body belonging to the Central Administration.

10 Initiated one year before the spill, the 'Migres' programme, funded by the Andalusian Government and coordinated by SEO/Birdlife and involving more than 200 volunteers, collected data on up to 25 different species of migratory birds (white stork, European honey buzzard, common vulture, griffon vulture, short-toed eagle, osprey, kestrel, etc.) as they passed through Doñana on their way to cross the Strait of Gibraltar.

References

ABC, (1998), 'Doñana: La Contaminación Podría Exportarse a Través De Las Aves Migratorias, Según La SEO', *Diario ABC*, 10 August.

Aparicio, A., Escartín, J., Santamaría, L. and Valverde, I., (1998), 'Toxic spill caught Spain off guard', *Nature*, 395: 110.

Barry, A., (2001), *Political Machines: Governing a Technological Society*, London: Athlone Press.

Bartolomé, J. and Vega, I., (2002), *Mining in Doñana: Learned Lessons*, Madrid: Artes Gráficas Palermo, S.L.

Bear, C. and Eden, S., (2011), 'Thinking like a fish? Engaging with nonhuman difference through recreational angling', *Environment and Planning D: Society and Space*, 29 (2): 336–352, doi: 10.1068/d1810.

Benito, V., Devesa, V., Muñoz, O., Suñer, M. A., Montoro, R., Baos, R., Hiraldo, F., Ferrer, M., Fernández, M. and González, M. J., (1999), 'Trace elements in blood collected from birds feeding in the area around Doñana National Park affected by the toxic spill from the Aznalcóllar mine', *Science of the Total Environment*, 242: 309–323.

Bennett, J., (2010), *Vibrant Matter: A Political Ecology of Things*, Durham, NC: Duke University Press.

Braun, B., (2008), 'Environmental issues: inventive life', *Progress in Human Geography*, 32 (5): 667–679, doi: 10.1177/0309132507088030.

Braun, B. and Whatmore, S., (2010), *Political Matter: Technoscience, Democracy, and Public Life*, Minneapolis: University of Minnesota Press.

Bravo, I., (1999), 'Doñana: lo peor ha pasado', *Mundo Científico*, 197: 73–77.

Brown, S. D. and Middleton, D., (2005), 'The baby as virtual object: agency and difference in a neonatal intensive care unit', *Environment and Planning D: Society and Space*, 23 (5): 695–715, doi: 10.1068/d354t.

Callon, M., (1986), 'Some elements of a sociology of translation: domestication of the scallops and the fishermen of St Brieux Bay', in J. Law (ed.), *Power, Action and Belief: A New Sociology of Knowledge?*, 196–223, London: Routledge.

Castree, N., (2003), 'Environmental issues: relational ontologies and hybrid politics', *Progress in Human Geography*, 27: 203–211.

CSIC (Centro Superior de Investigaciones Científicas), (1999), *11° Informe del Grupo de Expertos del Consejo Superior de Investigaciones Científicas y otros Organismos Colaboradores sobre la Emergencia Ecológica del Río Guadiamar*, Madrid: CSIC.

Clark, N., (2011), *Inhuman Nature: Sociable Life on a Dynamic Planet*, London: Sage.

Connolly, W. E., (2010), 'Materiality, experience and surveillance', in B. Braun and S. Whatmore (eds), *Political Matter: Technoscience, Democracy and Public Life*, 63–87, Minneapolis: University of Minnesota Press.

De Lucio, J., (1997), *Espacios Naturales Protegidos del Estado Español*, Madrid: Comunidad de Madrid.

Deleuze, G. and Guattari, F., (1988), *A Thousand Plateaus: Capitalism and Schizophrenia*, London: Athlone Press.

Departamento Confederal de Medio Ambiente de CC.OO, (1998), 'Editorial: Lecciones de un desastre', *Daphnia: Boletín informativo sobre la prevención de la contaminación y la producción limpia*, 13: 1.

Díaz Pinedo, F., (1998), 'Doñana, más allá de los límites', *Ecosistemas*, 24/25: 8–10.

El Mundo, (1998a), 'Tocino y Chaves critican el «alarmismo injustificado»', 4 May, available at: www.elmundo.es/papel/hemeroteca/1998/05/04/sociedad/412219.html

El Mundo, (1998b), 'El acuífero 27 de Doñana está contaminado, según un informe de la Confederación Hidrográfica', 9 May, available at: www.elmundo.es/papel/hemeroteca/1998/05/09/sociedad/417397.html

Foucault, M., (1998), *Aesthetics, Method, Epistemology* (Essential Works, Vol. 2), New York: The New Press.

Fritz, C. E., (1961), 'Disaster', in R. K. Merton and R. A. Nisbet (eds), *Contemporary Social Problems*, 651–694, New York: Harcourt.

García-Acosta, V., (2002), 'Historical disaster research', in S. Hoffman and A. Oliver-Smith (eds), *Catastrophe and Culture: The Anthropology of Disaster*. Santa Fe, NM: School of American Research Press.

García-Novo, F., (1998), *Informe de seguimiento de los efectos del accidente de Aznalcóllar*, Sevilla: Junta de Andalucía.

Garrido, H., (2008), *Guadiamar, Ciencia, Técnica y Restauración: El Accidente Minero Diez Años Después*, Madrid: CSIC Press.

Gilbert, C., (1998), 'Studying disaster: changes in the main conceptual tools', in E. L. Quarantelli (ed.), *What Is a Disaster? Perspectives on the Question*, New York: Routledge.

The Sociological Review, 62:S1, pp. 38–60 (2014), DOI: 10.1111/1467-954X.12123

Greenpeace, (1999), *Doñana: Un Año Después De Vertido De Aznalcóllar*, Internal Report Madrid, Greenpeace.

Greenpeace, (2002), *Corporate Crimes: The Need for an International Instrument on Corporate Accountability and Liability*, Report.

Grimalt, J. O., Ferrer, M. and MacPherson, E., (1999), 'The mine tailing accident in Aznalcollar', *The Science of the Total Environment*, 242 (1–3): 3–11.

Guardian, The, (1999), 'Toxic timebomb', 6 January, available at: www.guardian.co.uk/society/1999/jan/06/guardiansocietysupplement7.

Guerrero, F. M., Lozano, M. and Rueda, J. M., (2007), 'Spain's greatest and most recent mine disaster', *Disasters*, 32 (1): 19–40, doi:10.1111/j.0361-3666.2007.01025.x.

Hailwood, S., (2000), 'The value of nature's otherness', *Environmental Values*, 9 (4): 353–372.

Harada, T., (2000), 'Space, materials, and the "social": in the aftermath of a disaster', *Environment and Planning D: Society and Space*, 18 (2): 205–212.

Harman, G., (2009), *Prince of Networks: Bruno Latour and Metaphysics*, Melbourne: Re.Press.

Harman, G., (2010), *Towards Speculative Realism: Essays and Lectures*, Winchester: Zero Books.

Heidegger, M., (1971), *Poetry, Language, Thought*, trans. A. Hofstadter, NewYork: Harper and Row.

Hernández, L. M., Gómara, B., Fernández, M., Jiménez, B., González, M. J., Baos, R., Hiraldo, F., Ferrer, M., Benito, V. and Suner, M. A., (1999), 'Accumulation of heavy metals and As in wetland birds in the area around Doñana National Park affected by the Aznalcollar toxic spill', *Science of the Total Environment*, 242 (1–3): 293–308.

Hinchliffe, S., Kearnes, M. B., Degen, M. and Whatmore, S., (2005), 'Urban wild things: a cosmopolitical experiment', *Environment and Planning D: Society and Space*, 23: 643–658

Hird, M. J. and Roberts, C., (2011), 'Feminism theorises the nonhuman', *Feminist Theory*, 12 (2): 109–117.

Holloway, L., (2003), 'What a thing, then, is this cow . . . : positioning domestic livestock animals in the texts and practices of small-scale "self-sufficiency" ', *Society and Animals*, 11: 145–165.

Ingold, T., (2006), 'Up, across and along', *Place and Location: Studies in Environmental Aesthetics and Semiotics*, 5: 21–36.

Ingold, T., (2007), *Lines: A Brief History*, London: Routledge.

Ingold, T., (2008a), 'Bringing things to life: creative entanglements in a world of materials', available at: www.reallifemethods.ac.uk/. . ./vital-signs-ingold-bringing-things-to-life.pdf

Ingold, T., (2008b), 'When ANT meets SPIDER: social theory for arthropods', in C. Knapepett and L. Malafouris (eds), *Material Agency*, 209–215, New York: Springer.

Ingold, T., (2011), *Being Alive: Essays on Movements, Knowledge and Description*, London: Routledge.

Junta de Andalucia, (1998), 'Disposición Proyecto Control y Permeablización de la Marisma de Doñana Frente al Río Guadalquivir, al Brazo de la Torre y Entremuros', 3 October: 1–2.

Junta de Andalucía, (1999a), 'Informes científicos sobre el seguimiento de accidente de Aznalcóllar', Junta de Andalucía, Sevilla: Consejería de Medio Ambiente.

Junta de Andalucía, (1999b), 'El accidente minero de Aznalcóllar', Medio Ambiente en Andalucía, Informe 1998, Junta de Andalucía, Sevilla: Consejería de Medio Ambiente.

Latour, B., (1991), 'Technology is society made durable', in J. Law (ed.), *A Sociology of Monsters: Essays on Power, Technology and Domination*, Sociological Review Monograph No. 38: 103–132.

Latour, B., (1993), *We Have Never Been Modern*, Hempstead: Harvester Wheatsheaf.

Latour B., (2007), 'Turning around Politics: A Note on Gerard de Vries', *Social Studies of Science*, 37 (5): 811–820.

Latour, B., (2013), *An Inquiry into Modes of Existence*, Cambridge, MA: Harvard University Press.

Latour, B. and Weibel, P., (2005), *Making Things Public: Atmospheres of Democracy*, Cambridge, MA: MIT Press.

Law, J. and Mol, A., (2008), 'Globalisation in practice: on the politics of boiling pigswill', *Geoforum*, 39 (1): 133–143, doi: 10.1016/j.geoforum.2006.08.010.

Lefebvre, H., (1991), *The Production of Space*, Oxford: Blackwell.

Marres, N., (2012), *Material Participation: Technology, the Environment and Everyday Publics*, Basingstoke: Palgrave Macmillan.

Meharg, A. A., Pain, D. J., Ellam, R. M., Baos, R., Olive, V., Joyson, A., Powell, N., Green, A. J. and Hiraldo, F., (2002), 'Isotopic identification of the sources of lead contamination for white storks (*Ciconia ciconia*) in a marshland ecosystem (Doñana, SW Spain)', *Science of the Total Environment*, 300 (1): 81–86.

Michael, M., (2000), *Reconnecting Culture, Technology and Nature: From Society to Heterogeneity*, London: Routledge.

Mol, A. and Law, J., (1994), 'Regions, networks and fluids: anaemia and social topology', *Social Studies of Science*, 24: 641–671.

Murdoch, J., (1997), 'Inhuman/nonhuman/human: actornetwork theory and the potential for a non-dualistic and symmetrical perspective on nature and society', *Environment and Planning D: Society and Space*, 15: 731–756.

Pastor, N., López-Lázaro, M., Tella, J. L., Baos, R., Hiraldo, F. and Cortés, F., (2001), 'Assessment of genotoxic damage by the comet assay in white storks (*ciconia ciconia*) after the Doñana ecological disaster', *Mutagenesis*, 16 (3): 219–223.

Pastor, N., Baos, R., López-Lázaro, M., Jovani, R., Tella, J. L., Hajji, N., Hiraldo, F. and Cortés, F., (2004), 'A 4 year follow-up analysis of genotoxic damage in birds of the Doñana area (south west Spain) in the wake of the 1998 mining waste spill', *Mutagenesis*, 19 (1): 61–65.

Perry, R., (1998), 'Definitions and the development of a theoretical superstructure for disaster research', in E. L. Quarantelli (ed.), *What Is a Disaster? Perspectives on the Question*, New York: Routledge.

Perry, R., (2007), 'What is a disaster?', in H. Rodríguez, E. L. Quarantelli, and R. R. Dynes (eds), *Handbook of Disaster Research*, New York: Springer.

Prince, S., (1920), *Catastrophe and Social Change*, New York: Columbia University.

Sauri, D., Domingo, V. and Romero, A., (2003), 'Trust and community building in the Doñana (Spain) toxic spill disaster', *Journal of Risk Research*, 6 (2): 145–162, doi: 10.1080/1366987032000078910.

Schillmeier, M., (2011), 'Unbuttoning normalcy – on cosmopolitical events', *The Sociological Review*, 59 (3): 514–534, doi: 10.1111/j.1467-954X.2011.02019.x.

Schmidt, G., de Stefano, L., Robles, P. and Royo, E., (2002), *Minería en Doñana, Lecciones Aprendidas*, Ed. WWF ADENA.

SEO/Birdlife, (1998), 'Doñana: Preliminary environmental assessment', available at: www.c3.hu/~mme/madar/donana2.htm.

Simón, M., Ortíz, I., García, E., Fernández, J., Dorronsoro, C. and Aguilar, J., (1999), 'El desastre ecológico de Doñana', *Edafología*, 5: 153–161.

Spector, M. and Kitsuse, J., (1977), *Constructing Social Problems*, Menlo Park, CA: Cummings.

Stallings, R., (1997), 'Sociological theories and disaster studies', available at: http://dspace.udel.edu:8080/dspace/bitstream/handle/19716/135/PP2?sequence=1.

Stengers, I., (1991), *Cosmopolitiques. Tome 1: la guerre des sciences*, Paris: La Découverte.

Stengers, I., (2010), 'Including nonhumans in political theory: opening pandora's box?', in B. Braun and S. Whatmore (eds), *Political Matter: Technoscience, Democracy and Public Life*, 3–32, Minneapolis: University of Minnessota Press.

Vega, I. and Bartolomé, J., (1998), 'Doñana envenenada', *Panda, revista trimestral del WWF/Adena*, 16.

Whatmore, S., (2002), *Hybrid Geographies: Natures, Cultures, Spaces*, London: Sage.

Whitehead, A. N., (1985), *Process and Reality: An Essay in Cosmology*, New York: Free Press.

WWF, (2010), *Hacia un Nuevo Modelo de Gestión del Sistema Socio-Ecológico de Doñana Basado en la Construcción de una Visión Compartida Sobre Sus Ecofuturos*, Madrid: WWF.

WWF/ADENA, (2004), *Report on the Situation of the Aznalcóllar Mine and the Guadiamar Green Corridor*, Madrid: WWF.

The Sociological Review, 62:S1, pp. 38–60 (2014), DOI: 10.1111/1467-954X.12123

Misrecognizing tsunamis: ontological politics and cosmopolitical challenges in early warning systems

Ignacio Farías

Abstract: The failure of the Chilean tsunami warning system on the night of 27 February, 2010, opens up the question of the ontological politics of inquiry processes at the two national centres of recognition and civic protection involved. Focusing on approximately two hours of intense activity and communication, I identify three critical features of how non-human phenomena are enacted by these agencies and show how these features shaped the process of misrecognizing the ongoing tsunami. They involved, first, the problem of information and the tension between local and global assessments; second, the problem of interpretation and the tension between scientific evidence and political intervention; and, third, the problem of conclusions and the tension between certainty and uncertainty. The ensuing public and legal controversy about responsible actors of this fatal failure also offers an opportunity to reflect upon the precautionary principle as a model for action in uncertain situations. I suggest here that the failure of the tsunami warning system reveals the need of associating precaution to a cosmopolitical duty of recognition of non-human entities and forces.

Keywords: disasters, organizations, ontological politics, cosmopolitics, recognition

Inquiry and the politics of recognition

At 3:34 a.m. on 27 February, 2010, the sixth largest earthquake ever registered hit Central and South Chile. In the following hours, destructive tsunami waves battered 1,000 km of coastline, causing the loss of 181 lives, including 25 bodies that were never found, and putting many thousands of people in mortal danger. Some minutes after the earthquake, the national Hydrological and Oceanographic Service (SHOA) activated a tsunami warning, but after approximately one hour the warning was cancelled. During this hour, the civic protection office decided against the activation of the protocol for evacuation of coastal populations. Subsequently, the message that a tsunami had been ruled out was spread through different channels to various state agencies, national and local authorities, the media and the population, causing many people to return to their

The Sociological Review, 62:S1, pp. 61–87 (2014), DOI: 10.1111/1467-954X.12124

homes, which in some cases became a mortal trap. Even at noon of the next day, hours after the tsunami was over, military officers and civil officials responsible for tsunami monitoring and civic protection continued to ignore the fact that a tsunami had taken place. Such complete failure of the tsunami warning system makes one not only furious, but also puzzled and astonished about how this could ever happen.

A short revision of disaster research suggests that there are two major approaches to disasters resulting from accidents. The first one involves a pigeon-hole perspective based on a compartmental understanding of sociotechnical systems that searches for causes of disasters in bounded technological or human entities. Sociologists of disasters have, for example, pointed to organizational and cognitive aspects as causes of human errors (Woods *et al.*, 1994). Turner (1978), a pioneer in studying 'man-made' (as opposed to 'natural') disasters, shows that these are often preceded by many different warning signals that remained unnoticed by the people in charge. Accordingly, he described 'man-made' accidents as failures of foresight. Vaughan (1996) has provided a very convincing description of this type of failure as involving the normalization of deviance. The second approach to disasters is based on the idea that system failures cannot be located at any particular entity, human or non-human, but are the result of organizational dynamics (Weick, 1993) and complex interactions between large numbers of elements, subsystems and sites. The latter is the understanding developed by Perrow (1984) in his normal accidents theory. He suggests that the more complex and tightly coupled sociotechnical systems are, the more difficult it becomes to predict all possible interactions between their elements. Normal accidents are thus the improbable, but inevitable, result of such imperfection. Law's (2000) study of the Ladbroke accident follows in part this approach, while emphasizing that imperfections are not just unavoidable, as Perrow suggests, but also necessary to keep systems working smoothly. Thus, while Law challenges the totalizing system logic underlying Perrow's approach by stressing the overlapping of fluid impartial orders, both coincide in their morale of learning to live with failing systems.

These certainly are very useful approaches to studying the failure of the tsunami warning system in Chile. However, they all seem to miss a crucial characteristic of tsunami warning systems, namely, that these are research devices, socio-technical systems for inquiring into natural realities and producing knowledge about them (see also Petersen, in this volume). In this sense, a tsunami warning system works in a similar fashion as a laboratory (Latour and Woolgar, 1986), an oligopticon (Latour and Hermant, 1998) or even a centre of coordination (Suchman, 1997), and accordingly the kind of failure we need to study involves a certain way of constructing knowledge more than an accident or an error. This turn is absolutely necessary, if one considers that what distinguishes warning systems from other complex sociotechnical systems is that inquiry and reflexivity are an intrinsic part of their normal functioning.

The study of the failure of the tsunami warning system thus needs to be framed in a knowledge production perspective and focus on the actual process of inquiry occurring the night of 27 February 2010. A similar move towards merging disaster studies with social studies of science has recently been proposed by Downer (2011), who speaks of epistemic accidents for cases in which 'a scientific or technological assumption proves to be erroneous, even though there were reasonable and logical reasons to hold that assumption *before* (although not after) the event' (2011: 752, my emphasis). There is, however, a small but crucial difference in the tsunami misrecognition case. Here we are not dealing with a technical accident that followed from a prior process of scientific inquiry. The process of inquiry we need to study did not take place before the disaster, for inquiry is what this system does and how it fails.

Taking this into account, it becomes necessary to deploy analytical approaches and conceptual vocabularies centred on inquiry, rather than on accidents, in order to understand disasters such as the tsunami warning failure in Chile. In this article, I argue that the notions of recognition and misrecognition can play a particularly relevant role here. In cognitive psychology, recognition envisages a highly specific cognitive operation that involves acknowledging, on the basis of familiarity and/or recollection, the existence or occurrence of an entity or phenomenon (Diana *et al.*, 2006). As I elucidate in the following pages, recognition in sociotechnical warning systems involves a multi-sited distributed ascertainment of entities or situations predefined as potentially harmful. Recognition thus defines the way inquiry is being performed in these complex systems, defining not just a particular type of knowledge as relevant, but also an ontological politics (Mol, 1999). Moreover, I shall argue that recognition is a core aspect of what the philosopher of science Isabelle Stengers (2005) has called cosmopolitics.

Let me briefly introduce these notions of ontological politics and cosmopolitics and how they are connected with the problem of recognition. The notion of ontological politics was introduced in STS by Annemarie Mol (1999) to account for not just the sociomaterial construction or, to be more precise, enactment of reality, but most importantly to emphasize that the enactment of reality is always coupled with political choices. By studying the multiple ways in which anemia as a condition is enacted in hospitals, laboratories and health systems, Mol shows how each way of enacting its medical reality considers only certain sets of sociomaterial relationships and conditions of possibility for anemia, while disregarding others. By understanding ontology as what belongs to the real and as defining the conditions of possibility we live in, she observes that ontologies are plural and that they do not precede technoscientific practices, but are rather shaped by the latter. This is particularly critical, when it comes to institutions, such as health systems, that are constructed upon a specific ontology of anemia, for instance, as a clinical condition instead of a laboratory phenomenon. Studying ontological politics of technoscientific practices and institutions thus involves looking at the options and choices made regarding what is included and what is excluded.

Accordingly, the notion of ontological politics enables us to emphasize an important aspect of the inquiry and recognition processes of tsunami warning centres. Recognition does not just involve an epistemic process oriented towards a stable reality 'out-there', but enacts the reality of tsunamis in a very specific way. This involves not just a way of understanding or imagining tsunamis, but a full-fledged sociomaterial and sociotechnical network within which tsunamis can exist and be recognized. Accordingly, the recognition of even the tiniest sea rise cannot occur if an entire network of elements is not brought into being as well. The consequence of this is that different ways of practising tsunami recognition, just as different ways of diagnosing and treating anemia, bring along different ways of enacting the natural-technical-social reality of tsunamis (cf. Law, 2004). Thus, institutional arrangements and choices not only respond to epistemic or technical issues, but also involve ontological and political aspects, for they imply making certain entities and relationships present, while making others absent (cf. Law, 2004).

The ensuing disaster also made evident yet another political issue, namely, how entities that have been excluded, or made absent, become again included or present. In *Politics of Nature*, Bruno Latour argues that the main contribution of politicians to a parliament of things should be adding 'a certain sense of danger stemming from the multitude of excluded entities that can return to haunt the collective and demand to be taken into account this time' (2004a: 144). Latour (2004a) indicates that taking into account (or making present) those excluded entities and relationships is a moral obligation which, following Stengers (2005) could be understood with the notion of cosmopolitics (cf. Latour, 2004b).

The notion of cosmopolitics should not be confused with that of cosmopolitanism, which commonly refers to forms of universal citizenship and morality. Cosmopolitics sharply contrasts in two key regards such modern political ideals. The first divergence stems from the understanding of what the cosmos is. In cosmopolitanism, cosmos designates the world in the sense of the planet earth, of which cosmopolitical subjects would be citizens despite states or national boundaries. For cosmopolitanism, the world thus is a given and the key issue is how political belonging and citizenship is organized. The notion of cosmopolitics, on its part, problematizes the notion of cosmos. Instead of taking it for granted and focusing on forms of global citizenship, politics is conceived as a transformative activity oriented and concerned with how the world is composed, that is, with the entities and relationships that are defined as constitutive actors of a common world. The second contrast that follows from the first is that while cosmopolitanism imagines that the only political actors are human subjects capable of clearly defining and articulating their interests, visions and values, as well as morally justifying their preferences and actions, the cosmopolitical proposal requires considering the role and capacity of non-humans as political actors. Politics thus becomes increasingly intermeshed with science and other practical forms of exploring our sociomaterial worlds, while requiring experimentation with new forms of representing non-human's affordances, tendencies, capacities. In the work of Stengers, the cosmopolitical proposal also involves vindicating the figure of the idiot as a political actor who slows down processes of expert deliberation, thereby opening space for the emergence of the unexpected. Thus, while Latour (2004a) proposes imagining a new parliament of things and a new constitution, Stengers (2005) is more concerned with the ethical principles of techno-scientific practices. In the conclusion of this article, I will explore the possible consequences of taking a cosmopolitical approach to the problem of tsunami recognition.

Studying tsunami warning failure

In order to unveil these various politics of recognition and misrecognition, I focus on the actual inquiry process carried out on this fatal night. Thereby, I propose taking a symmetric, situated and onward perspective, assuming that the same type of work that led to misrecognition could have led to a successful recognition (Knorr-Cetina, 1981; Latour and Woolgar, 1986). It is only from a backward or *ex-post* perspective that courses of action can be reconstructed as errors, misperceptions or illusions. Accordingly, instead of trying to explain *why* the tsunami warning system failed, we need to describe *how* it failed. In the ensuing controversy about this failure, all sorts of explanations have been given pointing to larger institutional arrangements, organizational cultures, investment deficits, world economic crises and so forth. In this context, description understood as the minute study of the chains of actors and events involved in the actual process of decision-making (cf. Akrich, 1992; Latour, 2005b) is a helpful strategy to overcome the easy recourse to such external causes. Like the actors responsible for the failure, we need to remain pragmatists, concentrating on the situations. Sometimes, it is true, they will also look for institutional excuses: 'it was the budget'. But mostly, they stick to the situational factors and processes that lead to one particular result. This is the approach we need to take.

This is not to say that the study of failure and misrecognition should be bottom-up, extrapolating from the local to the global level. Misrecognition could be better understood if we follow a lateral approach, different from bottom-up as well as top-down strategies; an approach that focuses on the lateral movements among the different sites in which recognition is produced (Latour, 1988). Accordingly, our description will focus on two key sites, which were the main centres of translation and decision during the night in question. The first is the Hydrographical and Oceanographic Service of the Chilean Navy (SHOA), a state organization existing since 1966 and located in the port-city of Valparaiso. It is in charge of research, monitoring and warning about seismic and hydrological phenomena and, as such, it is responsible for the National System of Tsunami Alarm. The second key site, the Early Alert Centre (CAT) of the National Office of Emergency (ONEMI), is located in Santiago de Chile. It was founded in 1974 and is responsible for civic protection in the context of disasters.

In order to reconstruct the inquiry process unleashed by the earthquake and eventually leading to the cancellation of a tsunami alert, I rely on five types of secondary empirical materials. First, with the research assistance of Felipe Torres, we read and summarized the transcripts of the 22 sessions of the first Inquiry Parliamentary Commission on Natural Disasters, in session in 2010 and during which 28 key actors testified and were interrogated by the parliamentarians. Second, I revised the publicly available transcripts of six testimonies of key actors to the General Attorney in Chile, who runs a juridical investigation against the individuals that might result responsible for the tsunami warning failure. Third, I checked various official documents from the two governmental agencies involved, the ONEMI and SHOA. Fourth, I have profited greatly from three very detailed journalistic investigations published by the Chilean Centre for Journalist Investigation and Information (www.ciperchile.cl). And, finally, I have been reading and collecting hundreds of articles, interviews and media reports on the matter published in different Chilean newspapers.

This enormous proliferation of secondary empirical data is due to the fact that the tsunami warning failure amounts to one of the largest public controversies occurring in Chile during the last years. Relatives have presented criminal demands for their losses activating juridical and police investigations; internal investigations of the institutions involved have been made; a second Inquiry Parliamentary Commission was created, as many parliamentarians were unsatisfied with the conclusions of the first inquiry commission; the decisions of the former president became an electoral topic and a media topic. Accordingly, judges, police investigators, prosecutors, journalists, citizens, politicians, social scientists, lawyers and many other actors have kept collecting data, producing knowledge, passing judgements and allocating responsibilities about the tsunami warning failure. It is thus important to recognize here that the empirical data used for this article comes from a small fraction of the available sources. However, it is also important to say that the bulk of the current public controversy centres on the responsibility of political authorities, especially the then-president of Chile, and decisions made by these actors after they arrived at the Tsunami Alert Center almost three hours after the tsunami had started. In this article, I focus rather on the inquiry process and decisions made by technical actors during the first three hours of activity; matters that are not so much in the centre of the heated public debate.

Misrecognition in action: ontological politics of tsunami warning systems

Only a few weeks after the earthquake and tsunami, a Chilean TV network disclosed a 45-minute video showing what the civic officers, military officials and political authorities, including the Chilean president, were doing and discussing between 5 a.m. and 6 a.m. at the Centre of Early Alert (CAT). The images are quite impressive, as they show the lack of information, the confusion, hesitation and indecision that prevailed in that office. The video then became a public piece of proof for the predominant view of what occurred that night, namely, that the tsunami warning system failed because nothing was done by those in charge. As

The Sociological Review, 62:S1, pp. 61–87 (2014), DOI: 10.1111/1467-954X.12124

one deputy member of the ad-hoc Parliamentary Inquiry Commission (PIC) put it: 'Nobody did anything at all. The question is why?' (PIC, Session 6, 13 May 2010).

At the same time, actors from the responsible agencies argue they had insufficient and contradictory information about what was going on outside, so that nothing could be done. Moreover, it would have been irresponsible to make certain decisions, such as to evacuate, for this could have put the population at an unnecessary risk. The former Army Chief Commander even suggests that under such circumstances, acting would have been something appropriate only for a hero:

> One expects that under these circumstances the hero appears, who stands up and does everything that has to be done. But in the night of 27F, there were no heroes. (*La Tercera*, 20 February 2012)

This is, however, a very bad description of what occurred that night. Inaction on the part of the tsunami monitoring and civic protection technical agencies was neither the result of a refusal nor an impossibility to act. Looking at the testimonies, documents and reports collected for this study, it is clear that, quite to the contrary, much was done: data was retrieved, information communicated, visual inscriptions interpreted, protocols of action followed, discussions held, decisions made, etc. It was in such a context of intensified activity and hectic rush that apparently straightforward matters, such as what counts as a tsunami hazard, what is a tsunami alert or what is a tsunami, were put into question. It indeed took a lot of work, as well as decisions of various kinds to achieve inaction. This is what we need to understand in the first place.

The problem of information: becoming a recognition centre takes time

Misrecognition probably started with some swear words, as journalists Ramírez and Aliaga (2012) have uncovered in their detailed story. The former chief of one of ONEMI's regional offices was, technically speaking, a 'trained observer': a human individual trained to evaluate his sensory perception of an earthquake according to the Mercalli intensity scale. At 3:34 a.m., as the earthquake started shaking his house, he woke up and immediately focused on the building's and his own body's reaction to the earthquake. The building structure was cracking and he couldn't stay on his feet. He estimated an intensity of IX to X degrees on the Mercalli scale. Since he was only 3 km from the coast, he thought of the possibility of a tsunami. At 3:37 a.m., even before the earthquake had ceased, he called the Centre of Early Alert (CAT) of the National Office of Emergency (ONEMI) in Santiago de Chile, to report his observations. The official who received his call said that they had information indicating an earthquake of much less intensity. The trained observer got upset: 'Listen to me, you asshole. This is an earthquake and it is IX to X degrees' (see Ramírez and Aliaga, 2012). Two minutes later CAT officials sent out an earthquake intensity report indicating VIII degrees for the Biobio Region, thus dismissing this observer's assessment. Months later, as the story of this call came up, the former National Chief of ONEMI regretted that 'if this information would have circulated that morning, different decisions would probably have been made' (Ramírez and Aliaga, 2012).

But, can that be all? Have we already explained why the system failed? Would the report of this trained observer have been sufficient for CAT officials to order the imminent evacuation of at least three mid-size cities, several small cities and hundreds of smaller coastal settlements? As Ramírez and Aliaga (2012) rightly observe, the answer is probably negative. Indeed, powerful reasons would have made CAT officials refrain from immediately sending out an evacuation order.

To start with, there is the law. Accordingly, the Hydrographical and Oceanographic Service of the Chilean Navy (SHOA) is 'the only official authority responsible in the country to generate, evaluate or cancel messages or information issued during the operation of the National System of Tsunami Alert' (Presidential Decree No. 26 from 1966). The main reason mentioned in this decree for this arrangement is 'the aim to avoid the panic and confusion that tends to arise in the population towards the indiscriminate diffusion of news related to the approximation of tsunami waves to our coast' (*ibid.*). The rationale for the restriction of this prerogative to the SHOA is not that other state organisms would be unable to recognize the imminent hazard of a tsunami, but rather that they could arrive at contradictory conclusions, generating a communicational chaos. Here the ONEMI is a case in point, as it has trained observers distributed throughout the country who report their sensory observations to the CAT. The latter is obliged to transmit this information to the SHOA and to take action only after a tsunami alert has been issued by SHOA. But the CAT cannot order an evacuation without an official tsunami alert.

The central question then is what counts to emit a tsunami alert. While the direct sighting of a tsunami wave is reliable information enough, when it comes to recognizing a tsunami hazard the SHOA relies on instrumental measures regarding geological characteristics of the earthquake, such as the magnitude calculated on the Richter scale (not to be confused with intensity, a sensorial measure), the seismic moment or the amount of energy released, the type of telluric movement, and the size and location of the geological rupture. However, retrieving these instrumental measures from other national and international organisms takes the SHOA between 15 and 20 minutes, which in the case of near-shore tsunamis is more than enough time for the first destructive waves to reach the coast. This is exactly what happened on the night of 27 February.

At 3:44 a.m., only 10 minutes after the earthquake, an 'observation message' from the Pacific Tsunami Warning Center (PTWC) in Hawaii arrived. With this data, the SHOA officer in charge proceeded to georeference the coordinates, locating the epicentre inland at only 17 km from the coast. With this information, plus the Mercalli data about perceived intensity that also suggested a large rupture close to the coast, he arrived at the conclusion that the earthquake could produce a tsunami. With the computer software *Tsunami Travel Time*, the

The Sociological Review, 62:S1, pp. 61–87 (2014), DOI: 10.1111/1467-954X.12124

arrival times of tsunami waves for 12 cities along the 5,000 km long Chilean coast were estimated. At 3.51 a.m., 17 minutes after the earthquake, an alert was sounded. But as the former SHOA director explains:

> [t]he alert was not useful for some zones, which we know as 'sacrifice zones'. In the case of San Antonio, [the first wave arrived] at 3:50 a.m. and in Constitución at 3.49 a.m., I mean, we are talking about 15 minutes after the earthquake occurred. (PIC, Session 8, 20 May 2010)

Accordingly, the problem is that producing reliable information for assessing tsunami hazard takes time. Information is not just an automatic signal that can be spread in real time. Data needs to be retrieved, put together, entered and interpreted. Only then, after this has been done anew for every emergency, can SHOA and CAT become centres of recognition and protection.

At this point, one option is to abandon the situated process of recognizing a tsunami hazard to suggest that, if there are any responsible actors, they are those who delayed the implementation of a more rapid and effective system of seismologic assessment. Indeed, in 2007, the government announced the implementation of a new National Seismologic Network, which should allow a precise characterization of an earthquake in only 5 to 10 minutes. But this never materialized. The responsibility then, some argue, lies with the government. According to the former president, however, it was the fault of the slow bureaucracy of the Universidad de Chile, a key partner for the establishment of this network. But the funding, university speakers have replied, was only transferred in 2009 and could not be used, because, as the former ONEMI chief explained in an email to the presidency, it was assigned to expenditures 'exclusively in steel [but neither] in human resources nor in the installation and operational logistics' (*El Mercurio*, 26 February 2012).

But can that be the explanation? Do we now know where the problem lays? Perhaps. But if we stay with the actors in the situation, we learn that, since moving from local data to central assessments takes critical time, the National Emergency Office (ONEMI) had long ago developed the so-called 'Accemar' methodology for municipal tsunami prevention and action plans. Accordingly, it should be in the hands of local civic protection committees, comprised of municipal authorities, local police, fire departments and citizen organizations, to decide in a decentralized manner, and on the basis of sensorial perception, about tsunami alerts and evacuations (see ONEMI, 2001). So, the problem that the Accemar methodology makes evident is not just the tension between sensorial and instrumental earthquake data, but the movement from local and partial data (sensorial or instrumental, that's not the point) to a central and integral assessment of a situation. And the challenge is that the sites where this movement from local to global should be made are yet another locality in the network: offices located in Santiago de Chile and Valparaiso that need to become centres of recognition. For the ONEMI, the result is quite paradoxical. While its Accemar methodology teaches that coastal populations should evacuate immediately after a big earthquake, its Center of Early Alert, the CAT, should wait for the SHOA to generate the official alert, and only then officially initiate the evacuation.

In the meantime, failure can only be local. This is a key argument made by SHOA officers and ONEMI officials, who suggest that it was the local level and the population that failed to react as they should. At the Parliament, the Navy's Chief Admiral concluded his declaration by asking:

> So, is the alert important? It is important. Was this an extreme case, in which the only thing one could do was to act by conviction and education? Undoubtedly yes. (PIC, Session 4, 6 May 2010)

Accordingly, it is the population that has to react independently from the information and recommendations coming from the central level. And, indeed, in many cities and towns, this is exactly what the population did. And for the cases where this didn't occur, the explanation would then involve the lack of tsunami prevention and education programmes. We move out of the situation again and a new larger number of possible responsible actors suddenly come into sight. Did ONEMI offer risk prevention courses beyond the Accemar methodology? How many evacuation simulacra did the ONEMI perform in the last years? Certainly not enough, argue Members of Parliament, the media, the public. The cause for this, replies the former ONEMI Chief, was the limited budget of the institution. And the reason for budget reduction was none other than the world economic crisis of 2008 that constrained the national budget. Perhaps the economic crisis can count as the ultimate explanation for why local inhabitants didn't evacuate on their own initiative, but it is also the last factor necessary to understand how things failed. For this reason, I have not focused on explanations, but rather on description. And the description of this first chain of events indeed reveals a critical tension that is perhaps inherent to early warning systems in general: that becoming a centre of recognition requires time, mostly a matter of minutes, but critical minutes that are associated with local costs: the 'sacrifice zones'.

Centres of recognition are thus based on a sacrificial logic: some localities are the cost that needs to be paid for other localities to produce global and reliable assessments of the situation. Certainly, the Accemar Plan that empowers local committees to locally decide upon coastal evacuation offers a counterweight to such sacrificial logic, as it encourages communities to escape a possibly tragic destiny. But this does not change the fact that national centres of recognition slow down the communication of assessments. This slowing down does not just result from a concern with false alarms and mass panic, but also from a commitment to producing global, certain and definitive assessments. Different would be the case of a more decentralized and precautionary warning system, where each municipality or region would decide upon alerts and where interim decisions would be made upon incomplete and inconclusive information and eventually reversed as new information arrives. Instead of such precautionary logic, a sacrificial logic is inscribed in the system's orientation to producing global assessments and warnings.

The Sociological Review, 62:S1, pp. 61–87 (2014), DOI: 10.1111/1467-954X.12124

But this is still a very incomplete analysis, as it suggests that once this sacrifice has been made, there would be no more space for ambiguity, uncertainty or hesitation, and civic protection protocols would be enforced. But none of this happened in Chile on the night of the tsunami. In order to understand this, it is necessary to have a more detailed look at *how* the instrumental measurement of the earthquake became a further source of uncertainty.

The problem of interpretation: heuristics don't travel easily

Let us go back to the moment when SHOA officers interpreted that there was a tsunami hazard and an alert must be sent out (see Figure 1). Geological data had arrived from the Pacific Tsunami Warning Centre (PTWC) in Hawaii at 3:44 a.m. The PTWC geologist who dispatched this information testified that: 'Once we determined the location and the magnitudes [. . .] we realized that it was going to be an earthquake with a high tsunami potential' (see Oficina de la Fiscalía, 2010). Such a realization was not included in the observation message, which, as such, should not include any interpretations. Indeed, the PTWC didn't send out a tsunami warning until one hour later, as they received more information about the earthquake and sea level variations. At the SHOA, however, a decision had to be made immediately, on the grounds of the locally available data. As the Navy Chief Admiral explained, this was far from an easy task:

> A scientific rule accepted and valued says that if the epicentre is deeper than 60 kilometres, buried in the earth, the possibility for a tsunami is zero [. . .] This was a very difficult test for the lieutenant oceanographer on duty that day, who, nevertheless, acted very well. First, because the result was an epicentre inland, but he considered that it was close to the coast and, therefore, dangerous. Second, the measured depth was very close to the 60 kilometres depth. (PIC, Session 4, 6 May 2010)

It is easy to suspect these congratulatory words, repeated in the Navy Internal Investigation Report about the events of the night (see Armada de Chile, 2010), and criticize them as an institutional strategy for exculpating SHOA officers. But it is also true that the SHOA produced an even more precise estimation of possible arrival times of tsunami waves than the one sent one hour later by the PTWC. The point, however, is that producing a good interpretation of partial data at one particular location does not suffice to act as a national centre of recognition. The real challenge is making this local interpretation into the unique possible interpretation for all other locations in the network. As we will see, communicating this local interpretation is not just a matter of transmitting information. An alert requires more than just the statement declaring it. Data, rationales and context need to be sent along in a very precise way to ensure that other actors will not just receive a statement, but could also arrive at the same interpretation.

Put differently: does sending out my interpretation of an event suffice to ensure that other actors will comply with it? Certainly not, and precisely for this reason, the protocol establishes that when the SHOA sounds a tsunami alert, it has to check that all recipients send back a confirmation of receipt. In the case

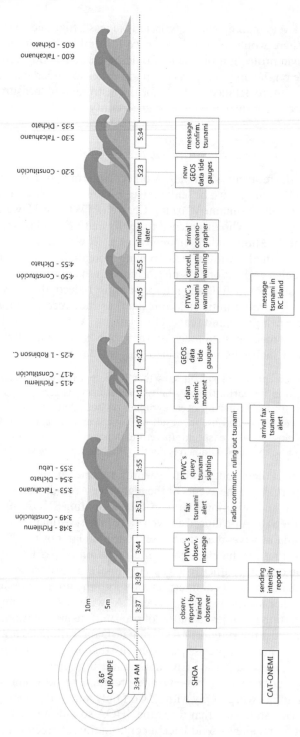

Figure 1: *Timeline of tsunami (mis) recognition process correlated with tsunami arrival times at main coastal settlements.*
Sources: El Mercurio, Section D, p. 6, 4 March 2012; Armada de Chile, 2010; Pontificia Universidad Católica de Chile, 2010.

The Sociological Review, 62:S1, pp. 61–87 (2014), DOI: 10.1111/1467-954X.12124

of the so-called Genmercalli national security network, which includes ports, Navy stations and maritime administrations, only 8 of 70 contact points sent back a confirmation. However, SHOA officers assumed the whole maritime network had received the message. This turned out to be a terrible mistake, for their very good interpretation of the partial data remained merely a local warning. Indeed, it is not just that the Navy stations, ports and other maritime institutions of the Genmercalli network didn't receive the information, but also that many local authorities who, due to the lack of other communication channels, are dependent upon these maritime institutions for information about a possible tsunami, never heard of it. This was, for example, the case of the Governor of the Biobio Region who, after communicating with the Admiral in charge of the local Navy port, transmitted a message to the population ruling out a tsunami and recommended going back to their houses. The case of this Admiral has been highly controversial, as he had a privileged view of the bay and assumed that what was taking place under his nose was a 'sea rise'. But, more interesting than discussing his incompetency is understanding the more fundamental problem that the whole tsunami warning system was facing that night, namely, that the right interpretation of the available data could not travel smoothly within the network.

This is particularly evident in the perhaps most controversial matter of the night, namely, the communications between the SHOA and the CAT and, especially, a fax with the subject 'Tsunami alert' (see Figure 2). According to SHOA officers, at 3:51 a.m. a simple and clear message was sent via the VHF radio system: 'Attention Omega Zero [CAT's radio code] . . . From SHOA . . . Tsunami alert in course'. After sending this message, SHOA officers proceeded to calculate the estimated arrival times and, with that information, prepared a fax issuing the alert, which finally went through at 4:07 a.m. According to CAT officials, when SHOA communicated with CAT at 3:51 a.m., SHOA officers were actually responding to a message sent out by the CAT two minutes earlier. In their answer, which CAT officials describe as much more articulated than a mere short instruction, SHOA officers would have conveyed instrumental information about 'the epicenter, indicating that it was inland and that the tsunami alert is ruled out, for the epicenter is inland' (ONEMI, 2010). It is perhaps tempting to stop here and think that we merely need to get the facts straight to find out which of the two parties is actually guilty: what did the SHOA officer really say during this call? Who is telling the truth and who is lying? An angry member of the Inquiry Parliamentary Commission suggested that the only way to arrive at the truth was to call a face-to-face confrontation between the two parties (PIC, Session 10, 3 June 2010).

But the question is not just whether the SHOA officer ruled out the tsunami at 3:51 a.m. or not, but rather the fact that his controversial words were articulated in a situational context in which multiple other communications were taking place in multiple directions. Even if he did, he was not the only reason why CAT officials understood the fax with the subject 'Tsunami alert' as a 'readiness and vigilance notice' only, assuming that in case a tsunami were to

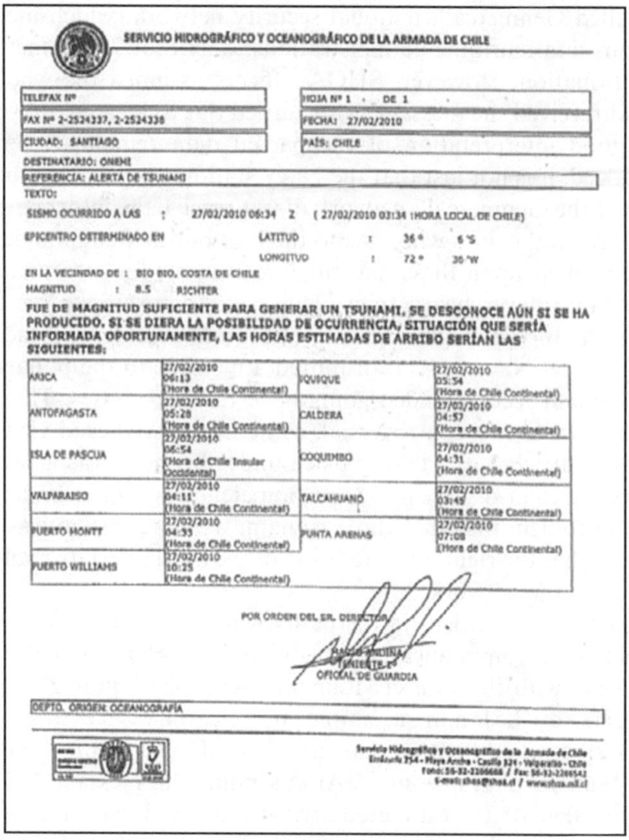

SERVICIO HIDROGRÁFICO Y OCEANOGRÁFICO DE LA ARMADA DE CHILE

TELEFAX Nº

FAX Nº 2-2524337, 2-2524338

CIUDAD: SANTIAGO

HOJA Nº 1 DE 1

FECHA: 27/02/2010

PAÍS: CHILE

DESTINATARIO: ONEMI

REFERENCIA: ALERTA DE TSUNAMI

TEXTO:

SISMO OCURRIDO A LAS : 27/02/2010 06:34 Z (27/02/2010 03:34 HORA LOCAL DE CHILE)

EPICENTRO DETERMINADO EN LATITUD : 36 º 6 'S

LONGITUD : 72 º 30 'W

EN LA VECINDAD DE : BIO BIO, COSTA DE CHILE

MAGNITUD : 8.5 RICHTER

FUE DE MAGNITUD SUFICIENTE PARA GENERAR UN TSUNAMI. SE DESCONOCE AÚN SI SE HA PRODUCIDO. SI SE DIERA LA POSIBILIDAD DE OCURRENCIA, SITUACIÓN QUE SERÍA INFORMADA OPORTUNAMENTE, LAS HORAS ESTIMADAS DE ARRIBO SERÍAN LAS SIGUIENTES:

ARICA	27/02/2010 06:13 (Hora de Chile Continental)	IQUIQUE	27/02/2010 05:54 (Hora de Chile Continental)
ANTOFAGASTA	27/02/2010 05:28 (Hora de Chile Continental)	CALDERA	27/02/2010 04:57 (Hora de Chile Continental)
ISLA DE PASCUA	27/02/2010 06:54 (Hora de Chile Insular Occidental)	COQUIMBO	27/02/2010 04:31 (Hora de Chile Continental)
VALPARAISO	27/02/2010 04:11 (Hora de Chile Continental)	TALCAHUANO	27/02/2010 03:45 (Hora de Chile Continental)
PUERTO MONTT	27/02/2010 04:33 (Hora de Chile Continental)	PUNTA ARENAS	27/02/2010 07:08 (Hora de Chile Continental)
PUERTO WILLIAMS	27/02/2010 10:25 (Hora de Chile Continental)		

POR ORDEN DEL SR. DIRECTOR

TENIENTE 1º

OFICIAL DE GUARDIA

DEPTO. ORIGEN: OCEANOGRAFÍA

Servicio Hidrográfico y Oceanográfico de la Armada de Chile

Figure 2: *Tsunami alert fax from SHOA to ONEMI.*
Source: http://ciperchile.cl/wp-content/uploads/FAX-Shoa-a-ONEMI-Tsunami.pdf

occur, the SHOA would notify them immediately. Thus, the central question is how it was possible for CAT officials to produce their own different interpretation of what was going on.

The short answer is that the interpretation rationale that led SHOA officers to one conclusion was not shared in the CAT, and that the communication of the tsunami alert via radio and fax was not sufficient to make this interpretation rationale travel from one place to the next. One could even argue that if arriving at this interpretation had been a difficult task, they should have assumed that it would find resistance at other network sites. In a sense, this is what CAT officials complained about, when they point, not just to the call before, but to the fax itself as being highly ambiguous.

Three elements of the fax have been at the centre of the controversy. First, the data itself: 'The epicentral data didn't coincide with what is technically necessary for tsunami probability' (see Ramírez and Aliaga, 2012). This is, however, a

The Sociological Review, 62:S1, pp. 61–87 (2014), DOI: 10.1111/1467-954X.12124

simplification of the matters, for what should count is the whole rupture area, not just the epicentre. Accordingly, a repeated question has been where this wrong assumption or simplified rule came from. One possibility denounced in the media is that the criteria for ruling out tsunamis included in official ONEMI and SHOA manuals leave too much room for interpretation (see Ramírez and Aliaga, 2012). But for CAT officials the problem is not related to manuals, but rather to the concrete inscriptions shaping the actual situation and leading to one conclusion or another. They claim, second, that the fax message was very ambiguous. The fax read: 'It is still unknown if it has occurred. If the possibility of occurrence is given, a situation that it would be reported when opportune, the estimated arrival hours are the following'. When asked why they didn't immediately sound the alert after receiving the fax, CAT officials argued that the fax was poorly formulated and that it was unclear what was meant by the situation 'would be reported when opportune'. And they went further, arguing that the font size of the fax's subject line reading 'Tsunami alert' was too small and that the whole layout imprecise – even though the phrasing and the format exactly corresponded with the officially mandated layout.

> I think that a clear enough document to declare an alert of this magnitude would be, for example: 'Given the occurrence of significant differences in sea level, a tsunami alert is declared'. That is enough for me. We wouldn't have any reservations in declaring tsunami alert if the information is clear and precise. But, in my understanding, this was not the case. (PIC, Session 10, 3 June 2010)

Interestingly, the controversy around the fax has come down to one key question, namely, whether the fax should be interpreted at all. In the words of a Member of Parliament: 'the first point that must be clarified relates to whether . . . the civic authority responsible for ONEMI has the possibility or liberty to interpret it' (PIC, Session 4, 6 May 2010). According to the Navy's Chief Admiral, there are many reasons why the fax should not be interpreted under any circumstances. To start with, there is the law: the SHOA is the only national agency responsible for issuing, assessing or cancelling a tsunami alert. The ONEMI should not interpret, but automatically react to the alert by activating the civil protection system: 'Why should another institution interpret the data? In that case it would suffice with interpretations and there would be no need for a responsible technical organism' (PIC, Session 4, 6 May 2010). Apart from the law, CAT officials would have been incapable of assessing technical information, for none of them had any training in geology, oceanography or the like. As it could be expected, this point has led to a different question, namely, who is responsible for putting together a team with no appropriate expertise; a question that rapidly leads to accusations against the former president, who designated a journalist as ONEMI chief in the first place. But, apart from this, SHOA officers argue that even if CAT officials were to interpret the fax, the only possible conclusion was to proceed immediately with the evacuation. The SHOA, they explain, sends three to four faxes per month to the CAT titled 'Seismic information', specifying that the reported seismic activity 'doesn't generate conditions for a tsunami'. In this context, a fax with the subject 'Tsunami Alert' should have been interpreted as a sufficient reason to activate the alert.

So the question is posed again: why didn't they? One way of explaining this has been to point out that the interpretation of the fax was shaped by the diverging definitions of alert and alarm prevailing in these two institutions. The National Office of Emergency (ONEMI) and hence also the CAT distinguishes between three types of alerts: green, yellow and red alerts, whereas only the latter requires actually taking action and mobilizing all available resources to control a harmful event. The SHOA, on the other hand, knows no coloured alerts, but only alerts and alarms, and none of these involve just vigilance or readiness, but rather a distinction between high probability and certainty of occurrence: 'Regarding alert and alarm, the truth is that for practical effects there is no difference at all, for in both cases people should be evacuated to secure zones' (Former Navy Chief Commander, PIC, Session 4, 6 May 2010). But, apparently, CAT officials didn't know SHOA's nomenclature and interpreted the tsunami alert as a yellow alert that only required them to prepare for a red alert. This mismatching makes evident the critical role of shared mental models in disaster management, when different institutions need to work together (cf. Smith and Dowell, 2000).

But, apart from this, the controversy around the interpretability of the fax reveals a much more fundamental tension: while the tsunami warning system is based on a profoundly modern separation between facts and power, evidence and intervention, and science and politics, this is not reflected in the actual practices of both institutions involved. As Latour (1993) has suggested, the purification of science and politics as two fields of human activity concerned with two distinct and irreconcilable objects, namely, nature and society, is a central axiom of modernity. In such a modern scheme, the SHOA is supposed to produce evidence about natural facts, while the CAT is supposed to have the power to intervene and eventually protect society from natural threats. But, looking at the actual practices of these actors, it is evident that SHOA officials are very aware that tsunami alerts are not just based on incontestable scientific facts, but on circumstanced interpretation work. In consequence, they see themselves confronted with decisions, which are simultaneously scientific and political, regarding whether to sound an alert or not. Similarly, the ONEMI understands that evacuating coastal populations cannot be an automatic and uncritical consequence of what is stated in a fax. From their perspective, the SHOA provides highly relevant information, but before ordering an evacuation, the CAT needs to evaluate the information available and the foreseeable consequences of such a decision. Thus, in practice, we have two organisms that are engaged in both science and politics, asking themselves which natural facts and which social interventions are right.

And how else could it be, if the facts regarding the earthquake were far from being precise or stable. Indeed, only several days later, international seismological services would release the significantly revised data. As it turned out, the earthquake was quite an obvious candidate for generating a tsunami. But this

The Sociological Review, 62:S1, pp. 61–87 (2014), DOI: 10.1111/1467-954X.12124

'fact' could only be construed later on after a great amount of highly specialized work was done. But neither this work nor a neat separation between evidence and intervention are things a tsunami warning system could afford.

The problem of conclusions: falsification is too costly

There are basically two ways of recognizing a tsunami. One has to do with seismic activity and involves interpreting earthquake data. The other has to do with water. When you sight a huge mass of water advancing through the ocean, or when tide gauges report sudden sea rises, you should know that a tsunami is taking place. This should be quite unequivocal. More important, this should be conclusive.

The first query about sightings of tsunami waves came at 3:55 a.m. from officials of the PTWC in Hawaii (see Figure 1). One of them explained in his witness declaration that tsunami sightings are the most reliable information, especially given the small number of tide gauges Chile has. The problem, he adds, is not just that tsunami waves could reach the coast without being detected, but also that the information of the tide gauges must be correctly interpreted. The SHOA corporal who answered this call confirmed that they didn't have any information about tsunami sightings whatsoever, and promised to call back when such information was received. Actually, tide gauges should have been delivering data about the ongoing tsunami with a maximal delay of 2 to 4 minutes. But the earthquake cut the optic fibre lines connecting them with the SHOA, so that data collected by tide gauges could only be retrieved via the GEOS satellite system to which these send their information in the 23rd minute of every hour. Accordingly, only at 4:23 a.m., 49 minutes after the earthquake took place, SHOA officers had the first information about sea levels. The data, transformed into a graphic, showed a small sea level rise right after the earthquake and, for most stations, a posterior diminution. In the case of Robinson Crusoe Island, the rise had been only 18 to 20 centimetres and was still below the high tide. In the case of Talcahuano, the rise registered was 1.8 to 2 metres, but only a couple of centimetres over the high tide mark (see Figure 3). The conclusion at which SHOA officials arrived was that a tsunami had not taken place and, accordingly, cancelled the tsunami alert at 4:55 a.m., 81 minutes after the earthquake.

There has been much debate about why this one conclusion was reached. An important factor, mentioned by SHOA officials in their defence, was their precaution regarding the danger of a false alarm that would trigger an evacuation in which people's lives could be put at risk. To paraphrase one SHOA official: 'If the tsunami hadn't occurred, and we had maintained the alert, now we would be giving explanations about why we didn't cancel'. One could thus argue that it was the institutional memory of a false tsunami alarm in 2005, causing the loss of two lives that led SHOA officials to this particular conclusion (cf. Peña, 2010). But SHOA officials, just as ONEMI officers, systematically contest contextual, institutional or historical explanations of their actions and decisions. They prefer to stick to the situation. And when they do so, they

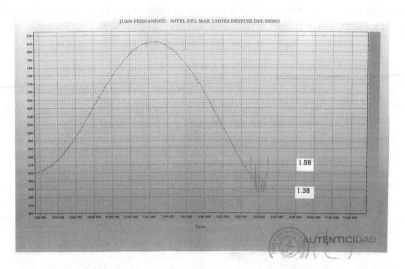

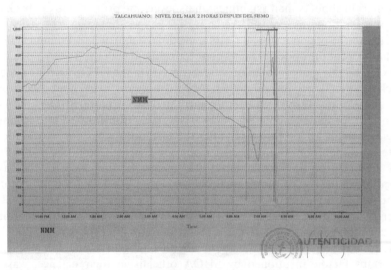

Figure 3: *Sea level graphs for Juan Fernandez (Robinson Crusoe Island) and Talcahuano.*
Source: http://ciperchile.cl/wp-content/uploads/Gráficos-Mareografos.pdf.
Intervened by the author.

recognize that the conclusion they arrived at was the result of having overlooked key information that was already available, such as the data regarding the seismic moment, available from 4:10 a.m. that indicated an amount of energy liberation large enough to produce a tsunami. And they also overlooked the

The Sociological Review, 62:S1, pp. 61–87 (2014), DOI: 10.1111/1467-954X.12124
© 2014 The Author. Editorial organisation © 2014 The Editorial Board of the Sociological Review

tsunami warning that the PTWC sent out at 4:45 a.m., ten minutes before the SHOA decided to cancel. The PTWC warning is interesting because it was issued with the same information from the GEOS satellite available at the SHOA. PTWC officials considered that the data coming from the tide gauges was very strange, for also Easter Island, which is located thousands of kilometres away from the epicentre, showed a slight rise of sea level. Their interpretation of the data was that this showed the effect of so-called 'surface waves', which spread out much faster than tsunami waves, which could yet come.

Conclusions, thus, are not the univocal result of empirical data or theoretical propositions. But neither can they be reduced to cultural contexts or institutional memories. They are rather situated and contingent forms of producing alignments of data, of ordering a chaotic set of information and excluding contradictory or mismatching data, in order to make sense of the world. Indeed, different conclusions are often possible. When the SHOA's chief oceanographer arrived at the SHOA some minutes after the alert was cancelled and saw the available mareographs, she reached a different conclusion. The diminution in sea rises visible in some of the graphs was interpreted by her not as a tendency to normalization, but as the occurrence of a 'resonance effect'. This was the instrumental confirmation that a tsunami was occurring.

But why did the SHOA fail to reactivate the tsunami alert or sound a tsunami alarm? Apparently, she communicated her conclusion to her direct superior, but it was not him, but his superior, who had made the decision to cancel the alert. Somehow her conclusion was lost in the Navy's hierarchical structure of communication and command. And, apart from that, critical voices add, she is a woman and a civilian, so that basically nobody listened to her. Let this organizational culture be the explanation for that. But what should we do with these three other contradictory pieces of information?

First, at 4:45 a.m., the Valparaiso Police Chief reported to the regional office of the ONEMI that the police station on Robinson Crusoe Island had confirmed via IP phone connection that between 4:20 and 4:30 a.m. a tsunami had devastated the small town of Bay Cumberland. According to the SHOA logbook, the CAT called at 5:17 a.m. asking whether they had information about anomalies in sea levels on Robinson Crusoe Island. Their answer was that they had information of a sea rise of only 18–20 cm. For SHOA officers and ONEMI officials it was then easier to assume that there was confusion on Robison Crusoe Island regarding what counts as a tsunami than to question their own conclusion. Second, at 5:23 a.m., new information from the tide gauges should be available for download. But when the time came, the satellite revealed that the tide gauge from Robinson Crusoe Island was disconnected. This should have been understood as a clear signal that the data from 4:23 a.m. that indicated only a 18–20 cm rise was also questionable. Perhaps, when hit by the wave, the tide gauge could only register a 20 cm rise before collapsing. But these alternative conclusions appeared to be out of the question given the already reached conclusion. Third, at 5:34 a.m. a tsunami confirmation sent by the former chief of SHOA's Oceanography section was also dismissed. His message read: 'I confirm tsunami in basetalc [Talca's maritime base]. Measured sea level 6 meters in Force Sub. A flood wave without breaker' (see Ramírez and Aliaga, 2012). Journalists cite internal SHOA sources that indicate that the current chief of SHOA's Oceanography section, whose conclusions were lost in the gender-biased chain of command, received this message and immediately read it aloud to the officials in charge, who just remained silent. Whether true or not, this story makes evident the obduracy of data alignments.

The problem then is when conclusions are treated as definitive. As the verb 'to conclude' suggests, conclusions are also powerful ways of finishing a discussion, of declaring something as over. Conclusions are thus quite dangerous, for they declare the process of inquiry and data alignment as over, producing certainty and, in this particular case, a huge relief: 'Ok, one problem less'. These were, for example, the now infamous words of the former ONEMI chief as she heard that the SHOA ruled out the tsunami (PIC, Session 5, 12 May 2010). And in such a context, new data is either made to fit the already achieved conclusion or questioned and kept apart. Only much later, after 7 a.m., as contradictory information started to overflow the SHOA office, was it decided to sound a preventive tsunami alert for Easter Island, still assuming that a near-shore tsunami had not taken place. Even as long as 5 hours later, shortly after noon, as the ONEMI chief met the elected president, she would still explain to him how unusual the earthquake had been, as it produced several sea rises, but no tsunami.

The fundamental problem underlying such unfortunate scenes is that when conclusions are arrived at, inquiry as a form of open exploration into the actual and possible states of the world stops. Data keeps being collected, information flowing, but once a conclusion has been reached, such data could only be used to either corroborate or falsify the already existing conclusion. But, as science studies have shown, falsification is a costly and difficult process. It involves a process in which a proposition is disproven with an empirical test. In the extreme case, counter-laboratories need to be construed, in order to contest the conclusions of one laboratory (Latour, 1987). In other words, producing a dissenter capable of questioning an already achieved alignment of data – a conclusion – is a costly process that takes time; time that a tsunami warning system just can't afford. Indeed, none of this occurred or even could have occurred during the night of the 27F at the offices of the SHOA.

Responsibility and precaution: for a cosmopolitics of recognition

One day after the tragedy, the former Chilean Minister of National Defence declared: 'What we saw occurring along the coast, from regions 6th to 8th is a tsunami, here and in Burundi; and a mistake was made' (*La Nación*, 28 February 2010). The Minister's reference to Burundi, by the way, a landlocked country, was an attempt to emphasize that the tsunami, as a natural phenomenon, was to be universally, univocally and immediately recognized as such. If this did not

The Sociological Review, 62:S1, pp. 61–87 (2014), DOI: 10.1111/1467-954X.12124

occur, this could only be the result of human errors. Two years after the disaster, in February 2012, Chile's general public attorney announced the prosecution of eight individuals from the CAT and SHOA for their 'participation in decision-making by technical agencies charged with issuing and disseminating tsunami warnings to the population' (*Agence France Presse*, 10 February 2012). Evidence against these individuals would suggest 'criminal negligence' in the performance of their duties. Law experts have observed that this prosecution resulted more from a simplistic application of the penal law principles of personal responsibility and guiltiness than from an informed juridical investigation of the subject matter (*El Mostrador*, 12 February 2012). The latter should make evident that the prosecuted individuals were making decisions in a situation of radical uncertainty, so that the penal law retrospective understanding of responsibility, connecting consequences to causes, does not apply so easily.

Moreover, as we have seen above, a clear-cut distinction between natural facts and human errors cannot be traced for the inquiry process that led to misrecognition (cf. Bloor, 1991). Much more relevant, for example, was the movement from local to centrally assessed facts; a movement that does not only require a critical time, but also taking into account some, but excluding other local facts. Accordingly, it seems that rather than improving the reaction time of central assessment and recognition, the challenge is to empower local committees, so that they can decide upon local facts without being overruled by national centres. Beyond this, it also became evident that an institutional design that assumes a separation between facts and power, the production of evidence and intervention contradicts the actual practices of both, the CAT and the ONEMI, which are simultaneously involved in science and politics. Accordingly, interaction between these centres cannot be reduced to the transmission of information, for the scientific and politic criteria required to arrive at certain interpretations of data must support each other. Instead of a further formalization and automation of communications, it thus seems important to introduce communication protocols to ensure that interpretations are shared. Lastly, perhaps the most critical tension crisscrossing the tsunami warning system was between scientific certainty and uncertainty. As we have seen, the key should be learning how to act with uncertainty rather than arriving too quickly at conclusions that reveal themselves to be practically irreversible. I'd like to dwell now on this latter tension to approach the issue of responsibility.

In the last decades, advances in legal thought have led to the introduction of the so-called 'precautionary principle' (Harremoës *et al.*, 2001) which, formulated in negative terms, indicates that lack of scientific proof does not justify inaction. More positively formulated, the precautionary principle brings along the obligation to make decisions in situations of uncertainty that are not definitive, thus introducing a prospective notion of responsibility based on a 'duty of prudence' (Callon *et al.*, 2009: 202). UNESCO (2005) gives a list of key common elements of various definitions of this principle, which can be summarized in three points: (1) this principle applies when scientific uncertainty exists about nature, causality and probability of harms that are morally 'unacceptable' and when this is not based on 'mere fantasy or crude speculation'; (2) this principle involves an intervention before the possible harm occurs and it should be proportional to the possible magnitude of that harm; and (3) intervention involves a need for ongoing systematic empirical research for evidence. The ascertainment of uncertainty is then the key for the application of the precautionary principle.

Based on this, one could ask why SHOA officers and CAT officials didn't act in a more precautionary mode, thus fulfilling their duty of prudence. But, interestingly, these actors justify their (now we know) non-precautious decisions in terms of prudence, responsibility and precaution. The ONEMI, for example, argues that not ordering an evacuation was done precisely to protect the population from an ungrounded decision:

> [I]f the technical organism . . . rules it out, how could I expose all communities to go out in the middle of the night, in the dark, just because it occurred to me, because one of three parameters is fulfilled? This seemed to me irresponsible, Mr. President. (Former ONEMI Chief, PIC, Session 5, 12 May 2010)

The SHOA, on its part, explains that they cancelled the alert, because maintaining it would have hindered rescue operations:

> Maintaining the alert . . . also has an effect. . . . Imagine all the people trapped, with a tsunami alert, and we keep it for several hours: rescue teams could not go to the places where that could happen . . . For example, if we had obeyed what the PTWC indicates . . . we would have kept the alert until 9:15 p.m., this is 17 hours with an alert . . . What occurs in a country with such an alert, with the people that can't be rescued or the people in hospitals. It is a discussable issue. (Former SHOA Director, PIC, Session 8, 20 May 2010)

As these explanations suggest, both SHOA and CAT evaluated the situation they were in with regard to the well-known risks of a false alarm, but not as one entailing scientific uncertainty regarding the tsunami hazard.

It is important to distinguish between risk and uncertainty (cf. Knight, 1921). Risk involves some knowledge about the probability of occurrence of a certain event, although this does not have to be mathematically measurable, as Knight classically suggested. Luhmann (1993), for example, contests the idea of risk as an objective measurable threat to redefine it as a by-product of decision-making between alternative courses of action. In either case, in order to be measured or taken, risks need to be known. Uncertainty defines a very different situation: one in which individuals and institutions know that they don't have any information about the probability of occurrence of a certain event (Callon *et al.*, 2009). The latter would have involved acknowledging the lack of reliable data regarding a tsunami hazard and acting accordingly. While risk-taking decisions resemble a more or less informed bet, decisions under conditions of uncertainty need to be temporary and reversible, so that alternative courses of action are not foreclosed in advance. Instead, SHOA officers and CAT officials trusted their data and heuristic models and risked falsely ruling out the tsunami. Had they evaluated the situation as one of uncertainty, as a situation in which you know that you don't really know what's going on, they would have possibly made a different call.

The key question here is whether one can hold actors responsible for having evaluated the situation in terms of some known risks instead of as one entailing radical uncertainty. One is tempted to say yes, but this is not easy. Definitions of the precautionary principle emphasize that the ascertainment of uncertainty should not be based on 'mere fantasy and crude speculation', but on a functional system of vigilance; this is, 'a more or less formalized set of sociotechnical arrangements that enables the collection, recording, and collation of information which, while dispersed and heterogeneous, is likely to reveal the broader collective problem' (Callon *et al.*, 2009: 211). What happens, however, when the very system of vigilance arrives at a false conclusion and acts accordingly?

Perhaps the key to this dilemma is that the ascertainment of uncertainty and thus the application of the principle of uncertainty cannot be based on a sociotechnical system of vigilance and inquiry alone, but also on a cosmopolitical form of vigilance and inquiry (Stengers, 2005; Latour, 2004b). Uncertainty thus would not just be a technoscientific problem, but a cosmopolitical one. Accordingly, I suggest that a cosmopolitical problematization of tsunami recognition would involve recognizing non-human forces as capable of acting, affecting and transforming the world in contingent and non-fully predictable ways. In the remainder of this article, I would like to explore this argument in two key regards: specifying the notion of a moral recognition of non-humans within the cosmopolitical proposal, and speculating about the practical consequences that fulfilling such a duty would have had for a tsunami warning.

The cosmopolitical proposals of Stengers and Latour, aimed as they are to open up the question regarding the entities and relationships that compose the common world, emphasize processes and procedures different from recognition. For Stengers (2005), cosmopolitics is fundamentally about *exploration*. Her vindication of the figure of the idiot is precisely about making possible a more open type of exploration, one that is even based on prejudice, 'fantasy and speculation', to paraphrase the UNESCO, but which slow down the process of producing technoscientific certainty. Latour (2004b; 2005a) stresses more the problem of *representation* (and demonstration) and how representation informs decisions about the entities and relationships that compose a common world or cosmos. Accordingly, the key cosmopolitical challenge is opening up traditional forms of political representation (and demonstration) to other forms of scientific or artistic representation.

The notion of *recognition* adds, I think, a third element to these cosmopolitical accents on exploration and representation. Certainly, one could imagine recognition as a middle step between the open exploration of the world and the experimental representation of its heterogeneous constituents. Attending, however, to the central role this notion plays in current moral philosophy to ensure the right to legitimate participation of human individuals and social groups within common worlds (Fraser and Honneth, 2003), one could start thinking of recognition as a cosmopolitical process in its own right. Nancy Fraser's work on recognition, even when it is confined to humans, offers some interesting insights here. Recognition, she argues, is not about individual self-realization, as Axel Honneth (1996) has classically suggested, but about ensuring that all those actually involved in social life are recognized as full social partners. Accordingly, misrecognition occurs '[w]hen . . . institutionalized patterns of cultural value constitute some actors as inferior, excluded, wholly other, or simply invisible' (Fraser, 2003: 29). In the case of humans, the only type of entities Fraser considers, recognizing someone means acknowledging him or her as an irreducible and unique individual whose actions cannot be explained by any broader model of action or category, such as race, gender or class. She calls her approach the status model of recognition, for the key is the relative standing of social actors and the achievement of participatory parity. In a sense, participatory parity is also what Actor-Network Theory (ANT) and more generally Science and Technology Studies (STS) have been arguing for over the last 30 years but with regards to non-humans. But there is an important difference. While for ANT the participatory parity of non-humans has been an empirical issue, Fraser's argument is a moral one. Accordingly, recognizing non-humans for their intrinsic capacities to affect collectives could be thought of as a moral operation that occurs even before exploration has been initiated, as a matter of principle, and which is not oriented to represent non-humans, but to affirm their ontological irreducibility, variability and volatility (cf. Clark, in this volume).

Recognition thus is to be thought of as shaping and even enabling inquiry and representation, not just as a middle step between the two. This is also the argument one encounters in Honneth's (2007) more recent work on recognition. He proposes looking at recognition not from the perspective of those who are recognized or misrecognized, but from the perspective of those who recognize. From this perspective, recognition involves an attitude towards an object, by which this object is constituted as something of interest and value. The enterprise of knowledge, Honneth suggests, is thus grounded in recognition and not vice versa. Despite Honneth's idea that recognition is done only by humans, as though this cognitive process would not be distributed and shaped by material inscriptions, technical devices and social arrangements, this line of reasoning permits us to further stress the central role of recognition for any cosmopolitical proposal.

As for the practical implications of this cosmopolitical approach, recognizing tsunamis as contingent non-human forces capable of behaving in surprising ways, as full-blown actors of our common world, should have allowed responsible individuals to ascertain the situation of scientific uncertainty they were in, leading them to act according to the precautionary principle. This, again, would have involved not just taking necessary action to avoid possible harms, but also engaging in an open exploration of the world. None of this occurred. Neither did the CAT, inspite of their doubts regarding the first tsunami alert, intervene in any way to avoid the worst, nor did the SHOA engage an open exploration of the possible tsunami after the alert was cancelled. Instead, the tsunami was

The Sociological Review, 62:S1, pp. 61–87 (2014), DOI: 10.1111/1467-954X.12124

assumed to be a predictable entity which could be modelled and reduced to a set of univocal indicators. In such context, even incomplete pieces of evidence were considered reason enough to conclude that a tsunami was not possible and the evacuation inadequate.

If this analysis points to the right problem, it then also follows that prosecuting individuals for criminal negligence in the fulfilling of technical duties is completely misleading. And not so much because individual responsibility would be distributed along sociotechnical networks of human and non-human actors, as the argument often goes, but most importantly because misrecognition was a result of an exclusively technical assessment of the situation. Failure did not follow from a misuse of technical procedures, but rather from a lack of capacity to reflect about the limits of technical models to predict tsunami hazard and act accordingly. Individual responsibilities were thus not related to negligence regarding technical duties, but to a moral failure of recognition. The ontological irreducibility of non-humans to technical models needs to be assumed and built into such warning systems, if coastal life with tsunamis is to be facilitated in Chile in a sustainable way. This is neither a problem of self-realization (Honneth, 1996) nor a problem of social justice (Fraser, 2003). Recognizing powerful non-human forces, such as tsunamis, is rather an ecological problem, a problem regarding the composition of a secure and sustainable common world.

Acknowledgements

I am particularly grateful to the organizers and participants of the workshop 'How do we manage? Unravelling the situated practice of environmental management' held in May 2012 at the Centre for Interdisciplinary Research of the Bielefeld University and especially to Israel Rodríguez-Giralt and Roger Strand for their encouraging comments. I also would like to thank the two anonymous reviewers who provided detailed comments, critique and suggestions.

References

Akrich, M., (1992), 'The de-scription of technological objects', in W. E. Bijker and J. Law (eds), *Shaping Technology / Building Society: Studies in Sociotechnical Change*, 205–224, Cambridge, MA: MIT Press.
Armada de Chile, (2010), 'Informe de la investigación efectuada al SHOA', Fiscal de Investigación Técnica, 25 March, available at: www.armada.cl/informe-tecnico-armada–shoa/prontus_armada/2010-03-25/094239.html (accessed 18 August 2013).
Bloor, D., (1991), *Knowledge and Social Imagery*, Chicago: University of Chicago Press.
Callon, M., Lascoumes, P. and Barthe, Y., (2009), *Acting in an Uncertain World: An Essay on Technical Democracy*, Cambridge, MA: MIT Press.
Diana, R., Reder, L., Arndt, J. and Park, H., (2006), 'Models of recognition: a review of arguments in favor of a dual-process account', *Psychonomic Bulletin and Review*, 13: 1–21.

Downer, J., (2011), ' "737-Cabriolet": the limits of knowledge and the sociology of inevitable failure', *American Journal of Sociology*, 117: 725–762.

Fraser, N., (2003), 'Social justice in the age of identity politics: redistribution, recognition, and participation', in N. Fraser and A. Honneth (eds), *Redistribution or Recognition? A Political-Philosophical Exchange*, 7–109, London: Verso.

Fraser, N. and Honneth, A., (2003), *Redistribution or Recognition? A Political-Philosophical Exchange*, London: Verso.

Harremoës, P., Gee, D., MacGarvin, M., Stirling, A., Keys, J., Wynne, B. and Guedes Vaz, S., (2001), 'Late lessons from early warnings: the precautionary principle 1896–2000', Environmental issue report No. 22, European Environmental Agency.

Honneth, A., (1996), *The struggle for recognition: the moral grammar of social conflicts*, Cambridge: MIT Press.

Honneth, A., (2007), *Reification: A Recognition-Theoretical View*, Oxford: Oxford University Press.

Knight, F. H., (1921), *Risk, Uncertainty, and Profit*, Boston, MA: Hart, Schaffner and Marx; Houghton Mifflin.

Knorr-Cetina, K., (1981), *The Manufacture of Knowledge: An Essay on the Constructivist and Contextual Nature of Science*, Oxford: Pergamon Press.

Latour, B., (1987), *Science in Action*, Milton Keynes: Open University Press.

Latour, B., (1988), *The Pasteurization of France*, Cambridge, MA: Harvard University Press.

Latour, B., (1993), *We Have Never Been Modern*, Cambridge, MA: Harvard University Press.

Latour, B., (2004a), *Politics of Nature: How to Bring the Sciences into Democracy*, Cambridge, MA: Harvard University.

Latour, B., (2004b), 'Whose cosmos, which cosmopolitics? Comments on the peace terms of Ulrich Beck', *Common Knowledge*, 10: 450.

Latour, B., (2005a), 'From realpolitik to dingpolitik or how to make things public', in B. Latour and P. Weibel (eds), *Making Things Public: Atmospheres of Democracy*, 14–43, Karlsruhe: ZKM; Cambridge, MA: MIT Press.

Latour, B., (2005b), *Reassembling the Social: An Introduction to Actor-Network-Theory*, Oxford: Oxford University Press.

Latour, B. and Hermant, E., (1998), *Paris Ville Invisible*, Paris: La Découverte.

Latour, B. and Woolgar, S., (1986), *Laboratory Life: The Construction of Scientific Facts*, Princeton, NJ: Princeton University Press.

Law, J., (2000), *Ladbroke Grove, Or How to Think about Failing Systems*, Centre for Science Studies, Lancaster University.

Law, J., (2004), *After Method: Mess in Social Science Research*, London: Routledge.

Luhmann, N., (1993), *Risk: A Sociological Theory*, New York: de Gruyter.

Mol, A., (1999), 'Ontological politics: a word and some questions', in J. Law and J. Hassard (eds), *Actor Network Theory and After*, 74–89, Malden, MA: Blackwell.

Oficina de la Fiscalía del Departamento de Justicia de Estados Unidos, (2010), *Declaración de Testigo, Vindell Hsu, PhD*, 15 December, Edificio Federal PJKK, Honolulu, Hawaii, available at: http://ciperchile.cl/wp-content/uploads/Declaraci%C3%B3n-Vindell-Hsu.pdf (accessed 28 September 2012).

ONEMI, (2001), *Accemar. Metodologia básica para la elaboración de un plan comunal de prevención y de respuesta ante tsunami*, Departamento de Protección Civil, ONEMI, available at: www.elmostrador.cl/media/2010/03/Plan-de-Onemi-de-Prevencion-y-Respuesta-ante-Tsunami-.pdf (accessed 28 September 2012).

ONEMI, (2010), *Sumario Interno. Declaración. Osvaldo Malfanti*, 15 June, available at: http://ciperchile.cl/wp-content/uploads/Declaracion-Osvaldo-Malfanti1.pdf (accessed 28 September 2012).

Peña, C., (2010), 'Falso tsunami de 2005: El bochorno que anticipó los errores del 27/2', in *CIPER*, Santiago de Chile: Centro de Investigación Periodística.

Perrow, C., (1984), *Normal Accidents: Living with High-risk Technologies*, Princeton, NJ: Princeton University Press.

The Sociological Review, 62:S1, pp. 61–87 (2014), DOI: 10.1111/1467-954X.12124

Pontificia Universidad Católica de Chile, (2010), *Definición de áreas de peligro de tsunami diferenciado para las localidades de Talcahuano, Llico, Tubul, Dichato y Constitución*, Santiago de Chile: Ministerio de Vivienda y Urbanismo, Gobierno de Chile/ Instituto de Geografía, Laboratorio de Investigación de Tsunami, available at: www.minvu.cl/aopensite _20100901145818.aspx (accessed 18 August 2013).

Ramírez, P. and Aliaga, J., (2012), 'Tsunami paso a paso: los escandalosos errores y omisiones del SHOA y la ONEMI', in *CIPER*. Santiago de Chile: Centro de Investigación Periodística.

Smith, W. and Dowell, J., (2000), 'A case study of co-ordinative decision-making in disaster management', *Ergonomics*, 43: 1153–1166.

Stengers, I., (2005), 'A cosmopolitical proposal', in B. Latour and P. Weibel (eds), *Making Things Public: Atmospheres of Democracy*, 994–1003, Cambridge, MA: MIT Press; Karlsruhe: ZKM/ Center for Art and Media in Karlsruhe.

Suchman, L., (1997), 'Centers of coordination: a case and some themes', in L. B. Resnick, R. Säljö, C. Pontecorvo and B. Burge (eds), *Discourse, Tools, and Reasoning: Essays on Situated Cognition*, 41–62, Berlin: Springer Verlag.

Turner, B., (1978), *Man-Made Disasters*, London: Wikeham.

UNESCO, (2005), *The Precautionary Principle*, World Commission on the Ethics of Scientific Knowledge and Technology.

Vaughan, D., (1996), *The Challenger Launch Decision: Risky Technology, Culture, and Deviance at NASA*, Chicago: University of Chicago Press.

Weick, K. E., (1993), 'The collapse of sensemaking in organizations: the Mann Gulch disaster', *Administrative Science Quarterly*, 38: 628–652.

Woods, D., Johannesen, L., Cook, R. and Sarter, N. (1994), 'Behind human error: cognitive systems, computers and hindsight', Defense Technical Information Center Document, available at: www.dtic.mil/dtic/tr/fulltext/u2/a492127.pdf.

Section 2
Experiments: Governance

Producing space, tracing authority: mapping the 2007 San Diego wildfires

Katrina Petersen

Abstract: This article explores the materiality of disaster politics through the practice of mapping during the 2007 wildfires in Southern California. It examines the process of production of two different maps, the maps produced by San Diego County and a popular Google My Map created by local media and academic institutions, in order to explore how an unfolding disaster comes to be understood. This article argues that the interplay between different technological and human entities to produce each map in turn produced different spaces of disaster in ways that challenged priorities of disaster preparedness and response. Specifically, the different mapping practices in 2007 produced different relationships to temporality, boundaries and responsibility, making different aspects of the disaster visible while constructing different threats and definitions of danger. They juxtaposed representational and relational knowledge as well as the value of prevention and demonstration. This article draws on data collected through textual analysis of government and scientific documents as well as interviews and observations of key actors, their mapping practices, and socio-technological networks.

Keywords: disasters, authoritative knowledge, materiality, maps, Southern California, geographical imaging technologies, boundaries, temporalities, practice

Introduction

In October 2007, Southern California was ablaze with wildfires. San Diego County was particularly hard hit when seven fires ignited within three days, burning 13 per cent of the county. There was an estimated $2 billion in damage, 2,500 buildings destroyed, 6,200 firefighters deployed, and evacuation orders for 515,000 residents (County of San Diego, 2007; California Department of Forestry and Fire Protection [CALFIRE], 2008; The San Diego Foundation, 2008).[1] The spatial expanse, rapid timing, inconsistent movement, and diversity of human and natural terrains affected by the flames made it difficult for any single institution or perspective to portray the situation. During the turmoil, maps became tools to facilitate comprehension of the burning space. Though firefighters had been using maps in the field for decades, this was among the first

The Sociological Review, 62:S1, pp. 91–113 (2014), DOI: 10.1111/1467-954X.12125
© 2014 The Author. Editorial organisation © 2014 The Editorial Board of the Sociological Review. Published by John Wiley & Sons Ltd, 9600 Garsington Road, Oxford OX4 2DQ, UK and 350 Main Street, Malden, MA 02148, USA

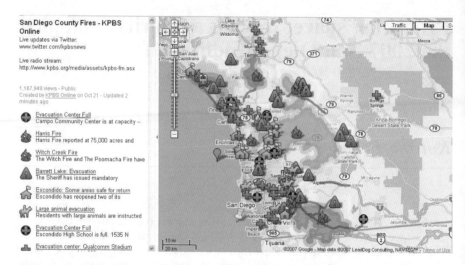

Figure 1: *The ad-hoc group's Google My Map. The screenshot was taken on day 4 of the wildfires.*
Source: KPBS.

times maps were used to aid inter-agency and public communication during a wildfire response. Yet over the course of the wildfires, there was a profound disconnect between what could be known and what could be represented at any given moment creating a space of uncertainty. The scale of these unknowns helped transform the flames into a disaster.

In order to explore the materiality of disaster politics, this article considers two attempts to make sense of the 2007 wildfires through mapping. Specifically, I examine the production of maps created by San Diego County's Emergency Operations Center (EOC) and a Google My Map (Figure 1) created by an ad-hoc group started by a public media outlet, KPBS, and San Diego State University (SDSU). I argue that the socio-technical practices involved in making these maps produced two different spaces of disaster. The different ways of encountering the burning space had consequences for how priorities in planning and response were determined, including questioning what qualifies as valued information, challenging the authority of jurisdictional boundaries and formal procedures, and establishing different time scales for action. Thus, this article asks: how did the different practices of mapping these wildfires produce different spaces of disaster? What was at stake epistemically and politically in the various mapping strategies employed?

Consider, for instance, how the fire perimeter for one of the fires, dubbed the Harris Fire, was drawn as it burnt through a less populated area to cross the San Diego County border into Mexico. The county maps (Figure 2) showed the fire perimeter ending with a straight line along the border, ending the space of the disaster at the edge of the county's responsibility to protect, excluding a section of the people affected by the flames and smoke. The ad-hoc map (Figure 1)

The Sociological Review, 62:S1, pp. 91–113 (2014), DOI: 10.1111/1467-954X.12125
© 2014 The Author. Editorial organisation © 2014 The Editorial Board of the Sociological Review

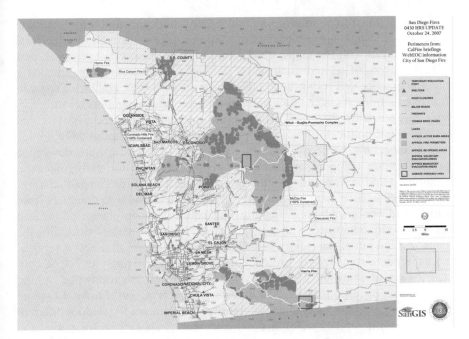

Figure 2: *One of San Diego County's maps. This PDF was released on day 3 of the wildfires.*
Source: San Diego Office of Emergency Services/SANGIS.

traced the perimeter into Mexico presenting a fire disaster that maintained continuity in where the fire went and who it affected rather than whose land it was on or whose responsibility was to fight it. By contrast, the county limited the perimeter on its maps because to represent more required the exchange of data over an international border, jumping multiple levels of jurisdiction and transforming the wildfires into a federal issue, changing the entire practice of response. Meanwhile, the ad-hoc group declared the straight line at the bottom of the county map artificial. In order to draw a fire perimeter that went over the border, the group worked with academic institutions that had access to the same satellite data as the county but were not bound by political limits. For them, it was a technological challenge grounded in social networking. These two ways of mapping the fire at the border place in juxtaposition the hierarchy of action (who is responsible) with the lived experience of the fires (who is affected). One suggests a priority of government response and protection of the region, whereas the other a priority of public understanding enabling residents to take their own actions.

By looking at map making as a form of situated knowledge production grounded in material practices rather than just looking at maps as artefacts or analytical tools, I look to how these practices produce specific ways of understanding disaster and politics of action. Because the volatile nature of disaster necessitated much to be impromptu and largely undocumented, I approximate these tacit and interactive elements of map production through interviews of actors involved with the maps, observation of their present day practices, and textual analysis of related documents.[2] To begin, I discuss how mapping is a material practice that stabilizes specific conceptions of space, and how a space in flux, like that of a disaster, challenges this practice. I focus on how technologies were engaged with, data was gathered, information deemed necessary, social networks and political infrastructures relied upon, and the maps were used. I then analyse how, as necessitated by the wildfires, the two groups developed unique wildfire mapping practices, including techniques for gathering data, negotiating and representing boundaries, and accounting for constant change. Interviewees include geographers from SDSU, editors and web designers from KPBS, field workers who provided fire data, county cartographers, and the lead county information officer who managed the flow of information – including the maps – in and out of the county's EOC. Textual analysis of after action reports, annual reports, standards of protocol, and environmental analyses helped construct ways of knowing wildfires in 2007, social and environmental values, expectations of responsibility, and existing plans for action. Lastly, I explore how the two practices assembled different spatial elements to produce different values, priorities and expectations and discuss the implications for policy and response.

Producing maps, producing spaces

Disasters bring into question previously accepted analytical categories or systems of classification and make it hard to know what to include on a map, let alone how to map a space in crisis. This messiness makes visible how the material pushes back on the social and political, problematizing attempts to make universal claims from individual patterns. Focusing on these material practices makes it possible to examine representations, like maps, that typically naturalize underlying cultural and historical relationships as if single, stable, shared and a priori (Harley, 1989; Monmonier, 1997).

These material practices are integral to the production of knowledge (Lynch, 1991; Alač, 2008) and social organization (Suchman, 2007). While representational choices grounded in social interests and personal beliefs inform what gets included on a map and influence causal explanations (Monmonier, 1997; Koch, 2011), how a map produces the represented space is not determined by a map's technology, the physical world, nor the map-maker alone. Rather, the technological and their users co-produce each other, materially and in practice (Pinch and Bijker, 1984; Woolgar, 1991). As Latour (1999: 30) writes, 'knowing the world and the knowing world are always performed in concert with each other'. Moreover, these practices are multiple, grounded in collective histories and future imaginaries, and are mutually constructed along with the artifacts and objects of those practices (Suchman, 2000).

As Sarah Whatmore (2002) argues, the question 'who has a say' ignores vital elements of the spatial practice, namely: how that say comes to be and how it gets turned into something that can be represented. The form and intensity a disaster will take and how it will be visually represented are shaped in some measure by how and where we build houses, who lives in those neighbourhoods, communication infrastructures, as well as the underlying geology (Davis, 1998; Wood and Fels, 2009). The distribution of responsibility, what is deemed proper aid and recovery, and whose voice will be given the authority to speak are influenced by assumptions of what is at stake, preferences for types of data, mapping software used, the direction of a given satellite, and the physical landscape (Fortun, 2001; Klinenberg, 2002; Barrios, 2011). Introducing new representational forms and practices, especially when normal patterns of action are under duress, have the potential to destabilize existing relationships and shift power relations.

Artefacts and systems of engagement are inseparable; one cannot isolate an object from the practices that produce it. This article joins others in this volume that consider how our engagements with the material world – be it the burning flames or the satellite capabilities – push back on political and cultural forces to help shape how we ascribe meaning to a disaster. Like Tironi (this volume), I consider how the material objects of a disaster are multiple and emerge during the disaster, not prior to it. This is the case even for technologies and material structures that exist prior to a major event, like the shelters described by Deville *et al.* (this volume). Similar to Easthope and Mort (this volume), I explore these relationships by looking at the situated nature of knowledge production. In this chapter I examine how the practices of mapping relate to the production of knowledge and authority to help explain how wildfires become disasters with specific shapes for which society needs to plan and respond.

Drawing the San Diego County's fire maps

San Diego County produced maps of the fires every six to twelve hours as part of their common operating picture for internal decision-making and for use by first responders in the field.[3] The maps were drawn in ArcGIS, a geographic information system (GIS) mapping software that requires specialized training and encourages data integration. Every time the county updated their data they produced a distinct map often including new stylistic features because of changing representational needs. However, the maps were consistently drawn to be comparable to each other and to regularly maintained maps, such as regional burn histories, population densities and wind patterns.[4] The maps were released to the media after they were transformed into pdfs and only after the necessary decisions were made using them, sometimes 24 hours after they were produced (County of San Diego Office of Emergency Services, 2007; County of San Diego Geographic Information Systems [SANGIS], 2008). While not initially released to the public, versions of the pdf maps were placed online for public access partway through the week of the flames. As these maps were made, they constructed a disaster that was unfolding at the edges of jurisdictional boundaries, along the lines of hierarchical structures, and tied to prior ways of engaging with the space of San Diego.

The county mapmakers harnessed a variety of data-gathering techniques and technologies to accomplish their task. During the first day of the fires, their maps consisted of fire perimeters overlaying basic infrastructure – the minimal needed to help first responders identify threats – primarily drawing on data gathered by teams fighting the fires. Though detailed, this data was limited to the regions visited by the firefighters and was only received by the mapmakers every twelve hours.[5] To help extrapolate between points, the mapmakers listened to fire radio for landmarks to pinpoint and drove around the burn area to get information firsthand.

As the fires progressed, the maps accounted for an increasing number of features to help not just contain the flames, but coordinate the larger response and manage the displaced public. In some cases, this involved overlaying already existing maps, such as jurisdictional boundaries for national forest service areas and Indian reservations. Other elements came verbally from the EOC, like locations for local assistance and road closures, and were added as the job of the responders changed from fighting the fires to managing a continually displaced public.[6] The mapmakers also refined the fire perimeters to better reflect the nuances of the situation. To do so, they incorporated eyewitness reports and GPS data about offensive lines created to limit where the fire went as well as burn area flyovers. But these sources were inconsistent and routes were limited by wind, smoke and debris. After about two days, the mapmakers incorporated data derived from satellites and thermal photography. This data, though less detailed and always delayed compared to the movement of the fires, was consistent and offered expansive snapshots of the situation.

Aligning actions by mapping space

Reconciling all these data forms was not an easy task. The sources varied in resolutions, scale, subjectivity, and spread – features that had to be resolved in order to create a continuous polygon representing a fire perimeter, let alone a whole map of a disaster. Moreover, some of the data contradicted each other, forcing the mapmakers to choose between sources.

> *Field Mapmaker*: I knew where the origin was. I also know that the purple part of this map is wrong. Here's another thing: never believe these [points to fire perimeter]. I'm telling you not to believe mine. I just did a project in a GIS class looking at the origins of fires. So I got all the data, I started looking at it. Well that fire didn't start there [points to origin on map]. That fire didn't start there [points to another]. But I mean some of them are like, okay, there the fire started because the helicopter hit a power line. Well, you can argue all you want but it's got to be on the power line somewhere. So at any rate, this fire never moved ten feet in the easterly direction from when it started. The official fire propagation map he was pointing to depicted the fire moving

The Sociological Review, 62:S1, pp. 91–113 (2014), DOI: 10.1111/1467-954X.12125

east, but he knew better. To resolve the dilemmas, the mappers often depended on what they saw with their own eyes or previous experience to inform their interpretations.

Some information arrived in ways difficult to map as a result of translations required for it to be shared. For instance, responders in the field relied on visual references, but they had to deliver that information over the phone, verbally. Confusion was a common result.

> *Head of San Diego County's Joint Information Center (JIC)*: When the incident command post would call for an evacuation, sometimes they would say, we need to evacuate north of Del Dios Highway and south of this and east of this. And, the mapmakers would look at the map and Del Dios Highway would look like a snake. It'd go south and north and west and east and it just. . .What do you mean north of this highway? Because it's all over the map.

The mapmakers struggled to turn the words into shapes. The directional data designed to orient the mapmaker had no shared meaning without some point of reference off the map. The mapmakers often had to delay plotting the data until they confirmed specific spatial interpretations and visual relationships.

Not only were the data potentially contradictory and difficult to translate spatially, they often arrived in irreconcilable forms. Despite the pervasiveness of ArcGIS, five other real-time mapping platforms that were previously established as part of spatial data practices were still used by various factions in the response (Holt, 2008). For example:

> *Head of JIC*: The one thing now that is a limitation is that there is, well, currently in San Diego anyway, there's no way to get the map that I drew in, say, reverse 911 to show up as a layer in GIS. Whether that's through some kind of service or down-loaded as a GIS layer or feature class or whatever, there's no way to get that one database to talk to the other database.

Compiling data from these platforms was difficult. Mapmakers either redrew the data from one map onto another or printed out the maps to compare side-by-side. Moreover, they had to decide if redrawing the data was more valuable than the time the task took.

County mapmakers also added features to facilitate map use and communication. One of these was the gridlines from the Thomas Brothers brand of paper maps. Adding this design feature that represented something separate from how the disaster was unfolding on the ground increased the value of the maps for the first responders and field observers because they used this brand of map to determine regions of responsibility.[7] Other newly recorded features included hot spots and fire movement within the perimeters. These were added because everything within the exterior boundaries of a fire did not burn, so displaying the fires as full polygons could be misleading to those who did not understand fire burning patterns. This increased the usefulness of the maps to help determine which jurisdiction was facing the majority threat and should be put in charge of the unified command.[8]

Over time, features were also removed from the maps. This was especially the case when the maps were released to the public.

> County GIS Specialist: And so the director had a brief discussion with the policy group and they said yeah sure, release it, I mean this isn't secret information . . . we wouldn't be putting out where the hazardous materials are, we wouldn't be putting out where critical infrastructure was. We were just putting out: okay here's the area that's evacuated, here's where the fire is that we know about, here's your shelter locations. Here is, you know, the stuff the public needs to know.

The county predetermined what qualified as essential public information. This helped them avoid revealing information that would place the county in a position of liability, for example, making it harder for the public to question the county's priorities in response. This also helped control public behaviour, discouraging personal interpretations that might contradict evacuation orders.

Transposing data onto the map was more than a technological act. It required the mapmakers to negotiate the relative values of accuracy, details and timeliness. They could not have all three and maintain the connections and social organization they desired. They continually modified and included more features on their fire maps to make them valuable across socio-political lines prominent in non-disaster times, increasing the maps' authority as firefighting tools. They removed features to maintain a specific social order. Putting a variety of actors on the same page was more important than establishing consistency in data representation. The county wildfire maps became a tool for alignment of actions *in* the space of the wildfires rather than accurate description *of* the burning space.

Drawing lines to manage boundaries

While drawing their maps, the county mapmakers struggled to know what to include or what style of mapping to use. Part of this was due to changes in how people lived on the land that necessitated new and different forms of protection. Over the decades prior to the 2007 fires, San Diego residents increasingly pushed the boundaries of urban life into open spaces, interspersing suburban styles of living with wildland methods for maintaining land. Urban fires were fought based in city planning with maps that included structures, fuels, and building patterns (California and United States, 2008). Wildland firefighters drew their fighting styles from forestry practices, using maps that considered wood fuel patterns, proximity to urban spaces, drop points for aid, and previous burns (California and United States, 2008). The 2007 wildfires crossed between these two practices, requiring the mapmakers to make unprecedented decisions to accommodate the new kind of disaster and response.

As the county mapped the fire's movement over land, jurisdictional boundaries pushed back. San Diego had no centralized fire department; each city had its own, eighteen in total. In addition, San Diego County is divided by state forests and bureaus of land management regions (state responsibility), national parks

The Sociological Review, 62:S1, pp. 91–113 (2014), DOI: 10.1111/1467-954X.12125
© 2014 The Author. Editorial organisation © 2014 The Editorial Board of the Sociological Review

(federal responsibility), and Indian reservations (sovereign responsibility). It is bordered to the north by military bases and to the south by Mexico. Where each fire fell in relation to these lines changed who fought it and managed the information about it, a determination that was difficult, variable, and often entailed careful negotiations (California and United States, 2008).

This complexity was exemplified when two fires, the larger Witch fire and smaller Poomacha fire, merged over wildland and urban spaces:

Fire Mapmaker: It's burning in the forest it will be a forest service fire. It's burning down in private lands which is the state responsibility. Poomacha wound up being a fed team. The Witch Fire was 50/50 . . . started out as a fed team and then it became a state team and then they split in half with another fed team.

Q: How'd that work?

Fire mapper: Terrible, but . . .

Q: But how'd it go from federal back down to state?

Fire mapper: Well, it's not down.

Q: Oh?

Fire mapper: They're equal or at least the state thinks they're equal. But it depends on who owns the land. So the Witch Fire started and it was mostly burning Forest Service when it started, and then when it started burning mostly private lands it got into Rancho Santa Fe and down into Escondido and all that, then it became a state. . .the whole east end of it was a fed team, the west end of it was a state team.

In the end, the merged fire included three different authorities, with six teams total: state (California Department of Forestry and Fire Protection), federal (United States Forest Service), and regional (Heartland Fire Zone).[9] Also involved were the California Highway Patrol, San Diego County Sheriff, San Diego Red Cross, Animal Control, San Diego Police Department, Escondido Police Department, San Diego Gas and Electric, Bureau of Indian Affairs, Bureau of Land Management, Department of Corrections and Rehabilitation, and local fire agencies (CALFIRE, 2007). The work of negotiating responsibility placed different levels of responsibility as equals and juxtaposed different styles of fighting, each with their own priorities and interests to protect.

The authorities, though, often worked in isolation. Red Cross workers, often put in the middle as they supported the needs of the groups involved, described such experiences like this:

Red Cross Worker 1: In many cases – I've seen quite a few recently – they say they are a unified command but PD [police department], Fire, and Sheriff don't actually talk to each other.

Red Cross Worker 2: Incident commander's view of the disaster is like this [makes blinders around his eyes with this hands]. They might not even know what is going on around them.

The various authorities either had no time or interest in coordinating outside their immediate responsibility. To overcome these formal limitations and barriers, the mapmakers appealed to their socio-technological networks. As one of the county GIS specialists described:

The Sociological Review, 62:S1, pp. 91–113 (2014), DOI: 10.1111/1467-954X.12125
© 2014 The Author. Editorial organisation © 2014 The Editorial Board of the Sociological Review

Really what happens is I call to get imagery. . .I know somebody at USGS for the State of California. I know that person. I have their email address. I have their cell phone number. I call them up. I say, hey here's our situation, what imagery do you have available? Is there anything coming out? And that started a whole email chain of all the fires in California at that time and we were getting, what, 20, 30 messages a day.

Who was in the mapmakers' cell phones and who they trusted for information was just as important as the protocols and standards for mapping. This informal network was frequently used to fill in the gaps in data that were created by the formal boundaries. This was especially the case when it came to mapping around the border with Mexico, which was a delicate barrier to manage for the county.

Head of JIC: We can't even do anything. That's not to say we don't. Because we have relationships. So we, over the years, have shared things, shared equipment, taught classes. For example environmental health, the Hazmat Team, will go and train the firefighters in Mexico and we can communicate. We have duty officers that can communicate kind of off the record, I guess you'd say. But as far as coordinating at an EOC level, or higher government level, it's not allowed until you get to the federal government.

Many informal relationships exist between the border communities, but remain social or technological, neither officially documented nor openly displayed to the public.[10] This informal networking counterbalanced the official classifications and procedures when producing representations of the unfolding disaster.

Landscapes, even natural environments, are culturally constructed ways of engaging with the world, grounded in histories of labour practices, imagined travels, and urban experiences (Cronon, 1996; Weaver, 1996; Wood and Fels, 2009). Consequently, the power to represent and the power to organize are not to be found in the people alone, but in the hybrid formations that tie together society, technology, and nature (Spirn, 1996; Gandy, 2002). As the mapmakers tried to delimit the disaster in terms of what was represented on the map and who was responsible for taking action, the hybrid nature of the space pushed back.

For the county, mapping the disaster meant creating and maintaining relationships outside of the lines on a map, while simultaneously focusing on drawing those lines accurately. The intricate relationship between the formal and informal required to produce these maps reveals a multiplicity of spaces that push past categories that structured daily life in San Diego. The boundaries to be drawn could not be constrained within a single scale of action. Plotting lines on the maps initiated interactions between different scales of power and response, creating a friction in proper response between local action, cultures of practice, and international relations (Tsing, 2005). But to focus on already existing categories of difference – such as US vs Mexico, city vs state, or public vs private – reifies preconceived notions of a space (Rose, 1993; McDowell, 1999). Instead of looking at economics, politics and labour relations, these mapmakers had to look to the in-betweens and alternative imaginations of the space in order to map the disaster (Thrift and Amin, 2002; Whatmore, 2002).

Representing time to share in time

With ArcGIS integrated as a common platform throughout the county's response, compatible maps emerged from the field as they were made instead of individualized hand-drawn maps that remained at their sites of origin (SANGIS, 2008).[11] The ability to compare information between maps offered responders an unprecedented level of hazard analysis and fire prediction (County of San Diego, 2007). For the disparate and physically scattered groups of actors involved, corresponding maps enabled a shared vision of disaster and the possibility for a shared culture of engagement that previously was not possible through wildfire maps (Goodwin, 1995).

But there was a tradeoff. Mapping in GIS, though more networked, required extra time for production. As one of the fire mappers noted when asked if any specific requests were made of him as he mapped:

> Hurry up. And you know I probably would have had it done faster if I'd have just drawn it on a topo map and printed it. But I wouldn't be able to send it to anyone.

It is easier to draw by hand, but drawings on scraps of paper can neither be shared nor easily made into overlays for other information. The delay did not stop there. The pdfs created for disseminating the maps were so large that the Internet traffic to download the files crashed the county's servers, adding to the time between what was being mapped and what was on the map (County of San Diego, 2007). GIS brought responders closer together in action, but simultaneously created temporal distance between representation and experience.

The county amplified this gap in time by strategically holding back information. For example, they withheld news about a subsiding fire so information about a new evacuation zone would not be overshadowed. Their rationale was one of public safety: they needed the roads clear from people returning home so evacuees could leave. As the county mapmakers maintained the maps in the past, they incorporated into the representations how they wanted the general public to act at present.

When drawing lines on maps, past data, present descriptive perimeters, and future offensive perimeters were treated as equal. The data gatherers and fire fighters understood this temporally calculated nature of wildfire mapping.

> *Field Mapper*: Everybody knows that.
> *Q*: Everybody knows it?
> *Field Mapper*: What it's really telling you is that you're sitting back here, and you think it's here [points to a spot on the map] and someone walks in with a map that shows it here [points to a different spot], and then it's just useful for predicting where it's going to go.

The field mapper then described the maps use as this:

> First off, it's a planning tool. . .By the time this briefing is held this map is wrong. And in fact it's very wrong probably. And a lot of times they'll go in there and stick the map on the wall and somebody will bring their pen and go, now it's here, now it's here, now it's here. So it's dynamic.

The maps were intended for prediction, not an accurate representation of the disaster; they were temporally relational not merely representational. They included elements of where the fires could be and where they had been. To arrive at the present or an impression of the future, the maps had to be analytically connected to other previously mapped data.[12]

These maps were far from self-explanatory to someone unfamiliar with reading maps relationally. Yet, according to the county, the media and public treated the maps as literal.

> *County GIS Specialist*: They would take these and go, oh, okay we're on page whatever and they'd open the Thomas Brothers page, and go it looks like half of this page is burnt. If you're in this half . . . So our PIOs [public information officers] had to call very quickly and say no, no, that's not what a fire perimeter is. It doesn't mean every single house inside this gigantic polygon that is on a countywide map is burned.

> *Head of JIC*: The media would zoom in, okay let's look at that street. If you're on that side of the street, you're okay. But if you're on this side of the street, you're not. We had to call them up and say don't do that. Because it is just kind of a wide line of where we think the fire perimeter is. So there's no zooming. Don't zoom in and don't give people a false sense of security.

These maps were treated the same as a Google map, not how the county intended. In the end, when the maps were released to the public, the GIS specialists had to, in their words, include 'a detailed description of what it's saying'.

How these maps were drawn and used demonstrates that time is more than something stamped in the key. For the county, including past and future, not just what was happening at present, was necessary to depict disaster over space. Knowledge of the disaster emerged through associations and expectations in time. Fortun (2001) argues that the time limits given to a disaster shape its form just as much as tracking its movement over space. Their mapping practice made it possible to plan future action and predict the extent of the disaster, whereas treating a map as stand-alone would have turned it into a description of the present to be challenged for accuracy and detail.

Drawing the ad-hoc fire My Map

One local media news station, KPBS, started a map of its own. It was a single, continually updated, map drawn in Google My Maps. My Maps, new in 2007, was designed for non-cartographers to create simple overlays on top of the already familiar Google map background.[13] And, it was continuously accessible even while being modified.[14] Users were not limited to orienting themselves to the county as a whole; they could centre on or zoom in to any point, like their residence, to personalize their perspective and continually track their position as the fires moved around them. Like the county maps, this map utilized a wide range of sources. But rather than struggle for compatibility, their network of data coalesced around its variety. KPBS worked with geographers at SDSU to mimic the lines from the county maps, but also to solicit other sources to bring those traced lines more up-to-date. Over the week of the fires, this map became so popular it received over five million hits.[15] Assembling this map produced a disaster unfolding through local experiences, built on expectations for those affected to participate in the response, and focused on the immediacy of the moment. While the county maps provided a starting point for this ad-hoc mapping project making it not a true alternative mapping practice, the production of this ad-hoc map pushed back on the county mapping practice and on its definition of the disaster.

These mapmakers were not bound to the hierarchical rules of the county, so they could take advantage of SDSU's relationships with other academic institutions and federal institutions, like NASA, to access their infrastructures of research satellites, remote sensors and unmanned airplanes. They also relied on people who were well connected to events on the ground, such as Red Cross volunteers or the affected public, to provide details about evacuations, burnt houses, road closures and other information pointing to the lived experience of the fires. While the county mapmakers relied on their own experiences to interpret their data, the makers of this ad-hoc fire map benefited from interpretation from all sources. All of these sources were used to try to bring the always behind-in-time fire perimeters up-to-date to offer a map of the present situation. Overall, the ad-hoc group of mapmakers exercised their socio-technological networks in order to fill in the temporal gaps in a manner similar to how the county worked with its networks to fill in the spatial gap.

Mapping action to align space

These maps did not try to bring all the users into a single sighted action plan. Rather, it took its shape based on its users, technologies and sources for data. One of the unique sources for data was the general public. Because the map was available to the public and connected to a public radio station where the public could call in and offer experiences and observations, this relationship provided a set of single data points that refined, and often corrected, more official sources.

> *GIS student*: There was another situation in which we overestimated the fire over a freeway. We started receiving calls from listeners saying the fire had not jumped over the freeway. So at that point we modified the map because that was the most recent information we had from the ground. Our overestimation was also possibly because of the different resolution that we were working with.

> *Web developer*: If some guy's calling from his car and we say this is what we heard, we don't know if it's true. I wasn't waiting for some government official to confirm things. We were just working with what was flowing in.

> *Managing Online Editor*: The shelters, we would update it when we would hear that something was full. The official list wouldn't be updated yet, but someone would call up on the radio and say we're full. . .and it would get updated on the map. We got a

The Sociological Review, 62:S1, pp. 91–113 (2014), DOI: 10.1111/1467-954X.12125
© 2014 The Author. Editorial organisation © 2014 The Editorial Board of the Sociological Review

couple of calls from people saying your map says the shelter in Imperial Valley is taking such and such but we can't take that, and we would have to go and correct it.

The data from the public amended other sources in terms of time, location and condition. In some cases the information was rumours supplied as fact. Despite the risk of repeating incorrect information – something the county could not ignore for the sake of liability – this participation provided overall up-to-date information for the ad-hoc fire map. Rather than train the public to engage with the map in a specific way, these mapmakers incorporated the public into the production of the map bringing their expectations into the representation.

But however flexible, Google My Maps was not the most capable program. The mapmakers struggled with its predefined features intended to simplify cartographic practice. They found it limited how much and what could be put onto the map, dampening the mapmakers' ability to visually express detailed location and status.

> *KPBS web producer*: It was like there's a fire and there's a fire icon so there's a fire icon on the map. But the icon doesn't really tell you where it is; it's just generally in that area.

A dot in the middle of an entire burn area does not provide much information about an evolving fire scene. Moreover, the limited number of icons forced the mapmakers to get creative and write explanation into the map, something abnormal for a traditional map.[16] The limited number of items allowed at any single time caused the map to crash multiple times when the mapmakers tried adding one too many things at a time.

In 2007, Google My Maps had practically no compatible data forms, making it difficult to relate to other representations. Whereas the county relied on the technology to combine data layers, those working in My Maps had to do that layering by hand, repeating much of the work already done. For example:

> *GIS mapmaker helping KPBS*: We started taking the MODIS imagery, converting it to the GIS format, detecting the perimeter, overlaying it on top of Google, and tracing the perimeter so to update the Google My Maps.

Translating the data from one system to another relied upon individual skills. Any consistency in the process came from who was doing it rather than how it was done or what program was used. The ad-hoc group of mapmakers creatively aligned the data through their practice of mapping, rather than aligning their practice to a specific data standard.

This does not mean this map was any less authoritative; it could even be considered more so than one produced by inflexible rules. Authority is contingent upon the variables within the network of knowledge, not some pre-imposed structure (Wynne, 1992). For example, in some contexts (such as the science laboratory) standardization creates credibility, yet in other contexts (like disaster response) too much standardization can deny important local differences and culture. The success of this ad-hoc fire map, despite all of its limitations and contradictions, demonstrated the value of locally contingent ways of knowing

The Sociological Review, 62:S1, pp. 91–113 (2014), DOI: 10.1111/1467-954X.12125

and doing rather than de-contextualized rules of behaviour (Jordan and Lynch, 1992; Suchman, 2000, 2007). For this scattered network of interaction, variation in practice was necessary for any representational standards to work from one situation to the next.

Mapping through networks instead of boundaries

Unlike the specific protocols, categories, and organizations that drove the design of the county maps, those working on the ad-hoc map had neither an assumed hierarchy of responsibility nor predetermined set of roles and skills. These different approaches were partly responsible for the different treatments of the border on the maps:

> *Visualization Specialist at SDSU*: [KPBS] had a map to say there is the perimeter. There was actually a person that made the decision that we are going to do Mexico. And then because they did it and then in the county they said, oh, you're right, we need to do that. And that was [Head of San Diego County's EOC JIC] pounding on people's heads and they're going, yeah, but it's not in our jurisdiction, the rules . . . it's not our problem. And him going, but it really could be our problem.

The county struggled to address unique issues of the specific space and situation but the network around the ad-hoc map was versatile enough that it could address new developments and unexpected obstacles by involving different actors and technologies. The malleable structure of the socio-technical network involved with the ad-hoc map was as dynamic as the wildfires themselves. The practice that emerged constructed a hybrid space rather than wrangling a hybrid space into a bounded representation. It also encouraged a different way of engaging with the diverse data sources.

> *Visualization Specialist at SDSU*: But say instead of trying to put everything into the same format, the same standard . . . there's enough utilities that are going around so that if you just do something consistently that's probably the wiser thing.

By mapping consistently rather than through standards for compatibility, a wider range of data opened up to these mapmakers. As a result, the production of the ad-hoc map highlighted and showcased the networking, using the networks as its guidelines instead of a priori regulations. The scale of the institutional action did not matter, only the ability to share data.

Another unique data source these mapmakers had access to involved traversing the air above the fires. SDSU accessed one of NASA's unmanned aerial vehicles (UAV), the Ikhana, that could both see through the smoke with high resolution thermal imaging and provide the images within 20 minutes rather than 12 to 24 hours.[17] Though untested prior to the fires, it proved invaluable to the representation of the disaster.[18] This data source was originally just used by SDSU and the mapping data provided to the ad-hoc network. Only after seeing the success of this data source for SDSU were the county mapmakers convinced that this new technology was worth modifying procedure for and incorporating.

The Sociological Review, 62:S1, pp. 91–113 (2014), DOI: 10.1111/1467-954X.12125
© 2014 The Author. Editorial organisation © 2014 The Editorial Board of the Sociological Review

This technology introduced a new boundary to negotiate in order to map the disaster airspace. While not bound by the limits of the landscape, fire perimeters, or transportation infrastructure, the UAV was limited by the rules of the air.

> *Visualization Specialist at SDSU*: So NASA is asking should we fly over Malibu? But with the predator you have a limited amount of where you're going to go, what are you going to do? How high is it, what air space do you have to fly through? How do you get there? Do you fly around LAX? Do you fly off shore? Those were all concerns.

Managing how the plane could travel had implications for which fires were deemed important.[19] He continued:

> They were saying, oh, the Witch Fire is the big one, but the Harris Fire which was right on the border they were going, ohhhh, we can't go close to the border because there is the international boundary that's 10 miles and we don't want to be within 20 miles because we don't want to be anywhere close to getting State Department smacked for doing something that's the US spying on Mexico.

Though the fire along the border had less people and structures immediately in its path than other simultaneous fires, because it was an unknown entity for this data source it became a greater threat. Rather than maintaining the status quo and discussing the disaster in terms of what could burn, this new practice of data gathering changed what issues were discussed, how danger was perceived, and opened the conversation about what criteria should be used to determine the greatest threat.

Rather than map the space of the wildfires by transforming the phenomena into data in a particular way, this group of ad-hoc mapmakers worked with translations in their practice to represent the disaster. Though the mapmakers did not all adopt the same understanding of the wildfires, even their most mundane practices demonstrated how both the space and lived experience of the disaster were hybrids of technology, humans, and land (Michael, 2002). Examining the maps through practice makes it hard to discern which elements were included because of a decision made by a mapmaker, a result of technology, or a circumstance of the physical environment. It becomes problematic to separate human from non-human (Latour, 1987).

Though difficult to plan for, networks like this can help make visible what expert practices or political structures fail to see (Barrios, 2011; Frickel and Vincent, 2011; Weichselgartner and Breviere, 2011). In this case, this network grounded in material practice exposed new boundaries to negotiate and transcended others, in the process changing the fundamental nature of the threat, constituting priorities in response, and generating criteria by which the disaster would be understood and characterized. Producing a wildfire map in this way aligned actions *with* the space of the wildfires instead of actors *in* the space of the map.

Balancing consistency over time with thoroughness over space

The ad-hoc group did not have that same responsibility as the county to manage response or liability, and saw as their goal to provide the public with the most

The Sociological Review, 62:S1, pp. 91–113 (2014), DOI: 10.1111/1467-954X.12125

complete, relevant, and up-to-date picture as possible about the wildfires. The county mapmakers and responders focused on planning and prediction, thus designing the maps to show the disaster over time through interactions with and comparisons between various maps. Their maps presented the immediate present only as a moment in this interactive process rather than on the maps themselves. However, the modifiable nature of Google My Maps meant movement was built into its structure and the ad-hoc group could keep up with the changing space in the map itself. This made it possible for them to focus on simply keeping things as timely as possible.

Limited neither by technology nor liability, with no need to delay information any further, the ad-hoc group of mapmakers focused on representing the status of the elements being mapped.

SDSU Graduate Student: The strength of the KPBS news side was that they were keeping track of the opening and closing of certain areas for evacuation and things such as the capacities and the reports on capacities of evacuation centers, things like that. Not just location update on time related data.

Location and status, though intimately related, are very different questions that require very different engagements with temporality and representation. To provide the most up-to-date overall map, this team sacrificed the ability to make the specific details perfectly accurate. For example:

SDSU Geography student: I would try to always do the most recent one, maybe skipping some of the previous updates that were high resolution. I might do the MODIS that was just released four hours ago that is lower resolution than DigitalGlobe that was one day ago just because that's the best information for the current situation. Later I might go back and reuse the DigitalGlobe to draw a finer perimeter of how the fire was at that time . . . But for us the most recent one was the most important.

Rather than older data of higher resolution, they worked with less detailed data that was more recent.

In addition to omitting pixels, they omitted elements, even if deemed important, in order to continuously offer status information. Sometimes this was because of limitations in the software. For example, My Maps had a limited number of data points that could be active at any given time, forcing the mapmakers to simplify their representation and decide what was absolutely essential. At other times it was because there was no consistent source of information.

Web Developer: If your house wasn't on fire but there was a lot of smoke and you wanted to know the evacuation area . . . they released that in Thomas guide grid numbers, which is a box shape, or they would say Northern Rancho Penasquitos is evacuated. Where's the line from north and south? The fire didn't follow grid lines. That was really hard and we really wanted to be able to notify. I think towards the end we took it off, the last days, because it was basically everything, and it was shifting and hard to keep up with.

Web Developer: Road closures, those came and went, and it was hard to maintain because it was changing so fast. Specific exit and entrance points.

Managing Online Editor: The road closure information, there wasn't a good regular source for that. Caltrans didn't have a map that we could reference. We gave up on the roads after a while.

Web Developer: There were lines that were tracking roads, but they were just using up a bunch of our potential data. It was limited to 200 things, so we ended up tossing them completely.

The mapmakers did not want to display incomplete information that could potentially mislead users who assume a level of completeness, in space and time, to the map. Inconsistently representing information was worse, they decided, than not representing it at all. To produce a glimpse of 'what's happening now' in this disaster, they chose as their epistemic priorities consistency in time over thoroughness in space.

Drawing maps, drafting priorities

The two maps produced different views of the disaster. The county focused on predicting the disaster's path while the ad-hoc map focused on describing the disaster's present. The sense of what will come was a necessary way of knowing disaster for those fighting it, but was difficult to comprehend and accept for those living through it, often requiring an expert to mediate its meaning. Consequently, the county mapping practice centralized meaning which made sharing across the space of the fire possible, creating a common vision for how the maps' users were to engage with the wildfires. Its focus on aligning actors made it possible to have group action with responders all working towards the same priorities and the public acting in a coordinated manner. This mapping practice drew its authority from its ability to connect to normative social structures and systems of classification from non-disaster times. It defined clear roles for and maintained distinctions between the groups as it drew boundary after boundary, layer after layer. Such aligning made disaster planning easier to do in the abstract, but struggled to see other possible perspectives that could prevent future fires from becoming disasters. This practice made the unplanned and individual less visible. Doing so reinforced pre-existing social divides in how responses are organized and missed some of what was unique about the specific disaster space. To deal with these aspects, the county mappers had to use informal and undocumented networks to compensate for the formal limitations. The result is that what went into making the maps and what was decided with the maps did not follow the same rules.

The ad-hoc map looked in-the-moment and focused less on boundaries and predetermined lists of elements, instead represented what emerged from the messy situation, making space for the unexpected and otherwise marginalized aspects of the disaster. It organized its practice by distributing power over

The Sociological Review, 62:S1, pp. 91–113 (2014), DOI: 10.1111/1467-954X.12125

its network, hybridizing data formats, sources, people, land and technology through practice, aligning goals rather than meaning. It accounted for local experience and incorporated into its form user participation rather than training its users to engage with the map in a specific, top-down, manner. Drawing its values and priorities from the production process itself, it seemed to take no sides or value no specific social position over another. It made this easier by focusing on the immediacy and continuity of information rather than its completeness or accuracy. However, in trade, this practice erased entire catego-ries of action or experience. This map's authority emerged from its ability to account for the exceptional and individual. In doing so, it makes space for the atypical and assumes individual responsibility but at the cost of common action, shared meaning, or connecting present decisions to past events and future potentials. Doing so both ignores how social structure influences how a disaster unfolds and makes it possible to claim an end to the disaster when the map ends, limiting claims of responsibility and potentially challenging future requests for aid.

The two maps carry with them different assumptions about the public's relation to disaster response. The county, in its top-down build, is very focused on the first responders who are the people on the front lines fighting the fires, taking care of the displaced, or addressing medical emergencies. However, the general public, especially those nearby but not immediately affected, are com-pletely left out of their picture, both in their ability to engage with the maps as intended and in being represented within the map. But the public does not just wait for action, they are proactive and help each other; they do not fall into disorder unless there is a hierarchy imposed, rather they create a new order (Tierney *et al.*, 2006). The flexibility of the ad-hoc fire map, whether intentional or not, was built in a way to accommodate this type of public engagement during the disaster. Such assumptions built into these maps as communication tools can influence organizational and government response, as well as public acceptance of their claimed authority during disaster.

Yet these maps were not pure alternatives to each other. The ad-hoc map was grounded in the county map as a starting layer of information. If that layer had not existed for the first couple of days of the fire, the ad-hoc map would neither have taken its form nor been able to focus on presenting the immediacy of the situation. In turn, the county map modified goals, priorities and even techno-logical practices and sources for data in response to the existence and practices employed in the production of the ad-hoc map. For instance, it would not have been released to the public if the ad-hoc map had not existed. Nor would the mapmakers have modified procedure mid-disaster to incorporate the Ikhana data if there had not been another map that focused on representing the present rather than predicting the future. Their forms emerged through their mutual interactions; neither way of representing disaster existed in isolation from the other.

The making of both sets of maps demonstrates how there is no clear line to draw between nature and society – between flame and disaster (Wood and Fels,

2009). Representing the situation required the interaction of natural phenomena, social structures and technological mediations. While many of the preparedness plans account for human ignorance of nature or human manipulation of nature, they perpetuate false assumptions about how disasters work (Oliver-Smith, 2002; Hilgartner, 2007). Preparedness and response plans need to be modified to include these hybrid relations rather than lay blame along a spectrum between two distinct ends. These plans need to be rethought, regardless of the shape of the response and attributions of responsibility, in terms of the hybridity that pushed back on both sets of maps.

Finally, while many studies have pointed out that different affected groups construct a disaster differently (Hoffman and Oliver-Smith, 2002; Henderson, 2011), this chapter shows that even when the groups overlap or are working together, different constructions can still emerge. While both maps relied on much of the same data, social networks, and cultural understandings of the space, the actual mapping practices constructed very different disasters and potentials for response. In both cases, the practices highlighted the importance of accounting for material influences such as the physical world, the technologies used, and types of data gathered, not just social or cultural, on how a specific understanding of a disaster gains authority to represent the situation.

Acknowledgements

This material is based upon work supported by the National Science Foundation under grant no. 1127760.

Notes

1 These were among the largest wildfires in Southern California history and caused what, at the time, was the largest evacuation in the nation's history.
2 New methods in science and technology studies, as exemplified by Fortun's (2009) ethnography of open systems and Beaulieu's (2010) digital co-presence as an approach to fieldwork, propose ethnographic techniques that bound the field not by physical location or time, but by the networks and interactions that create knowledge. The field is not bound by physical space but by interactions and relationships over space and time. This way of treating the space of an analysis is important as the production of knowledge becomes increasingly grounded in interdisciplinary and collaborative work.
3 A common operating picture (COP) is a shared representation of all that is important in a disaster designed to be used by all actors responding to the disaster to coordinate their actions. Despite its name, different institutions or networks of actors can each have their own COP.
4 For example, knowing the fuel history – where a region had burnt in previous fires – helped fire fighters guess where the 2007 fires would burn. If an area had recently burnt, even if it was in the middle of a larger 2007 fire perimeter, it would likely be left unscorched (Holt, 2008).
5 At the change of firefighting shifts.
6 This became increasingly important as multiple shelters wound up in the line of the flames requiring the already evacuated to either shelter in place with fire around them or to pick up and move.

7 This sentiment of increased value was reiterated by multiple reports (SANGIS, 2008; Holt, 2008). In addition, the news media saw this value and took advantage of these gridlines in their own reporting.

8 Fires ebb and flow, jump around, and change intensity with the sun, wind, and available fuel (Holt, 2008).

9 Teams were coordinated under a unified command created for each fire, physically based at an incident command post, situated along an edge of the burn area and headed by a fire chief or police commander. For each fire there was staff in charge of operations, logistics, plans, and intelligence, and in some cases a mapmaker trained in GIS. Twice a day, with the shift change in response teams, the incident command posts (ICPs) held debriefings that relied on maps based on field data. Those maps were then sent to the county Emergency Operation Center for their response planning (California and United States, 2008).

10 Consequently it often appears to the public as if the border relations are being neglected and the people living near its edges ignored by the responders. This issue became a popular topic after the 2007 fires.

11 There were GIS trailers with wireless capabilities that mapmakers drove to the ICPs to map onsite instead of mapping only through indirect communication channels.

12 Including previous maps of the same fire, structures in the fire's path, historical burns, and weather patterns.

13 This was a feature SDSU needed in order to translate their more technical information into a publically accessible form. While some of the data required geographical expertise, the mapping software did not.

14 Except for a twelve-hour period when the frequency of updates crashed Google's My Map server.

15 Google provided this estimate to KPBS because the official counter was turned off to accommodate the high volume of traffic.

16 The software was designed to have pop up layers appear so that the verbal information could be directly connected to each icon, instead of in a separate statement accompanying the map as a whole. A few days into the fires, they found time to finally develop icons of their own.

17 It could provide data within 20 minutes of gathering it, fully interpreted, and in a format ready to be mapped. No waiting hours for the data, as required by traditional satellite imagery. It also provided much higher resolution data than the satellites (10-metre imagery compared to 250-metre). This new data format, though untested, provided the ability to have close to real-time and detailed data.

18 This UAV was part of a joint research project by SDSU, NASA and the US Forest Service to see how high resolution thermal imaging, a form of imaging that could see through smoke, could be useful during wildfires. While very useful in providing immediate data, it only provided a swath of data along a line of flight rather than regionally as would a satellite.

19 Though the social relationships that surmounted hierarchical boundaries were already in place when the 2007 fires ignited, the political relationships and boundaries still required negotiations.

References

Alač, M., (2008), 'Working with brain scans: digital images and gestural Interaction in fMRI laboratory', *Social Studies of Science*, 38 (4): 483–508.

Barrios, R., (2011), 'Post-Katrina neighborhoods recovery planning in New Orleans', in R. Dowty and A. Irwin (eds), *Dynamics of Disasters*, 97–114, Washington DC: Earthscan.

Beaulieu, A., (2010), 'From co-location to co-presence: shifts in the use of ethnography for the study of knowledge', *Social Studies of Science*, 40 (3): 453–470.

California Department of Forestry and Fire Protection, (2007), *Incident Information: Witch Fire*, available at: http://cdfdata.fire.ca.gov/incidents/incidents_details_info?incident_id=225 (accessed 3 March 2012).

California Department of Forestry and Fire Protection, (2008), *2007 Wildfire Activity Statistics*, State Board of Forestry and Fire Protection. Sacramento, CA: State Printing Office.

California and United States, (2008), *California Fire Siege 2007: An Overview*, Sacramento, CA: California Department of Forestry and Fire Protection.

County of San Diego Geographic Information Systems, (2008), *Emergency Standards of Operation*, San Diego, CA: SANGIS.

County of San Diego, Office of Emergency Services, (2007), *2007 San Diego County Firestorms After Action Report*, San Diego: EG&G Technical Services.

Cronon, W., (1996), 'The trouble with wilderness: or, getting back to the wrong nature', in W. Cronon (ed.), *Uncommon Ground: Rethinking the Human Place in Nature*, 69–90, New York: W. W. Norton & Co.

Davis, M., (1998), *Ecology of Fear: Los Angeles and the Imagination of Disaster*, New York: Vintage Books.

Fortun, K., (2001), *Advocacy after Bhopal: Environmentalism, Disaster, New Global Orders*, Chicago: University of Chicago Press.

Fortun, K., (2009). 'Figuring out ethnography', in J. Faubian and G. Marcus (eds), *Fieldwork Is Not What it Used to Be*, 167–183, Ithaca, NY: Cornell University Press.

Frickel, S. and Vincent, M. B., (2011), 'Katrina's contamination: regulatory knowledge gaps in the making and unmaking of environmental contention', in R. Dowty and A. Irwin (eds), *Dynamics of Disasters*, 11–28, Washington DC: Earthscan.

Gandy, M., (2002), *Concrete and Clay: Reworking Nature in New York City*, Cambridge, MA: MIT Press.

Goodwin, C., (1995), 'Seeing in depth', *Social Studies of Science*, 25: 237–274.

Harley, J. B., (1989), 'Deconstructing the map', *Cartographica*, 26 (2): 1–20.

Henderson, K., (2011), 'Mind maps, memory and relocation after Hurricane Katrina', in R. Dowty and A. Irwin (eds), *Dynamics of Disasters*, 77–97, Washington DC: Earthscan.

Hilgartner, S., (2007), 'Overflow and containment in the aftermath of disaster', *Social Studies of Science*, 37 (1): 153–158.

Hoffman, S. and Oliver-Smith, A., (2002), 'Introduction: why anthropologists should study disasters', in S. Hoffman and A. Oliver-Smith (eds), *Catastrophe and Culture: the Anthropology of Disaster*, 3–22, Santa Fe: School of American Research Press.

Holt, J., (2008), *Southern California Fires 2007: What We Learned, How We Worked*, Initial Impressions Report, Tuscon, AZ: Wildland Fire Lessons Learned Center, available at: http://wildfirelessons.net/documents/2007_SO_Cal_ICT_FINAL_REPORT.pdf (accessed 11 December 2012).

Jordan, K. and Lynch, M., (1992), 'The sociology of a genetic engineering technique: ritual and rationality in the performance of the plasmid prep', in A. Clarke and J. Fujimura (eds), *The Right Tools for the Job: At Work in 20th Century Life Sciences*, 77–144, Princeton, NJ: Princeton University Press.

Klinenberg, E., (2002), *Heat Wave: A Social Autopsy of Disaster in Chicago*, Chicago: University of Chicago Press.

Koch, T., (2011), *Disease Maps: Epidemics on the Ground*, Chicago, IL: University of Chicago Press.

Latour, B., (1987), *Science in Action: How to Follow Scientists and Engineers through Society*, Cambridge, MA: Harvard University Press.

Latour, B., (1999), 'Circulating reference: sampling the soil in the Amazon Forest', in *Pandora's Hope: Essays on the Reality of Science Studies*, 24–79, Cambridge, MA: Harvard University Press.

Lynch, M., (1991), 'Laboratory space and the technological complex: an investigation of topical contextures', *Science in Context*, 4 (1): 81–109.

McDowell, L., (1999), *Gender, Place, Identity: Understanding Feminist Geographies*, Minneapolis: University of Minnesota Press.

Michael, M., (2002), *Reconnecting Culture, Technology and Nature: From Society to Heterogeneity*, London: Routledge.

Monmonier, M., (1997), *Cartographies of Danger*, Chicago: University of Chicago Press.

The Sociological Review, 62:S1, pp. 91–113 (2014), DOI: 10.1111/1467-954X.12125

Oliver-Smith, A., (2002), 'Theorizing disasters', in S. Hoffman and A. Oliver-Smith (eds), *Catastrophe and Culture: the Anthropology of Disaster*, 23–48, Santa Fe: School of American Research Press.

Pinch, T., and Bijker, W., (1984), 'The social construction of facts and artefacts: or how the sociology of science and the sociology of technology might benefit each other', *Social Studies of Science*, 14 (3): 399–441.

Rose, G., (1993), *Feminism and Geography: The Limits of Geographical Knowledge*, Minneapolis, MN: University of Minnesota Press.

San Diego Foundation, The (2008), *October 2007 Fires Community Needs Assessment Update: Executive Summary*, available at: www.sdfoundation.org/Portals/0/Newsroom/PDF/Reports/Executivesummary_AFTFlr.pdf (accessed 13 May 2012).

Spirn, A., (1996), 'Constructing nature: the legacy of Frederick Law Olmstead', in W. Cronon (ed.), *Uncommon Ground: Rethinking the Human Place in Nature*, 91–113, New York: W.W. Norton & Co.

Suchman, L., (2000), 'Embodied practices of engineering work', *Mind, Culture, and Activity*, 7 (1&2): 4–18.

Suchman, L., (2007), *Human-machine Reconfigurations: Plans and Situated Actions*, Cambridge: Cambridge University Press.

Thrift, N. and Amin, A., (2002), *Cities: Reimagining the Urban*, Malden, MA: Blackwell.

Tierney, K., Bevc, C. and Kuligowski, E., (2006), 'Metaphors matter: disaster myths, media frames, and their consequences in Hurricane Katrina', *Shelter from the Storm: Repairing the National Emergency Management System after Hurricane, Annals of the American Academy of Political and Social Science*, Vol. 604, *Katrina*: 57–81.

Tsing, A., (2005), *Friction: An Ethnography of Global Connection*, Princeton, NJ: Princeton University Press.

Weaver, B., (1996), ' "What to do with the mountain people?" The darker side of the successful campaign to establish the Great Smoky Mountains National Park', in J. Cantrill and C. Oravec (eds), *The Symbolic Earth: Discourse and our Creation of the Environment*, 151–175, Lexington, KY: University Press of Kentucky.

Weichselgartner, J. and Breviere, E., (2011), 'The 2002 flood disaster in the Elbe Region, Germany: a lack of context-sensitive knowledge', in R. Dowty and A. Irwin (eds), *Dynamics of Disasters*, 141–158, Washington DC: Earthscan.

Whatmore, S., (2002), *Hybrid Geographies*, Thousand Oaks, CA: Sage Publications.

Wood, D., and Fels, J., (2009), *The Natures of Maps: Cartographic Constructions of the Natural World*, Chicago: University of Chicago Press.

Woolgar, S., (1991), 'Configuring the user: the case of usability trials', in *A Sociology of Monsters: Essays on Power, Technology and Domination*, 58–99, London: Routledge.

Wynne, B., (1992), 'Misunderstood misunderstanding: social identities and public uptake of science', *Public Understanding of Science*, 1 (3): 281–304.

Atmospheres of indagation: disasters and the politics of excessiveness

Manuel Tironi

Abstract: This article examines how specific political arrangements are articulated to govern disasters. I suggest that disasters give rise to political experiments in which uncertainties are sensed, ordered and managed. I argue, however, that when the world is uncanny and indeterminacies are excessive and radically vital, the search for stability is messier than experimental politics might assume. Drawing on the cases of PRE Talca and Talca con Tod@s, two post-disaster participatory experiments that unfolded in Talca, Chile, I call *atmospheres of indagation* the expanded and enhanced political experimentalism unearthed by disasters. Of indagation because the inquiry was meticulous, open and agonically needed. And atmosphere because this indagation unfolded under the form of an overarching, multiform and ambiguous ambience in which everything could be explored, scrutinized and contested – including the experiments themselves. More concretely, I describe how these two experiments, via different participatory technologies, enacted different versions of Talca. But I attempt to show, as well, how PRE Talca and Talca con Tod@s were configured by openly contesting the principles and assumptions of each other. The result was a highly complex topological arrangement in which political publicness was expanded and re-articulated, thus defying conventional understandings on political experiments.

Keywords: political experiments, atmospheres of indagation, public participation, excessive controversies, Talca

Introduction

In the morning of 27 February 2010, an 8.8 Richter scale earthquake battered south-central Chile. It was the sixth largest earthquake in recorded history. Five large cities, 45 mid-size cities and more than 900 rural and coastal villages were devastated (Bresciani, 2010).

Talca, a mid-size city located 255 km south of Santiago, Chile's capital city, was one of the most heavily impacted. The earthquake affected 20 per cent of the city and 64 per cent of all its housing units had to be demolished or needed urgent repair (ELCI, 2010a). For at least three weeks after the earthquake Talca was a city with no formal political power. The first days were critical. Without water, electricity or basic services, episodes of looting abounded. Humanitarian

The Sociological Review, 62:S1, pp. 114–134 (2014), DOI: 10.1111/1467-954X.12126

help could not enter into the city because roads were destroyed, but also because trucks were diverted and ransacked. Neighbours organized defence committees. Stories about residents plundering their own neighbourhood almacenes (grocery shops) began to multiply. Talquinos[1] were in shock. Their world had collapsed and they couldn't recognize what was left of it. The earthquake had propelled all sorts of uncertainties and collective disorganizations. Soon political conflicts arose. By the sixth day after the disaster, hundreds of neighbours marched through the Alameda, Talca's central avenue, demanding faster and better solutions to the government. Political dislocations accrued when two different participatory rebuilding processes were assembled in Talca, called PRE Talca and Talca con Tod@s. The particularity of these engagement exercises was that they did not only mobilize different sets of assumptions, goals and techniques; more importantly, each experiment was openly and synchronously configured in opposition to the other.

How can we make sense of this political situation? In this article I suggest that disasters give rise to political experiments in which attempts are made to order and make sense of uncertainties. But as I will argue, when the world is uncanny and indeterminacies are excessive and radically vital, the search for stability is messier than experimental politics might assume. Drawing on the case of Talca, I call *atmospheres of indagation* the multi-experimental and topological field unearthed by disasters.

Political experiments and disasters

Disasters have gained methodological relevance within sociology because, as a 'punch' to the system, they make visible the material, institutional, cultural and political consensuses configuring normality (Kreps, 1998; Oliver-Smith, 1999, 2002; Oliver-Smith and Hoffman, 2002; Perry, 2005). In this sense, disasters may well be assumed as a form of controversy similar to those analysed by Science and Technology Studies (STS). Both, indeed, derive their sociological appeal from a Garfinkelian experimentalism: in both a breaching situation renders problematic otherwise stabilized elements of our domestic, political, scientific or organizational routines.

STS have argued that insofar as controversies problematize objectual, epistemic and institutional arrangements, they are ripe for the emergence of democratic experiments. Whether under the shape of formalized public participation exercises (Braun and Schultz, 2010; Lezaun and Soneryd, 2007) or as spontaneous engagement arenas (Latour, 2001), displayed as large-scale *in vivo* processes (Mitchell, 2005) or circumscribed to *in vitro* settings (Muniesa and Callon, 2007), conforming to conventional public realms (Nelkin, 1992) or revolving around domestic spaces (Marres, 2010, 2012), sociotechnical controversies push for more experimental ways of doing politics. And here experimental has a twofold meaning. First, these political articulations are experimental because materials, entities and relations are approached carefully and openly, guided by tentative trials and material evidences (Callon *et al.*, 2009; Marres, 2012; Millo and Lezaun, 2006; Whatmore and Landström, 2011). In these arenas spokespersons, delegates, objects, the common good, experts, laypersons, problems and solutions are not defined a priori but are generatively produced according to 'due process' within the experiments themselves (Latour, 2004). The experimentality of these arrangements thus lies in the possibility of undertaking politics as an 'encounter with what we can't yet "determine" – [with] what we can't yet describe or agree upon' (Rajchman, 2000: 20 in Hinchliffe, 2007: 100).

These political arrangements are also experimental, secondly, because like experiments in the biological and physical sciences, political experiments are material apparatuses designed to unveil the world and make it speak (Stengers, 2000). And they do so by a twofold movement of controlling and staging the phenomena under scrutiny.

Indeed, the effects of experiments do not exist outside the experimental apparatus. The experimental object is dependent on the arrangements purposefully set up 'to create, produce, refine and stabilize phenomena' (Hacking, 1983: 230). Likewise, in democratic experiments there is always some kind of ontological production at work. Political experiments are generative. As material devices they enact the subjects or publics engaged in and with them. Assumptions, theoretical projections and normative principles about agents' rationality, optimal communication and the common good are scripted into – and fleshed out by – the methodological apparatuses put forward to perform the experiment, even if these are as simple as chairs around a table (Girard and Stark, 2007). The public then 'is never immediately given but inevitably the outcome of processes of naming and framing, staging, selection and priority setting, attribution, interpellation, categorisation and classification' (Braun and Schultz, 2010: 406).

The validity of experiments, however, lies in their ability to configure an isolated environment. In order to project and produce, experiments have to control, and distance themselves from, the world (Knorr-Cetina, 1999; Latour, 1993): they need to draw a distinction between the regime of the *experientia*, the sheer liveliness and messiness of quotidian practices, and that of the *experimentum*, the controlled setting of conjectures and materials by which newness is brought to the world (Callon *et al.*, 2009; Licoppe, 1996). To be sure, as Isabelle Stengers (2000) has stated, the distancing from the world does not mean that experiments are abstract. It rather means that they create a *locality*: a set of intersecting references that forces any attempt of contestation to follow the experiment's terms. It is only by defining and fixing this set of internal and out-of-the-world principles and assumptions that an experiment may actually enact its objects of inquiry. For example, Lezaun and Soneryd (2007) have shown how participatory methodologies are usually designed based on specific assumptions about human rationality and communication, and it is only by fixing these references that political experiments produce particular results for policy making.

In short, experiments have an ambivalent relation with *publicness*: while experiments approach the world openly and tentatively, their internal references have to remain secluded from publicity in order to function as such.[2] It is precisely this seclusion, however, that is problematized in post-disaster political experiments.

Disasters, as a form of controversy, are privileged sites for the unfolding of experimental politics. Disasters also give rise to a type of politics in which objects, figurations and articulations are dynamically, although cautiously, produced during the political staging itself. But it wouldn't be fair to fully equate disasters as just another form of controversy. While STS accounts describe controversies as breakdowns triggering generalized uncertainties, all too often these accounts seem to clash with the actual controversial situations at hand. Notions such as 'crisis of objectivity' (Latour, 2004) or 'radical uncertainty' (Callon *et al.*, 2009) have been typically utilized to grasp the profound dislocations that are brought to the fore in and by controversies and the dramaturgy that comes with them. However, sometimes confined to experts/scientific disputes, and at other times to extremely well-tempered public arenas, the controversies studied by STS usually *do not* involve the vital and immediate integrity of the world and its objectual constitution. In contrast, disasters imply a situation in which reality is violently and materially disturbed. Affection (Dewey, 1991 [1954]) cannot be taken light-heartedly. In disasters like earthquakes, pandemics, tsunamis, wildfires or oil spills, something is ferociously destroyed, killed, displaced or reshuffled.

Disasters, in this sense, could be understood as an *excessive* type of controversy: situations in which the matter controversial is always outstripping, vitally plethoric and abundant, involving life's sheer liveliness itself. A *hypercontroversy*, paraphrasing Morton (2010): a type of extended, scale-less controversy that 'confound[s] our limited, fixated, self-oriented frameworks' (Morton, 2010: 19). First, disasters are not just about the disturbance of consensuses, the challenges on objectivity or the clashes between different world-making assemblages. They are about extreme differences: about asymmetric exchanges between humans and non-humans and the reworking of the world by recalcitrant entities. In contrast to sociotechnical controversies, with disasters there is always a material surplus, an objective and ontological resistance: forces – made of incandescent magma, mineral matter, water masses or toxic metalloids – that defy any attempt to establish an assemblage manageable – and even apprehensible – by humans (Clark, 2012).

Second, disasters as excessive and recalcitrant entities are 'totalizing events' (Oliver-Smith, 1999: 20): they account for situations in which life in all its functional, material and metabolic forms grinds to halt. As they unfold, 'all dimensions of social-structural formation and the totality of its relations with its environments may become involved, affected, and focused' (Oliver-Smith, 1999: 20). What is involved in disasters is not the functioning of discrete networks or the problematization of specific technoscientific knowledges, however complex they may be, but the operational stability of life-supporting systems (Lakoff and

Collier, 2010: 243). However persistent are the efforts made by STS scholars to convince us that technoscientific controversies end up 'switching off the whole society' (Callon, 2006 [1981]: 137), this 'switching off' is always limited and benevolent when compared with the 'switching off' implied in the uncontrollable and unpredictable movement of geological bodies or meteorological forces: the radicality of uncertainty is of a different kind when the world can *literally* not be reckoned.

And thirdly, disasters dissolve any attempt to draw teleological diagrams. While most methods for controversy analysis rest on procedural templates that emphasize the sequential nature of controversial events (for example Bijker and Pinch, 1984; Yaneva, 2012), disasters 'can in part be understood as a kind of narrative implosion where there [is] not simply meaninglessness, but also too much meaning, an excess' (Law and Singleton, 2006: 9). This extreme abundance contests any attempt to frame disasters in rigid past/present/future, pre-event/event/post-event, or introduction/development/conclusion temporalities and storylines.

It is worth asking, then, how political experimentalism can (has to) be revisited and expanded in the face of disasters' excessiveness. If uncertainty is the engine propelling democratic experiments, do disasters, as forms of radical uncertainty, impose upon democratic arrangements new political challenges? What does 'experimental politics' mean and what are its features when the world loses its material and ontological support?

The tentative hypothesis of this article is that the ontological breakdown brought by disasters sparkles wider forms of political experimentalism. In situations of radical dislocation in which *everything* loses its epistemic and ontic stability, political experiments become ways of searching that are, in turn, searched upon – or experiments that are themselves objects of experimental inquiry. Put differently, disasters congeal a kind of extended, iterating and all-encompassing exploratory search, or what could be labelled as an *atmosphere of indagation*. Of indagation because here the exploration is urgent and purposeful, and because it is done tentatively, collectively and carefully: the inquiry at work is meticulous, open and agonically needed. And atmosphere because this indagation unfolds under the form of an overarching, multiform and ambiguous ambience – a 'gynaecological' (Sloterdijk, 2011 [1998]) political climate: an ecological condition configured by 'vibes, inspirations, energies, and resonances or sympathies' (Laermans, 2011: 115) that allow, reinforce and immunise this excessive indagation. In this *climate* exploration cannot be confined to the settings and affordances of an experiment, because experiments themselves are reintroduced into these atmospheres as objects of political inquiry as well. In these exploratory climates, experimental devices overflow and multiply, implicating themselves iteratively as objects of the very same search they help to enliven. Thus atmospheres of indagation denote a type of political experimentalism that cannot be cut or delimitated: they do not point at particular experimental arrangements, but at the coagulation of enhanced and extended political climates in which anything can be explored, scrutinized and contested, therefore

The Sociological Review, 62:S1, pp. 114–134 (2014), DOI: 10.1111/1467-954X.12126

raising new questions and zones of uncertainty. Bruno Latour has compelled us to recognize that within controversies there is 'No possible agreement on what makes up the world, the beings that inhabit it, that have inhabited it, that shall inhabit it. Disagreements are not superficial, passing, due to simple errors of education or communication, but fundamental' (Latour, 2011: 39). Atmospheres of indagation signallize the type of political arrangement that arises when, taking Latour's words seriously, the world cannot be easily agreed upon.

In what follows I draw on the cases of PRE Talca and Talca con Tod@s, the two post-disaster participatory experiments developed in Talca, to empirically describe these atmospheres of indagation. The story of Talca's post-disaster participatory exercises is about two experiments unfolding at once, each one enacting its own version of the world. But I want to claim that it is also a story about a broader form of political experimentalism, one in which each experiment openly challenged the references of the other, disclosing for public scrutiny elements that are usually kept behind scenes in experimental settings. Insofar as these public contestations were taken up by each experiment as their starting points from which to uphold their methodological and theoretical apparatuses, the result is a highly complex topological arrangement in which the way experimentality is conceptualized may need to be expanded.

A tale of two participatory experiments: PRE Talca and Talca con Tod@s

By May 2010, two months after the earthquake, two participative reconstruction plans had coalesced in Talca. The first was the official PRE Talca (PT).[3] As devised by the government, the basic structure of the PRE was an agreement between the central government, the municipality and a private donor financing the plan. In the case of Talca the donor was the Hurtado-Vicuña group, well known in the region for its various agricultural enterprises and for being an important construction firm. The Hurtado-Vicuña group hired Polis, a prestigious architectural and planning firm, to design the master plan and all the necessary participatory exercises.

But PT was severely contested. Although it expressly stated that public participation was one of its main policy objectives, neighbourhood associations and NGOs were dubious about the role of a private corporation in the planning process and how its stakes in the city's real estate industry could undermine equity goals within the planning process. Thus, against PT, citizen organizations, professional associations and NGOs established Talca con Tod@s (Talca with Everyone, TcT hereafter).

Thus two experiments in government unfolded at unison. Each one with its own set of assumptions and techniques, therefore each one producing a different world. In this section I will follow PT and TcT, as two political experiments, in their attempts to elicit different versions of Talca. But I will attempt to show, as well, how an atmosphere of indagation was enlivened in Talca, one in which all elements, including the experiments themselves, could be potentially politicized.

Producing a context (or, what is Talca?)

The formal launching of PT was on 12 May 2010. The agreement mandated a 90-day deadline to hand in the rebuilding proposal to the municipality. The professional team in charge of PT had to devise and apply all the necessary methodologies to secure an inclusive and participative process 'both in the design and in the implementation of the solutions' (MINVU, 2010: 4). Interestingly, however, PT's very first activity was not to engage neighbours in a broad citizen appraisal, but to draft a technical diagnosis of Talca. Before any participatory exercise, the internal structure of the city had to be disclosed – and this meant to unveil the geo-economic features of the city.

Analyses, calculations and maps were done, and PT arrived at a very singular conclusion: Talca's problem was not its actual devastation but its previous deterioration; not the earthquake but the severe and deep-rooted obsolescence of the city. Talca, PT argued, was a declining city that needed not so much a rebuilding plan as an urban rehabilitation programme. In the words of one of the architects of PT:

> [Central neighbourhoods] were already very, very deteriorated neighbourhoods before the earthquake, and what the earthquake did was to deteriorate them even more . . . So in this sense more than to rebuild [what we want] is to recuperate. Instead of just rebuilding what existed, this [PRE Talca] has to do with the capacity to identify the problems coming from before [the earthquake]. (Interview, September 2010)

Interestingly then, the earthquake was not viewed as an obstacle to be solved but as an opportunity to be capitalized in order to transform Talca into a more competitive city. 'Now it is cheaper than ever to go underground, to bury electric cables, make underground parking, to do a lot of things that are much more expensive when they involve demolishing a house' (Interview, September 2010), assessed optimistically the governor.

Many critical scholars have denounced the utilization of disasters as political exceptions for the unrolling neoliberal policies, often under the argument of a unique 'opportunity' to be tapped (Gunewardena and Schuller, 2008; Klein, 2008; Rozario, 2007). These approaches seldom recognize, however, all the work that has to be invested to technically produce these 'opportunities' and a world accordingly. In Talca a myriad of economic and geographical analyses, cartographies and models were performed to locate Talca's competitive advantage (PRE Talca, 2011). The results, which became the touchstone of PT's programme, indicated that Talca was a 'sub-optimal' city in geo-economic terms. As one of PT's architects declared, 'We did a super interesting map. Talca is in the middle of the region. It could therefore be the [region's] touristic epicentre, but there isn't anything [in Talca]. There is nothing to see in Talca'

The Sociological Review, 62:S1, pp. 114–134 (2014), DOI: 10.1111/1467-954X.12126

(Interview, September 2010). PT thus argued that the key for a sustainable rebuilding of Talca was to transform the city into the central node within the region's economic networks.

In June 2010, one month after PT's launching, TcT was established by an ensemble of citizen organizations. At the heart of TcT's launching was a very different diagnosis of the city – a diagnosis made openly in opposition to PT.

PT and TcT were in many senses convergent. For TcT it was also crucial to delineate a context. But the context delineated by TcT did not highlight the endemic decay of the city but, on the contrary and against PT's political position, its rich civic life. What the disaster unveiled was not the economic fragility of Talca but its unique density of civil associations. In direct reference to PT, TcT thus emerged as a collective whose primordial task was not to retool Talca's competitiveness but to trigger 'a process of social dialogue' in order 'to rise and articulate a massive and including social force, with critical and purposeful vision, that will position the citizenry as a valid counterpart to the public and private institutions related to the reconstruction' (ELCI, 2010a).

TcT's contra-argument began to circulate. SUR Maule and Reconstruye, two NGOs with extensive expertise in political communication, were fundamental in spreading TcT's principles. More specifically, they created the idea that another definition of 'opportunity' was plausible. What had to be capitalized was not Talca's untapped geo-economic advantages but the city's abundant social capital. And just as cartographies, calculations and measures were deployed by PT to enliven Talca's economic features, a myriad of technologies of democracy (Laurent, 2011) – online media and a multiplicity of workshops, seminars and public lectures, leaflets and posters (see Figure 1) – were mobilized by TcT to produce a civic regime. Suddenly Talca became an extraordinary communitarian city. 'The particularity of Talca', says enthusiastically an architect from TcT, 'is that it has a level of [communitarian] resources that you don't find elsewhere. There is a significant level of social capital in the city' (Interview, September 2010).

Thus in an archaeological operation sought to dig out the hidden features of Talca, TcT framed the civic opportunity opened by the earthquake in terms of latent forces being reactivated by the disaster. And the embodied expression of this awakening was the *community leader*. Useless in the depoliticized post-Pinochet environment, 'the earthquake connected the leaders again with their social bases' said a NGO member (Interview, September 2010). The earthquake proved that the community leader was alive and demanded political agency. Moreover, the community leader became an embodied way to publicly contest the political architecture of PT's participatory experiment. TcT's message was that PT had neglected the inclusion of community leaders as integral parts in the planning process. In the words of TcT, the political relevance of the initiative was 'the capacity to articulate and understand the diversity of social actors, to renovate the protagonism of *community leaders* and to welcome new post-disaster leaderships' (Letelier and Boyco, 2011: 65, emphasis added). PT's position was thus not only challenged abstractly by TcT's definition of

Figure 1: *Promotional poster for first* cabildo *organized by Talca con Tod@s.*
Source: Talca con Tod@s

'opportunity', but also materially by denouncing PT's unwillingness to include the community leader in the political arena.

Enacting Talquinos

PT and TcT, as experimental apparatuses, enacted different versions of Talca. But the technical diagnosis was inseparable from the social one. PT and TcT also enacted differently the citizens inhabiting their singular worlds. And they did so, as well, by publicly disclosing and problematizing each other's experimental references regarding whom the Talquinos were and how their political subjectivity and willingness to participate had to be calibrated.

If Talca was a city abundant in civic consciousness, then any post-disaster planning had to be slowed down in order to cautiously engage Talquinos into the process, TcT argued. 'We demand to be heard, we won't allow being ignored', read the first manifesto of TcT (ELCI, 2010b). And to be heard meant to accept that rapidity and executive efficiency were not the first priority:

Talquinos, TcT asserted, had many things to say. Indeed, TcT assumed that neighbours were engaged. Following a liberal understanding (Cruikshank, 1999), Talca's surplus of civic virtues was embodied in an interested citizen. Or put differently, the emphasis on social capital as the main asset of the city – praised and promoted through a number of demonstrational devices – implied the existence of vocal individuals eager to connect and participate. Among the Talquinos 'there was a desire of city- and citizen-making' explain Letelier and Boyco (2011: 65).

A battery of blog posts, letters to the editor, magazine articles and NGO manifestos brought to life the figure of a civic neighbour ready to participate. The expression 'Si no nos dan la palabra ¡nos la tomamos!' (If they don't give us a chance to speak, we take it by force!) became TcT's tagline (see Figure 1). The slogan moulded an image of subjects ready to proactively jump into the public sphere, but also one of individuals with something to say. Indeed, TcT also assumed that citizens were experts. Talquinos were capable of bringing technical knowledge into the planning discussion. An architect from TcT puts it succinctly:

> I've been gifted with many life experiences working with social organizations . . . I like the clarity they have, it is like one is drawn into an office, into a world that is unaware of the problems and they [community organizations] have a much clearer solution, and you just have to write it down. (Interview, September 2010)

The assumption of an engaged and expert citizen, crucial for the development of TcT's participatory experiment, was, however, heavily criticized by PT. PT exposed TcT's criteria in the public debate. And by doing so, PT built its own set of assumptions regarding the nature of citizens in Talca.

Against TcT, PT assumed that Talquinos were practical. They wanted action and change, not deliberation. They were tired of being asked; now they wanted solutions. Talquinos, in PT's account, were anthropologically at odds with TcT's assumptions. PT circulated this conviction throughout Talca and public officials involved in PT's process – mainly from the municipality – were instrumental in this task. Social workers, planners and all types of experts of community (Rose, 1999) were in charge of spreading the word and publicly explicating TcT's ill-conceived assumptions about Talquinos. An urban planner from the municipality summarizes the main message:

> People are sick of participation, of surveys . . . they have responded the same so many times . . . they want solutions and not so much *blah blah*. Because there are all these characters coming here! [Saying] 'Let's do a survey to know this and that'. That has been done so many times that people are angry. No more discussions, they want solutions. (Interview, September 2010)

This practical subjectivity implied a very particular version of political life. Citizens were political, but only insofar as this meant to engage in the *evaluation* of solutions and not in the *design* of them. Talquinos were tired of all the deliberative but inefficient proposals devised by TcT – which invited neighbours to engage in the definition of issues, rather than in the selection of alternative solutions. This matched the technical diagnosis advanced by PT: the city needed to urgently revert its endemic and deep-rooted decay and Talca could not afford to squander precious time in excessive deliberation. Citizens, PT confirmed, agreed. Therefore to fast-forward without obstructing the rebuilding process with pointless civic engagements was a way of *adjusting* the plan to Talquinos' epistemic and political identity.

The reactiveness of Talquinos – their unwillingness to engage in the deliberative design of solutions – was explained, PT claimed, by their *non-expert* nature. Indeed, PT assumed Talquinos as being at odds with technical knowledge. 'One can't expect,' says a municipal officer explaining their technical illiteracy, 'that a neighbour will come [to PT's public meetings], voice an idea and that that idea will be done, it is not like that' (Interview, September 2010). Neighbours, therefore, were invited to share their perceptions and aspirations, even their technical opinions, but the complexity of the rebuilding plan would always be insurmountable for them. 'A reconstruction plan is a very technical thing', said the governor reflecting on PT's public participation processes, 'so neighbourhood leaders will hardly have the real opportunity to confront their opinions against [PT's] professionals' (Interview, September 2010). This decision – to exclude citizens from participating in technical issue due to the complexities involved – was aimed directly at denouncing TcT's inefficient principles and was publicly aired by PT and local authorities as a sign of reasonableness. Through public discourses, community meetings and leaflets, the message was that participation hinged as the basic condition for PT, but that this participation had to be done – unlike TcT – intelligently. Thus PT wouldn't reduce participation, only engineer it to the needs and characteristics of Talquinos. As the mayor of Talca explains, participation within PT was abundant, although focused on opinions and comments:

> Several massive meetings were made . . . there was a weekly consulting committee where people could come and everyone that wanted to comment could go to the [PT] website, in addition to the surveys. So I don't know what else could have been done . . . Many meetings were had with neighbourhood associations, explaining to them [the plan] and asking for their opinions.

Eliciting technologies

Thus two contexts had been created. Two worlds: two different sets of economic, political and anthropological assumptions, parameters and restrictions operating as the background against which each experiment was erected and evaluated. PT articulated the problem as a city in decay that needed urgent economic revitalization and a political subject that, matching this diagnosis, was tired of being asked, had no technical knowledge and, consequently, craved for concrete solutions. TcT put forward a world configured by a city plethoric in civic life and, concomitantly, a citizen eager to participate and ready to enthusiastically jump into the public sphere. The different conjectures and references of PT and TcT, moreover, were *never* protected from public scrutiny. Their staging was made in the wild, deprived from the isolation usually needed for experiments to work. And this open and extended experimentalism was reinforced when the techniques for eliciting Talca's context and citizens both experiments had assumed and fixed were also publicly displayed and challenged.

PT implemented two major participatory techniques. First, the *Encuesta Ciudadana* (Citizen Survey) applied by the end of May 2010 at the very beginning of the process. The survey was conducted both online through PT's website and face-to-face.[4] Based on the idea of Talquinos as functional, solution-oriented and technically illiterate, the survey was thought more as a narrative device than as an actual engagement platform or technical tool for controversy management.

The survey was a one-page questionnaire asking five questions, three of them with predefined response options.[5] Globally, the questions were intended at constructing an aestheticized narrative about Talca. A total of 3,473 face-to-face surveys were responded between June 2nd and June 9th. The results were transformed into charts depicting preferences and rankings that were publicized in several presentations as a snapshot about how Talquinos imagined their city.

These *Encuestas Ciudadanas* were severely criticized by TcT for patronizing residents and not having basic methodological reliability. PT reacted to these contestations and a polling firm was hired to conduct a 2,792-case survey between 22 July and 26 July. Conventional sampling protocols were followed, the questionnaire's phrasing was revised and new sociodemographic questions were added. But the survey's objective remained the same: respondents were asked to 'imagine' their city, give information about preferred locations and to rank potential interventions. Criticisms arose again, mainly pointing at the extreme simplification of the rebuilding challenges scripted in the survey (Azócar *et al.*, 2010).

The second technique applied by PT was the *Conversaciones Ciudadanas* (Citizen Conversations). These were community meetings organized in different neighbourhoods to present PT's projects and to receive feedback from the community. Progressively, these *Conversaciones Ciudadanas* became the core of PT's participatory methodology and were thought to silence critiques coming from TcT. A total of seven meetings were held between May and July, with attendance ranging from 7 to 60 people.

Interestingly, the call for participation was made by the municipality's Department of Community Development and not by PT. Meetings, in addition, were held in the quarters of *junta de vecinos* (neighbourhood councils), formal community-based organizations highly questioned for their lack of representativeness and their government-dependence. Thus *Conversaciones Ciudadanas* were usually attended by elderly citizens, most of them enrolled in or close to the municipal governance networks. PT's anthropological assumptions were thus confirmed: attendees had no technical knowledge and were eager to solve their punctual problems, not to discuss broader political issues. As shown in Figure 2, *Conversaciones Ciudadanas* resembled more conventional one-way, educational

Figure 2: Conversación Ciudadana *in El Prado, Talca.*
Source: PRE Talca 2011.

arenas (Callon, 1999) than dialogical deliberative forums. Debate, indeed, was generally missing from *Conversaciones Ciudadanas*. A note from fieldwork:

> While the objective is interaction and people can give their opinions, the options given by the architect are quite delimitated . . . for example, [in one of the *Conversaciones Ciudadanas*] an attendant wondered if future houses could have better doors, a requirement to which everybody adhered. The architect, a bit uncomfortable, responded that 'that is something that has to be evaluated'. . . (Fieldwork notes, September 2010)

The participatory techniques actualized and confirmed the theoretical citizen assumed by PT. The figure of an illiterate and a-political citizen only willing to engage in the (minimal) evaluation of solutions was produced in and by *Encuestas Ciudadanas* and *Conversaciones Ciudadanas*. With the former PT went out to retrieve images and symbols and thus citizens were mobilized, precisely, as individuals engaged solely in narrative making; with the latter PT invited a version of the community that matched, and hence confirmed, the conjecture of a practical, non-expert Talquino. If the political power of experiments resides in their capacity to make the world speak *without* the author (Stengers, 2000), PT assembled an experimental apparatus in which the world – a context constituted by a particular Talca and a particular Talquino – was ratified via the *Encuestas Ciudadanas* and *Conversaciones Ciudadanas*.

TcT openly criticized PT's participatory technologies. TcT had defined a context and an ideal Talquino in public opposition to PT. Thus, also in open disagreement with PT, TcT devised a different set of eliciting techniques, one that would unveil the ideological configuration of PT's experiment.

TcT's main participatory technique, and arguably the pillar sustaining its normative architecture, was the *Cabildos* (councils). These were open meetings

The Sociological Review, 62:S1, pp. 114–134 (2014), DOI: 10.1111/1467-954X.12126

in which all Talquinos were invited to voice out their opinions about the rebuilding process. *Cabildos* were the materialization of the critique against PT: they were demonstrational devices confirming that a different citizenness could be imagined and experimentally produced. It was thoroughly and publicly stressed that the aim of *Cabildos* was, in contrast to PT, to allow 'the very same community to decide what, where and how to reconstruct, creating a counterweight to the governmental initiative [PRE Talca]' (aMaule, 2010).

Two *Cabildos* were conducted. The first meeting brought together 300 people. Its goal was to discuss, adjust and validate a list of critical themes (the so-called *Agenda Ciudadana para la Reconstrucción*, Citizen Reconstruction Agenda). The second session was devoted to group discussions for each of the work-themes defined in the first council. As participatory experiments, *Cabildos* were complex methodological apparatuses and mobilized particular epistemic and political references. First, *Cabildos* were not thought as functional devices to guide the rebuilding process, but as arenas where a *new citizen* could be brought centre stage and, with her, a new political regime. In words of TcT, *Cabildos*

> Aim[ed] at a cultural change beyond the post-earthquake conjuncture. The commitment is to change the way citizenship is executed and to build the city we dream. For this, the *Cabildos* and the movement [TcT] represent the activation of a process of social capital construction, key in the development of a more equal and integrated society. (Talca con Tod@s, 2010)

Second, while TcT discourses were focused on and exalted the figure of the citizen, the main methodological subject and the key agent of political change were civic organizations. Or put differently, *Cabildos* mobilized a model of representative democracy: while ordinary citizens were invited and attended the *Cabildos*, it was their spokespersons who were the ultimate engine of the experiment. 'When we talk about spaces for an active civil society', indicates an architect from TcT, we must refer to '*local organizations* making the [rebuilding] process their own (Cociña, 2011: 57, emphasis added). In fact, the success of the first *Cabildo* was not measured by the quantity of people attending, but by the number of organizations represented. 'Five work commissions, three artistic activities, forty professional facilitators, eleven work-themes and *more than 60 organizations participating*, are some of the numbers of this process' (Levantemos Ciudadanía, 2010, emphasis added).

As a result, those attending *Cabildos* were not usual Talquinos but the political ones: community leaders, NGOs professionals and engaged residents. *Cabildos*, then, enacted and confirmed the political subjects idealized by TcT. The involved citizen was produced by TcT's experimental setting. And literally. Excerpts from our field notes taken at the second *Cabildo*:

> When there are dialogue problems or the tone of the conversations rises, a woman [from TcT staff] that was seated in front of the computer [taking notes of the *Cabildo*]

says that it is mandatory to eliminate fighting and that all must agree . . . people listen to her . . . she is the one preventing the Cabildo from becoming a usual [unconsensual] community meeting.

After a while, the same woman that intervened before to calm a discussion, says that it's necessary to write a common document with the proposals. And for that, she says, it might be useful to listen first to the architect . . . he [the architect] talks about the importance of staying downtown [instead of being relocated elsewhere with housing vouchers] . . .

After the talk, people give ideas and proposals . . . [one participant] demands faster solutions, which the women [typing the proposals] translate into 'more inclusion of the citizenry'. (Fieldwork notes, September 2010)

In *Cabildos* individuals were shaped to match the idealized figure of the 'engaged citizen'. First, a particular sociality and political performance was promoted. Sound political engagement required individuals to behave in a particular way: rules of good communication had to be followed, bodily expressions had to be managed and consensuses had to be reached. The political subject – her voice, opinions, gestures – was protocolized. The civic Talquino had to be, indeed, civic. Second, while *Cabildos* were open and citizens had the ultimate word, certain ideas were promoted, enhanced and prioritized. Particular assumptions about public space, equity and 'good living' were upheld: civic subjects not only had to behave as such, they had to think civically as well. This includes the actual manipulation of opinions, demands and expectations in order to align them in a 'real' programme of empowerment. The result was hence the public production of not only a methodological device that was in itself a contestation to PT's apparatus, but also of a citizen that was at odds with PT's conjectures.

Conclusions: from experiments to atmospheres of indagation

Talca – a mid-size city in south-central Chile – witnessed the emergence of two political experiments after the 2010 earthquake, PRE Talca and Talca con Tod@s. They were experiments because they attempted to organize collectively Talca's post-disaster political life, and also because they defined and fixed a number of epistemic, methodological and political references to enact singular worlds. As I have tried to show, one sought to enliven a world composed of a decayed city that was in need of urgent economic regeneration and that therefore understood the earthquake as an opportunity to revive its competitiveness; the other articulated a world that rested upon the abundant civility of the city, being the quake a unique occasion to awake and expand the already existing social capital. One world was populated by practical, technically illiterate individuals; the other by political, expert citizens. And these features and assumptions were enacted, in one case, with the material help of surveys and informational meetings aimed at capturing the perceptions and opinions of

The Sociological Review, 62:S1, pp. 114–134 (2014), DOI: 10.1111/1467-954X.12126

Talquinos; in the other case, they were brought to life by shaping them in and through open citizen councils and other empowering devices.

In many ways this is a story about multiplicity: about the more than one but less than many realities that were fleshed out in Talca (Mol, 2003). This story suggests that however vital and materially evident disasters might be, they have to be nonetheless interpreted, measured and projected, therefore enacted in different ways and sites. This, in turn, points at a paradoxical condition of disasters: while the collapse of the world requires enacting it anew, it also gives rise to modes of political experimentation that produce heterogeneous worldings (Tsing, 2010). The case of Talca indicates that when it comes to participatory experiments the question is not just about empowering or including an actor or community (Pearce, 2003; Pelling, 2007) but of formatting what an actor is, how this actor has to participate and which is the inventory of possible problems and solutions at hand. It is, hence, not a question about the strength of democracy, but about what are the conducts, contexts and ways of knowing assumed in democratic technologies.

But Talca's post-disaster story is also one about political experimentalism. Or better said, about wider and messier *ways of searching*. Indeed, a unique modality of political experimentalism unfolded in Talca, one – I want to argue – that cannot be merely framed as the unfolding of a singular experiment not to the emergence of a contentious *enjeu* between an intervention and its opponents. Laurent (2011), for example, has described how anti-nanotechnology activists resisted the NanoViv Debate, a series of public dialogues on nanotechnology set up in Grenoble, France. These activists skilfully mobilized social theories and demonstrational devices to contest nanotechnology development, arguing that the matter had advanced in Grenoble without collective discussion and neglecting negative long-term effects (Laurent, 2011: 661). Laurent calls 'counter-experiments' the manifold actions taken by these anti-nanotechnology groups, such as squatting, literary and artistic interventions, graffiti paintings and independent debates. But in contrast to the case of Talca, the relation between these contesting demonstrations and its critics was not symmetrical. While activists interfered in the official experiment's architecture, activists did not allow themselves to be affected by the NanoViv experiment. The case of Talca is thus significantly different. It doesn't suffice to say that the experiment became a controversy, with an experiment on the one hand and a more or less organized contestation to it on the other. For in Talca *two* experiments were staged, and both were proponents and contenders, exponents and antagonists, *at the same time* – and therefore they both had to arrange their experimental apparatuses openly. No straightforward diagram of interventions and their opposition as in Laurent's case can thus be delineated in Talca.

So how to make sense of the political experimentalism put forward in Talca? In situations of radical uncertainty, Talca's case seems to suggest, experimental politics can be scruffier and more far-reaching than has been usually assumed in STS. They assemble knowledge practices that seem to be characterized by what John Dewey calls *indeterminacy* (1939).[6] In his *Logic: Theory of Inquiry* (1939),

Dewey claims that inquiry is a particular form of search. As such, instead of separating the inquiry from the problematic situation, Dewey asserts that 'it is of the very nature of the indeterminate situation which evokes inquiry to be *questionable*; or, in terms of actuality instead of potentiality, to be uncertain, unsettled, disturbed' (1939: 105, emphasis in the original). Thus we inquire when we are uncertain and, concomitantly, when we seek for answers in regards to the uncertainty evoking the inquiry. But this does not mean that the problem has been identified *prior* to the inquiry. Inquiry is not anticipatory. On the contrary, 'the indeterminate situation becomes problematic in the very process of being subjected to inquiry' (1939: 107). Thus in uncertain or indeterminate situations, such as disasters, we put forward modes of inquiry in which the very definition of the problem is part of the inquiry. Or as Dewey put is, 'To see that a situation requires inquiry is the initial step in inquiry' (1939: 107). Hence indeterminacy not only poses the necessity of a search but forces a type of search in which you don't know what you are looking for (Stark, 2009: 2). Insofar as the object to be searched becomes evasive and is continuously being made within exploratory activities, the search itself emerges as a problematic and relational process (Farías and Weszkalnys, both in this volume, underline different although inter-related forms of knowledge ambivalence and non-knowledge put forward in catastrophic situations).

This heterarchic logic of search seems more appropriate to understand the case of Talca and the atmosphere of indagation put forward. As I tried to demonstrate, the worlds enacted by PT and TcT never stayed put. They were not just different; they were also constantly and topologically interfering with each other – for each experiment publicly challenged the principles and conjectures of the other, making these problematizations the centripetal points for the arrangement of their own experimental apparatuses. Their references, as key components of the experiments they were unearthing, did not remain in the shadows, protected from the spotlight of public scrutiny. PT and TcT diagrammed, carefully and tentatively, a city and a citizen, but the seclusion from the world, a requirement for every experiment, was not achieved. These diagrams, far from staying indoors, were publicized in the wild, opening ambivalent questions yet to be answered in the process of inquiry. PT and TcT were not just two searching technologies, for the search they were performing involved investigations about what was the search about and which were the appropriated technologies for the task. Thus the political search unleashed by the disaster was not (could not be) circumscribed to the unfolding of particular experiments, but expanded to articulate *them* as problematic matters that were included in the cosmogram that had to be recomposed. I have labelled this political experimentalism as an atmosphere of indagation in an attempt to emphasize its ecological condition: a political climate, a 'fog ball' (Sloterdijk, 2005: 225) that sustains the conditions for a generalized and recursive experimental *umwelt*.

The provisional conclusion is that political inquiry in situations of radical indeterminacy may invoke atmospheres of indagation in which the imposition of only *one* regime of truth, however experimental it may be, is doomed to fail. As shown by the case of Talca, the collapse of life congealed an atmosphere of indagation in which all materials, processes and decisions could be potentially transformed into objects of political inquiry – including PT and TcT themselves. In this sense, atmospheres of indagation may be an alternative way of thinking about search when the world has to be literally recomposed anew and references cannot be easily fixed. Atmospheres of indagation may be, as well, a way of thinking about politics when controversies prove to be radically recalcitrant and materially resistant. A politics of excessiveness: collective arrangements that confronted to ontological breakdowns demand for more plural and reflexive explorations – and therefore configuring new forms of publicness. Noortje Marres (2012) has suggested that the publicity of political experiments has to be revisited when materials are accounted as openly mediating heterogeneous practices in the articulation of participatory engagements. Atmospheres of indagation offer a second mode of expanding the nature and allocation of publicity within political experiments – one not associated with objects being front-staged within experimental apparatuses but with multiple experiments having their references openly and simultaneously questioned and performed. When disasters seem to be ubiquitously lurking in our daily lives, the acknowledgment of this type of excessive experimentalism seems crucial, and not only for a better understanding of the politics-disasters nexus but also for expanding our imagination on the political inventiveness of controversies at large.

Acknowledgements

Research support generously provided by FONDECYT Iniciación 11100034 and CIGIDEN/FONDAP 15110017. Versions of this paper were presented at the 2011 4S conference in Cleveland and at the Instituto de Sociología at Pontificia Universidad Católica de Chile. I am grateful to Israel Rodríguez-Giralt, Michael Guggenheim, Joe Deville and three anonymous reviewers for their invaluable comments and suggestions.

Notes

1 Gentilic for Talca.
2 It goes without saying that experimental 'intersecting references' might be contested, as they indeed are. Many experiments are expressly launched to dispute the results of prior ones. The contestation, however, is always *a posteriori*: the references of an experiment are problematized only once they have already accomplished their work and are out in the world open to criticism – and not while they are *in operation* configuring the experiment. There are, as well, cases in which two experiments unfold in unison, challenging each other from the outset. But quite often these experiments diverge only partially from each other, sharing most of the basic definitions, assumption and principles. Differences are methodological and not epistemological, and hence are *attributional* controversies unfolding in these situations (Pinch and Leuenberger, 2006). The crucial question is which experiment arrives faster and more efficiently, *ceteris paribus*, to the desired and shared goal.

3 PRE stands for Strategic Reconstruction Plan, *Plan de Reconstrucción Estratégica* in Spanish.
4 For the application of the face-to-face- survey, key points of the city were selected, such as the mall, the railway station and the square.
5 The questions were: (1) *What is missing in the city?*; (2) *Select a place for Talca's postcard*; (3) *If you could select an area in the city to live, which area would you choose?*; (4) *Indicate the area of Talca you like the most*; (5) *Indicate the area of Talca you like the least.*
6 Dewey's pragmatism has been revived by STS scholars in the last decade to rework the articulation between technosciences and politics, most prominently by Noortje Marres (2007, 2012).

References

aMaule, (2010), '¿PRETALCA o Cabildo Ciudadano? ¡Tú decides!', available at: www.elamaule.cl/admin/render/noticia/26000 (accessed May 2013).
Azócar, F., Miño, C. and Moreno, D., (2010), 'Encuesta ciudadana en Talca: lo que queda pendiente', available at: www.reconstruye.org/2010/07/encuesta-ciudadana-en-talca-lo-que-queda-pendiente/ (accessed May 2013).
Bijker, W. and Pinch, T., (1984), 'The social construction of facts and artifacts: or how the sociology of science and the sociology of technology might benefit each other', *Social Studies of Science*, 14 (3): 399–441.
Bresciani, L. E., (2010), '1.000 pueblos y ciudades que reconstruir', *La Tercera*, 2 April.
Braun, K. and Schultz, S., (2010), ' ". . . a certain amount of engineering involved": constructing the public in participatory governance arrangements', *Public Understanding of Science*, 19 (4): 403–419.
Callon, M., (1999), 'The role of lay people in the production and dissemination of scientific knowledge', *Science, Technology and Society*, 4 (1): 81–94.
Callon, M., (2006 [1981]), 'Pour une sociologie des controverse technologiques', in M. Akrich, M. Callon and B. Latour (eds), *Sociologie de la traduction. Texts fondateurs*, Paris: Presses des Mines [originally in *Fundamenta Scientiae*, 2: 381–399].
Callon, M., Lascoumes, P. and Barthe, Y., (2009), *Acting in an Uncertain World: An Essay on Technical Democracy*, Cambridge, MA: MIT Press.
Clark, N., (2012), *Inhuman Nature: Sociable Life on a Dynamic Planet*, Thousand Oaks, CA: Sage Publications.
Cociña, C., (2011), 'Ideología y reconstrucción. Levantar ciudades y ciudadanías', available at: www.reconstruye.org/wp-content/uploads/2012/02/Articulos-Catalogo_coci%C3%B1a.pdf (accessed May 2013).
Cruikshank, B., (1999), *The Will to Empower: Democratic Citizens and Other Subjects*, Ithaca, NY: Cornell University Press.
Dewey, J., (1939), *Logic: Theory of Inquiry*, New York: Henry Holt and Co.
Dewey, J., (1991 [1954]), *The Public and its Problems* (Athens, OH: Swallow Press/Ohio University Press).
ELCI (Escuela de Líderes de Ciudad), (2010a), 'Mapas de daño de Talca', available at: elci.sitiosur.cl/mapa_dano_postterremoto/mapas.htm (accessed May 2013).
ELCI (Escuela de Líderes de Ciudad), (2010b), 'Se lanzó cabildo de Talca', available at: http://elci2011.sitiosur.cl/not_home_8.htm (accessed May 2013).
Girard, M. and Stark, D., (2007), 'Socio-technologies of assembly: sense making and demonstration in rebuilding Lower Manhattan', in D. Lazer and V. Mayer-Schoenberger (eds), *Governance and Information: The Rewiring of Governing and Deliberation in the 21st Century*, New York and Oxford: Oxford University Press.
Gunewardena, N. and Schuller, M., (2008), *Capitalizing on Catastrophe: Neoliberal Strategies in Disaster Reconstruction*, Blue Ridge Summit, PA: AltaMira Press.
Hacking, I., (1983), *Representing and Intervening. Introductory Topics in the Philosophy of Natural Science*, Cambridge: Cambridge University Press.

Hinchliffe, S., (2007), *Geographies of Nature: Societies, Environments, Ecologies*, Thousand Oaks, CA: Sage Publications.

Klein, N., (2008), *The Shock Doctrine: The Rise of Disaster Capitalism*, New York: Picador.

Knorr-Cetina, K., (1999), *Epistemic Cultures: How the Sciences Make Knowledge*, Cambridge, MA: Harvard University Press.

Kreps, G., (1998), 'Disaster as systemic event and social catalyst', in E. L. Quarantelli (ed.), *What Is a Disaster? Perspectives on the Question*, New York and London: Routledge.

Laermans, R., (2011), 'The attention regime: on mass media and the information society', in W. Schinkel and L. Noordegraaf-Eelens (eds), *In Medias Res: Peter Sloterdijk's Spherological Poetics of Being*, Amsterdam: Amsterdam University Press.

Lakoff, A. and Collier, S. J., (2010), 'Infrastructure and event: the political technology of preparedness', in B. Braun and S. Whatmore (eds), *Political Matter: Technoscience, Democracy and Public Life*, Minneapolis, MN: University of Minnesota Press.

Latour, B., (1993), *The Pasteurization of France*, Cambridge, MA: Harvard University Press.

Latour, B., (2001), 'From "matters of facts" to "states of affairs": which protocol for the new collective experiments?', Lecture to the Darmstadt Colloquium, available at: www.bruno-latour.fr/node/372 (accessed May 2013).

Latour, B., (2004), *The Politics of Nature: How to Bring the Sciences into Democracy*, Cambridge, MA: Harvard University Press.

Latour, B., (2011), 'Il n'y a pas de monde commun : il faut le composer', *Multitudes*, 45 (2): 38–41.

Laurent, B., (2011), 'Technologies of democracy: experiments and demonstrations', *Science and Engineering Ethics*, 17: 649–666.

Law, J. and Singleton, V., (2006), 'A further species of trouble? Disaster and narrative', available at www.heterogeneities.net/publications/LawSingleton2006SpeciesOfTrouble.pdf (accessed May 2013).

Letelier, F. and Boyco, P., (2011), *Talca posterremoto: una ciudad en disputa*, Santiago de Chile: Ediciones SUR.

Levantemos Ciudadanía, (2010), 'Se viene el Cabildo ciudadano por la reconstrucción en Talca', 14 August, www.levantemosciudadania.cl/archives/2544 (accessed May 2013).

Lezaun, J. and Soneryd, L., (2007), 'Consulting citizens: technologies of elicitation and the mobility of publics', *Public Understanding of Science*, 16 (3): 279–297.

Licoppe, C., (1996), *La Formation de la pratique scientifique. Le Discours de l'expérience en France et en Angleterre, 1630–1820*, Paris: La Découverte.

Marres, N., (2007), 'The issues deserve more credit: pragmatist contributions to the study of public involvement in controversy', *Social Studies of Science*, 37 (5): 759–780.

Marres, N., (2010), 'Frontstaging nonhumans: publicity as a constraint on the political activity of things', in B. Braun and S. Whatmore (eds), *Political Matter: Technoscience, Democracy and Public Life*, Minneapolis, MN: University of Minnesota Press.

Marres, N., (2012), *Material Participation: Technology, the Environment and Everyday Publics*, London: Palgrave Macmillan.

Millo, Y. and Lezaun, J., (2006), 'Regulatory experiments: genetically modified crops and financial derivatives on trial', *Science and Public Policy*, 33 (2): 179–190.

MINVU (Ministerio de Vivienda y Urbanismo), (2010), 'Convenio de Cooperación PRE Talca', available at: www.minvu.cl/incjs/download.aspx?glb_cod_nodo=20100910155220&hdd_nom _archivo=Convenio%20firmado%20PRE%20Talca.pdf (accessed November 2012).

Mitchell, T., (2005), 'The works of economics: how a discipline makes its world', *European Journal of Sociology*, 46 (2): 297–320.

Mol, A., (2003), *Body Multiple: Ontology in Medical Practice*, Durham, NC: Duke University Press.

Morton, T., (2010), *The Ecological Thought*, Cambridge, MA: Harvard University Press.

Muniesa, F. and Callon, M., (2007), 'Economic experiments and the construction of markets', in D. MacKenzie, F. Muniesa and L. Siu (eds), *Do Economists Make Markets? On the Performativity of Economics*, Princeton, NJ: Princeton University Press.

Nelkin, D. (ed.), (1992), *Controversy: Politics of Technical Decisions*, Thousand Oaks, CA: Sage Publications.

Oliver-Smith, A., (1999), 'What is a disaster? Anthropological perspectives on a persistent question', in S. Hoffman and A. Oliver-Smith (eds), *The Angry Earth: Disaster in Anthropological Perspective*, New York and London: Routledge.

Oliver-Smith, A., (2002), 'Theorizing disasters: nature, power, and culture', in S. Hoffman and A. Oliver-Smith (eds), *Catastrophe and Culture: The Anthropology of Disaster*, Santa Fe, NM: SAR Press.

Oliver-Smith, A. and Hoffman, S., (2002), 'Introduction: why anthropologists should study disasters', in S. Hoffman and A. Oliver-Smith (eds), *Catastrophe and Culture: The Anthropology of Disaster*, Santa Fe, NM: SAR Press.

Pearce, L., (2003), 'Disaster management and community planning, and public participation: how to achieve sustainable hazard mitigation', *Natural Hazards*, 28: 211–228.

Pelling, M., (2007), 'Learning from others: the scope and challenges for participatory disaster risk assessment', *Disasters*, 31 (4): 373–385.

Perry, R., (2005), 'Disasters, definitions and theory construction', in R. Perry and E. L. Quarantelli (eds), *What Is a Disaster? New Answers to Old Questions*, Bloomington, IN: Xlibris Corporation.

Pinch, T. and Leuenberger, C., (2006), 'Studying scientific controversy from the STS perspective', concluding remarks on panel 'Citizen Participation and Science and Technology', 2006 East Asian Science, Technology and Society.

PRE Talca, (2011), Memoria: Síntesis Diagnóstica y Formulación de Objetivos Estratégicos.

Rajchman, J., (2000), *The Deleuze Connections*, Cambridge, MA: MIT Press.

Rose, N., (1999), *Powers of Freedom: Reframing Political Thought*, Cambridge: Cambridge University Press.

Rozario, K., (2007), *The Culture of Calamity: Disaster and the Making of Modern America*, Chicago: University of Chicago Press.

Sloterdijk, P., (2005), 'Foreword to the theory of spheres', in M. O'Hanian and J.-C. Royoux (eds), *Cosmograms*, Berlin: Lukas & Sternberg.

Sloterdijk, P., (2011 [1998]), *Esferas I: Burbujas. Microsferología*, Madrid: Siruela.

Stark, D., (2009), *The Sense of Dissonance: Accounts of Worth in Economic Life*, Princeton, NJ: Princeton University Press.

Stengers, I., (2000), *The Invention of Modern Science*, Minneapolis, MN: University of Minnesota Press.

Talca con Tod@s, (2010), Inaugural speech, first *Cabildo*, 14 August, available at: www .levantemosciudadania.cl/archives/2544 (accessed November 2012).

Tsing, A., (2010), 'Worlding the Matsutake Diaspora: or, can actor–network theory experiment with holism?', in T. Otto and N. Bubandt (eds), *Experiments in Holism: Theory and Practice in Contemporary Anthropology*, Oxford and Malden, MA: Wiley-Blackwell.

Whatmore, S. J. and Landström, C., (2011), 'Flood apprentices: an exercise in making things public', *Economy and Society*, 40 (4): 582–610.

Yaneva, A., (2012), *Mapping Controversies in Architecture*, London: Ashgate.

Technologies of recovery: plans, practices and entangled politics in disaster

Lucy Easthope and Maggie Mort

Abstract: Recovery practices following the loss of home, sense of security, space and possessions, have recently become a focus of UK government attention. How people recover from disasters is seen to have a direct bearing on individual, community and economic well-being, so that the recovery itself becomes a form of social change. A plethora of instruments: templates, checklists and guidance documents have been produced to effect this recovery. We term these 'technologies of recovery', which work within a wider context of disaster planning aimed at bringing order where much is uncertain, reactive and dependent on emerging relations between people, things and spaces. While such protocols are not necessarily unwelcome, they carry many assumptions. We show how these technologies are built from official, distal narratives, versions of recovery remote from situated practices or recovery-in-place. Official emergency planning builds on 'lessons' from previous emergencies, to be then applied to future crises. Knowledge that is situated, complex and partial is potentially useless because emergency planners seek accounts that don't depend on highly localized circumstances. From a five-year ethnography of both a flooded community and the development of government recovery guidance, it became clear that technologies or recovery became transformed and remade in localized practice when enacted by newly formed and precarious collaborations of residents and *local* responders. Operating alongside, and sometimes underneath, the official response, residents and local responders demonstrated a remaking of the politics of recovery.

Keywords: flooding, emergency planning, recovery practices, technologies

Introduction: flooding in Toll Bar, Doncaster, UK

Toll Bar is a settlement of 1,400 residents in Doncaster, South Yorkshire and is described as a 'village'. It lies in a bowl-like area in a part of the UK hit most severely socially and economically by the closure of the pits in the early 1990s following the 1984–5 miners' strike. In June 2007 parts of England experienced devastating and unseasonal storms and rainfall and South Yorkshire experienced severe flooding, with 48 areas of the large borough of Doncaster affected. In the borough 3,286 homes were flooded, with 2,275 suffering 'major damage' as defined by the local council and 283 businesses were also affected (Doncaster

The Sociological Review, 62:S1, pp. 135–158 (2014), DOI: 10.1111/1467-954X.12127
© 2014 The Authors. Editorial organisation © 2014 The Editorial Board of the Sociological Review. Published by John Wiley & Sons Ltd, 9600 Garsington Road, Oxford OX4 2DQ, UK and 350 Main Street, Malden, MA 02148, USA

Figure 1: *The purpose-built caravan park for council tenants in Toll Bar.*
Source: Photography by L. Easthope, 2007.

Metropolitan Borough Council, 2011). In the village of Toll Bar, a primary school, hundreds of homes, shops and small businesses were severely damaged.

The subsequent government-appointed 'Pitt Review' describes the flooding of 2007 across the UK (Pitt, 2008) as 'extreme', 'exceptional' and 'serious' and what happened in Toll Bar began as one of these extreme, exceptional, serious events. The flooding in this village started as a mingling of environmental frailties and human-made neglect ravaged by severe and unprecedented rainfall. But it also exposed a chronic weakness; this was not a one-off event but part of a way of life, part of what it means to live in that place.[1]

A number of developments then occurred in the wake of the Toll Bar floods that clearly differed from 'conventional' emergency planning practices.[2] Flooded out of their homes, many Toll Bar residents spent the first weeks sleeping in nearby leisure centres, re-imagined as 'rest centres', making home in places like squash courts. Then residents of the council-managed housing asked to be kept together rather than being dispersed to temporary accommodation across the county. Unusually, to facilitate this Doncaster Council created and managed a large park of 50 mobile homes and a laundry area built on a farmer's field (see Figure 1). Staying local proved critical to the way in which people were able to maintain or rebuild their networks after the floods. Importantly, the new caravan park was close by the majority of damaged homes and opposite the primary school. Not only did the residents stay local, but an adjacent temporary structure was set up by the council as a 'Neighbourhood Support Centre'. Here council staff, which we term 'local responders', relocated to Toll Bar village from their offices in Doncaster, working initially on a 24-hour shift pattern. This relocation and continuous presence was critical: over time it became clear that these local responders who had to follow the National Recovery Guidance (including technologies of recovery), were acting as intermediaries between the displaced residents and the distant authorities. This entanglement became a crucial aspect of the flood recovery.

This entanglement was new. Prior to the floods the Neighbourhood Manager explained that there was very little engagement between many Toll Bar residents and the Council; if you were seen talking to a council worker it was assumed that you were a 'grass'.[3] But the floods meant that people had to interact, and later chose to interact,[4] and then they got to know the council workers as individuals. The residents then became open to other council suggestions and suddenly there was 'take up' of things like council literacy and computing courses. People became aware of a council scheme that allowed them to access laptop computers and these started to appear at meetings of the residents and the 'One O'clock Club' (see later). They also obtained a 'dongle'[5] that residents shared to give them Internet access. If they met in each other's houses to do this, they referred to this as hosting 'the Internet café'. It was in these spaces and through these relationships, that the politics of recovery began to be reshaped, as field notes from 2009 illustrate:

> On a number of occasions [after the floods] I walked around the village with Pat. Everywhere we went people acknowledged him. Young boys and older teenagers would stop and chat to him. He explained to me that it was often these boys which had been considered 'trouble' before the floods. It was their 'anti-social behaviour' that had been included in the statistics before. Now if they were getting boisterous he could have a word and they would say to him 'Sorry about that Pat'. He knew their names; they knew his.

Planning and ordering: technologies of recovery

Many attempts are made to bring order to the messy realities of life after disaster and one formal attempt is undertaken through a process called Emergency Planning. More specifically, attempts to bring order to disaster settings in the UK are made through the use of particular emergency planning tools. Embedded in emergency plans, these instruments, often presented in the form of documents, tables and checklists, are developed centrally through a process of distilling and reducing accounts of previous emergencies. They are then sent out for use by those working in the field of emergency planning, which in the UK is a function of local government, police forces, health organizations and utility companies; a function given greater precedence since the passing of the Civil Contingencies Act 2004. The 'lead government department' for much of this work is the Civil Contingencies Secretariat, placed within the UK Cabinet Office. In 2007 the government initiated work to examine specifically the way in which communities and businesses 'recover' from disasters, subsequently issuing guidance and particular tools to emergency planners: the National Recovery Guidance (Cabinet Office, 2007).

We term these particular tools, 'technologies of recovery': they are human and non-human; material and discursive, designed to change or manage human behaviour. At the deepest level this perspective draws on Foucault's elaboration of technologies of power, perhaps most telling, that of biopower where the object of management is groups of people or populations. We then use 'technologies of recovery' in the sense that the tools and instruments we describe are embedded within policy networks, which can themselves be seen as technologies (Harrison and Mort, 1998). Drawing more particularly from Science and Technology Studies where empirical explorations of what counts as technology generated the sociotechnical perspective, in thinking about technologies of recovery we borrow from Pinch *et al.*'s discussion of 'social' technologies, which refers to artefacts and processes 'whose purpose is to produce changes in human behaviour' (1992: 266). In their case, Pinch *et al.* analyse devices and practices in health economics and show ways that such instruments work normatively. In our case the guidance documents, checklists, templates and other recovery tools developed in emergency planning are designed to effect a desired state or endpoint. To achieve the desired state multiple problems get reformulated in the 'terms of a narrowly conceived discourse of macroeconomics' (Ashmore *et al.*, 1989: 91) and in this discursive practice many diverse consequences can be subsumed into one set of aggregate figures: texts and plans are designed to produce outcomes within particular settings.

The 'technologies of recovery' are both social and material, made up of lots of small parts, which in the case of disaster recovery include guidance sheets, templates, flash cards, checklists and so on. They are a form of socio-technical intervention, acting on the simultaneous construction of a range of human and non-human actors, which include emergency planners, residents of the flooded village, household possessions, online forms and templates. Like the wildfire maps described by Katrina Petersen (this volume), actors produce artefacts that are imbued with different values, expectations and priorities. They are fashioned as objects, which shape a relationship between numbers of actors and 'gain sense and significance within everyday activities and ordinary experience' (Heath *et al.*, 2003: 77).

Initial policy level discussions about 'recovery' in Whitehall involved a collaboration of civil servants, academics, emergency planners and those considered representative of experiential disaster learning, such as in one case, survivors who had experienced the Carlisle floods in 2005.[6] The aim appeared to be that different knowledges would be brought together to make a nationally available set of tools to be called the National Recovery Guidance, available to download from a Cabinet Office website. It would include explanatory information, recovery decision templates, topic sheets, checklists and links to other useful pages on the Internet. It would include forms with empty boxes to be populated by local planners with their own disaster specificities and geographies and the nature of the emergency. The National Recovery Guidance was launched to emergency planners by the Cabinet Office in November 2007.

The Sociological Review, 62:S1, pp. 135–158 (2014), DOI: 10.1111/1467-954X.12127

C	Casualties
H	Hazards
A	Access
L	Locations
E	Emergency Services
T	Time

Figure 2: *Aide memoire.*
Source: Created by L. Easthope, 2007.

The Guidance is replete with textual devices such as flow charts to facilitate decision-making. The underlying ethos is that anything produced must be highly efficient and effective in a crisis. This is taken to mean clear and brief, and thus leads to a proliferation of field-based tools such as small laminated cards (eg with a list of instructions that a police officer could refer to on arrival at an emergency) that can withstand the effects of smoke or rain or whatever else a disaster may involve. Such instruments also act as a reminder to planners or to residents of a flood-prone area of points they should consider and so they aim to shape decision-making. An example is CHALET: a visual representation of how to get from A to B. CHALET provides stepping-stones through a messy, complicated time.

Figure 2 is an example of the Aide Memoire cards issued to emergency responders, who are expected to use this as a prompt to help them evaluate situations on arrival at the scene of an emergency. The mnemonic 'CHALET' is used in the sense of 'make sure you have your CHALET card with you'.[7]

Planning and preparedness activities, such as completing local registers outlining major hazards in the area, occupy the majority of an emergency planner's workload. To demonstrate and evidence that this work is being undertaken requires the generation of a plethora of plans and supporting documents. Again working from the view of policy as technology, Bloomfield and Vurdubakis in their analysis of information technology (IT manuals, consultancy reports and popular guides), state that in circumstances of technological development and implementation, texts constitute a 'particularly potent set of intermediary devices' (1997: 86). The texts they examine are involved in the implementation and development of 'information systems': an attempt to represent a heterogeneous network of people and machines and ideas, concerns, aspirations and project management tools. These plans, Gantt charts and checklists and templates 'represent and therefore mobilize the heterogeneous human and non-human actors and materials constitutive of a..[ ] system' (1997: 86), in the same way that the plethora of emergency plans aim to do. They have a kind of textual agency (Cooren, 2004), in that they try to perform a version of recovery. Law describes how sociotechnical innovations, (the writing, the map) 'open up the possibility of ordering distant events from a centre' (1994: 104).

This brings us to a further and influential trope in our thinking – the role of plans. Emergency planning and planners attempt to find a path from an initial state, such as the aftermath of a severe flood, to a desired goal state given certain conditions along the way. For the community to achieve the desired goal state of, for example, a normal transport infrastructure or re-established tourism, it must undertake certain actions that are outlined in the rest of the guidance document. In framing 'technologies of recovery' as a way of thinking through what came to happen in Toll Bar, we start not from Lee Clarke's version of plans as 'fantasy documents' (Clarke, 1999) though we find his work very persuasive for analysing other disaster settings, but in this context more from Lucy Suchman's critique of artifacts of social ordering in her article 'Plans, Scripts and Other Ordering Devices':

> I have argued that to treat a plan – or any other form of prescriptive representation – as a specification for a course of action shuts down precisely the space of inquiry that begs for investigation; that is, the relations between an ordering device and the contingent labors through which it is produced and made reflexively accountable to ongoing activity. Naturalizing plans as representations (mental or otherwise) existing prior to and determining of action obscures the status of planning as itself a form of culturally and historically situated activity, manifest in specific practices and associated artifacts. Taking plans as artifacts, in contrast, recommends a research agenda dedicated to examining the heterogeneous practices through which specific ordering devices are materialized, mobilized, and contested, at particular times and places, with varying effects. (Suchman, 2007: 187)

Recovery instruments may be presented as neutral and applicable to multiple situations (for example, because they are nationally available on an open-access website) but the 'recovery' that these tools are trying to effect is actually highly variable, messy and situated. Such recovery instruments may, like many social technologies, such as telecare alarm systems or public health leaflets, be presented as products of science, but this is highly problematic. These technologies may be highly unrealistic because they are only as good as the data and statistics fed into them; that is, any input such as a completed box on a template. They need to behave in a uniform, stable way, untainted – in the case of the Toll Bar floods – by the vagaries of the loss of home or space or things. They are attempting to idealize and singularize the multiple, messy world of disaster and they may attempt to be uniform and stable but the world of practice cannot reflect that. As Bijker and Law state, 'Technologies always embody compromise' (1992: 3).

Because both residents and council responders stayed local in Toll Bar the materialization, mobilization and contestation of technologies of recovery became visible. This also opened the way for detailed ethnographic work. 'Contingent labours' came into view: the local responders (acting as intermediaries)

The Sociological Review, 62:S1, pp. 135–158 (2014), DOI: 10.1111/1467-954X.12127

and the residents worked on, and with, the National Recovery Guidance protocols to do something different.

As John Law puts it, there is function in the plan as a written document:

> . . . some materials last better than others. And some travel better than others. Voices don't last for long and they don't travel very far. If social ordering depended on voices alone, it would be a very local affair. (Law, 1994: 102)

Of course plans can be lost, burned, misinterpreted but if cared for and maintained Law suggests that then they will appear to travel well, across time and space; in this case from Whitehall out to Toll Bar.

Official narratives of disaster

> The Symposium offers a range of subjects; choosing from over 20 sessions, aimed at tackling the most important issues in our profession, including case studies, (lessons identified from the past 12 months,) expert insights, master classes, energising practitioner skills and importantly offers an opportunity to horizon scan and gain insight into future risks and the environments we face. (UK Emergency Planning Society, 2011)

Events staged for disaster managers, such as the seminar advertised above, are often centred on the most recent disasters. At these events participants are asked to give presentations in a particular, formulaic style: 'PowerPoint' presentations conclude with a final slide listing lessons identified from an earlier operational response. These events are also used to launch new recovery devices. Certain disasters become particularly emblematic and in UK emergency planning circles (and now also in the media and even public awareness) are known simply by names or numbers such as '7/7', '9/11', 'Lockerbie', 'Buncefield'.[8] These numbers are thrown into the dialogue: for example, 'we have learnt a lot about communications since 9/11', without further elaboration or explanation.

Ironically, even though these disasters are often known by their geographical name, situating them within the context of place is problematic. They are seen to be of little use to other planners if lessons cannot be taken back to their own practice and applied to their own problems. Yet knowledge that is situated, complex, and partial is potentially useless because what emergency planners also want is lessons identified that do not depend on a highly localized set of circumstances.

Access to telling disaster stories at these events is strictly limited so although planners sitting in the audience may believe that they are hearing 'everyone's' perspective, certain filters act to screen and reduce the narrative. Even when 'affected people' are invited to give a presentation, their experience is organized in particular ways. In 2009, a number of Toll Bar residents, who had become particularly and eloquently vocal about life after the floods had been invited to speak at a national planning event. The letter of invitation, in the jargon of the UK Civil Service, asked them to speak for no more than 25 minutes and to submit their 'PowerPoint slides' two weeks in advance (field notes, May 2009).

The women did have access to computers but were not employed in roles that involved using PowerPoint and they immediately felt alienated, saying that this event 'probably was not really for them'.[9] Outwardly, the Whitehall based planners employed strategies to ensure community engagement, but in practice they illustrate that they either do not understand how to undertake this or actually have no real interest in this kind of engagement or consultation. By requesting residents to produce only an 'overview' of their story, the most situated realities get occluded. But it is these realities that often reveal critical insights about recovery and the 'contingent labours' involved.

Of course there are numerous and competing accounts of any emergency. An official narrative is written/presented by emergency planners and other 'official actors' in one specific register, using terminology from a particular lexicon. It is promoted through specific artefacts, such as 'debrief reports' that are given meaning when they are shared by other emergency planners. Clarke points out that this is primarily concerned with making organizations work better, respond better, plan better. 'But much of this . . . is about how organizations create the categories in the first place. As they create those categories they fashion a language with which to speak about uncertainty' (Clarke, 1999: 136).

Consider this extract from the Pitt Review:

> The floods that struck much of the country during June and July 2007 were extreme, affecting hundreds of thousands of people in England and Wales. It was the most serious inland flood since 1947. In the exceptional events that took place, 13 people lost their lives, approximately 48,000 households and nearly 7,300 businesses were flooded and billions of pounds of damage was caused. In Yorkshire and Humberside, the Fire and Rescue Service launched the 'biggest rescue effort in peacetime Britain'. (Pitt, 2008: 3)

Pitt received numerous submissions from flood-damaged communities, but more commonly their interpreters. In this extract, there is an attempt to convey the scale of the floods; to include deaths, injuries, homes but the narrative is still constructed through operational facts and statistics and there is almost no sense of space or place or person within the discussion. As Law points out, there is no method here for simultaneously juggling the social and the technical (1991: 8). Emergency planning speaks of the 'technical' easily enough, and then tries to bring in the 'social', but cannot shake off the technical frame.

Since 2008 the Cabinet Office produces a biennial register of the major risks facing the UK. This is a tool available online to demonstrate to both emergency planners and the public where risk management strategies need to be focused (eg terrorism, pandemic flu). Influenced by studies following the 2001 UK foot and mouth disease disaster (Mort *et al.*, 2005) a new category was introduced into this National Risk Register in 2010: there would now be an assessment of 'psychological impact'. However, the extract in Figure 3 illustrates that the discourse about how people are affected by emergencies is framed in terms of facts and statistics: 'ten different types of disruption are to be taken into account, from an inability to gain access to healthcare or schools to interrup-

> **Social disruption** – the disruption to people's daily lives.
>
> Ten different types of disruption are taken into account, from an inability to gain access to healthcare or schools to interruptions in supplies of essential services like electricity or water and to the need for evacuation of individuals from an area. In addition, the National Risk Assessment (but not, at present, Community Risk Registers) also attempts to estimate the psychological impact emergencies may have. This includes widespread changes to patterns of behaviour or anxiety, loss of confidence or outrage that may be felt by communities throughout the country as the result of an emergency. (Cabinet Office, 2010)

Figure 3: *Extract from the National Risk Register, 2010.*
Source: National Risk Register, 2010 released to the public on 22 March 2010.

tions in supplies of essential services like electricity or water and to the need for evacuation of individuals from an area (Cabinet Office, 2010).' Despite naming this 'social disruption', these cannot recognize the messier aspects of disaster such as relationship breakdown, alcoholism, suicide, domestic violence.

The intermingling (and sometimes unhappy co-existence) of a multiplicity of stories after disaster has been explored by authors such as Phil Scraton (1999), writing about the aftermath of the 1989 Hillsborough football stadium disaster and John Law's exploration of multiple perspectives on the Ladbroke Grove rail disaster. Each narrative has its own truth and there is competition for them to be heard:

> There is a regional dimension to the Ladbroke Grove Rail Inquiry. There are pigeon-holes for this, and pigeonholes for that. Different days deal with different topics. And different bodies with an interest in the outcome of the Inquiry are represented, bodies which occupy a patch of socio-technical space, together with the rights, duties, responsibilities, problems and benefits which go with that space. (Law, 2000: 3)

There appears to be a link between dominant narratives of emergency and the roots of emergency planning and management as a discipline in a masculine, militaristic culture.[10] Emergency planners, predominantly men, often embark on a second career in later life after many years of military or police service. They bring their past training with them and there were no additional formal qualifications required to become an emergency planner (Coles and Easthope, 2009). This militaristic and civil defence paradigm creates an unfavourable context for other stories to be articulated; emergency planners express an acceptance that these other stories are important but ultimately have little time for debates on multiple perspectives.

Adhering to the classical unities of drama, the 'Aristotelian rules of plot', much critiqued by Erikson (1994, 2008), the official narrative has a beginning, middle and an end; it is coherent and the role provided for each actor/actant is clear. There are opportunities for certain actors to contribute to the formalized, 'on the record' emergency planning narrative in the UK such as in debriefing events held for the response agencies, to public inquiries, inquests and court proceedings. In Doncaster the official narrative was promulgated through reports produced by elected council members, submissions to the Pitt Inquiry between 2007 and 2009, and a 'lessons learned' event for emergency planners. The notion that there is definitive and objective knowledge about producing recovery is, however, an illusion. As Manuel Tironi (this volume) describes, 'disasters dissolve any attempt to draw teleological diagrams' and the abundance of meaning exploding out from them challenges a neat framing within the boundaries of pre-event, event and post-event.

In her argument for situated knowledges, Haraway calls for doctrine and practice that 'privileges contestation, deconstruction, passionate construction, webbed connections, and hope for transformation of systems for knowledge and ways of seeing' (Haraway, 1988: 585). However, there was little opportunity to undertake this contestation, construction, transformation at the national 'Recovery Planning' events held in 2007–2011 and attended by the authors. Many of the presenters at these events stated that the community must be 'engaged with' as part of the recovery plan. But the language used was simply not the language of the local communities, or indeed the vast majority of the population not engaged in emergency planning and response.

> It is a principle of recovery that it must be conducted at the local level with the active participation of the affected community and a strong reliance on local capacities and expertise. (Field notes, September 2011)[11]

A statement such as the above cloaks the entire process of talking with people, helping people and assisting them to access information and resources, in mystery. This suggests that the way that emergency planning is done actually impedes the meaningful engagement of those affected by the emergency and stifles other voices from the start. Emergency planners don't always know how to ask questions, listen to answers and avoid alienation of the residents at the earliest stages of a supposed 'process of engagement'.

The resulting technologies are blind to the subtleties that affect both recovery and also preparedness for future emergencies such as hope and trust, for example trusting that the emergency planners would be able to prevent a future flood now they had seen what had happened and how to stop it. There were times when Toll Bar residents openly challenged the official narratives.

> 'I don't know who they thought they were writing it for . . .'. (Field notes, September 2011)

This comment was made during a scathing critique of a new draft document sent out by the UK Environment Agency. The 'opinions' of residents had been sought but it was felt that this consultation was, in residents' words, a 'tick box exercise' (field notes, September 2011). Other, different, competing narratives of what was happening in Toll Bar were not always heard at these official events, but they were aired elsewhere:

> How many times have we said this? Are we interested in the process or are we interested in the product? This is about doing things right and doing the right things and I think that's what, that's what we did. I know what WE did and I'm not saying it didn't happen anywhere else, but when we had to do something we did it. How many people went out on Saturday evenings knocking on doors asking people if they wanted washing machines and cookers and things like that. (Discussion Group with local responders, June 2008)

In the above quotation it is the responders who are demonstrating that they have seen that there are critical gaps in the official guidance. However, this alienation of the residents' experiences, coupled with a close relationship between local responders and local residents, does leave both space and support for the creation of new local recovery practices to be 'trialled' and the official protocols to be transformed: in practice, in Toll Bar local responders and local residents reformed and reimagined the guidance. Below we focus specifically on an account of one meeting to show the way in which this happened.

Toll Bar gets put on the map: reclaiming 'the recovery'

> It's nice to have Pam . . . she is a voice for us. (Discussion group transcript, March 2008)

Much of what was observed in the first year after the flood involved day-to-day efforts by residents to reclaim their lives. The effort that was required to function while living in caravans, managing children, visiting the laundry, arranging the delivery of new possessions was a major burden. However, in the second year, it became clear that as some people returned to their refurbished homes they were galvanized to undertake activities that would rebuild their community and also prepare it for future flooding. Measures that were put in place by residents as an initial response to the flooding stayed in place.

One resident, Pam Sutton, had a sister in London who ran a 'One O'clock Club' in a school. This was a meeting of local residents using a school room and Pam explained that she 'decided to copy the idea' in the aftermath of the floods (field notes, December 2011). Just weeks after the floods Pam initiated this on a Monday at the primary school in Toll Bar as a way of 'bringing the community together' (field notes, December 2011).

Pam talked frequently about wanting to bring the villagers together and how the village had lost its identity over the years before the floods. This became a particularly strong theme during and immediately after the flooding when the residents felt that they had been forgotten and abandoned. In echoes of commonly held beliefs about New Orleans (Lee, 2006), residents even raised concerns that flood water had been specifically diverted into the village to protect the newly built college and commercial sector in the town centre:

> Pam says: 'The Council has done us proud . . . although we were a compromise . . . we were cheaper to redo than the rest of the town or The Hub (the newly built college)', I ask her what she means by this and she says that she does believe that the water was diverted and Toll Bar was sacrificed to save the newer city centre areas. This is a view many residents have expressed to me but the council strongly deny. It is a view that the Mayor openly mocked in his presentation to emergency planners in June 2008. (Field notes, April 2009)

In their earliest days in the rest centres, residents were expressing concerns that the Council would use the flooding as a reason to 'erase' Toll Bar. They feared dispersal across the rest of Doncaster and the closure of the badly damaged primary school. This then influenced their concerns that the village was being marginalized. Pam, with support from members of the 'One O'clock Club' and local responders, frequently mentioned that there was nothing to mark the entrances to the village. Toll Bar was just 'merged' between two other villages. She worked with the local council to obtain funding for stone signage to welcome drivers and visitors entering Toll Bar (see Figure 4).

The marker stones took many months to arrange (completion of grant forms and national funding applications and local government contract tenders) but when they were positioned they were a clear, obvious symbol that the village was 'still there':

> Pam says very fervently that the one good thing from all this is that Toll Bar is now on the map . . . 'we fought for that..we had to have a disaster to get a Christmas tree with lights on in the village.' They tell me that before the floods the council Christmas lights used to go up in Bentley and Askern on either side, but they would leave out Toll Bar. They had to rely on the lady with the paper shop who used to put lights in her big windows. 'We got bins in the village too' Pam adds. The stones at the entrance clearly are part of this naming and valuing that they feel has been omitted in the past. (Field notes, April 2009)

With a number of other residents and support from Rosalind McDonagh, the Emergency Planner at Doncaster Council, Pam went on to form a group that would alert the rest of the community to a possible flood:

> Pam says she has become a flood warden so that she can be kept informed . . . . 'You need to be involved to get the information'. Pam says how she now has arrangements with friends to let each other know as soon as they hear anything. (Field notes, April 2009)

This group of residents, some in their 60s and 70s, now undertake flood prevention measures: taking it in turns to walk the length of the problematic Ea Beck[12] and feed back to the Environment Agency any problems such as obstructions they find. In December 2011 we watched as Pam and another resident spoke at a Cabinet Office event to explain this work to other communities. They

Figure 4: *The welcome stones placed at the entrances to the village.*
Source: *Photography by L. Easthope, 2009.*

reflected that since 2007 they had been given new powers[13] as residents to do things such as close roads and to speak directly to the Environment Agency. The local council responders, working collaboratively, arranged to fund the radios and torches and fluorescent jackets for the residents.

One resident said:

> . . . in 2007 we were on the Outside but now we are on the Inside. Now if we ring up and say there is a problem they [the EA and the Council] listen to us. (Field notes, November 2011)

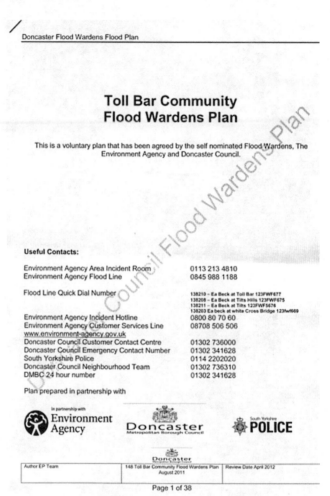

Figure 5: *Toll Bar community flood wardens plan.*
Source: Doncaster Metropolitan Borough Council, 2009.

This group of concerned residents was then described, documented, written about as 'self nominated flood wardens' (Figure 5). They had become 'something else', not just residents, and were now named actors within new technologies of recovery.

These plans in paper and electronic form were an important part of this change in Toll Bar. They gave the residents' new status, permanence and transferability. These documents could be transferred between residents, the police or the Environment Agency in advance of the flood and therefore allowed Pam and the others to be 'on the inside' of a future response. The differences and discrepancies between the National Recovery Guidance and the local practices have

The Sociological Review, 62:S1, pp. 135–158 (2014), DOI: 10.1111/1467-954X.12127

enabled something new to happen here: Whatmore and Landström (2011) explain that these differences are:

> important in the context of flooding in which controversies often centre on discrepancies between the firsthand experience of flood events, the vernacular knowledge accumulated in affected localities, and the flood science that informs 'evidence-based' flood-risk management.

Their work draws on involvement with a group of social and natural scientists working with flooded residents, 'to interrogate the science that informs local flood management and intervene in the public controversy to which it had given rise'. A particular synergy with the Toll Bar study is how Whatmore and Landström focus on the artifacts that 'mediated a collective flood apprenticeship in Ryedale' and were then 'recharged as publicity devices through which the working practices and knowledge claims . . . gathered political force in the wake of the group's work' (2011: 585). In Toll Bar too, these artefacts of flooding recovery became potent devices of mediation that scaffolded attempts to support a recovering community.

Only by understanding the way that technological change is contingent is it possible to comprehend how recommendations in a government inquiry report written in Whitehall (the Pitt Review) are inextricably linked to a collective of people who walk the length of a river every four weeks; stopping for cakes baked by the children of an emergency planner, who walks alongside them. The recommendations of greater community engagement and the use of flood warden schemes made by the Pitt Review were to be followed up/enacted/audited. How they were to be enacted was a local affair. The strategic support meant that some resources were available, accessed through new instruments. Toll Bar has now been described, by 'outsiders', as having an 'effective' flood wardens scheme. In fact this was shaped by its history, politics and people. There was no internal logic here, no cause and effect: Pitt did not recommend something that the planners then put in place. Nor did the residents engineer this on their own. The flood warden's scheme was heterogeneously engineered by local residents and local council responders, using resources and shaping recovery technologies created far away.

The meeting

To effect what happened next in Toll Bar required a network that could link together heterogeneous and disparate groups and individuals. Residents and council responders were both part of this network. Together they began to shape the physical recovery tools: the texts such as community flood plans, the equipment (a flood response box and their own fluorescent jackets). How this was done was often most visible at occasions when the council responders and residents came together.

In September 2011 a 'Flood Wardens' meeting was held in a refurbished community building located opposite the school. Rosalind from the Council was attending with a colleague, and a representative from the Cabinet Office. Previous encounters at early public meetings after the flood had been tense, uncomfortable experiences where the women of the village seemed cowed and diminished. This 2011 meeting could not have been more different: the chairs were arranged on all four sides of a square and there was no 'top or bottom'. Pam chaired the meeting but was sat amongst other residents. The meeting broke off while a cup of tea was made and there was some hilarity over which guest had brought the best biscuits; the Cabinet Office representative or the researcher (he had brought chocolate biscuits as well and laughs saying: 'Lucy said you will expect good biscuits').

A further difference was the presence of Easthope's seven-month-old daughter Elizabeth at the meeting. She started off in her pushchair listening to the voices intently and nodding at key points, which led to much laughter around the table. Rosalind leant over and lifted her out of the pushchair; she was then opposite Pam and started to engage her in a game of 'Peepo'. The meeting came to a halt while this game was played.

> There is never any sense that the meeting is outside of Pam's control: she allows the chatter and the laughter, laughs herself and then moves on to the next point. Everyone gets a chance to speak and a photocopy of letters of correspondence between Pam and the Cabinet Office and Pam and the Environment Agency and the handwritten notes of the previous meeting are passed amongst us. Later, copies of these documents will also be distributed to villagers (by Pam, who goes door to door) who cannot make the meeting but have asked to be kept informed. She addresses many of the issues at this particular meeting specifically to the colleague from the Cabinet Office with the preface of: 'You'll want to know this' or 'You can take this back with you'. She has copies of everything for him. Later the Cabinet Office representative thanks Pam and Rosalind: 'a lovely day' and says he: 'has never attended a meeting like it'. (Field notes, September 2011)

As Figure 6 shows, the notes of the meeting were later written in longhand, flowing script by Pam. Rosalind understands this from her position as intermediary and explains to us later that this is how the residents say they want it. They do not want the council to type them up despite this offer being made. Pam writes them out and arranges for them to be copied and distributed to residents.

Perhaps, here a new technology is created. It is different from something that the Council would produce on its headed notepaper and 'Microsoft Word' template but it has many of the same intentions. These notes allow the 'recovery' to be carried and transported to other villagers and then to other, more distant audiences such as the Cabinet Office. It does not matter that these notes are not formally typed: they will still get things done and enable new things to be enacted. The residents' actions are no less potent by being less 'formal': in this handwritten form they are personal and real. The residents also could retain control over the notes by not allowing them to be 'typed up'. Almost four years after the flood happened, this group of residents' relationship with the Council and in some respects the Government, is transformed.

The Sociological Review, 62:S1, pp. 135–158 (2014), DOI: 10.1111/1467-954X.12127

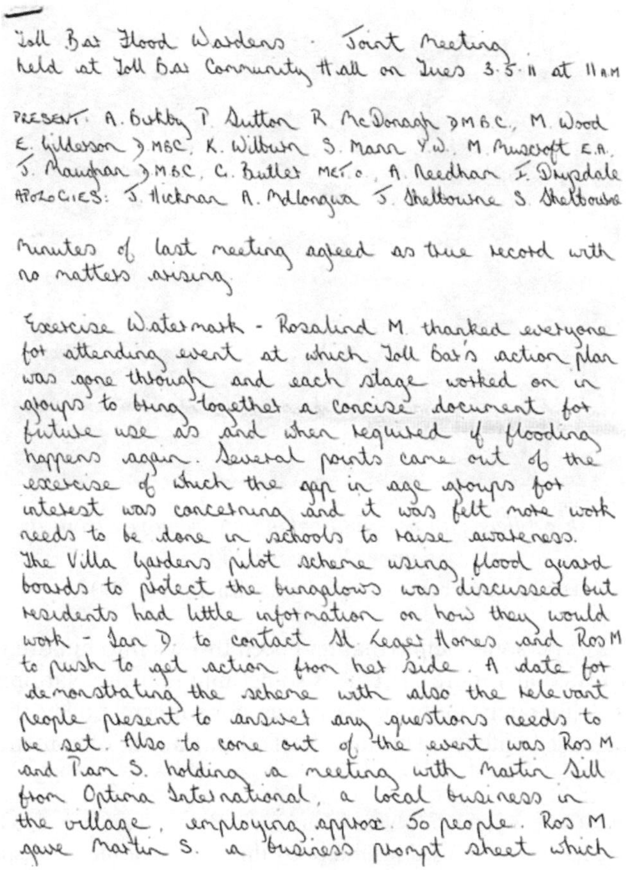
Toll Bar Flood Wardens · Joint Meeting
held at Toll Bar Community Hall on Tues 3.5.11 at 11AM

PRESENT: A. Bukby P. Sutton R McDonagh DMBC, M. Wood
E. Gilderson DMBC, K. Wilburn S. Mann Y.W. M Muscroft E.A.
J. Maughan DMBC, C. Butler MET.O, A. Needham I. Drysdale
APOLOGIES: J. Hickman A. Mdlongwa J. Shelbourne S. Shelbourne

Minutes of last meeting agreed as true record with no matters arising

Exercise Watermark - Rosalind M. thanked everyone for attending event at which Toll Bar's action plan was gone through and each stage worked on in groups to bring together a concise document for future use as and when required if flooding happens again. Several points came out of the exercise of which the gap in age groups for interest was concerning and it was felt more work needs to be done in schools to raise awareness. The Villa Gardens pilot scheme using flood guard boards to protect the bungalows was discussed but residents had little information on how they would work - Ian D. to contact St Leger Homes and Ros M to push to get action from her side. A date for demonstrating the scheme with also the relevant people present to answer any questions needs to be set. Also to come out of the event was Ros M and Pam S. holding a meeting with Martin Sill from Optima International, a local business in the village, employing approx. 50 people. Ros M gave Martin S. a business prompt sheet which

Figure 6: *Handwritten notes of Flood Wardens meeting (September 2011).*
Source: Toll Bar Flood Wardens Group.

Replacing lost items

The need for something different to be co-produced by residents and council responders first appeared in relation to lost personal items from the homes of the residents. Here, a deviation was necessary from the 'pathway' specified in the National Recovery Guidance (NRG). The politics of transformation in Toll Bar is not a story of obvious dissent and conflict. Instead where the NRG was mute or did not match the situated realities of life in this place the residents and the local responders found their only option was to work around the guidance. The situated responders came to see that the technologies of recovery would not work here without transformation.

A critical issue concerned uninsured residents, that is, those who did not have a contents insurance policy and therefore did not have a financial 'safety net' to

Figure 7: *A skip filled with personal belongings removed from the residents' homes, February 2008.*
Source: Photography by L. Easthope, 2007.

replace their lost personal items (that had been thrown into hundreds of council skips as illustrated at Figure 7). This is something that the National Recovery Guidance is deliberately mute on as it was government policy that everyone should have house contents insurance. In Toll Bar a lack of contents insurance was endemic:

> They say a lot of people didn't have insurance and now some people who are trying to get some, have been refused insurance by three different high-risk specialist companies. Those that have claimed on it can't seem to get renewals ... she (the responder) was surprised when she found out how few people had insurance at the start and thought 'everyone would have it'. They tell me about the set of bungalows in Toll Bar that is occupied by the elderly. As they were bungalows, there was no upstairs to take things to and everything was ruined. The responder said that because the people were old she had assumed that they would be good with money and would have something like insurance but they didn't.. She says that they lost everything. It was heartbreaking as they had to watch everything they owned being put into skips in the front garden. She says that she can't see why insurance isn't taken out with rent [for council house residents]. (Field notes, March 2008)

In its guidance document 'Dealing with Insurance Issues' (Cabinet Office, 2011) the National Recovery Working Group set out starkly its stance towards the uninsured:

> Dealing with the uninsured: Although Local Authorities have discretionary powers to commit expenditure in an emergency situation, Section 138 of the LG act 1972 and amended by Section 156 LG and Housing Act 1989, this is not usually used to cover the costs of the uninsured, but rather to fund the response and to deal with welfare needs of those affected. (Cabinet Office, 2011)

The Sociological Review, 62:S1, pp. 135–158 (2014), DOI: 10.1111/1467-954X.12127

It also promotes the following statistics on the downloadable template:

93% of all homeowners have Home Buildings insurance in place, although this falls to 85% of the poorest 10% of households owning their own home. This insurance is a standard condition of a mortgage . . . . . . 75% of all households have Home Contents insurance in place . . . Half of the poorest 10% of households do not have Home Contents insurance. (Cabinet Office, 2011)

These figures become highly problematic in an area such as Toll Bar where there is a high number of low-income households and a much diminished uptake of contents insurance. The local council responders had to deal with this issue as it affected so many people, but this meant much more than just a deviation from the guidance documents. They instead had to develop an entire strategy themselves. They had to 'get around' the strong resistance expressed in the official guidance to funding or assisting uninsured residents. There was also equally strong resistance from other residents who had prioritized insurance. As one (insured) resident said: 'We don't have a Sky subscription but they do, and then they got help for not being insured' (field notes, March 2008).

However, the lack of insurance actually also presented an opportunity in Toll Bar. It was, in the first few months after the floods, an early example of co-production of recovery. Without this deviation from the guidance, many residents would have been unable to replace many of their lost items. Solutions involved utilizing support that was available from voluntary organizations and church groups, but with local responders acting as a gateway to put uninsured residents in touch with organizations that were supplying free electrical goods as a charitable gesture or grants for the purchase of small items. As one responder said to me:

What else were we supposed to do . . . these were people with nothing . . . we could have obeyed the official guidance but there were two little kids in there and just bare floors. (Informal discussion with Neighbourhood Management Team members, March 2008)

A further deviation in Toll Bar, and an opportunity for residents and responders to collaborate, was the embracing of donated items and other charitable items:

At a conference last week they mentioned that people in the UK don't tend to accept second hand and charitable items after floods but here I notice a big poster entitled 'List of Donated Items' with things like 'pair of curtains' on it. In an accompanying newsletter that I read it says that this is proving popular with people being able to swap things and you should bring along your things. (Field notes, January 2008)

The entanglement of council responders (the Neighbourhood Management Team) and residents, who were physically placed together, and whose lives entwined through cups of tea and frozen pipes and sandbags meant that omissions in the National Guidance could be worked around locally. The production of these solutions also enabled the forging of relationships, which sustained throughout this work and served to scaffold it:

> They need you as well, you feel like the community needs you. (Discussion Group with Neighbourhood Team, June 2009)

> What the local council have set up that and they're a wonderful team, and it's not just for the council people they've done it for all the people in the village . . . they've really been supportive of everybody in the village. And you know, I just hope that it continues and I don't want them to leave (laughs). (DMBC, 2008)[14]

> Is it all going to regress [if Toll Bar neighbourhood team is wound up]. You can't just do that to a community. They need support. We're the fourth most-deprived school in Doncaster. I don't want you to go. Things would deteriorate. Other people in the community have told me the same. You've got ideas, you don't sit in an office and do nothing, you carry out tasks, you listen to people, and it's working together as a team with everybody, with the school and the community. I think that's what makes the difference, I really do. It's been a unique experience that I don't want to lose it. (DMBC, 2008)

> Oh no I don't want them to leave, they've been fabulous for the school and the neighbourhood, for the school and the community. We've been able to work together for the betterment of the community really . . . they've been really useful. (DMBC, 2008)

Conclusions

The National Recovery Guidance was provided to emergency planners by the Cabinet Office to help them 'produce' recovery in localized settings. Generic and applicable to multiple situations, once these instruments arrived in Toll Bar they began to be locally re-imagined. Perhaps this transformation is unremarkable, for Toll Bar after the floods is like all of the social world: 'multiple and para-doxical' (Ashmore *et al.*, 1989: 192). Generic tools get appropriated at a local level. Plans and protocols leave the environment in which are created (White-hall) and are then reformulated by residents and responders. The daily interaction and entanglement of local residents and local council responders allowed the Guidance created far away to be made to work locally. This process has often been explored in Science and Technology Studies. What became visible is that, like so many other 'social technologies', technologies of recovery, when appropriated by new users were capable of being 'employed in ways quite different from those which were originally intended' (Bijker and Law, 1992: 8). Using the Guidance and intermediaries to access grant money for a carnival or for a commemorative stone placed in a garden created by men and women who came together at a club initiated by one resident was a novel act, part of the politics of recovery. Each time technologies of recovery are used in this way they get reshaped a little. They are not on a trajectory of change powered by their own momentum, they continue to be shaped by the way that they are put to work.

But the politics does become remarkable. It became clear that what was being observed in the localized setting was not always a story of 'them and us'. Council staff found themselves co-located with displaced residents, boundaries began to dissolve and the Neighbourhood Management Team, for the first time, were seen as 'on the same side' as the residents. This was an emergency where the operational responders were placed within the recovery, so proximately and for such a long period of time, that identities began to merge – people were 'in this together'. What was also remarkable was that this co-production had ever been allowed to happen at all. As described in the introduction, this entanglement of council responders and local residents was precarious. Residents slowly began to engage with their council neighbours and experience joint working, whereas before the floods there had been times of little engagement and minimal trust. What began as a fragile relationship, slowly strengthened, could so easily never have happened.

The presence of the Guidance and its material forms served an additional purpose as reassurance, and this reassurance played its part in forming these relationships. Initially for planners, when faced with scenes of devastation and incongruous images of displaced people setting up home in community centres, or personal possessions mingling with wastewater and rubble in streets, a template that appears to categorize chaos into workable themes and then provide a lead for action is essential. Also initially, for residents, the presence of actors wearing jackets embellished with official logos and holding clipboards (containing documents to which they, residents, have not had access) provides the impression that experts have specialist knowledge which will necessarily help them. However, in the process of 'meeting the locals' (in the shape of people, spaces, intermediaries, local temporalities) what was a reduced and distilled approach requiring the erasure of those features, instead got entangled with them. As we said in the introduction, the flooding of Toll Bar is not a one-off event but part of a way of life, part of what it means to live in that place. Entangled responders and residents, placed together, co-produced a transformed set of practices which enabled other things to happen. Such transformation may also be omitted from the official narratives and analysis of life after disaster and instead, once again, much of the variety, dilemmas and tensions may be occluded. In the wake of the disaster at Toll Bar, entangled politics produced a recovery which could be recognized locally and processed nationally.

The many factors that collided to form a perfect storm in the recovery of Toll Bar shaped outcomes that may be unique and may certainly be problematic to replicate. A different set of factors may collide in other places to produce an aftermath that is so very different. Guidance on how to perform 'recovery' to effect any positive action must take these networks and intersections into account. By remoulding recovery instruments both residents and responders showed that they never saw the technologies as static; they took them and made them do something that needed to be done. Together, they had found a way to make the technologies work in this place.

Acknowledgements

We wish to acknowledge the support of all the residents and the responders of Toll Bar who contributed to this study.

Notes

1 As part of the study Easthope staged an exhibition with local responders and local residents that displayed art work, poetry, video testimonies relating not just to the 2007 floods but to the many years of earlier flooding. This included records that demonstrated over 700 years of flooding in that area of Doncaster.
2 Easthope has worked in the UK field of emergency planning for 15 years.
3 A 'grass' is a colloquial term for somebody who informs on other members of the community to the police (eg for a crime) or to the local council (eg for benefit fraud).
4 'People don't think we are grassing any more. I will come back here' (field notes, April 2008).
5 An electronic key that provides Internet access.
6 Easthope was a member of these working groups and was able to draw on her notes here.
7 An example of its inclusion in a hospital emergency plan is at p. 21 on the webpage www.miltonkeynes-northamptonshire.nhs.uk//resources/uploads/files/PH_10.pdf (accessed 8 February 2013).
8 7/7 refers to the terrorist attacks by four suicide bombers that occurred in London, 7 July 2005. Lockerbie refers to the terrorist bombing of a Pan Am airline, which blew up over 800 square miles of England and Scotland. The majority of the wreckage devastated the Scottish town of Lockerbie and killed 11 people on the ground as well as the 259 people on the plane. Buncefield was an oil storage depot in Hertfordshire that caught fire and became Europe's biggest peacetime blaze.
9 Field notes, May 2009.
10 Characteristics such as nurturing or listening may be derided. This can be illustrated through the use of the derisory term *'pink and fluffy'* by emergency planning practitioners and emergency responders to describe either negatively or apologetically any work that is related to supporting people after death and disaster. Anne Eyre (2007: 29) explores the way in which the specific term, 'pink and fluffy' is directed towards Police Family Liaison Officers deployed to support families after sudden deaths. It is used with other derogatory phrases such as their work being concerned with 'hand holding'.
11 'Recovery Planning' presentation by Lincolnshire Emergency Planning Unit in 2011.
12 This beck was identified as a major cause of much of the flooding in Toll Bar and surrounding villages. Since 2007 it has been a focus for much of the improvement works carried out by the Environment Agency.
13 These are not statutory powers but by this they mean that the 'official' response agencies have 'given' them a role in the response.
14 In 2008 Doncaster Metropolitan Borough Council (DMBC) commissioned a research student to gather opinions of the Neighbourhood Management Team. The council supplied the authors with the data and with the report supplied to the council. They had asked team members, residents, other local responders and primary school teachers to reflect on their experiences in the year after the floods.

References

Ashmore, M., Mulkay, M. and Pinch, T., (1989), *Health and Efficiency: A Sociology of Health Economics*, Milton Keynes: Open University Press.

The Sociological Review, 62:S1, pp. 135–158 (2014), DOI: 10.1111/1467-954X.12127

Bijker, W. and Law, J., (1992), *Shaping Technology/ Building Society*, Cambridge, MA: MIT Press.

Bloomfield, B. and Vurdubakis, T., (1997), 'Paper traces: inscribing organizations and information technology', in B. Bloomfield, R. Coombs, D. Knights and D. Littler (eds), *Information Technology and Organizations: Strategies, Networks and Integration*, Oxford: Oxford University Press.

Cabinet Office, (2007), *National Recovery Guidance*, available at: http://webarchive.nationalarchives.gov.uk/+/http://www.cabinetoffice.gov.uk/ukresilience/response/recovery_guidance/generic_issues/structures_processing.aspx (accessed 8 February 2013).

Cabinet Office, (2010), *National Risk Register*, available at: www.gov.uk/government/publications/national-risk-register-of-civil-emergencies (accessed 1 May 2013).

Cabinet Office, (2011), *National Recovery Guidance – Infrastructure Issues – Dealing with Insurance Issues*, available at: www.gov.uk/national-recovery-guidance-infrastructure-issues#dealing-with-insurance-issues (accessed 1 May 2013).

Clarke, L., (1999), *Mission Improbable*, Chicago: University of Chicago Press.

Coles, E. and Easthope, L., (2009), 'Back to school qualifications, competences and cultural change', presentation to the FEMA HE event, Washington 2009 and reproduced in *Blueprint – Journal of the Emergency Planning Society*, Autumn: 22–24.

Cooren, F., (2004), 'Textual agency: how texts do things in organisational settings', *Organization*, 11 (3): 373–393.

Doncaster Metropolitan Borough Council (DMBC), (2008), 'Neighbourhood Management Team Data – Notes', unpublished.

Doncaster Metropolitan Borough Council (DMBC), (2011), 'Presentation given by emergency planners', Emergency Planning Society Conference, Coventry, UK, July.

Erikson, K., (1994), *A New Species of Trouble*, New York: W.W. Norton & Co.

Erikson, K., (2008), 'Preface', in I. Convery, M. Mort, J. Baxter and C. Bailey, *Animal Disease and Human Trauma: Emotional Geographies of Disaster*, Basingstoke: Palgrave Macmillan.

Eyre, A., (2007), 'Family first', *Police Review*, 14 December: 28–31.

Haraway, D., (1988), 'Situated knowledges: the science question in feminism and the privilege of the partial perspective', *Feminist Studies*, 14 (3): 575–599.

Harrison, S. and Mort, M., (1998), 'Which champions, which people? Public and user involvement in healthcare as a technology of legitimation', *Social Policy and Administration*, 32 (1): 60–70.

Heath, C., Luff, P. and Svensson, M., (2003), 'Technology and medical practice', *Sociology of Health and Illness*, 25: 75–96.

Law, J. (ed.), (1991), *A Sociology of Monsters: Essays on Power, Technology and Domination*, London: Routledge.

Law, J., (1994), *Organizing Modernity*, Oxford: Blackwell.

Law, J., (2000), 'Ladbroke Grove, or how to think about failing systems', Centre for Science Studies, Lancaster University, available at: www.lancs.ac.uk/fass/sociology/research/publications/papers/law-ladbroke-grove-failing-systems.pdf (accessed 1 May 2013).

Lee, S., (2006), *When the Levees Broke: A Requiem in Four Acts*, Home Box Office.

Mort, M., Convery, I., Baxter, J. and Bailey, C., (2005), 'Psychosocial effects of the 2001 UK foot and mouth disease epidemic in a rural population: qualitative diary-based study', *British Medical Journal*, 331 (1234): doi: 10.1136/bmj.38603.375856.68.

Pinch, T., Ashmore, M. and Mulkay, M., (1992), 'Technology, testing, text': clinical budgeting in the UK National Health Service', in W. Bijker and J. Law (eds), *Shaping Technology/ Building Society*, 265–289, Cambridge, MA: MIT Press.

Pitt, M., (2008), *Learning Lessons from the 2007 Floods: An Independent Review by Sir Michael Pitt*, available at: http://webarchive.nationalarchives.gov.uk/20100807034701/http://archive.cabinetoffice.gov.uk/ (accessed 1 May 2013).

Scraton, P., (1999), *Hillsborough: The Truth*, Edinburgh: Mainstream Publishing.

The Sociological Review, 62:S1, pp. 135–158 (2014), DOI: 10.1111/1467-954X.12127

Suchman, L., (2007), *Human – Machine Reconfigurations: Plans and Situated Actions*, 2nd edn, Cambridge: Cambridge University Press.

UK Emergency Planning Society, (2011), *Condition Critical: The EPS Resilience Symposium*, Conference web page (archived).

Whatmore, S. and Landström, C., (2011), 'Flood apprentices: an exercise in making things public', *Economy and Society*, 40 (4): 582–610.

Section 3
Preparedness: Anticipation

Creating a secure network: the 2001 anthrax attacks and the transformation of postal security

Ryan Ellis

Abstract: The 2001 anthrax attacks transformed the US postal network into a site of uncertainty and danger. Five individuals died as a result of anthrax exposure, while 22 individuals were infected; estimates place the cost of the attacks, including sanitation and lost revenue, at $6 billion. The attacks highlighted the limitations and particularities of pre-existing biological-defence efforts and led to the adoption of new practices of postal security. In this article I examine the failure of pre-attack planning and critically analyse the creation and implementation of new security standards within the postal network in the wake of the 2001 attacks. Through archival research conducted at the Smithsonian Institution and documents obtained under the Freedom of Information Act (FOIA), the article traces the politics inscribed within the architecture of new security technologies. The creation of new forms of security was a contentious and fraught process that brought together a cross-section of interest groups, including postal labour, large-volume mailers, and postal management. Ultimately, however, these new forms of security serve to reinforce, rather than disrupt, pre-existing structures of power. New security practices serve the interests of large-volume commercial mailers – long-entrenched and central players in postal politics – at the expense of postal workers and the general public. The article emphasizes the possibilities and limitations of disasters to create moments of disruption and undergird new political interventions.

Keywords: infrastructure, risk, information and communication technologies

In 2001 an unknown number of letters containing spores of anthrax were sent through the US postal system, exposing scores of postal workers and patrons to possible harm.[1] Five individuals died as a result of anthrax exposure (22 were infected); while over 30,000 people were given prophylactic antibiotic treatment (Dellafera, 2007; Inglesby *et al.*, 2002: 2237). According to estimates compiled by the National Research Council, one-third of the US population took extra precautions in handling the mail during the attacks (Committee on Standards and Policies for Decontaminating, 2005: 1–22). The economic impact of the attacks was staggering: clean-up of postal facilities ran into the hundreds of

The Sociological Review, 62:S1, pp. 161–182 (2014), DOI: 10.1111/1467-954X.12128

millions of dollars, while declines in letter volume, productivity and new security measures amounted to roughly $6 billion (Committee on Standards and Policies for Decontaminating, 2005: 1; Congressional Research Service [CRS] 2002a, 2002b; Potter, 2001). Suddenly, one of the more mundane aspects of daily life – opening the mail – became imbued with danger and unease. Panic ran high: hoaxes and false-alarms involving letters thought to contain anthrax became common disruptions; the investigative arm of the United States Postal Service (USPS), the United States Postal Inspection Service (USPIS), dealt with over 17,000 such incidents and evacuated over 600 postal facilities in the year following the attacks (USPIS, 2002: 12). As Chief Postal Inspector Lee Heath (2003) noted, the anthrax letters were a 'weapon of mass disruption'. While not reaching catastrophic levels of harm, the tragic deaths of five individuals compounded by widespread anxiety and far-reaching economic consequences elevated the attacks into a disaster. The attacks destabilized the continued flow of mail, imperiled, to a degree, the health of workers and patrons, and introduced potentially ruinous costs for the already financially precarious USPS.

In response to the attacks, the USPS adopted new technologies to counter further incidents of biological terrorism. The attacks – occurring just days after the terrorist strikes of 9/11 – were initially viewed through the prism of international terrorism: policymakers interpreted the letters as an indicator of the rising terrorist threat (Rhodes, 2010).[2] Defence officials and public health experts had prepared for a possible biological attack involving anthrax for decades. The 2001 attacks, however, highlighted the limitations of these pre-existing biodefence efforts and quickly spurred calls for new forms of security. The USPS eventually installed two new surveillance systems – the 'Biohazard Detection System' (BDS) and 'Intelligent Mail' – to counter future attacks. These systems of control transform the operation of the postal network in explicit and subtle ways. As will be argued in detail below, these technologies embody clear political choices and commitments: new forms of postal security privilege particular types of uses and users at the expense of others, sort suspect or at-risk network flows from 'normal' and accepted flows, and prioritize particular types of threats while ignoring others. It is within these new standards that the legacy and politics of disaster are recorded and made durable.

The politics of infrastructure security: overview and aims

The article examines the failure of pre-attack planning and the creation and installation of the BDS and Intelligent Mail. Through archival research conducted at the Smithsonian Institution and documents obtained under the Freedom of Information Act (FOIA), the article examines the politics of new forms of postal security; it considers how, by whom, and to what end new control technologies have been integrated into the postal network. Examining these systems highlights how disasters can become encoded within new infrastructure standards. As Star (1999) points out, behind the seemingly mundane

The Sociological Review, 62:S1, pp. 161–182 (2014), DOI: 10.1111/1467-954X.12128
© 2014 The Author. Editorial organisation © 2014 The Editorial Board of the Sociological Review

and normal working of infrastructures rest explicitly political decisions that are all-too-often overlooked. Opening the 'black box' of infrastructure standards uncovers conflicts and constitutive choices that otherwise remain below the surface. Ultimately, as I will show below, peering within the inner workings of new postal security practices reveals the re-entrenchment of powerful interests. The adopted forms of surveillance reproduce the prevailing hierarchies of power that dominate postal politics: the centrality of large commercial mailers, the ongoing subordination of labour, and the marginalization of the public all find clear expression within the BDS and Intelligent Mail.

While biological terrorism has been considered from a variety of vantage points within the social sciences (see Cooper, 2006), the BDS and Intelligent Mail have received little scholarly attention; the development, operation, and broader implications of these technologies have not yet been assessed. Reviewing their creation and deployment contributes to the growing literature on the politics of risk (see Beck *et al.*, 1994; Fortun, 2001; Mueller, 2006; Robin, 2004; Sunstein, 2007; Tironi, in this volume), and joins the growing discussion centring on the contemporary expansion of the use of surveillance technologies within infrastructures (see Coaffee and Wood, 2006; Graham, 2004; Lyon, 2003). The process through which new forms of security emerge is never simple or inevitable: how to build new security standards into the postal network – determining what constitutes an acceptable 'fix' for the problem of biological terrorism – was an open question subject to intense debate among postal management, commercial interests that used the network for business, and postal workers. As the work of Ulrich Beck (1992, 2009) makes clear, novel risks alone compel little. As Beck is quick to point out, risks circulate in unpredictable ways, alternately providing an impetus for new political engagement and the reordering of power, or conversely serving as a means for foreclosing political deliberation and reifying existing centres of power. It is how risks are seized and translated into action that shapes their lasting significance. Tracing the adoption of the BDS and Intelligent Mail underscores the relevance of this insight. As we will see, key interest groups are central in dictating how the disruptive potential of risks is concretized into routine practices.

At the same time, the case of postal security can be usefully seen as an example of a more general ongoing shift in infrastructure management. Both in the US and internationally, surveillance technologies are increasingly used to police infrastructure flows. Efforts to graph new forms of security onto the postal network are part of the larger post-9/11 recategorization of infrastructures as sites of danger and anxiety. As Stephen Graham (2004, 2011), Andrew Lakoff (2008), and others note, infrastructures are increasingly viewed as problematic 'insecure' spaces requiring new forms of state intervention. These 'vital systems' are seen as critical resources in need of protection (Lakoff, 2008). New security practices are reordering, in ways that are both obvious and obscure, the basic material systems that underpin daily life. Transportation systems, telecommunications networks, electric power grids, and myriad other infrastructures have seen the introduction of new barriers to access, filtering technologies, and surveillance techniques designed to counter the disruptive effects of terrorism (Graham, 2011; Lyon, 2003, 2004). New security practices require interrogation not only through the lens of normative questions concerning their efficacy, but also in reference to questions of power and social relations (Monahan, 2006). As Torin Monahan (2006) notes, when critically examining surveillance techniques, the question to be posed is not 'do they work?' but rather, 'what type of social relations do techniques of surveillance produce? How do technologies of control create or reaffirm inequalities?' Importantly, the question 'Do they work?' can be productively reframed as: For whom do they 'work'? Who is authorized to decide whether or not a particular technology is judged as a success or a failure? It is here, in examining these questions and revealing these choices, that the political implications of security technologies can be brought into focus. To understand the politics of disaster, the BDS and Intelligent Mail must be viewed through the prism of these concerns. It is precisely to these questions – and this mode of interrogation – that the article now turns.

Old fears and new challenges: the 2001 anthrax attacks and the limits of planning

The anthrax attacks of 2001 were, in many ways, unsurprising. Defence strategists and public health officials worried about the possibility of a biological attack since at least World War II. Anthrax, due to its durability and relative ease of production, often topped the list of likely agents to be used (Cieslak and Eitzen, 1999; Henderson, 1999; Inglesby, 1999; Inglesby et al., 1999; Mangold and Goldberg, 2000). Historically, planners assumed that an attack using anthrax would fall into one of two categories: a mass-casualty attack targeting a large concentrated population; or a limited-exposure attack, perhaps using the letters containing anthrax, targeting a small number of individuals. While the mass-casualty scenario received far greater attention – and had a much longer history – both models led to the development of preparedness efforts.[3]

Thomas V. Inglesby, writing in *Emerging Infectious Diseases* in 1999, offers a narrative description of the mass-casualty scenario:

> On the evening of November 1, a professional football stadium before an audience of 74,000. The evening sky is overcast; the temperature mild, a breeze blows from west to east. During the first quarter of the game, an unmarked truck drives along an elevated highway a mile upwind of the stadium. As it passes the stadium, the truck releases an aerosol of powdered anthrax over 30 seconds, creating an invisible, odorless anthrax cloud more than a third of a mile in breadth, The wind blows the cloud across the stadium . . . the anthrax is detected by no one. (Inglesby, 1999: 556)

Similar speculative formations circulated within US defence, public health, and scientific communities during the cold war, appearing in public information campaigns produced by the Federal Civil Defense Administration and the Department of Defense, and serving as the basis for numerous tests undertaken

The Sociological Review, 62:S1, pp. 161–182 (2014), DOI: 10.1111/1467-954X.12128

by the US and the World Health Organization (WHO) (see Fee and Brown, 2001; Inglesby *et al.*, 2002; Pile *et al.*, 1998; WHO, 1970). After the cold war, the model was again cited to caution against the insecure stocks of bio-weapons in the former Soviet republics, the threat posed by so-called 'rogue nations' (such as Iraq), and terrorist organizations (Henderson, 1999; US Office of Technology Assessment [OTA], 1993). In each instance, planners presumed that an attack would target an area with a high population-density, such as a subway or stadium, in order to inflict maximum harm.

A series of hoaxes during the late 1990s pointed toward another model of attack – limited exposure – and highlighted the possibility that the postal system could be used to spread anthrax. During this period, letters purporting to contain anthrax were sent to government offices, health clinics and private businesses throughout the US and Canada (Centers for Disease Control and Prevention [CDC], 1999; Kournikakis *et al.*, 2001). Although none of these letters actually contained anthrax spores – they were doctored in most instances with a harmless powder – the hoaxes pointed toward a model of attack that was far different from the continually recycled 'mass-casualty' scenario. Public health officials and postal management took note. They began to consider the possibility of a narrowly targeted attack delivered through the mail.

The mass-casualty and limited-exposure models underpinned different public health interventions (see Ethridge, 1992; Fee and Brown, 2001; Zajtchuk and Franz, 2004). The mass-casualty model sat behind a number of high-profile efforts, including: the creation of the CDC's Epidemic Intelligence Service (EIS), which placed epidemiologists in the field to watch for signs of a biological attack; the establishment of the National Pharmaceutical Stockpile; and the organization of special biohazard rapid-response teams (General Accounting Office [GAO], 1999, 2000; Ethridge, 1992). In 1999, in response to the anthrax hoaxes, the CDC released interim guidelines outlining how to respond to alleged incidents of anthrax in the mail. The USPS subsequently adopted the CDC's recommendations and issued a new management instruction, 'Emergency Response to Mail Allegedly Containing Anthrax', in October of the same year. The new policy was simple: in the event of the discovery of a suspect piece of mail, workers were to notify their supervisors, isolate the area containing the suspicious item, and wash their hands.

The limits of normative cases: the 2001 anthrax attacks

In the fall of 2001, the possibility of an anthrax attack ceased to be purely hypothetical. In late September and early October, letters packed with anthrax were sent to various media outlets in New York and Florida and the offices of Senators Tom Daschle and Patrick Leahy (Dellafera, 2007; Government Accountability Office, 2004). The actual attack looked much different from the established scenarios: it was neither a large-scale release, nor a single instance of limited-exposure. Both the mass-casualty scenario and the limited-exposure model assumed a single moment of peril and a limited, well-defined, radius of exposure. The 2001 attacks were different. The anthrax letters seemed to 'infect' the entire postal network through cross-contamination. As the malicious letters were processed, anthrax spread to other letters and postal equipment. Rather than subjecting a narrowly defined population to exposure, or impacting a few well-defined 'at-risk' sites, cross-contamination potentially exposed everyone that came into contact with the postal system to harm (GAO, 2003b).

The attacks exploited the particular architecture of the contemporary postal system. Beginning in the 1970s, the USPS invested billions of dollars in the adoption of automated equipment in order to streamline postal processing (GAO, 1997). By the late 1990s, the postal network was structured around massive centralized processing plants that relied on automated equipment. The concentration of automated processing in these dense hubs make the network cheaper and more efficient, but it also bred cross-contamination. As the initial malicious letters moved through automated postal processing equipment, spores of anthrax escaped and mixed with the regular mail. The mechanics of automated processing facilitated cross-contamination: high-speed automated processing rapidly compresses letters, forcing air and, in the case of letters filled with anthrax, spores of anthrax out of sealed envelopes through minute tears and pores in the envelopes. As the anthrax letters were processed, spores spilled out of the envelopes and travelled through the air, contaminating other pieces of mail, processing equipment, and the larger postal workspace. Spores eventually spreading to over 60 different locations is six states (GAO, 2003b). Anthrax appeared in disparate places – the Federal Reserve Board, Howard University, Walter Reed Hospital, a home in rural Connecticut, to name a few – linked only by the common thread of postal service (Center for Counterproliferation Research, 2002). CDC Director Dr Jeffrey Koplan offered a bleak assessment, stating that '[t]here seems to be the potential for not just hundreds and just thousands, but tens of thousands and maybe more letters to be potentially at risk for some level of cross-contamination' (quoted in Center for Counterproliferation Research, 2002: 73). Cross-contamination revealed a hidden downside of automation and centralized processing: the long-standing pursuit of efficient network operation created new vulnerabilities that were open to malicious appropriation (see Luke, 2004). The attacks, in this fashion, illustrate Beck's wry observation that it is the very triumphs of modernization that now produce new forms of risk (Beck, 1992, 2009).

The protocols developed by the CDC and the USPS in response to the hoaxes of the late 1990s offered little comfort. Established protocols assumed that only a letter that had been deliberately treated with anthrax was dangerous. Importantly, in-place emergency response procedures also assumed that anthrax exposure would be obvious: previous hoax letters contained explicit threats and noticeable heaps of white powder. A person who came into contact with an anthrax letter, it was assumed, would be well aware of their exposure. Neither the CDC nor the USPS previously considered the possibility of cross-contamination.[4] As instances of cross-contamination began to appear, US

Surgeon General Dr David Satcher noted the rapidly shifting landscape: 'Until a week ago, I think all of the experts would have said [that cross-contamination was not a danger]. The fact of the matter is, we were wrong' (quoted in Center for Counterproliferation Research, 2002: 45). Cross-contaminated mail did not bear suspicious markings, threatening language, or other outward signs of malicious intent. Spores of anthrax in low, though still dangerous quantities, were invisible to the naked eye; cross-contaminated mail appeared indistinguishable from the familiar mix of bills, letters, and magazines that typically arrived in mailboxes across the country. A person receiving a cross-contaminated letter would likely have no idea that they had been exposed. Cross-contamination placed postal employees at risk as well. Workers labouring in close proximity to contaminated automated equipment faced unwitting exposure. With each new case of cross-contamination, the limitations of CDC-USPS guidelines became increasingly apparent. New forms of security would have to be created.

Searching for security: risk and interest group politics

The anthrax attacks, in isolation, compelled little. The content of new security protocols was an open – and contentious – question. While the 2001 attacks revealed the limitations of in-place protocols, what was to come next – the shape of a new security posture – was by no means clear. The two interest groups most closely linked to the fortunes of the postal network – postal workers and the commercial mailing industry – wrestled to define the terms on which new forms of postal security would rest. Labour and commercial mailers viewed the problem of biological terrorism through starkly different frames: workers viewed biological terrorism as a workplace safety issue, while the mailing industry – companies that rely on mailings as a central component of their businesses, including direct mailers that create advertising mail for clients and catalogue merchants – worried about disruptions to the smooth functioning of the postal network. These interpretations focused on different objects of concern – the protection of worker health on the one hand, and the preservation of network functionality on the other – and, unsurprisingly, led to disagreements over the contours of new security standards.

Unions representing postal labour viewed the attacks as assaults on the postal workforce. Labour was sharply critical of the initial failure of postal management to contain the spread of anthrax. Cross-contamination impacted postal workers directly: nine postal workers contracted anthrax from cross-contamination and testing eventually confirmed the presence of anthrax in over 23 different postal facilities.[5] The American Postal Workers Union (APWU), the largest postal union, led a walkout of workers in New York City and filed three lawsuits in US District Courts, charging the USPS with failing to provide a safe workplace (see APWU, 2001a, 2001b, 2001c; Reaves 2001; USPS Office of Inspector General [OIG], 2002c). APWU President William Burrus publicly accused postal management with offering different levels of safety for government officials and postal workers. Burrus pointed out that Supreme Court and Congressional offices were closed at the first hint of possible anthrax exposure, while postal facilities, in some cases, remained open even after anthrax had been discovered. As Burrus framed the issue: 'Are the lives of postal workers less valuable than the lives of U.S. senators? Are the lives of postal workers less valuable than the lives of Supreme Court justices? What value do our lives have?' (quoted in APWU, 2001d). William Smith, president of New York Area Metro Postal Union, drew the same conclusion, tartly offering: 'I realize that [postal] employees are not Supreme Court justices or senators or Congress, but they are God's children; they have the same right to life as the aristocrats' and that '[n]o one piece of mail is worth a human life' (quoted in Finn, 2001).

While labour viewed biological terrorism as an attack on the bodies of postal workers, the mailing industry saw the 'health' of the network as the central object in need of protection. The interpretation of biological terrorism as a problem of network functionality, fits well within what Andrew Lakoff (2008) describes as the logic of 'vital systems security'. As opposed to security logics structured around the protection of populations (or the sovereign), infrastructures are increasingly viewed as vulnerable spaces to be protected. Commercial mailers moved to protect the network. They worried that if the public lost confidence in the safety of the mail – refusing to accept 'junk mail', catalogues, and other forms of mail out of an abundance of caution – their businesses would be destroyed (Odell, 2001; Riggs, 2001; Viveiros, 2001). Trade associations such as the Association for Postal Commerce, Mailers Council, and the Direct Marketing Association, called for postal management to take steps to quell safety concerns. Yet, commercial mailers also worried about the side-effects of new layers of security. They warned that adopting poorly designed security efforts could jeopardize the two qualities that make the mail an attractive commercial medium: low-cost and timely delivery (Anon, 2002; Oser, 2001; Riggs, 2001; Schultz, 2001). The concerns of large, bulk, mailers were not to be taken lightly: roughly 75 per cent of all mail is sent by bulk mailers (GAO, 2003a). Large mailers, as a result, have historically played a significant role in dictating postal policy. Although both labour and industry advocated new forms of postal security, commercial mailers offered a crucial caveat: new security measures could not increase the postage rates charged to large, bulk, mailers, or impose delivery delays (GAO, 2001; Rowan, 2002a). Commercial mailers wanted new forms of security to restore confidence in the mail, while preserving the speed and economy of the network.

The Postal Service found itself in a difficult position. Its two most powerful and vocal constituents, labour and large mailers, aggressively pushed for new forms of security – implicitly and explicitly questioning postal management's initial response to the attacks – though their aims chafed: labour's prioritization of worker safety would likely lead to added costs and delays in postal processing; mailers called for security, but refused to accept new security practices that will add costs or jeopardize the speed and convenience of the mail. In order to reconcile this tension, the head of the USPS, Postmaster General Potter, created

The Sociological Review, 62:S1, pp. 161–182 (2014), DOI: 10.1111/1467-954X.12128

a new working group, the Mail Security Task Force (MSTF), in October 2001 to consult with the Postal Service on new security practices (see Rowan, 2002a). The taskforce broke with long-standing postal policy and brought together management, senior leadership from the postal labour unions and management associations, and representatives of the mailing industry (USPS, 2001). This was a significant change. For decades powerful mailers had exclusive access to postal management through the Mailers' Technical Advisory Committee, a public-private partnership run by the mailing industry and the Postal Service that is closed to union participation (see APWU, 2008; Mailers' Technical Advisory Committee, n.d.). The MSTF was different: it included both union leaders and the voices of commercial mailers.

The MSTF underscores the limitations of the political potential of novel forms of risk. In this case, labour's agitation, indeed, sparked institutional innovation. The anthrax attacks, and the uneven initial response by the USPS, provided labour with a highly visible management 'failure'. The USPS's initial inability to grapple with cross-contamination allowed labour to level powerful charges of unequal treatment. Labour seized the salient threat of biological terrorism to secure a more prominent place in postal policy. As Beck (1992, 2009) highlights, risks can, in certain instances, serve as a catalyst that supports the democratization of formerly closed institutions. Postal workers leveraged safety concerns to wedge open postal governance. While in other domains invocations of 'security' post-9/11 were used to justify the foreclosure of political participation due to 'exceptional' circumstances, here, something different unfolded. The MSTF, on the face of it, offered a more democratically minded form of governance that, at least nominally, enfolded those most directly subject to the bodily harm inflicted by the anthrax attacks – postal workers – within its deliberations.

Yet, the power of the MSTF was in important respects circumscribed. The MSTF's recommendations were informal and non-binding; the Postal Service retained final authority over security policy. The invitation to join the MSTF placated, for a time, the concerns of postal workers. Now, finally, labour could join commercial mailers in providing postal management with advice outside of the highly formal rate cases or through the negotiation of collective bargaining agreements. However, postal workers soon realized that access is not quite the same as power. Labour would quickly find out that commercial mailers still held the power to shape postal policy. Risk, as a political resource, transformed to a limited degree the governance structure of postal decision-making, but, as the contours of newly adopted security standards would make clear, risk did not reorganize the basic structure of power at play within postal politics.

From irradiation to ICTs: the politics of selection

The USPS, with the assistance of the MSTF, considered a number of different possible 'technical fixes' to the problem of biological terrorism, including a host of sanitation technologies, process changes, and information and communication technologies (ICTs) that provided surveillance and detection capabilities (GAO, 2001; USPS, 2002a). The eventual adoption of ICTs over other competing technologies was neither inevitable nor obvious. Rather, the key ICT systems that were finally installed, the Biohazard Detection System (BDS) and Intelligent Mail, emerged largely thanks to the efforts of commercial mailers, a key interest group in postal politics, and the timely intervention of external groups, including congressional staffers and select local governments. The adoption of the BDS and Intelligent Mail was a triumph for commercial mailers. Unlike competing technologies, ICTs offered the promise of seamless operation – security that did not disrupt the flow of mail – and did not saddle commercial mailers with burdensome additional costs. As security technologies, they prioritized the 'health' of the network over the prevention of physical harm to postal workers.

The reliance on ICTs was a reversal. Initially, postal management looked to sanitation technologies, irradiation in particular, to be the most promising security option (Day, 2002). Irradiation uses targeted ionizing radiation to kill or neutralize harmful biological agents. It is routinely used in industrial settings, such as food processing and medical equipment sterilization (General Counsel of the Office of Compliance, 2002). Unquestionably, irradiating mail would destroy any spores of anthrax.

Widespread adoption of irradiation faced stiff opposition. The USPS began irradiating mail sent to federal agencies in the November 2001 (USPS OIG, 2002d). Operational problems and safety concerns marred efforts to expand the use of irradiation to cover the entire postal network. Delays were rampant. Mail subject to irradiation on average took over twice as long to reach its final destination (eight days, as opposed to two or three days) (Government Accountability Office, 2008). For commercial mailers, the side-effects of irradiation were even more troubling. Irradiation damages routine items sent through the mail. Plastics (such as credit cards), electronics and other materials sent through the mail experienced varying degrees of damage (Day, 2001). Even regular letters could become brittle and discolored as a result of the process (CRS, 2002a). Irradiation sanitized the mail, but at the expense of damaging, and in some cases rendering useless, the contents of the mail. Shortly after the introduction of irradiation for federal mail, commercial mailers argued against expanding the programme (Rowan, 2002a).

Federal employees and local governments provided mailers with support. They were also hostile to irradiation. Federal employees receiving irradiated mail claimed that it caused nausea, headaches, nosebleeds and other forms of sickness. Both the Congressional Office of Compliance and the National Institution for Occupational Safety and Health (NIOSH) opened investigations into the possible side-effects of handling irradiated mail (General Counsel of the Office of Compliance, 2002; NIOSH, 2002). Both reviews noted that there were no known long-term health effects associated with irradiated mail, but concluded that handling such mail may be a cause of the reported health symptoms.

The Sociological Review, 62:S1, pp. 161–182 (2014), DOI: 10.1111/1467-954X.12128

Local governments were nervous about irradiation as well. They were not eager to have irradiation facilities operating in the midst of their communities. In order to test the feasibility of expanding irradiation system-wide, the USPS invested $40 million in new equipment and began constructing specialized facilities near Washington, DC. Local officials reacted swiftly. One week after USPS started outfitting a new sanitation facility in Temple Hills, MD, local officials shut off the building's utilities in response to concerns over the safety of bringing sanitized mail into the county. Local officials in Montgomery County, MD similarly derailed USPS plans to operate an irradiation facility (USPS OIG, 2002d).

The combination of operational problems, health concerns and local opposition blunted efforts to implement system-wide irradiation.[6] The USPS shifted course and embraced a strategy primarily focused on ICTs. The BDS and Intelligent Mail emerged as a palatable alternative to sanitation technologies. As a technical 'fix' to the problem of biological terrorism, they promised security without upsetting day-to-day operations or, importantly, increasing the costs ascribed to large mailers. Both the BDS and Intelligent mail are political artifacts that, in different ways, embody the triumph of bulk mailers at the expense of postal labour and, to a degree, the general public. Encoded within these new infrastructure standards are implicit and explicit political judgements about the relative importance of the commercial features of the postal network and the safety of workers, assessments of how to define 'safe' and 'at-risk' mail, and assumptions about who should ultimately be responsible for the costs of added layers of security. Labour leaders felt an acute betrayal. While the MSTF promised them a more active role in postal governance, the shift to ICTs, in their estimation, bent to the demands of powerful mailers at the expense of workplace security (Burrus, 2003).

Toward a bifurcated postal system: the biohazard detection system

The BDS is an automated detection system that tests air particles above automated mail processing equipment for the presence of anthrax and, in the event of a positive result, triggers on-site and off-site alarms (USPS, 2004b; USPS OIG, 2006). Effective lobbying by commercial mailers guided key decisions concerning the system. The BDS splits the postal network into two separate processing networks: one for individuals and small organizations sending mail from their homes, street collection boxes or post offices; another for commercial mailers sending letters in large batches at discounted rates. The BDS, and its associated costs and extra handling, apply only to the first, while bulk mailers are able to opt out of the costs and extra handling tied to new security screening. The BDS treats as safe mail originating from large mailers, while scrutinizing the mail from individuals, homes and other small entities. The interests of large commercial mailers are embodied in the BDS: it provides a measure of security designed to reassure the public that the mail is safe, but does so without adding to the postage rates or delivery times of bulk mailings.

The USPS and Northrop Grumman, the defense contractor, began developing the BDS in 2002; it became fully operational in 2005 (see USPS, 2005, 2006b; USPS OIG, 2002a, 2006). The BDS is installed in large postal Processing and Distribution Centers across the country. The BDS is attached to a specific piece of automated postal processing equipment, Advanced Facer Canceller System (AFCS) machines, which are used to scan mail for proper postage. The mechanics of the BDS are straightforward: as letters are processed on an AFCS, air samples are continually collected by the BDS and analysed for the presence of anthrax; a positive test signal stops mail processing equipment, triggers alarms within the facility, and notifies emergency responders (Rowan, 2002a; USPS OIG, 2002a, 2002b). The system allows the AFCS to operate at regular rates and, absent a positive result, does not delay mail flow (USPS, n.d.[a]).

Deciding where to place the BDS within the postal processing chain – on which pieces of automated equipment to attach the BDS – is significant: deciding where to locate the BDS rests on assumptions concerning which mail is considered 'at risk' and, crucially, determines who is responsible for the costs associated with the provision of security. The decision to integrate the BDS with the AFCS, rather than other pieces of automated postal machinery, was not guided by the technical features of automated equipment, the precise outlines of the 2001 attacks, or even intelligence reports concerning how a future attack may unfold. Indeed, AFCS machines are only one of many different pieces of automated equipment that process mail. What is unique about AFCS machines, however, is that they exclusively process collection mail – letters sent from street collection boxes, homes, small businesses and individuals – while other automated equipment, such as Delivery Bar Code Sorters (DBCS), process both collection mail and bulk mailings from large mailers. By placing the BDS on the AFCS, the BDS only 'scans' collection mail and avoids bulk mailings (USPS, 2002a; USPS OIG, 2002b). AFCS machines are not the only type of automated equipment that can cause cross-contamination: during the 2001 attacks, both AFCS and DBCS machines spread cross-contamination within postal facilities (see Dewan *et al.*, 2002; Dull *et al.*, 2002; Teshale *et al.*, 2002). Although in 2001 the majority of anthrax letters were sent through collection mail, at least one mailing was sent as a parcel (a category of mail that is not currently subject to the BDS) (see Cole, 2003). The USPS did collect intelligence to assess the threat of another bioterrorist attack using the mail, but the threat assessment was not completed by the independent contractor until May 2003 and presented to the USPS in June 2003 – nine months *after* the outlines of the BDS were approved by the USPS management (USPS, 2004a, 2004b).

The organization of the BDS reflects the wishes and power of large volume mailers to define new security standards. As it first became clear through their opposition to irradiation, industry trade groups sought to avoid any costs or delays associated with added security. They argued that bulk commercial mailings were safe, while collection mail was potentially dangerous (see Alberta,

The Sociological Review, 62:S1, pp. 161–182 (2014), DOI: 10.1111/1467-954X.12128

2001; GAO, 2001; Rowan, 2002a). By bypassing the BDS, bulk mailers avoid the added costs associated with security. Since their mail is deemed 'safe' and bypasses the BDS, the costs of the BDS are not included in the calculation of rates charged to bulk mailers. These costs are not trivial: according to audits by the USPS Office of Inspector General and published figures from the *Washington Post*, as of 2011 total system costs range between $1.05 and $1.4 billion, with continuing operating costs above $100 million annually (Hsu, 2005; Lester *et al.*, 2004; USPS OIG, 2006). While a fraction of these costs have been paid through federal appropriations, the majority of the costs, including annual operating costs, are expenses that are recovered through postal rates.[7] With bulk mailers effectively opting out of the BDS, the system's costs are borne by individual mailers and small entities that do not have the opportunity of opting out and, to a lesser degree, the public through limited federal homeland security appropriations. In place of involvement with the BDS, large mailers have the option of enrolling in a voluntary mail security programme – known as the B.2.2 Security Initiative for Commercial Mailers – that offers participants confidential and non-binding security recommendations (Rowan, 2002b; USPS, n.d.[b]).

While industry trade groups initially joined labour in supporting new security efforts as a means of assuaging customers' fear of anthrax, they successfully worked to limit the scope of new security practices and displace the costs onto the public at large (through appropriations) and small and individual mailers. While the threat of biological terrorism briefly served to democratize postal governance, the BDS demonstrates the limits of risk as a disruptive or transformative political resource. At its core, the BDS is a conservative response to the attacks: it reinforces the privileged position that commercial mailers hold in postal politics. In its selective deployment and distribution of costs, the BDS creates a tiered system of security within which bulk mailers are free from added burdens. The USPS Office of Inspector General and postal labour unions criticized the exclusive application of the BDS on collection mail and called for an assessment of all categories of mail (see USPS OIG, 2002b). APWU President Burrus noted (2003) during Congressional Testimony in forceful terms that:

> [The BDS] will go on specified postal equipment, not all of the equipment . . . Over 50 percent of [mail] bypasses the [BDS] . . . That mail would never come through . . . biodetection equipment. It will go directly to the letter carrier, to the bag, to the American customer, to the American citizens.

Burrus's estimate may have been generous: mail sent from (largely commercial) mailers at bulk rates – roughly 75 per cent of all mail – avoids scanning by the BDS (GAO, 2003a). In calling for an expanded program of detection, the USPS OIG and APWU highlight the political choices inscribed within the BDS.

Intelligent mail: revenue, cost and security

The BDS was not the only new security system adopted after the anthrax attacks. Postal management also introduced a new suite of services, known as

'Intelligent Mail', to confront biological terrorism. Intelligent Mail is an assemblage of interlinked technologies – including data-rich barcodes, scanning equipment and software – that generate, store and manipulate real-time data from the postal network. As a security tool, Intelligent Mail data can be used to reroute mail flows away from 'trouble areas' where anthrax has been identified. It also allows investigators to reconstruct the path of identified contaminated mail through the system. Intelligent Mail is, however, not exclusively a security technology: it also serves as a tool for revenue generation and cost control. It fuses what are typically discrete domains of surveillance: consumptive behaviour, the workplace and security (see Lyon, 2003). Intelligent Mail underpins the production of new product lines and new forms of workplace control. It is part of a larger ongoing transformation of postal service into a 'flexible' enterprise: one that is less hospitable toward a unionized workforce and less interested in providing uniform services to a broad customer-base. While the politics of the BDS are largely defined by absence – the ability of large mailers to opt out – the politics of Intelligent Mail are defined by whom it includes, both as customers of newly designed commercial products and as subjects under supervision. Intelligent Mail produces a specific matrix of social relations: within its operation, we find the concurrent prioritization of commercial interests and marginalization of labour. Here, as in the BDS, we find the politics of disaster encoded within the workings of new infrastructure standards.

The development of Intelligent Mail began in the mid-1990s as a joint effort of postal management, commercial mailers and postal equipment manufacturers. Initially, the project had little to do with security: the aim was to create new value-added products for commercial mailers and new managerial tools for the USPS to control costs (see Intelligent Document Task Force, 1999, 2001, 2004; Mailing Industry Taskforce, 2001). The 2001 anthrax attacks pointed out another application for the then in-development technology: security. Postal management and the mailing industry scrambled to reposition Intelligent Mail as a security technology, arguing that its security applications were a 'logical extension' of its commercial and operational aims, and pushed for its adoption in the March 2002 *Emergency Preparedness Plan* (see Gibert, 2001; Intelligent Document Task Force, 2001; Mailing Industry Taskforce, 2003).

After a decade of development, Intelligent Mail launched in 2006 (Government Accountability Office, 2009). Intelligent Mail aims to create a perfect real-time rendering of the postal network, what the USPS refers to as 'total mail visibility'. Intelligent Mail combines new information-rich barcodes, scanning equipment, and computer systems to create and manage data charting mail flow and worker behaviour (USPS, 2009). Intelligent Mail barcodes contain a range of information – including a unique identifier indicating mailer and recipient, routing details, and service type – and are placed on individual pieces of mail and aggregates, such as transportation containers. As mail moves through the network, automated processing equipment and postal workers using hand-held scanners, known as Intelligent Mail Devices, scan barcodes to create a detailed real-time record of postal operations (USPS, 2009). Intelligent

The Sociological Review, 62:S1, pp. 161–182 (2014), DOI: 10.1111/1467-954X.12128

Mail, however, offers not only a snapshot of mail flow, but also of worker behaviour. As letter carriers travel through their assigned routes, Intelligent Mail Devices create a digital record of the carrier's behaviour. All collected data are stored in the USPS's information-backbone service, the 'Intelligent Mail Visibility Service' (USPS, 2002b).

Key players from across the postal industry – including bulk commercial mailers such as American Express and Capital One; marketing companies, including ADVO, Acxiom, Young & Rubicam; catalogue and greeting card manufactures; and communication companies, such as Siebel Systems, Symbol Technologies, and R.R. Donnelley – initially envisioned Intelligent Mail as a way to cater to the needs of large mailers (Mailing Industry Taskforce, 2001). Intelligent Mail data is used to create a host of value-added services sought by commercial mailers, such as bulk track-and-trace services and advanced notification of incoming mail (USPS, 2009). These services allow commercial mailers to better manage their logistics, but offer little to the more general mailing public. In this respect, Intelligent Mail represents the fracturing of the postal network: general users are offered a set of basic services, while sought-after markets – commercial mailers – are provided with enhanced, value-added, upgrades (see Graham and Marvin, 2001). Intelligent Mail is an important strategic initiative for the USPS. As postal volumes decline, value-added services structured around the commodification of information offer the USPS one of the few possibilities of revenue growth (Intelligent Document Task Force, 1999; USPS, 2002c).

Intelligent Mail is also critical to the reorganization of labour relations within the postal network. The collection of fine-grained, real-time, network data offers the opportunity to shift how labour is deployed (Mailing Industry Taskforce, 2001). 'Total mail visibility' not only enables mailers to peek inside the postal network and track the circulation of their mailings, but also generates data tracking postal workers as they travel outside the office. Expanded surveillance is critical to the ongoing expansion of the use of temporary, casual, labour. Since the mid-1980s, the USPS has prioritized the use of temporary workers as a means of controlling costs. Non-union, non-career, employees work for lower wages and, in most cases, do not receive the benefits afforded career employees.[8] Intelligent Mail data provides management with the ability to quickly evaluate individual performance, information that is increasingly useful when applied to the management of temporary workers that, unlike career employees, can be added and subtracted from employee rolls with little difficulty. Further, Intelligent Mail enables management to finely calibrate the deployment of temporary workers to meet short-term fluctuations in workload – adjusting staffing levels in response to temporary spikes and depressions in mail volume (USPS, 2009). Historically, postal labour has been dominated by a highly unionized career workforce, with workers typically occupying stable roles day after day. The move to flexible labour allows management to hire and fire low-cost workers as needed and, importantly, shift workers to meet changing demand. Intelligent Mail, seen within this larger context, appears not only as a way of creating new products, but also as part of the larger ongoing reorganization of postal labour.

The positioning of Intelligent Mail as a security technology was an afterthought. The USPS and its corporate partners developed it for quite different purposes in response to issues unrelated to security. Yet, as Intelligent Mail was being reviewed and considered for adoption, the Postal Service and industry used the threat of biological terrorism to justify moving forward with the project (see Gibert, 2001; Mailing Industry Taskforce, 2003). The Postal Service argued that Intelligent Mail offered clear security benefits. Real-time processing and distribution data generated through Intelligent Mail could be used to isolate cross-contaminated mail and reroute other mailings away from sites of cross-contamination. Additionally, the wealth of data produced through Intelligent Mail, the Postal Service argued, would assist investigators by allowing them to retroactively trace the movement of contaminated mail through the network (USPS, 2002a). The only real distinction between Intelligent Mail's security features and its commercial and managerial uses relates to how data are used. In the context of debates about postal security, it emerged as a possible new 'fix' that could complement the BDS (see GAO, 2001; Gibert, 2001; Rowan, 2002a). The same qualities that make the collection of real-time postal data attractive as a commodity and operational tool – increased customization, visibility and control – make it a useful security instrument.

Although 'security' offered a rationale for the adoption of Intelligent Mail, it is important to see the programme as a key element of a larger transformation of the Postal Service. The shifts that Intelligent Mail enables – toward boutique customized products tailored to commercial mailers and toward a greater reliance on temporary workers – are not value neutral. Intelligent Mail, like the BDS, is inscribed with a certain politics. The remaking of the Postal Service into a flexible, informational, enterprise benefits particular users and categories of workers at the expense of others. With Intelligent Mail, the Postal Service moves away from offering uniform services available to all customers, and embraces new product lines that cater to the needs of commercial mailers. Intelligent Mail, like the BDS, prioritizes bulk mailers over small-scale or individual mailers. At the same time, Intelligent Mail undergirds the ongoing transformation of postal labour: it supports the replacement of career workers with low-cost, temporary, workers.

Conclusion: excavating the 'sunk' politics of biohazard security

The 2001 anthrax attacks illustrate the power of disasters to destabilize the gridlock of politics as usual and the limitations of these moments of fissure. The attacks did not conform to the established narratives of how an anthrax attack would unfold and undermined long-standing bio-defence efforts. The newly created Mail Security Task Force departed with traditional modes of postal

The Sociological Review, 62:S1, pp. 161–182 (2014), DOI: 10.1111/1467-954X.12128
© 2014 The Author. Editorial organisation © 2014 The Editorial Board of the Sociological Review

governance and brought together in a deliberative setting labour, mailers, management and relevant experts to discuss how to confront the cross-cutting challenges of postal security. In this sense, the anthrax attacks were a catalyst for a new mode of inclusive postal politics. For decades, mailers have largely steered postal decision-making through formal and informal linkages to postal management, while labour has been marginalized. Here, the attacks appear to illustrate the political potential of novel risks to spark inversion and new political formations.

The catalytic potential of the anthrax attacks to upend hierarchies of power, however, is qualified and temporary. Opening the 'black box' of security standards reveals the re-entrenchment of hierarchies of power. The assemblage of technologies designed to counter the threat of biological terrorism are not apolitical or neutral: they privilege certain forms of use over others; distribute costs unequally across different categories of users; prioritize commercial concerns over worker safety; and engage in the policing of labour in an effort to aid the shift toward temporary labour.

The legacy of the 2001 anthrax attacks in part resides and endures within these new technologies. The BDS and Intelligent Mail are now regular features of the postal network – standards embroidered within the infrastructure. More than a decade after the last documented case of an anthrax mailing, the BDS and Intelligent Mail remain in place. As the novelty of these systems fade, they morph into taken-for-granted components of how the postal network operates – an unremarkable and unquestioned aspect of how things are done. They are now pieces of the 'sunk' politics of infrastructure. Yet, before the BDS and Intelligent Mail become obscured by the regularity of their operation and hidden in plain sight, it is worth taking a moment to revisit and analyse the values encoded within their operation. As the proceeding pages makes clear, examining the creation and operation of these technologies of control pushes to the fore the politics of postal security, and serves as a reminder that although disasters may be fleeting and transitory, their impacts linger.

Acknowledgements

Research support generously provided by the Smithsonian National Postal Museum/National Philatelic Exhibitions of Washington, DC (NAPEX) Scholarship and the Institute for Research on Labor and Employment, University of California, Los Angeles. Additionally, this work is funded by the Office of Naval Research under award number N00014-09-1-0597. Any opinions, findings and conclusions or recommendations expressed in this publication are those of the author and do not necessarily reflect the views of the Office of Naval Research. The article was begun while serving as a Postdoctoral Fellow at the Center for International Security and Cooperation, Stanford University and completed while at the Belfer Center for Science and International Affairs, Harvard Kennedy School.

Notes

1 Anthrax is the disease caused by spores of the bacterium *Bacillus anthracis*. Infection can take three different forms: inhalation, cutaneous and gastrointestinal. As is colloquial, 'anthrax' will be used to refer to both the spores of *Bacillus anthracis* and the disease that can result from exposure.
2 The investigation into the anthrax mailings eventually identified a US bio-defence researcher as the likely source of the mailings.
3 For a discussion of the importance of anticipatory strategies, see Weszkalnys, in this volume.
4 Canadian defence researchers conducted the only known laboratory tests of the distribution of anthrax through the mail prior to the fall of 2001 and echoed the conclusions reached by the CDC and USPS (Kournikakis *et al.*, 2001).
5 It is likely that testing did not identify the full scope of cross-contamination. For a discussion of the limitations of the testing process (see Government Accountability Office, 2005).
6 Select federal mail remains subject to irradiation.
7 Based on available USPS cost data and OIG audits, it appears that appropriated federal funds have paid for less than half of the costs of the BDS (see USPS, 2002a, 2004a, 2006a, 2006b; USPS OIG, 2002a, 2006).
8 Since the mid-1980s, the growth of casual workers has outpaced the growth of career employees: from 1987 to 2007, total career employees declined by 8.8 per cent, while non-career employees increased by 106.5 per cent (CRS, 2008).

References

Alberta, P. M., (2001), 'USPS expected to seek as much as $10 billion in aid from Congress', *Direct*, 7 November.
American Postal Workers Union (APWU), (2001a), 'Oct. 25 teleconference a success', available at: www.apwu.org/news/burrus/2001/update57-2001-102601.htm.
American Postal Workers Union (APWU), (2001b), 'Steps to insure protection from anthrax', available at: www.apwu.org/news/burrus/2001/update58-2001-110801.htm.
American Postal Workers Union (APWU), (2001c), 'Anthrax-contaminated facilities must be decontaminated and tested', available at: www.apwu.org/news/burrus/2001/update59-2001-111901.htm.
American Postal Workers Union (APWU), (2001d), 'Union, management reach fork in the road on anthrax policy', available at: www.apwu.org/news/nsb/2001/nsb31-2001-112701.htm.
American Postal Workers Union (APWU), (2008), 'Federal judge dismisses APWU lawsuit against Bush', 4 December, available at: www.apwu.org/news/webart/2008/08118-bushlawsuit-081204.htm.
Anon., (2002), 'Reader's Digest Hurt by 9/11 and Anthrax Scare', *Direct*, 24 January.
Beck, U., (1992), *Risk Society: Towards a New Modernity*, trans. M. Ritter, Thousand Oaks, CA: Sage.
Beck, U., (2009), *World at Risk*, trans. C. Cronin, Malden, MA: Polity.
Beck, U., Giddens, U., and Lash, S. (eds.), (1994), *Reflexive Modernization: Politics, Tradition and Aesthetics in the Modern Social Order*, Stanford, CA: Stanford University Press.
Burrus, W., (2003), 'Testimony before Subcommittee on National Security, Emerging Threats and International Relations, Committee on Government Reform', House of Representatives, 19 May.
Center for Counterproliferation Research, (2002), 'Anthrax in America: A chronology and analysis of the fall 2001 attacks', Working Paper, November, available at: www.fas.org/irp/threat/cbw/anthrax.pdf.
Centers for Disease Control and Prevention (CDC), (1999), 'Bioterrorism alleging use of anthrax and interim guidelines for management – United States, 1998', *MMWR Weekly*, 48 (04): 69–74.

The Sociological Review, 62:S1, pp. 161–182 (2014), DOI: 10.1111/1467-954X.12128

Cieslak, T. J. and Eitzen Jr, E. M., (1999), 'Clinical and epidemiological properties of anthrax', *Emerging Infectious Diseases*, 5 (4): 552–555.

Coaffee, J. and Wood, D. M., (2006), 'Security is coming home: rethinking scale and constructing resilience in the global urban response to terrorist risk', *International Relations*, 20: 503–517.

Cole, L. A., (2003), *The Anthrax Letters: A Medical Detective Story*, Washington, DC: John Henry Press.

Committee on Standards and Policies for Decontaminating Public Facilities Affected by Exposure to Harmful Biological Agents: How Clean is Safe? National Research Council of the National Academies, (2005), *Reopening Public Facilities after a Biological Attack: A Decision Making Framework*, Washington, DC: National Academies Press.

Congressional Research Service (CRS), (2002a), 'The U.S. Postal Service Response to the Threat of Bioterrorism through the Mail', RL31280, 11 February.

Congressional Research Service (CRS), (2002b), 'Postal service financial problems and stakeholder proposals', RL31069, 11 September.

Congressional Research Service (CRS), (2008), 'U.S. Postal Service Workforce Size and Employment Categories, 1987–2007,' RS22864, 22 April.

Cooper, M., (2006), 'Pre-empting emergence: the biological turn in the war on terror', *Theory, Culture and Society*, 23: 113–135.

Day, T., (2001), 'Mail sanitization', presentation to Mailers' Technical Advisory Council, USPS Headquarters, Washington, DC, November, available at: https://ribbs.usps.gov/mtac/documents/tech_guides/.

Day, T., (2002), 'Mail sanitization update', presentation to Mailers' Technical Advisory Council, USPS Headquarters, Washington, DC, February, available at: https://ribbs.usps.gov/mtac/documents/tech_guides/.

Dellafera, T. F., (2007), 'Affidavit in support of search warrant', United States District Court, District of Columbia, 31 October.

Dewan, P. K., Fry, A. M., Laserson, K., Tierney, B. C., Quinn, C. P., Hayslett, J. A., Broyles, L. N., Shane, A., Winthrop, K. L., Walks, I., Siegel, L., Hales, T., Semenova, V. A., Romero-Steiner, S., Elie, C., Khabbaz, R., Khan, A. S., Hajjeh, R. A., Schuchat, A. and members of the Washington D.C. Anthrax Response Team, (2002), 'Inhalational anthrax outbreak among postal workers, Washington, D.C., 2001', *Emerging Infectious Diseases*, 8 (10): 1066–1072.

Dull, P. M., Wilson, K. E., Kournikakis, B., Whitney, E. A., Boulet, C. A., Ho, J. Y., Ogston, J., Spence, M. R., McKenzie, M. M., Phelan, M. A., Popovic, T. and Ashford, D., (2002), '*Bacillus anthracis* aerosolization associated with a contaminated mail sorting machine', *Emerging Infectious Diseases*, 8 (10): 1044–1047.

Ethridge, E., (1992), *Sentinel for Health: A History of the Centers for Disease Control*, Berkeley, CA: University of California Press.

Fee, E., and Brown, T. M., (2001), 'Preemptive biopreparedness: can we learn anything from history?' *American Journal of Public Health*, 91 (5): 721–726.

Finn, R., (2001), 'Union chief's battle is with the postal service', *New York Times*, 1 November.

Fortun, K., (2001), *Advocacy after Bhopal: Environmentalism, Disaster, New Global Orders*, Chicago: University of Chicago Press.

General Accounting Office (GAO), (1997), 'Postal service: automation is taking longer and producing less than expected', GAO/GGD-93-89BR, February.

General Accounting Office (GAO), (1999), 'Combating terrorism: observations on biological terrorism and public health initiatives', GAO/T-NSIAD-99-112.

General Accounting Office (GAO), (2000), 'Combating terrorism: linking threats to strategies and resources', GAO/T-NSIAD-00-218.

General Accounting Office (GAO), (2001), 'Highlights of GAO's conference on options to enhance mail security and postal operations', GAO-02-315SP, 20 December.

General Accounting Office (GAO), (2003a), 'U.S. Postal Service: a primer on worksharing', GAO-03-927, July.

General Accounting Office (GAO), (2003b), 'Bioterrorism: public health response to anthrax incidents of 2001', GAO-04-152, 9 October.

General Counsel of the Office of Compliance, United States Congress, (2002), 'Investigation of the health effects of irradiated mail', OSH-0201,0202, 2 July.

Gibert, P., (2001), 'Using intelligent technology for mail security', presentation to Mailers' Technical Advisory Council, USPS Headquarters, Washington, DC, 8 November, available at: https://ribbs.usps.gov/mtac/documents/tech_guides/.

Government Accountability Office, (2004), 'U.S. Postal Service: better guidance needed to ensure appropriate response to anthrax contamination', GAO-04-239, September.

Government Accountability Office, (2005), 'Anthrax detection: agencies need to validate sampling activities in order to increase confidence in negative results', GAO-05-251, March.

Government Accountability Office, (2008), 'United States Postal Service: information on the irradiation of federal mail in the Washington, D.C., area', GAO-08-938R, 31 July.

Government Accountability Office, (2009), 'U.S. Postal Service: intelligent mail benefits may not be achieved if key risks are not addressed', GAO-09-599, May.

Graham, S. (ed.), (2004), Cities, War, and Terrorism: Towards an Urban Geopolitics, Malden, MA: Blackwell.

Graham, S., (2011), Cities under Siege: The New Military Urbanism, New York: Verso.

Graham, S. and Marvin, S., (2001), Splintering Urbanism: Networked Infrastructures, Technological Mobilities, and the Urban Condition, New York: Routledge.

Heath, L., (2003), 'Weapons of mass disruption', presentation to Mailers' Technical Advisory Committee, USPS Headquarters, Washington, DC, 7 May, available at: https://ribbs.usps.gov/mtac/documents/tech_guides/.

Henderson, D., (1999), 'The looming threat of bioterrorism', Science, 283 (5406): 1279–1282.

Hsu, S. S., (2005), 'Anthrax alarm uncovers response flaws', Washington Post, 17 March.

Inglesby, T. V., (1999), 'Anthrax: a possible case history', Emerging Infectious Diseases, 5 (4): 556–560.

Inglesby, T. V., Henderson, D. A., Bartlett, J. G., Ascher, M. S., Eitzen, E., Friedlander, A. M., Hauer, J., McDade, J., Osterholm, M. T., O'Toole, T., Parker, G., Perl, T. M., Russell, P. K. and Tonat, K., (1999), 'Anthrax as a biological weapon: medical and public health management', Journal of the American Medical Association, 281 (18): 1735–1745.

Inglesby, T. V., O'Toole, T., Henderson, D. A., Bartlett, J. G., Ascher, M. S., Eitzen, E., Friedlander, A. M., Gerberding, J., Hauer, J., Hughes, J., McDade, J., Osterholm, M. T., Parker, G., Perl, T. M., Russell, P. K., Tonat, K.; Working Group on Civilian Biodefense, (2002), 'Anthrax as a biological weapon, 2002: updated recommendations for management', Journal of the American Medical Association, 287 (17): 2236–2252.

Intelligent Document Task Force, (1999), Pursuing the Intelligent Document: A Vision for Paper-Based Communications in the Information Age, Phase I Report.

Intelligent Document Task Force, (2001), Pursuing the Intelligent Document: A Review of Technologies Impacting the Future of Mail, Phase II Report.

Intelligent Document Task Force, (2004), The Internet of Things: The Final Report of the Intelligent Document Task Force.

Kournikakis, B., Armour, S. J., Boulet, C. A., Spence, M. and Parsons, B., (2001), 'Risk assessment of anthrax letters', Defence Research Establishment Suffield, DRES TR-2001-048, September.

Lakoff, A., (2008), 'From population to vital system: national security and the changing object of public health', in A. Lakoff and S. Collier (eds), Biosecurity Interventions: Global Health and Security in Question, 33–60, New York: Columbia University Press.

Lester, E., Bearman, G. and Ponce, A. (2004), 'A second generation anthrax smoke detector: an inexpensive front-end monitor that detects bacterial spores', IEEE Engineering in Medicine and Biology, 23 (1): 130–135.

Luke, T. W., (2004), 'Everyday techniques as extraordinary threats: urban technostructures and non-places in terrorist actions', in S. Graham (ed.), Cities, War, and Terrorism: Towards an Urban Geopolitics, 120–136, Malden, MA: Blackwell.

Lyon, D., (2003), Surveillance after September 11, Malden, MA: Polity.

The Sociological Review, 62:S1, pp. 161–182 (2014), DOI: 10.1111/1467-954X.12128

Lyon, D., (2004), 'Technology vs. "terrorism": circuits of city surveillance since September 11, 2001', in S. Graham (ed.), *Cities, War, and Terrorism: Towards an Urban Geopolitics*, 297–311, Malden, MA: Blackwell.

Mailers' Technical Advisory Committee, (n.d.), 'Mailers' Technical Advisory Committee Charter', available at: http://ribbs.usps.gov/mtac/documents/tech_guides/mtac_charter.pdf.

Mailing Industry Taskforce, (2001), *Seizing Opportunity: The 2001 Report of the Mailing Industry Task Force*, 15 October.

Mailing Industry Taskforce (2003), 'Promote Development of Intelligent Mail', Spring.

Mangold, T., and Goldberg, J., (2000), *Plague Wars: A True Story of Biological Warfare*, New York: St Martin's Press.

Monahan, T., (2006), 'Questioning surveillance and security', in T. Monahan (ed.), *Surveillance and Security: Technological Politics and Power in Everyday Life*, 1–26, New York: Routledge.

Mueller, J., (2006), *Overblown: How Politicians and the Terrorism Industry Inflate National Security Threats, and Why We Believe Them*, New York: Free Press.

National Institute for Occupational Safety and Health (NIOSH), (2002), 'NIOSH Health Hazard Evaluation Report: Department of Health and Human Services: HETA #2002-0136-2880 United States Senate and House of Representatives, Washington, D.C', July.

Odell, P., (2001), 'Live from Chicago: Wientzen, a tumultuous year for DMers', *Direct*, 29 October.

Oser, K., (2001), 'Boardroom braces for anthrax fallout', *Direct*, 24 October.

Pile, J. C., Mallone, J. D., Eitzen, E. M. and Friedlander, A. M., (1998), 'Anthrax as a potential biowarfare agent', *Archive of Internal Medicine*, 158 (5): 429–434.

Potter, J. E., (2001), 'Statement of Postmaster General/CEO John E. Potter before the Subcommittee on Treasury and General Government Committee on Appropriations United States Senate', 8 November, available at: www.usps.com/news/2001/press/pr01_1108pmg.htm.

Reaves, J., (2001), 'The anthrax saga continues', *Time*, 2 November.

Rhodes, R., (2010), *The Twilight of the Bombs: Recent Challenges, New Dangers, and the Prospect for a World without Nuclear Weapons*, New York: Knopf.

Riggs, L., (2001), 'Lettershops brace for slowdown', *Direct*, 18 October.

Robin, C., (2004), *Fear: History of a Political Idea*, New York: Oxford University Press.

Rowan, J., (2002a), 'Mail security task force update', presentation to Mailers' Technical Advisory Council, USPS Headquarters, Washington, DC, February, available at: https://ribbs.usps.gov/mtac/documents/tech_guides/.

Rowan, J., (2002b), 'Mail Security Task Force Update', presentation to Mailers' Technical Advisory Council, USPS Headquarters, Washington, DC, May, available at: https://ribbs.usps.gov/mtac/documents/tech_guides/.

Schultz, R., (2001), 'Direct hit: mail war', *Direct*, 16 October.

Star, S. L., (1999), 'The ethnography of infrastructure', *American Behavioral Scientist*, 43: 377–391.

Sunstein, C., (2007), *Worst-Case Scenarios*, Cambridge, MA: Harvard University Press.

Teshale, E. T., Painter, J., Burr, G. A., Mead, P., Wright, S. V., Cseh, L. F., Zabrocki, R., Collins, R., Kelley, K. A., Hadler, J. L., Swerdlow, D. L. and members of the Connecticut Anthrax Response Team, (2002), 'Environmental sampling for spores of *Bacillus anthracis*', *Emerging Infectious Diseases*, 8 (10): 1083–1087.

United States Office of Technology Assessment (OTA), (1993), *Proliferation of Weapons of Mass Destruction: Assessing the Risk*, OTA-ISC-559, Washington, DC: GPO.

United States Postal Inspection Service (USPIS), (2002), *Annual Report of Investigations of the United States Postal Inspection Service*, 12 December, available at: https://postalinspectors.uspis.gov/pressroom/pubs.aspx.

United States Postal Service (USPS), (1999), 'Emergency response to mail allegedly containing anthrax', Management Instruction EL-860-1999-3, 4 October.

United States Postal Service (USPS), (2001), 'Postmaster General announces mail security task force', Press Release No. 01-089, 15 October, available at: www.usps.com/news/2001/press/pr01_089.htm.

United States Postal Service (USPS), (2002a), *U.S. Postal Service Emergency Preparedness Plan for Protecting Postal Employees and Postal Customers From Exposure to Biohazardous Material and for Ensuring Mail Security Against Bioterror Attacks*, 6 March, Washington, DC: USPS.

United States Postal Service (USPS), (2002b), 'How to succeed with MSP', Delivery Support Headquarters, Washington, DC: USPS.

United States Postal Service (USPS), (2002c), *United States Postal Service Transformation Plan*, Washington, DC: USPS.

United States Postal Service (USPS), (2004a), 'Update on biohazard detection system in response to OIG Report #DA-MA-02-001', 7 July.

United States Postal Service (USPS), (2004b), 'Decision analysis report: biohazard detection systems', 24 September.

United States Postal Service (USPS), (2005), *Comprehensive Statement on Postal Operations*, Washington, DC: USPS.

United States Postal Service (USPS), (2006a), 'Response to the House Subcommittee on Transportation, Treasury, Housing and Urban Development, the Judiciary, District of Columbia and the Senate Subcommittee on Transportation, Treasury, Judiciary, Housing and Urban Development, Committees on Appropriations', January.

United States Postal Service (USPS), (2006b), *Comprehensive Statement on Postal Operations*, Washington, DC: USPS.

United States Postal Service (USPS), (2009), 'Intelligent Mail Vision', Rev. 2.0, July.

United States Postal Service (USPS), (n.d.[a]), 'Biohazard Detection System: National Communications Plan'.

United States Postal Service (USPS), (n.d.[b]), 'Security of the mail', available at: www.usps.com/communications/news/security/b22_faq.htm.

United States Postal Service Office of Inspector General (USPS OIG), (2002a), 'Postal service's efforts to implement prevention and detection technology', DA-AR-02-008, 4 September.

United States Postal Service Office of Inspector General (USPS OIG), (2002b), 'Biohazard detection system', DA-MA-02-001, 24 September.

United States Postal Service Office of Inspector General (USPS OIG), (2002c), 'Fact-finding review of actions and decisions by postal service management at the South Jersey processing and distribution center', LH-MA-02-004, 22 March.

United States Postal Service Office of Inspector General (USPS OIG), (2002d), 'Audit report – postal service strategy for processing at-risk mail and deployment of irradiation equipment', AC-AR-02-003, 29 March.

United States Postal Service Office of Inspector General (USPS OIG), (2006), 'Biohazard detection system consumables', DA-AR-06-006, 30 September.

Viveiros, B. N., (2001), 'NEDMA holds town meeting to discuss anthrax crisis', *Direct*, 2 November.

World Health Organization, (1970), *Health Aspects of Chemical and Biological Weapons*, Geneva: World Health Organization.

Zajtchuk, R. and Franz, D., (2004), 'Biological terrorism', in Committee on Counterterrorism Challenges for Russia and the United States, *Terrorism: Reducing Vulnerabilities and Improving Responses*, 214–221, Washington, DC: National Academies Press.

The Sociological Review, 62:S1, pp. 161–182 (2014), DOI: 10.1111/1467-954X.12128

Concrete governmentality: shelters and the transformations of preparedness

Joe Deville, Michael Guggenheim and Zuzana Hrdličková

Abstract: This article analyzes how shelters act as a form of concrete governmentality. Shelters, like other forms of preparedness, are political acts in the absence of a disaster. They are materializations and visualizations of risk calculations. Shelters as a type of concrete governmentality pose the question of how to build something that lasts and resists, and remains relevant both when the object that is being resisted keeps changing and when the very act of building intervenes so publicly in the life of the restless surrounding population. Comparing shelters in India, Switzerland and the UK, we highlight three transformations of preparedness that shelters trigger. First we analyse how shelters compose preparedness by changing the relationship between the state and its citizens. Rather than simply limiting risk or introducing 'safety', the building of shelters poses questions about who needs protection and why and, as we will show, this can generate controversy. Second, we analyse how shelters decompose preparedness by falling out of use. Third, we focus on *struggles to recompose* preparedness: Changing ideas about disasters thus lead to shelters being suddenly out of place, or needing to adapt.

Keywords: shelters, materiality, risk, nuclear war, preparedness

Introduction

Consider this: there are three countries that each protects some of their people from harm with concrete structures capable of preserving life in extreme physical circumstances. If these concrete shelters could talk, they might tell us stories: stories about what sets them apart from others, about the people they are meant to house, and about the experts and governments that surround them. Perhaps it might go a bit like this: When encountering the other shelters in our trilogy, shelters in country A might be tempted to adopt a certain swagger. These are a community of shelters whose population has grown rapidly in the last half century, heavily supported by their government, to the extent that they now sit embedded in the basements of every relatively new block of flats. 'We can protect an entire population!', they declare. But push a little and you begin to

The Sociological Review, 62:S1, pp. 183–210 (2014), DOI: 10.1111/1467-954X.12129

find a niggling sense of self doubt. The disaster that they depended on for so long, a disaster they assumed would never go away, seems to be fading from view. And there is another problem: there have been persistent whispers of a need for these shelters to adapt to new kinds of disasters. But this is no easy task. These shelters feel themselves old, solid, concrete and inflexible. Then: a ray of hope! After it seemed that its human population was about to stop the prolif-eration of shelters, a single disaster far away has shown some particularly influential members of this human mass that these shelters might, in fact, have a place in their society. The shelters can, for now at least, breathe a little easier.

Shelters in country B might be briefly taken aback by the lengthy experience and sheer scale of the community of shelters in country A; by comparison, this group of shelters is younger and can protect a smaller proportion of the popu-lation. This hesitation is only fleeting. 'Look', they say, 'we, at least, are rel-evant!'. They go on: 'For thousands of years our country has been whipped by disasters. Now at last, we can protect people from them. Yes, perhaps we were a little late on the scene, but now we are here, we are needed!' As seeming proof of this there are plans for their community to be expanded. And, what's more, they are being made to be flexible. They have no need to worry about the fate of one single type of disaster, seeing as they are *made* to be able to adapt. Once again though, probe a little, and things are not so rosy: these shelters should be ready for disaster, but many now stand dilapidated, or are used for purposes which limit their ability to protect people if, and when, a disaster should strike.

The shelters in country C crumble away silently, listening to the argument between the other two. These are a diverse and often ragged assembly of shelters built, in very different ways and to very different standards, by the rulers of their country and by some of their population. They know that they are now on the way out, with a decline that started many years ago. A few of their number, designed to house the most influential people in the land, are struggling on, true to their original purpose. A few survive as tourist attractions. A few more sit in people's homes and gardens and are used as wine cellars. But, although low in number, they feel as if they know something the other two don't: that shelters may not be about offering material protection at all, but instead about human power and about human protest, where what is important about building a shelter is the act itself and the ability of this act to demonstrate either protection or, in fact, its almost total absence.

What these stories begin to show, and what we will explore further is that the relationships between 'risk', material 'protection' and the uses of concrete shel-ters is not a given. Shelters are not simply responses to risks. Rather shelters produce, react to and transform risks and preparedness. Their material presence poses questions about the plausibility of a particular risk, as well as the shelters offering themselves up to be read as a visual representation of what constitutes an acceptable level of survival and for whom. Rather than unravelling geneal-ogies of preparedness we focus on *how shelters transform preparedness*.

We analyse three types of transformation. First, we focus on how shelters *compose* preparedness. That is, on how the building of shelters concretizes the

The Sociological Review, 62:S1, pp. 183–210 (2014), DOI: 10.1111/1467-954X.12129

idea of state-led preparedness, in turn changing the relationship between disasters, citizens and the state. Rather than simply limiting risk or introducing 'safety', the building of shelters poses questions about who needs protection and why and, as we will show, this can generate controversy.

Second, we focus on how shelters *decompose* preparedness.[1] That is, on changes in the shelter buildings themselves, and in particular their falling out of use. Shelters represent a particular form of preparedness intended to work through sheer materiality: the more concrete, the safer. However, as we will see, shelters become unusable when they lack support from the population or adopt other uses. Some are even built so frailly as to be proof of failed government policies.

Third, we focus on *struggles to recompose* preparedness. Shelters are designed according to the particular kinds of forecasting and disaster expertise of their time (and, indeed, place). Expertise evolves and changes, whereas shelters, as concrete, obdurate structures remain more or less the same. Changing ideas about disasters thus lead to shelters being suddenly out of place, or needing to adapt. We observe the different fates of shelters in the face of such changes in expertise by looking at the examples of shelters in Switzerland, India and the UK.

Concretizing preparedness

One of the main insights of disaster research is that disasters highlight the political constitution of reality. They show the way in which choices are made to do certain things one way and not another (see, for instance, Law, 2003; Perrow, 1984; Vaughan, 1996, 2004). Already in the 1930s Lowell Carr pointed out that disasters should be understood as a special case of social change (Carr, 1932). It was the unique empirical situation surrounding the disaster that attracted him, for the insights that could be gained about society in general. Disasters were less important as a specific type of field for research and more for their unique and total qualities, which made it possible to observe social change in action.

One obvious way in which disasters change society is that they have effects not only after they occur, but also before, or in what Carr called the prodromal period of disaster (Carr, 1932: 210–211, see also the introduction to this volume by Guggenheim). Research has shown that there are a variety of preparedness practices which operate according to different logics (Lakoff and Collier, 2010; Anderson, 2011). These range from the deployment of what Collier and Lakoff call archival statistical knowledge (Collier, 2008), as for example in the form of insurance (Ericson and Doyle, 2004), to training and exercises (Anderson and Adey, 2011; Davis, 2007), to planning documents (Clarke, 1999), to the complex set of preparedness discourses discussed in the article by Weszkalnys (this volume). For us, what is crucial about preparedness is the relationship between these practices and disaster, as a more or less present object. We are not interested in different kinds of preparedness and their historicity, but in analysing how one particular concrete form, the permanent concrete shelter,[2] produces different kinds of social change. Importantly, this social change, produced through and by the shelter, can take place in the very absence of disaster – this very absence, indeed, is a material effect of its own. In disaster preparedness, then, the disaster can often become an *absent transformer* and it becomes obvious that preparedness itself enacts particular kinds of social change, independently of the presence of the disaster itself. Assessing whether or not disasters are 'triggers' for preparedness, and why, becomes an empirical question.

Carr was also farsighted in his understanding of disasters as perfect exemplars of the need for a more materially sensitive sociology. Carr critiqued culturalist accounts by showing the way that the natural world could not be straightforwardly tamed – and in fact had direct influences on the course of society (Carr, 1932: 209). But more than that, the 'natural', non-human world was, for Carr, *transformative*. He followed disaster's social effects, ranging from the redesign of bulkheads after the Titanic disaster, to the sudden appearance of female conductors on streetcars after the major munitions explosion disaster in Halifax, Canada. Disasters, as Carr came to see it, co-produced the socio-material.

In disaster preparedness, and particularly in the case of shelters, this formulation is especially relevant. Shelters are *concretized* forms of preparedness produced by absent disasters. It is their very concrete existence, being made to withstand the worst kind of impact, be it from nuclear warheads or cyclones, which produces a lasting effect. They are not only material, but they are made of a material that is the very epitome of materiality: concrete, and as thick and durable as possible (Forty, 2012; Slaton, 2001). If technology is society made durable, this is one of the ultimate durable technologies. More than any other object or building type, the function and use of shelters is a direct effect of their sheer materiality. Unlike banks or churches, the successful functioning of shelters is not largely an outcome of sophisticated technological features or interior layout, but rather the sheer thickness of their walls and the rigidity of their design. We refer to this as *concrete governmentality*, building on Foucault's terminology. This refers to the ways in which the particularly durable, supposedly permanent aspect of concrete as a material through which to build protection, comes to both epitomize and shape relations between the state and the population. In concrete governmentality, governmental institutions use concrete structures to, quite literally, build up their conceptualizations of risk and the role of government in protecting civilians in the belief that the material properties of concrete can offer solutions to particular preparedness problems. While we focus on shelters, this could include a range of protective measures from levees, to embankments, to housing.

The sheer materiality of concrete also has particular effects where there is no disaster. Shelters remain present, even if the disasters for which they were originally built have ceased to be a threat or fashions of expertise have changed. This durability can have effects on reshufflings of the relationship between the state and the population. Preparedness is nowadays mostly a state-led practice.[3]

It is the state, acting through its standardization mechanisms and organizations of civil defence and protection, that organizes preparedness. This includes building shelters. However, precisely because of their durability, shelters can turn against their builders, while also standing as spaces which the public can use and adapt in various ways. As such, the population and the shelters shape preparedness as much as the state does, with the material as a specific mode through which the social is assembled, thus acquiring political capacity and actively shaping the course of political action (Marres and Lezaun, 2011).

Composing preparedness

What is a shelter? How might it compose preparedness? Introducing three shelter programmes in different countries, we start by looking at how concretized forms of protection come to shape relationships between the state and the population. We begin in Switzerland and India, to show how certain kinds of disasters are transformed through shelter building programmes, in turn changing the relationship between the state and the population. In both of these cases we can observe how, through the introduction of new, standardized sets of buildings, the state extends its reach by claiming responsibility for its citizens in relation to specific disasters.[4] In the case of India, the concrete governmentality represented by shelters protects parts of the population considered to be vulnerable to disaster, because of their geographic location and housing conditions. In Switzerland, by contrast, we can observe an attempt to compose a total form of protection. The population is understood as homogeneous, with a shelter space built for each and every individual. We then turn to the UK, where we can observe quite the opposite. Here, a small minority of concerned citizens attempt to challenge the state preparedness provision, through their own material practices, by themselves taking on responsibility for shelter building. Their aim is to use the shelter as something akin to concrete 'proof devices', as a way of demonstrating the very absence of state protection in the face of seemingly imminent and total disaster.

India frequently suffers from devastating cyclones,[5] with the east coast and parts of the west coast being extremely vulnerable (NDMA, 2008: 1–9). The level of vulnerability varies and some locations are more likely to be worse affected than others because of their latitude as well as topography.[6] Until the 1970s, cyclone disasters were understood by the Indian state as events to be *responded to*: their role was to provide care to victims after a disaster, potentially in collaboration with third parties. In this sense, in the preparatory or 'prodromal' phase, these disasters were rather *undermaterialized*. What materialization there was – largely in the form of organizational responses – occurred only once the disaster had already happened.

From the late 1970s, this began to change, in particular in the aftermath of the 1977 Andhra Pradesh cyclone. With extensive support from the Red Cross, over 200 new shelters were built in a period from 1978 to 1982 (McKerrow,

2010). This was followed by a second building programme in the aftermath of a sequence of disasters occurring in the late 1990s and early 2000s.[7] On the back of a sudden influx of funding and due to a new government disaster management framework[8] a new, 'second generation' of Indian shelters began to appear (interviews in South India, July 2012; and NDMA, 2008).[9]

These two periods of shelter construction should not be simply understood as having been 'triggered' by the disasters that preceded them. Rather, what we see in both periods is a shift in both the *temporality and materialization* of disaster, with a general shift in emphasis towards preparedness, and, in particular towards materialized preparedness through the built environment. Furthermore, in this process, as relevant as the disaster 'itself' are the changing forms of expertise and sources of funding available for preparedness activities, with the construction of shelters increasingly involving not only (local) government actors but also humanitarian/development organizations, along with community-based and other non-governmental organizations. Binding much of this diverse input of expertise together is a confidence in state-led forms of standardization, with the designs for the shelters being produced by (or in cooperation with) the Public Works Department (see Figures 1 and 2; interviews in South India, July 2012). The result of this new alliance of expertise, control, funding and practice, has been to transform disasters into manageable events, which can be affected by, in this case, concrete forms of action, *prior* to a future event.

The disaster to which the Swiss shelter was designed to answer – possible nuclear attack – was quite different to India's cyclones. This is not simply because of the quite different place of human agency in constituting the two threats, or the different way they distribute harm. It is also because, like virtually every other country in the cold war that was seeking to deal with the danger posed by the proliferation of nuclear weapons, Switzerland was faced by a threat of potentially catastrophic proportions *of which it had had no direct experience.* This is a small but important point: one needs to be cautious about drawing causal inferences between the presence of disaster and the presence of preparedness measures. Discussions within the Swiss government about the need for a comprehensive defensive response to the threat of nuclear proliferation started soon after the Second World War.[10] However, it wasn't until the early 1970s that this initial ambition began to be pursued in earnest, with a promise made by the Swiss government to its people in their entirety: that if there was a nuclear attack, there would ultimately be a space in a nuclear bunker for each and every Swiss inhabitant (Schweizerischer Bundesrat, 1979: 19). This commitment was backed with significant levels of funding, it was legally enshrined and its delivery was rigorously monitored (see Schweizerischer Bundesrat, 1979: 20). Fast forward around half a century and the results are startling: there are now enough spaces in these bunkers, designed to withstand a nuclear assault, for just under 100 per cent of the population. The backbone of this provision is around 300,000 private shelters (see Figure 3) – on top of 5,000 larger public facilities – built into many Swiss homes and apartment blocks (Eidgenössisches Departement für Verteidigung, Bevölkerungsschutz und Sport, 2012: 59).

The Sociological Review, 62:S1, pp. 183–210 (2014), DOI: 10.1111/1467-954X.12129

FRONT ELEVATION

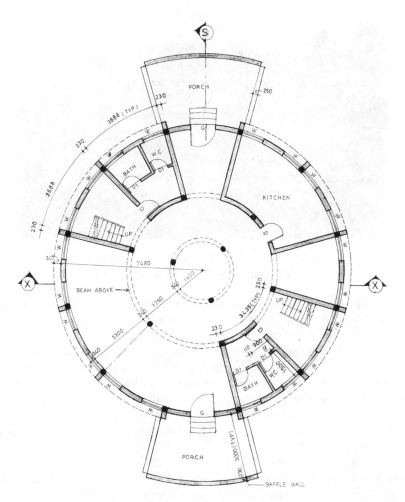

Figure 1: *Design of circular shelter.*
Source: Public Works Department of Puducherry (obtained with the permission of Mr Gopalakrishna, PWD architect, 19 July 2012).

Their differences notwithstanding, disaster preparedness epitomized by shelters in both India and Switzerland thus involves deeper engagements between the state and the population, mediated and shaped through concrete, that is through the state-sanctioned building of structures for the protection of the population. This is partly because the governing structures of both countries play a central role in maintaining a degree of control over the shelter programmes, with both envisioning that their duty is to ensure the survival of their

Figure 2: *Photo of circular shelter in Vadapattinam.*
Source: Photography by Z. Hrdličková, 20 July 2012.

civilian populations. Shelters also concretize a confidence in the value of dedicated, technical, material solutions to disaster, whether the disaster is apparently natural or man-made in origin (see Berger Ziauddin, 2010). The absent disaster, whether nuclear explosion or a cyclone expected to arrive sometime in the near future, is transformed into an entity that, with the right application of technique, as concretized into a built material response, can be if not eliminated then at least managed. In both cases, the shelters compose preparedness anew, uniting the state and the population in the imagined, or soon to be present disaster. As an instance of concrete governmentality, the shelter folds government and population together.

In the case of the UK, however, we can observe how shelters composed preparedness not through concrete presence, but absence. For, after the Second World War, the UK made virtually no attempt to provide the population *themselves* with protection in the form of nuclear shelters. This was a decision taken mostly for financial reasons as early as the 1950s (Smith, 2010) and it placed UK civil defence in an uncomfortable position: it was tasked with warning the population about an imminent nuclear threat while at the same time being unable to offer any significant material protection. Indeed, the civil defence establishment repeatedly complained about this situation, to no avail. The culmination of the lack of support, in 1968, was the total abolition of civil defence as an autonomous organization dedicated to disaster response (Grant, 2010; Stafford, 2011). The particularly stark contrast with Switzerland points to the inevitably political logic of disaster preparedness: although both nations were faced with very similar threats, the UK did not, in anything like a serious or sustained way, act to protect the population through the building of shelters.

Figure 3: *Family life continues in a Swiss bunker.*
Source: Robert Aeberhard, *Vom Luftschutz zum Zivilschutz: Aus der Geschichte des passiven (blauen) Luftschutzes und des Zivilschutzes,* Solothurn: Vogt-Schild, 1983, p. 145.

The government did build *some* shelters, but their principal effect was largely unrelated to their specific protective features. More important than how they might protect a few additional people was what the shelters revealed about the asymmetries of protection. As revealed first by 'the spies for peace' activists in 1963 (Anon., 2007), and then, more famously in 1982, by Duncan Campbell in *War Plan UK: The Truth about Civil Defence in Britain,* although the government denied the need for shelters for the population, it actually had built a number of shelters for its top civil servants (Campbell, 1982). Indeed not only had it built these exclusive shelters, but a whole governmental infrastructure designed to keep the country running during a nuclear war and in its aftermath. At least some of these buildings were constructed to the highest standards and were coupled to the most complete possible infrastructure. Ultimately, this amounted to transforming preparedness into an object involving multiple, increasingly visible asymmetries. The UK ended up as a country in which the state made an explicit decision that the government and parts of the administration was worth preserving even if it meant the ultimate absence of a population and an inhabitable territory.

The shelters that were built by the state thus had a double effect: the first was to *build in* a split in protection. The British shelters would have protected the government and some civil servants, who, in a very technical sense, would have been able to keep the country running, even in the perverse case of an extinct population. This fragmented the idea, so frequently invoked by the government in its public proclamations, of a unified nation, threatened *as a whole* by nuclear bombs (a similar notion to that routinely circulated in Switzerland). This particular vision and valuation of society became architecturally split in two by the concrete form of preparedness designed for the imagined bomb. If the disaster were to ever arrive, its effect would be to render visible, in the most brutal and extreme manner, cleavages between population and government.

This split could be disguised as long as the government shelters were not known to the public. But the fact that this kind of reasoning was eventually made public meant that the shelters became very visible and very real for the British population. The second effect was thus for the shelters to become demonstrations of the civil defence bureaucracy's non-belief in either its own assessment of the unlikelihood of a nuclear attack (otherwise why was it building shelters for itself), or, if an attack did come, in the adequacy of the kinds of improvised solutions recommended by the government to the British population (to be explored shortly). In the case of the UK the controversies around the concretization of preparedness very much obliterate the issue of the disaster itself and instead highlight the precarious relationship between the government and the population. The disaster is not thus simply an external force against which a defence is built.

As we will see in the next section, the full story of the composition of preparedness in the UK cannot be told only with reference to state-built shelters. Yet before we address this, it is important to illustrate how the transformation of preparedness that shelters effect, despite being so apparently obdurate, occurs also through their ongoing, processual interactions with other events, not necessarily limited to disasters. In other words, temporality matters, precisely because shelters are built before disasters happen.

Decomposing preparedness

Once shelters are built, they are testament to a particular idea of government preparedness. However, other constituencies apart from the government both build and use shelters for various reasons and in various ways, which are very often at odds with the ideas of preparedness originally informing their construction. This is not simply a story of the power of users to adapt technology to suit their needs (Oudshoorn and Pinch, 2003). Rather, what is at stake is the very functioning of shelters for their designed purpose. The problem here is twofold: First, because shelters are extremely obdurate structures, they exist for a very long time, but, since disasters are infrequent, are rarely used. They may thus either outlive the disasters for which they were built, as we will see in the case of Switzerland, or become used for other things, to the point that they become unusable in case of a disaster. This we refer to as the 'decomposition' of shelters.

Second, since the promise of a particular shelter is a function of both a disaster forecast and calculations about how materials might combine to withstand a disaster, shelters can be simply unusable from the outset. In the UK, as we will show, a hobbyist scene emerged in which people started to build shelters themselves to counter the absence of government provision, but these shelters were very often more a political statement than a usable shelter. Here the very composition of shelters in one social domain threatens to decompose the shelters in another.

In Switzerland, with its seemingly universal, egalitarian promise of protection, one of the features of the security establishment's historical relationship with the public was a sense that the population were not as signed onto the whole Swiss civil protection concept, including its network of concrete shelters, as much as they should have been; as Berger Ziauddin (2012) has shown, apathy about – and disengagement with – the shelter amongst the Swiss population is a key feature of its history. In the earlier cold war days, there was a concern with a Swiss public that was understood as problematic by virtue of being 'uninformed'. The suggestion was that, if the public understood the issue presented by the nuclear threat as well as their protectors did, their attachment to Swiss civil protection measures would be stronger. But, in nearly the same breath, the establishment wondered if perhaps the problem was, in fact, that the proliferation of imagery of nuclear destruction in various forms of visual media meant that the population was over-exaggerating the nuclear threat. There was talk within the Swiss civil protection establishment of a prevailing 'fatalism' which was impeding their work – a sense that, given the destructive power of nuclear weapons in the event of a third world war, its protective measures might be useless (Y. Meier, 2007: 136–137). This central problematic was summed up in a 1969 article, which acknowledged that it was 'exceptionally difficult, in both an understandable and convincing manner to, on one hand, acknowledge the ultimate possibility of total destruction and, on the other, show that this is only one variant, and a very unlikely one, amongst all the possible dangers' (Y. Meier, 2007: 137; citing Rimathé, 1969: 43 [our translation]). In other words, the shelter, on its own, could not solve the problem of protection for the Swiss establishment. To read accounts from the time is to be struck by the sense of frustration, perhaps even sometimes bafflement, at this fact.

Later, in the 1980s, alongside a marked increase in media attention to rising numbers of conscientious objections to civil protection (*Zivilschutzverweigerung*) (M. Meier, 2007: 186),[11] the increasingly powerful campaign for nuclear disarmament shifted the problem: this movement questioned the very definition of the concrete shelter as an entity that was primarily concerned with 'protection' (see also Berger Ziauddin, 2012). As most clearly expressed in a collection of critical essays published in the late 1980s, the shelter was described, in effect, as an anti-political device (Barry, 2002; Ferguson, 1994) that impeded broader debates about the very existence of nuclear weapons. It was, therefore, effectively contributing to making daily life *less* safe. The Swiss population, it was argued, imagining themselves safe underground as the

Figure 4: *Imagining nuclear war in Switzerland (child's painting).*
Source: Robert Aeberhard, *Vom Luftschutz zum Zivilschutz: Aus der*
Geschichte des passiven (blauen) Luftschutzes und des Zivilschutzes,
Solothurn: Vogt-Schild, 1983, p. 120.

nuclear bomb hit, could avoid engaging with, taking responsibility for, and challenging the global threat to humanity (Figure 4, see also Albrecht *et al.*, 1988; M. Meier, 2007).

Once again, the promise of protection materialized in the shelter itself is not enough: the Swiss population are a body of people that needs to be actively *attached* to the Swiss civil protection programme and to its network of bunkers. The problem in the 1980s was that not only was the security establishment encountering a population that was ambivalent about shelters, it was now encountering, in certain quarters, a population who were themselves trying to actively redefine the shelter: to themselves attach to its concrete fabric the idea that shelters might *generate* more dangers than they alleviated. The original promise of the shelters thus begins to decompose, as the shelters generate, amongst the population themselves, a very different way of doing and orienting the political.

Decomposition can also occur through practice. In India, for example, when cyclones have hit, these shelters have sometimes remained only partially employed. A local engineer told us that, during one of the larger cyclones of recent years, hurricane Thane, the new shelter in Veerampattinam, Puducherry, was used by around ten families. Although this could still be a sizeable number of people, there is no sense that the facility was used to anywhere near its capacity, despite the fact that the shelter is likely the safest building in the village. This matches accounts about the historical use of some of the older shelters. One reason is that other concrete or brick buildings – labelled '*pukka*' – are perceived as equally safe and so are also used in disasters (churches, temples, schools and new houses). Another is that many residents are reluctant to leave their homes for fear of looters, especially if it is also made of brick or other resistant materials, which are likely to keep them safe in the face of moderate disaster. This points to a tension within the promise of protection concretized in these shelters in South India: they promise only to protect life, not livelihood. Given that the financially more secure residents who are likelier to live in more resistant houses – as well as being residents who may perceive themselves as potentially at greater risk of looting given their status – this means that shelters, or other *pukka* buildings, are more likely to be used by the least well off. And the state knows it. As one of the senior officials implementing the cyclone mitigation programme said, shelters are for 'BPLs' – people 'below poverty line' (interviews in New Delhi, March 2013). Some local inhabitants also prefer temples, in particular, over shelters, given that – to put their argument in our terms – they offer a metaphysical mode of protection that escapes, and cannot be contained by, processes of concretization. Further, it should be noted that concrete and brick homes have proliferated since the building of the first generation of shelters, as incomes have grown. Whether or not these buildings are safer is not the point: particularly given the shelter's inability to protect livelihood (which staying in a *pukka* home might), it can no longer, by its mere presence, make an easy claim to offer the most effective form of protection. The promise of sheltering, by becoming distributed, has become decoupled both from one specific building type and from the strength of concrete.

There is another problem for the Indian shelter, centring on its frequent acquisition of novel uses. Some are used as schools (Lavanya, 2011) and crèches (McKerrow, 2010). One we have seen was transformed into a police station. Another is used by the Chennai University as an administrative building (Figure 6). Some shelters have become hang outs for unwelcome alternative uses – 'anti-social behaviour', as one interviewee put it. Although not of this kind, alternative use was envisaged in the design of the older shelters. For a little recognized fact is that, as shown in the original architect's model (Figure 7), these shelters were originally intended to serve, first and foremost, as community centres. The explanation popular among contemporary disaster management practitioners, saying that shelters from the 1980s failed because they were not owned by the community, does not therefore wholly stand up. The problem is rather what constitutes an acceptable 'community' and, as we will see, how, on its way down from the architect's table through the hands of organizations and local authorities, the very act of encouraging alternative use can begin to decompose the shelter's intended purpose.

The promise of protection and of multi-use is replicated in the newer centres (Figures 5 and 8): as their architect told us, it is key that the community use these buildings for other purposes during the year, otherwise they will become obsolete. So, for example, the first floor is designed as a marriage hall, with separate rooms for the bride and bridegroom. This mirrors a stipulation meant to accompany the original shelters: that they should not become permanent offices, because of the hardware and general clutter that comes with such use. Further, in line with the participatory mantra prevalent in today's governance, the 'Design Recommendations for the Construction of Cyclone Shelters' clearly state that the local community should be involved in the architectural design of the shelter (Ministry of Home Affairs, 2005: 9). As so often, however, the precise role of community participation remains unclear. In the more contemporary shelters, it is the local authorities that provide the specifications – shelter capacity required, for example, and the topography of the area – and based on this data, the architects of the individual states produce a design. So, as before, questions arise about the limits of community. Is a local authority a part of the community or is it not? (Hastrup, 2011). Is it 'true participation' when the architects speak to local authorities rather than to community groups directly?

The problem, as explicitly recognized in the flexible, ideally inclusive design of the newer shelters, is that more permanent alternative uses prevent people from using the buildings for their original purpose – protection during tropical storms. This is the case in the shelter that is now a police station, for example. And, indeed, in the case of those shelters that have come to be associated with unwelcome social practices. Protection therefore proves to be an entity that can easily 'leak out' of these concrete shelters, if they are not surrounded by the right combination of everyday practices.[12] The concrete governmentality embodied by Indian storm shelters thus faces an uneasy task: how to make the population dwell in the shelter without endangering the very purpose they were built for. They have to be dwelled in without too much clutter in order to serve as shelters.

The Swiss shelter shares some of these problems of decomposition with its Indian cousin. Until 2004, owners of individual houses and residential blocks in Switzerland had to ensure that their shelters could be clear and ready for use, in the event of a nuclear attack, within 24 hours. This meant that they could be used as storage places, much in the same way as other cellar spaces, but that no major alterations should be made, or devices installed that were permanent, or semi-permanent. The abolition of this requirement – with the argument that as the risk of a nuclear attack had decreased the likely forewarning time had increased – has meant that, in particular in the larger private shelters, some have

The Sociological Review, 62:S1, pp. 183–210 (2014), DOI: 10.1111/1467-954X.12129

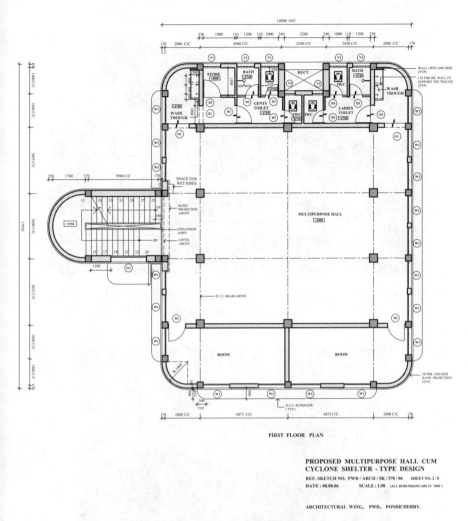

Figure 5: *Design of second generation of multi-disaster resistant multi-purpose cyclone shelters, also called community halls.*
Source: Public Works Department, Puducherry, obtained on 19 July 2012.

been converted to other uses – into temperature controlled wine cellars or saunas, for example.[13] Meanwhile public shelters, controlled by municipalities are, on occasion, rented out – for example, to host musical events. This has meant either the removal and storage of key machinery (filters, for example), or building work that has compromised the integrity of the shelter structure. The conversion back into a shelter thus becomes contingent on the *restoration* of shelter status: a process that could take weeks or even months. In both the Indian and Swiss cases the promise of sheltering has to coexist successfully with

Figure 6: *New use of old shelter for Chennai University, ECR, Tamilnadu.*
Source: Photography by Z. Hrdličková, 20 July 2012.

Figure 7: *Model of the first generation circular shelter called 'Community
Centre for Cyclone Affected Areas'.*
Source: Photography by Z. Hrdličková, 16 July 2012.

a range of everyday uses. For the shelter to be able to not only withstand a
disaster, but also successfully house people in a disaster, it often has to withstand
competing claims to alternative uses that emerge as the shelters interact with the
environments and populations around them. Imagining, then, the participation
of these now transformed, no-longer-quite-as-protective buildings in future dis-

The Sociological Review, 62:S1, pp. 183–210 (2014), DOI: 10.1111/1467-954X.12129

Figure 8: *Multi-purpose shelter/ community hall in Veerampattinam outside Puducherry.*
Source: Photography by Z. Hrdličková, 18 July 2012.

asters (whether cyclone or nuclear), we see how, in this now 'prodromal period' (to return to Carr's terms), the terrain upon which the disaster will intersect with both the shelter and their potential inhabitants, now likely to be housed elsewhere, is being shifted.

Decomposition does not have to refer solely to changes in the material fabric of a shelter. It can also occur when a competing protective materialization threatens the credibility of another. This is what happened in the UK. Here it is the state shelters that decompose, but not through neglect or criticism, but through the construction (or composition) *of a different way of doing sheltering*.

In the UK, rather than providing protection against the nuclear threat in the form of state built shelters, the government assigned the responsibility for protection onto the population. If anyone was going to protect the British population from the threat of the bomb, it would have to be the British themselves. The government, in this scenario, became a producer and distributor of expertise – and not (with some exceptions, as we have already seen) a builder and concretizer of expertise.

Particularly emblematic of this are the experiments that the British government undertook at a location called 'Rose Cottage' during the 1950s and 60s. Rather than build and test actual shelters, engineers pursued knowledge that might be adapted to the everyday lives of British homeowners: using books against windows, for example, as a way of giving some protection from the effects of a nuclear blast. The problem was that the results of these experiments highlighted the very limits of expertise, divorced from concrete support, to be able to significantly alter the possibility of nuclear survival. It was revealed, for instance, that 27 inches worth of books against a window would be needed to provide any kind of protection (Smith, 2010: 173), a figure not within reach of all but the most studious of British households.

Yet, far from deterred, successive British governments stuck to the task – of distributing, and not materializing, preparedness. The problem was that the limits of this soon became clear to much of the population. Particularly notorious were the 'Protect and Survive' leaflets. Their advice, which was widely ridiculed, included building a 'fall out room' for which 'bricks, concrete or building blocks, timber, boxes of earth, sand, books, and furniture might all be used' (HMSO, 1980). In these leaflets, and in British cold war preparedness more generally, it is thus clearly not state-led protection that is in play, but rather individualized bricolage.

It is of course not *impossible* for households to generate at least some measure of protection for themselves from a nuclear threat if the state chooses not to do it for them. This was the conclusion arrived at by a small group of people in the UK in the 1980s, whose work clustered around the journal 'Practical Civil Defence'. They believed not only that nuclear war was a real possibility, but also that it was survivable. Moreover, they believed it was worth funding the construction of nuclear proof shelters themselves.

To do so, they had to solicit the service of firms to deliver items including entrance doors and air filters. The technicalities of protection and the question of what a shelter should look like thus became a matter of what information was available and choice. For instance, a guide to shelter design from 1983 mentioned 'over two hundred companies selling prefabricated shelters, shelter designs and equipment' in the UK and included a list of suppliers.[14]

Here we find a peculiar twist: most of these suppliers were *Swiss* (Ormerod, 1983). And, when not, it is often adherence to 'Swiss Government Guidelines' that is proclaimed as a key selling point (Figure 9). Swiss standards became the blueprint for the UK as, for shelter builders, this provided access to a form of standardization. Sadly for British shelter builders, Swiss standards did not solve all their problems, for the shelter suppliers would generally only deliver parts of the home built shelter. The result was that both in their plans and in their construction, these shelters often did not approach the quality of Swiss shelters – in fact, many were rather makeshift. But this is not surprising. For, not only did the UK government step back from providing shelters, by itself proposing very makeshift forms of protection, it also had its own regulatory authority replaced by that of another state, Switzerland, but with no means to control it. Swiss shelter standards became hypothetical standards in the UK, but without any accompanying enforcement.

What kind of preparedness do these building practices actually *compose*? A certain form of protective material bricolage, perhaps. But more important, we suggest, is that these localized, individual compositions each enact a *decomposition of preparedness*: a decomposition of the idea of the state as materially responsible for the survival of its population.

200

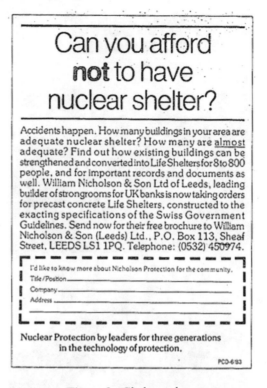

Figure 9: *Shelter advert.*
Source: Practical Practical Civil Defence, May/June 1983, p. 32.

This can be illustrated with an example: one Graham Bate built a 13ft by 10ft concrete shelter equipped with a 'radiation meter and a Swiss-designed system to filter out radioactivity' (Anon., 1983b: 31). This 30-year-old civil engineer at the Yorkshire Water Authority built it under a six-foot-high mound of earth to protect him, his wife and their three children (Figure 10). His justification for building it: 'Anything's better than the apathy evident in the UK about civil defence these days' (Anon., 1983b: 31).

As Bate is well aware, it is thus not only the practical responsibility for shelter building that is shifted onto the population, it is also keeping alive *the very issue* of materialized protection for the population. While we do not know whether such shelters would have withstood a nuclear attack, we do know that they never had to. Their role was to prove that, indeed, the state did not provide material protection for all, or even acknowledge the importance of doing so. The construction of these shelters demonstrated that these builders, in contrast to their own government, and many other citizens, did believe in both the *possibility* of nuclear war and the value of preparing to survive it.

Figure 10: *Bate Shelter.*
Source: Anon. (1983b: 31).

At the same time, doing protective, self-responsibilized protective politics meant overcoming apathy to show, through their activity and personal endeavour that 'anything is better than nothing'. This turned a technical problem – how to build a structure that can counter the effects of a nuclear attack – into a demonstration of an 'as if' mode of state-led politics. As captured in another article in Practical Civil Defence: 'Whilst politicians and civil servants procrastinate over the cost of "effective" civil defence measures men of "iron will" and foresight are applying hard won engineering skills to the job of answering this nation's need' (Anon., 1983c: 17). For these men (it seems they all were men), it did not matter so much whether their shelters provided adequate protection against a certain likelihood of attack. What mattered was proving that, even if buried in their garden, *protection could be made concrete, even if it would never withstand the bomb.*

The Sociological Review, 62:S1, pp. 183–210 (2014), DOI: 10.1111/1467-954X.12129

Struggles to recompose preparedness

The last transformation we want to focus on involves the struggles to recompose preparedness through shelters. As we have shown, shelters concretize particular ideas about preparedness. These relate in part to how the relationship between the state and the population is understood, but also to particular expertise about disasters. The idea, at its most simple, tends to be that the more expertise gets 'fed into' shelters, the better they will be able to withstand disaster. As we have seen, this expertise might range from the design of the shelter's protective features to ideas about how to ensure shelters are an ongoing success, by helping them fit cleanly into their surrounding populations. However, what often passes unrecognized is that it is not only unknown future disasters which the shelter might have to confront, but also unknown future changes in prevalent modes of expertise. It is in these moments that a shelter has to either recompose preparedness in such a way as to remain included, or face irrelevance.

The Indian cyclone shelters built in the late 1970s and early 1980s, the Swiss state-led nuclear shelters, and the British hobbyist shelters can be seen as all standing for a mode of disaster expertise in which disasters are viewed as distinct entities, that need to be prepared for in distinct ways. However, this heterogeneous approach to disasters has increasingly become unfashionable and an approach highlighting the necessity of multi-hazard preparedness has been on a steady rise since the 1980s and increasingly so since the 1990s. As Andrew Lakoff (2007) has documented, the roots can be found in the end of cold war. The US preparations for nuclear attack had to shift away from threats posed by a 'stable enemy' and towards those from a 'nonspecific adversary' (Lakoff, 2007: 263). Thus the all-hazards approach began to move towards its contemporary position as the world's pre-eminent mode of assessing disaster risk. The approach was firmly internationalized when the UN declared the International Decade for Natural Disaster Reduction in the 1990s, which targeted developing countries, and established that countries should strive for disaster preparedness through an all-hazards approach rather than through a reactive response mode (Lechat, 1990; Sharma, 2000).

The second generation Indian shelters, mentioned earlier, can be seen as attempting to recompose a concrete form of preparedness in such a way that it follows this new mode of expertise. The new shelters are no longer formally branded as cyclone shelters alone. They are instead envisaged as multi-disaster resistant structures, the specific design of which depends on the types of disasters the particular area is prone to. The shelters on the south-east Indian coast are therefore designed as earthquake-resistant structures that can also withstand strong winds and flooding, whether caused by cyclone, storm surge or tsunami. In contrast with the highly distinctive circular shape of the first generation shelters, the newer models in South India have a more conventional, rectangular appearance. Although, on second inspection, they retain specifically disaster-resistant features, with rounded corners to enable them to better withstand wind power and other features[15] that make them resistant to other disasters, such as earthquakes or flooding. If these shelters had a message it might be that concreteness and flexibility are not inherently antithetical.

Yet how safe are even these new shelters from future changes in fashions of expertise? Despite their promise of flexibility, they cannot escape the central problem at the heart of all shelters: that particular modes of expertise become *built into them*. What happens, then, when buildings stay the same but the disaster changes? The UK, after all, *did* at one point have a huge shelter infrastructure, built in response to the Second World War air raids. In 1983, the journal *Practical Civil Defence*, the same community that built makeshift shelters, was so desperate in its quest for shelters that, in an article entitled 'Dereliction?', it called upon its readers to participate in a 'nationwide derelict shelter survey' (Anon., 1983a: 25). Readers were invited to photograph these now seemingly irrelevant shelters and the journal would send the compiled documentation 'to the Minister of State for Home Defence, at the Home Office' (Anon., 1983a: 25). The idea was to rehabilitate a concretized form of preparedness from another age. This rehabilitation of course required an accompanying conceptual shift (a proto form of all hazards expertise, if you like): that a shelter ultimately need not necessarily be tied to one type of disaster, but could be adapted to different disasters, in which their re-use would happen 'at a fraction of the cost of starting all over again' (Anon., 1983a: 25).

This undertaking was unsuccessful, an outcome that might not have come as much of a surprise to the *Practical Civil Defence* community. Yet what they failed to recognize was that the fate of these forgotten shelters foreshadowed that of their own homemade shelters. After the waning of the cold war, these too lost their obvious use. Additionally, from the late 1980s onwards, the UK slowly moved towards an all-hazards approach, as officially embraced in the 2004 Civil Contingencies Act (HMO, 2004). With the apparent decrease in the nuclear threat, this implied there was no longer a need for the government to justify their (non) shelter building policy, nor were there any fringe groups calling for shelters. In 2010, a certain Mr Mike Thomas tried to sell his house including a nuclear proof shelter with, unavoidably, a 'Swiss-made ventilation system' that he built in 1985 (Daily Mail Reporter, 2010: no pages). Asked against which kind of disaster the shelter might now protect, Mr Thomas, answered: 'It could still be used as a panic room if someone came burgling the house' (Daily Mail Reporter, 2010: no pages). Mr Thomas struggles valiantly, by force of necessity, to recompose his own concrete form of preparedness as a private version of an all-hazards approach, in which the state plays no role.

There are clear echoes here between the struggles of Mr Thomas and his shelter and the recent history of the Swiss shelter. In Switzerland, nuclear shelters are buildings similarly tied to one threat: the threat of military, nuclear attack. At the same time, the Swiss government has mirrored many others by seeking to take into account and prepare for a diverse range of dangers, assessed according to an evaluation of their risks and potential impact. In Swiss civil protection discourse you therefore see a move from a cold war security stance, in which the bunker was placed at the absolute centre of civil protection strategy to the contemporary situation in which, despite much talk of risk analysis, and despite countless reports, there is never any justification made for shelters on the basis of a formalized risk calculation.[16] These infrastructural, cold war remnants still will not fit cleanly into a modern, risk based, ideally flexible – what in a 2010 report comes to be called ideally 'networked' – preparedness strategy (Schweizerischer Bundesrat, 2010).

In the struggles to recompose preparedness there is one phenomenon that helps shelters more than any other, and certainly more than any particular form of expertise: a disaster demonstrating their relevance. On 9 March 2011, the Swiss parliament in Bern looked to be taking the first significant step towards ending the Swiss shelter programme, as they voted to abolish the requirement for new buildings to include a shelter.[17] However, on 11 March, just under 6,000 miles away from Bern, a huge earthquake struck Japan, damaging a reactor at the Fukushima nuclear power plant. In the weeks that followed, it became clear that this might become the most significant nuclear accident since Chernobyl. Influenced by this turn of events, the Swiss senate rejected the decision of the parallel chamber and on 6 June the parliament reconsidered and reversed its original decision;[18] the duty to include a bunker in new Swiss homes was maintained. The shelter had escaped its end by a hair's breadth (Anon., 2011a, 2011b; Putzier, 2011). Indeed, it is not an exaggeration to say that it is now Fukushima that is being concretized into the Swiss shelter as it struggles through its post-cold war afterlife. A remote natural-human made disaster has, for now at least, given new life to this troublesome part of Switzerland's civil protection apparatus.

Conclusion: the concrete transformations of preparedness

In our account we have spoken for shelters, taking something of a liberty seeing as it is likely that these obdurate structures would prefer to sit silently and solidly as they always do. They don't talk to each other, and keep their secrets, their promises and opportunities as well as their futility and unusability with them. In India, shelters might look over at their neighbours – houses – increasingly made of concrete too, and wonder how much longer it will take before all houses are built sturdily enough to resist cyclones and other disasters. Swiss shelters perhaps wonder, why they were built in the first place, when nobody uses them. Maybe shelters in the UK might consider what would have happened, if they would ever have needed to be used. Would those that protected the government have felt ashamed for the population dying around them? Would those that were built by hobbyists have even had time for embarrassment before they collapsed in the face of a nuclear blast, which they were inadequate to resist? Behind all this wondering is a shared question: why, despite all being built to save lives, do they all seem to embody a certain futility? That is, why had nobody thought better about their fate beforehand?

The answer, as we have shown throughout this article points to the particular qualities of *concrete governmentality*. The broad lesson of the story is that it is not simply disasters that transform the relationships between the governing and the governed, between the state and the population, so too do practices of preparedness. And they do so even in the absence of disasters. Disasters do not merely serve as excuses for the state, to justify acting in ways not possible under normal circumstances. Disasters are absent transformers: They produce the very problem of preparedness even if they never occur.

As forms of concrete governmentality, shelters are some of the most para-doxical and puzzling forms of preparedness: First, through their very material existence they materialize and *compose*, in public, particular relationships between the state and the population. They materially and visibly enact what are usually thought of as the unseen mechanisms of governmentality. In Switzerland they embody the population as a unity, while in India and the UK they fracture the population vis-à-vis the state. Second, shelters also *decompose*. Their very material existence can become a problem, for example when the need to keep cyclone shelters operational becomes an affordance for other practices that, in turn, makes them unusable. Lastly, disasters themselves, as products of the same forecasting techniques and expertise as shelters, may simply disappear. Concrete shelters, precisely because they are so durable, then need to recompose, and to find new forms of expertise and new disasters, which can justify their continuing role in processes of concrete governmentality. One particular form of expertise that has played this role in all of our cases, in various guises, is all hazards. In India it is by demanding that cyclone shelters should also withstand earthquakes and floods. In the UK, the all-hazards ethos is deployed via private, improvised practices, while in Switzerland, the range of disasters is expanded with the help of an unexpected event: Fukushima.

Taken together, the problems that we have identified with preparatory shelter building is not a denunciation of concrete governmentality but rather an appraisal of the very concrete problem of preparedness: how to build something that lasts and resists, and remains relevant both when the object that is being resisted keeps changing and when the very act of building intervenes so publicly in the life of the restless surrounding population.

Acknowledgements

We gratefully acknowledge funding by a European Research Council starting grant (GA 263731 OD) that made research for this article possible. We would also like to thank the various interview partners. For critical comments we would like to thank the editors of the volume, the series editor Chris Shilling, the three external reviewers, as well as Silvia Berger Ziauddin, Aurora Fredriksen and Monika Krause.

The Sociological Review, 62:S1, pp. 183–210 (2014), DOI: 10.1111/1467-954X.12129
© 2014 The Authors. Editorial organisation © 2014 The Editorial Board of the Sociological Review

Notes

1 For another take on processes of composition and decomposition, see Marres (2011).
2 Concrete shelters should not be confused with the humanitarian temporary or semi-permanent 'shelters' which are usually set up in the aftermath of a disaster.
3 One might argue that in the global South preparedness is nowadays mostly led by international institutions such as the World Bank and the UN agencies. However, these preparedness building projects emphasize active partnerships with state actors with the ultimate envisioned goal that the state would become the leader in preparedness building.
4 On the importance of standardization see Timmermans and Epstein (2010).
5 'In the last 270 years, 21 of the 23 major cyclones (with a loss of about 10,000 lives or more) worldwide occurred over the area surrounding the Indian subcontinent (India and Bangladesh)' (NDMA, 2008: xxiv).
6 Four states (Tamil Nadu, Andhra Pradesh, Orissa and West Bengal) and the Union Territory of Puducherry on the east coast and Gujarat state on the west coast are more vulnerable to hazards associated with cyclones (NDMA, 2008: xxiv).
7 For example, the 1999 Orissa Cyclone, the 2004 Indian Ocean tsunami.
8 Based on the Disaster Management Act (DMA) 2005, the mitigation of the impacts of disasters became a priority for the Indian state and led to the setting up of a new structure of organizations headed by the apex body – National Disaster Management Authority (NDMA).
9 Disasters that are unexpected and/or cause a great loss of life can generate a reaction of shock which can become translated into an influx of donations by the public, organizations and other states and the political will to respond.
10 A nuclear deterrent was also actively pursued for a period, but ultimately rejected.
11 This itself needs to be understood as growing out of and related to an ongoing leftist critique of Switzerland's Total Defence (*Gesamtverteidigung*) concept, centring on the power and influence of the Swiss military. This is a critique that persists, in altered form, to the present day.
12 The line is thin indeed. As Hastrup pointed out quoting the work of Ingold, if structures are to be relevant and serve their intended purpose, they have to be dwelled in (Hastrup, 2011: 50) or as disaster management practitioners put it, they have to be owned by the community.
13 Drawing on interview data with Swiss civil protection officers, 2013.
14 It is worth noting parallels with the contemporary situation in the USA, where it is perfectly possible – if you can afford it – to pay a company to build a shelter to deliver what it promises will be 'the ultimate protection for you, your family, and valuables'. See http://disasterbunkers.com/plans-and-specs.php.
15 The use of materials like the RCC (reinforced concrete) frame, light-weight pre-cast concrete blocks, corrosion resistant steel and with structural specifications to withstand specified wind velocities, storm surges (up to 7m high), and earthquake loads (Ministry of Home Affairs, 2005: 13–14); and the requirement that the shorter side of the shelter face the coast (Chandra, 2005).
16 See Hagmann and Cavelty (2012) for an overview of the rise of the risk register as a technology of disaster management, including an exploration of some of the difficulties that have surrounded the adoption of this technology in Switzerland.
17 The so-called *Schutzraumbaupflicht.*
18 By 94 votes to 74.

References

Albrecht, P., Gross, A., Hohler, A. E., Hug, P., Lauterburg, W., Schnyder, T., Stocker-Meier, M., Stöcklin, J., Suchomski, J. and Tanner, J., (1988), *Schutzraum Schweiz: mit dem Zivilschutz zur Notstandsgesellschaft*, Gümligen and Bonn: Zytglogge.

Anderson, B., (2011), 'Preemption, precaution, preparedness: anticipatory action and future geographies', *Progress in Human Geography*, 34 (6): 777–798.

Anderson, B. and Adey, P., (2011), 'Affect and security: exercising emergency in UK civil contingencies', *Environment and Planning D, Society and Space*, 29 (6): 1092–1109.

Anon., (1983a), 'Dereliction?', *Practical Civil Defence*, May–June: 25.

Anon., (1983b), 'Do-it-yourself; safer than houses!', *Practical Civil Defence*, May–June: 31.

Anon., (1983c), 'The men of iron . . .', *Practical Civil Defence*, May–June: 16–17.

Anon., (2007), 'Archived Report – Danger! Official Secret – RSG6 Pamphlet', *28DaysLater.co.uk Urban Exploration Forums*, available at: www.28dayslater.co.uk/forums/showthread.php/9044-DANGER!-OFFICIAL-SECRET-RSG6-Pamphlet (accessed 5 October 2012).

Anon., (2011a), 'Nun also doch wieder Schutzräume: Nationalrat vollzieht Kehrtwende – bürgerliche Parteien schwenken um', *NZZ Online*, available at: www.nzz.ch/nachrichten/politik/schweiz/katastrophenschutz_nationalrat_schutzraeume_1.10838252.html (accessed 7 June 2011).

Anon., (2011b), 'Ständerat hält an Schutzraum-Pflicht fest: Maurer warnt vor Ländern mit Atomwaffen', *NZZ Online*, available at: www.nzz.ch/nachrichten/politik/schweiz/staenderat_haelt_an_schutzraum-pflicht_fest_1.10766938.html (accessed 31 May 2011).

Barry, A., (2002), 'The anti-political economy', *Economy and Society*, 31 (2): 268–284.

Berger Ziauddin, S., (2010), 'Wahre Schweizer Architektur ist unterirdisch – oder wie die Schweiz im Kalten Krieg zum Schutzbaumusterland wurde', in Historisches Seminar, Universität Stuttgart.

Berger Ziauddin, S., (2012), 'Apocalypse now? Swiss bunkers as (in)effective transition spaces into the postnuclear world', paper presented at the 'Organising Disaster' advisory board workshop.

Campbell, D., (1982), *War Plan UK: The Truth about Civil Defence in Britain*, London: Burnett.

Carr, L. J., (1932), 'Disaster and the sequence-pattern concept of social change', *The American Journal of Sociology*, 38 (2): 207–218.

Chandra, G. R., (2005), 'Revenue-disaster management – finalization of design criteria and model design for cyclone shelters under the national cyclone risk mitigation project (World Bank Assisted)' a letter from Ragesh Chandra, Collector-cum-Additional Secretary to Government of Pondicherry addressed to the Advisor (Disaster Management), National Disaster Management Division, Ministry of Home Affairs, New Delhi sent dated 15/2/2005 ref No. 48673/AS(R)/RO/TAH/D2/2005.

Clarke, L., (1999), *Mission Improbable: Using Fantasy Documents to Tame Disaster*, Chicago: University of Chicago Press.

Collier, S., (2008), 'Enacting catastrophe: preparedness, insurance, budgetary rationalization', *Economy and Society*, 37 (2): 224–250.

Daily Mail Reporter, (2010), 'For sale: four bedroom luxury home, sea views. . . and underground bunker able to withstand nuclear blast', *Mail Online*, available at: www.dailymail.co.uk/news/article-1322143/For-sale-Four-bedroom-luxury-home–underground-bunker-able-withstand-NUCLEAR-blast.html (accessed 6 August 2012).

Davis, T. C., (2007), *Stages of Emergency: Cold War Nuclear Civil Defence*, Durham, NC: Duke University Press.

Eidgenössisches Departement für Verteidigung, Bevölkerungsschutz und Sport, (2012), *Strategie Bevölkerungsschutz und Zivilschutz 2015+. Bericht des Bundesrates*, Bern: Eidgenössisches Departement für Verteidigung, Bevölkerungsschutz und Sport.

Ericson, R. V. and Doyle, A., (2004), 'Catastrophe risk, insurance and terrorism', *Economy and Society*, 33 (2): 135–173.

Ferguson, J., (1994), *The Anti-Politics Machine: 'Development,' Depoliticization, and Bureaucratic Power in Lesotho*, Minneapolis: University of Minnesota Press.

Forty, A., (2012), *Concrete and Culture: A Material History*, London: Reaktion.

Grant, M., (2010), *After the Bomb: Civil Defence and Nuclear War in Britain, 1945–68*, Basingstoke: Palgrave Macmillan.

Hagmann, J. and Cavelty, M. D., (2012), 'National risk registers: security scientism and the propagation of permanent insecurity', *Security Dialogue*, 43 (1).

The Sociological Review, 62:S1, pp. 183–210 (2014), DOI: 10.1111/1467-954X.12129

Hastrup, F., (2011), *Weathering the World: Recovery in the Wake of the Tsunami in a Tamil Fishing Village*, New York: Berghahn Books.

HMO, (2004), Civil Contingencies Act 2004, available at: www.legislation.gov.uk/ukpga/2004/36/part/1?view=plain (accessed 9 February 2011).

HMSO, (1980), 'Protect and survive', available at: www.atomica.co.uk/main.htm (accessed 9 February 2011).

Lakoff, A., (2007), 'Preparing for the next emergency', *Public Culture*, 19 (2): 247.

Lakoff, A. and Collier, S. J., (2010), 'Infrastructure and event: the political technology of preparedness', in B. Braun and S. Whatmore (eds), *Political Matter: Technoscience, Democracy, and Public Life*, Minneapolis: University of Minnesota Press.

Lavanya, M., (2011), 'School still in cyclone shelter', *The Hindu*, available at: www.thehindu.com/news/cities/chennai/article2745133.ece (accessed 1 October 2012).

Law, J., (2003), *Disasters, A/symmetries and Interferences*, Centre for Science Studies, Lancaster University, available at: www.lancs.ac.uk/fass/sociology/papers/law-disaster-asymmetries-and-interferences.pdf.

Lechat, M. F., (1990), 'The international decade for natural disaster reduction: background and objectives', *Disasters*, 14 (1): 1–6.

Marres, N., (2011), 'The costs of public involvement: everyday devices of carbon accounting and the materialization of participation', *Economy and Society*, 40 (4): 510–533.

Marres, N. and Lezaun, J., (2011), 'Materials and devices of the public: an introduction', *Economy and Society*, 40 (4): 489–509.

McKerrow, B., (2010), 'You smell like a fish and drink like one too!', *Bob McKerrow – Wayfarer Mountains, Travel, Humanitarian Work and Opinion*, available at: http://bobmckerrow.blogspot.co.uk/2010/04/you-smell-like-fish-and-drink-like-one.html.

Meier, M., (2007), *Von der Konzeption 71 zum Zivilschutz 95. Der Schweizer Zivilschutz zwischen Sein und Schein*, Freiburg: Lizentiatsarbeit.

Meier, Y., (2007), *Die gesellschaftliche und institutionelle Verankerung des schweizerischen Zivilschutzes in den 1950er und 1960er Jahren. Der Zivilschutz als Ausdruck des ambivalenten schweizerischen Selbstverständnisses im Kalten Krieg*, Freiburg: Lizentiatsarbeit.

Ministry of Home Affairs, (2005), *Design Recommendations for Construction of Cyclone Shelters: National Cyclone Risk Mitigation Project*, New Delhi: Government of India.

NDMA, (2008), *Management of Cyclones: National Disaster Management Guidelines*, New Delhi: Government of India.

Ormerod, R. N., (1983), *Nuclear Shelters: A Guide to Design*, London: Architectural Press.

Oudshoorn, N. and Pinch, T. J. (eds), (2003), *How Users Matter: The Co-Construction of Users and Technologies*, Cambridge, MA: MIT Press.

Perrow, C., (1984), *Normal Accidents: Living with High-Risk Technologies*, New York: Basic Books.

Putzier, K., (2011), 'Warum die Schweizer so gerne Bunker bauen', available at: www.morgenpost.de/politik/ausland/article1699108/Warum-die-Schweizer-so-gerne-Bunker-bauen.html (accessed 21 July 2011).

Rimathé, W., (1969), 'Glaubwürdigkeit der Aufklärung beim Zivilschutz', *Schutz und Wehr*, 35 (5/6): 42–44.

Schweizerischer Bundesrat, (1979), *Zwischenbericht der Sicherheitspolitik*, Bern: Schweizerischer Bundesrat.

Schweizerischer Bundesrat, (2010), *Bericht des Bundesrates an die Bundesversammlung über die Sicherheitspolitik der Schweiz*, available at: www.vbs.admin.ch/internet/vbs/de/home/documentation/bases/sicherheit.parsys.9457.downloadList.86387.DownloadFile.tmp/sipolbd.pdf (accessed 22 August 2011).

Sharma, V. K., (2000), 'Natural disaster management in India', in S. Narayan (ed.), *Anthropology of Disaster Management*, 53–67, New Delhi: Gyan.

Slaton, A. E., (2001), *Reinforced Concrete and the Modernization of American Building, 1900–1930*, Baltimore, MD: Johns Hopkins University Press.

Smith, M., (2010), 'Architects of Armageddon: The Home Office Scientific Advisers' Branch and Civil Defence in Britain, 1945–68', *The British Journal for the History of Science*, 43 (2): 149–180.

Stafford, J., (2011), ' "Stay at home": the politics of nuclear civil defence, 1968–83', *Twentieth Century British History*, available at: http://tcbh.oxfordjournals.org/content/early/2011/09/23/tcbh.hwr034.abstract (accessed 15 February 2012).

Timmermans, S. and Epstein, S., (2010), 'A world of standards but not a standard world: toward a sociology of standards and standardization', *Annual Review of Sociology*, 36: 69–89.

Vaughan, D., (1996), *The Challenger Launch Decision. Risky Technology, Culture, and Deviance at NASA*, Chicago: University of Chicago Press.

Vaughan, D., (2004), 'Theorizing disaster: analogy, historical ethnography, and the Challenger accident', *Ethnography*, 5 (3): 315–347.

The Sociological Review, 62:S1, pp. 183–210 (2014), DOI: 10.1111/1467-954X.12129

Anticipating oil: the temporal politics of a disaster yet to come

Gisa Weszkalnys

Abstract: Here, I analyse the temporal politics of economic disaster associated with prospective oil exploration in the African Atlantic island state of São Tomé and Príncipe (STP). I call this politics the 'not yet' of disaster – a temporality in which future disaster has effects in the present. The theories and practices of social scientists, global policy institutions, and advocacy groups have contributed to an ontology of oil as a disastrous matter that may cause a 'resource curse'. Focusing on STP's antici- pated oil resources, I ask what political forms, objects and effects are generated by what some consider a disaster in the making. I trace the role of anticipation as a specific temporal disposition, particularly among Santomean state officials and members of civil society, which substitutes fresh certainties and uncertainties about what oil might bring. These include suspicions and uncertainties regarding the opera- tions of anticipation itself. Suspicion, I suggest, is not the target of anticipation but implicated in its practice and may even call it into doubt, thus redirecting anticipation against itself.

Keywords: anticipation, economic disaster, oil, suspicion, temporal politics

Cursed resources

In the wake of the global financial crisis, citizens in the West have been encour- aged to develop a certain economic proficiency and exercise vigilance, lest such a disaster repeats itself. In Britain, there are TV programmes that teach hapless citizens to take care of their personal finances; hundreds of people famously camped outside St Paul's Cathedral as part of the Occupy London campaign; and my 16-year-old stepson submitted an account of his own attempted occu- pation of the Oxford branch of a high street bank as part of his GCSE coursework for 'Citizenship Studies'. These practices come alongside the post- 2008 austerity policies that purport to mitigate some of the worst effects of the crisis as well as ongoing deliberations about regulatory and institutional reforms (cf. Lakoff, 2010: 2). Embedded, here, are fresh proposals for individual and collective reorientation in the face of potential economic calamity. Arguably, the citizens of Europe and the US could also look for inspiration towards the

The Sociological Review, 62:S1, pp. 211–235 (2014), DOI: 10.1111/1467-954X.12130
© 2014 The Author. Editorial organisation © 2014 The Editorial Board of the Sociological Review. Published by John Wiley & Sons Ltd, 9600 Garsington Road, Oxford OX4 2DQ, UK and 350 Main Street, Malden, MA 02148, USA

experiences of their counterparts in the 'global South'. There, a sense of economic crisis has been an almost everyday condition and has been accompanied, for some time, by programmes designed to foster a public understanding of economics, broadly conceived, and to encourage a specific temporal orientation that might counteract corrupt practices and other economic misdemeanours in the future.

This article examines the temporal politics of such efforts to anticipate economic disaster, specifically disaster related to natural resource wealth. I consider anticipation as an 'affective state', that is, 'not just a reaction, but a way of actively orienting oneself temporally' (Adams *et al.*, 2009: 247, emphasis omitted). To anticipate is not simply to expect; it is to realize that something is about to happen and, importantly, to act on that premonition. Distinguishing between this and other possible orientations towards the future is critical to what I term the temporal politics of a disaster yet to come. I draw on ethnographic research in the African Atlantic island state of São Tomé and Príncipe (STP), a Portuguese colony until 1974 and currently the world's third smallest economy[1] but with potentially significant oil reserves in its maritime territory. In expectation of great resource wealth, the country's barely 200,000 inhabitants – its governors, public servants and citizens – have been admonished to be vigilant of a 'resource curse'.[2] Through the institutions they build, the laws they ratify, the accounts they publish or, in essence, through the ways in which they concern themselves with a future with oil, Santomeans are urged to display their preparedness.

Importantly, as a type of economic disaster, the resource curse is not sudden or unforeseen.[3] In the formulations of scholars, policy-makers, and activists, it emerges as a slow-burning phenomenon associated with resource booms or dependency on resource revenues, especially in developing countries, and is frequently identified with economic stagnation, social inequality, and even civil war (Auty, 1993; Collier and Hoeffler, 2000; Karl, 1997; Ross, 2012; Sachs and Warner, 2001). In this view, the curse eats away at a country's economic and political institutions or prevents them from fully developing in the first place, and may be exacerbated by the presence of despotic leaders, corrupt governments, and the rent-seeking behaviour of political elites. Given this, the assumption is that if the right measures are taken the curse may be preventable.

'Disasters do not just happen', write anthropologists Anthony Oliver-Smith and Susanna Hoffman (2002: 3). Not only do they require the presence of a human population as disaster's point of impact; they are compounded by specific political structures or cultural beliefs. I would add that they are co-produced by human and non-human factors in another sense as well. In my research to date, I have aimed to explore the complex articulations of the resource curse as an economic device and the worlds to which it applies itself, rather than to assess the validity of its empiricist claims (Weszkalnys, 2011).[4] Here, I show how within the contemporary epistemic practices of the international financial institutions, quasi- and non-governmental institutions, and the extractive industries, oil has acquired an inherently destructive or disastrous potential, in addition to the generative potential that is characteristic of resources *per se* (cf. Ferry and Limbert, 2008). Potentiality, as Giorgio Agamben (1999) writes, works as 'the presence of an absence'. I take up this notion in thinking about the effects of absent oil. Specifically, I raise the question of how social scientific and associated knowledge practices, such as those that underwrite the resource curse, help constitute ontologies of disastrous matter and of how this matter should be dealt with, for example, by technical or political means.

This article asks what political forms, objects, and affects are generated by disaster in the making, such as STP's anticipated resource curse? Conversely, how does this disaster that is yet to come articulate a particular temporal politics that demands close attentiveness to what the future holds? I do not seek to establish one (disaster) as cause for the other (temporal politics) but suggest their mutuality. Put briefly, anticipation unfolds with disaster in mind, *and* it confirms the need to be ready for the worst. Global policy and non-governmental agencies as well as international and Santomean actors have posited STP as the instantiation of a generalized, global phenomenon (the resource curse) to which anticipation is the appropriate response.

In my own analysis, the STP case becomes an instantiation of a broader contemporary anticipatory regime (Adams *et al.*, 2009). I infer from it a specific temporal politics that I call the 'not yet' of disaster.[5] I demonstrate that far from being an empty placeholder, the 'not yet' (or potentially disastrous oil) has been productive of new entities, organizational forms, and subjectivities. This is played out, for example, in the oil-related institutions set up as protection against an oil curse, and in the mobilization of civil society ready to hold government and industry accountable. In my conclusion, I shall suggest that rather than a bridging moment that takes us from the present to the future in a straightforward line, the 'not yet' is better seen as an unfolding, a faltering, and a distribution of temporalities – for suspicion (triggered not least by demands to be vigilant) seems to make anticipation an always incomplete endeavour.

The 'not yet' of resource disaster

What kind of disaster is the resource curse? Consider this cartoon that appeared in a leaflet about oil – its extraction, circulation, and effects – distributed in 2004 among large parts of the Santomean population. The leaflet was part of a consultation process run in the context of a so-called National Forum that was to bring unity to the Santomean people following an attempted *coup d'état* in the previous year. As a potentially divisive factor in Santomean society, oil had become a special focus of this consultative work. The leaflet was designed by an advisory team from the Earth Institute at Columbia University in New York City, headed by the renowned economist Jeffrey Sachs and sponsored by the Open Society Institute.[6] Among other things, the team had been instrumental in drawing up a resource-revenue management law for STP. The cartoon juxtaposed a landscape devastated by flooding, with houses submerged in water and trees uprooted, with another made fertile by the controlled flow of water for irrigation and populated by smiling people. The accompanying text read:

> Imagine what would happen if there were a big flood that hit us unprepared. It would wash over the land, then dry up as quickly as it arrived, and leave the country devastated. The water would be useless to us. If we knew the country were to be flooded, we would build dams to contain the water and channel it so that it would be used for our benefit. Oil money is similar. Other countries have seen a lot of oil money arrive suddenly, tear up old ways of doing things, then suddenly disappear and leave the countries worse off than they were before the oil. *The oil law creates a dam to turn the possible flood of oil money into a useful flow of real resources.*[7]

The new law, it was implied, would wall off an area of Santomean jurisdiction, perfecting it, making it watertight, and creating a legislative enclave in what is largely perceived as a sea of partiality and arbitrariness. It would thus prevent a future resource disaster.

Floods, tsunamis or earthquakes are perhaps more typical of the sort of phenomena described as disaster than the effects brought by the influx of large revenues from oil. Disasters are usually conceived as spatially and temporally circumscribed events, causing great physical destruction or loss of life, and evoking visceral responses, shock and anger among victims, witnesses and onlookers (Sims, 2007). Attempts to press these events into social scientific definitions struggle to include these affective dimensions, the profound sensation of loss of human mastery and control, that is, disaster's 'more-than-rational' aspects (cf. Clark, 2011). Disasters have been defined as 'combining a potentially destructive agent/force from the natural, modified, or built environment' and a population rendered vulnerable due to particular circumstances, including its geographic location, the absence of infrastructures, or a lack of adequate social organization (Oliver-Smith and Hoffman, 2002: 4). Disaster studies researchers have argued that social and political factors are crucial in exacerbating disaster, as is a lack (or overload) of information and data, and depending on their degree of vulnerability, some people may be hit harder than others (eg Hoffman and Oliver-Smith, 1999; Lakoff, 2010; Oliver-Smith and Hoffman, 2002; Quarantelli, 1998; Sarat and Lezaun, 2009).[8] Disasters are, therefore, seen as events that can be anticipated if not always wholly prevented.

Implicit in such struggles for definition are, in addition, persistent questions regarding the ontology of disaster: What dependencies does disaster imply between 'natural' and 'social' things? How does it give opportunities to stake out what is and what is not human? Should we judge disaster by its causes, its effects, or the responses it provokes? There are also questions about disaster's timing – when does it start?; when does it end? – vague temporal markers drawn out by practices of preparedness and recovery. In this section, I want to briefly address these questions in relation to the resource curse.

The cartoon's allegorical elision between floods of water and floods of revenue from a natural resource is suggestive of the ways in which resources, too, have been seen as 'natural agents' capable of causing catastrophic damage to the populations on which they act. Of course, it may be argued that oil's primary potential for causing disaster is not allegorical at all but derives from its undoubted polluting capacities, wreaking havoc and bodily suffering in human and non-human populations due to corporate neglect or technological failure (cf. McGuire and Austin, 2013). Oil's destructive capacity has been further associated with its plenitude or its finitude. On the one hand, humankind's ability to be a most forceful 'geological agent' (Clark, 2012: 261) causing irrevocable climatic damage is certainly underwritten by the seemingly continuous discovery of new hydrocarbon sources. On the other hand, such discovery is justified by gesturing towards the eventual exhaustion of hydrocarbon reserves, another resource disaster for which humankind has struggled to prepare.

The other disastrous potential of oil, the resource curse, which is the focus of this article, is similarly the outcome of a whole techno-social-material arrangement (Mitchell, 2009; Watts, 2004; Weszkalnys, 2013). It involves extractive infrastructures such as platforms and pipelines, administrative entities and government bodies, global policies, and work safety regulations typical of the industry, and is modulated, though not overdetermined, by the specific properties of the substance we call oil. However the curse has much to do with what scholars have identified as the manufactured scarcity of oil (Labban, 2008), and follows from oil's ontological conversion from a substance found in the subsoil into a financial asset, revenue, or sums of money. Occasionally, it is thought to be just the expectation of oil that causes the curse to happen.

In this view, the resource curse becomes, to mix metaphors, one of the 'original sins' of the Anthropocene:[9] That which Nature has given us to enable human flourishing and happiness is deemed to bear within itself a destructive potential, called forth by greedy and thoughtless human acts. The impacts of the oil curse are seen as gradual, to some extent foreseeable, and the damages it causes as largely indirect (eg Humphreys *et al.*, 2007a). There has been a continuous displacement of more resource-deterministic accounts of the curse with accounts that seek to explain the curse in terms of economic, institutional, or socio-cultural factors. As a consequence, greater emphasis is now placed on the curse's non-quantitative, or at least not fully calculable, aspects. Prudence and restraint, in the form of institutions, regulations, and corporate and public-sector ethics, are advocated as the remedy for the oil curse.

In STP, worries about the uncertain future of the nascent oil economy were not empirically unfounded. From the start, the country's involvement in the oil sector was troubled by unfavourable agreements, accusations of bribery and corruption, and diplomatic disputes. In 1997, the country signed a fateful contract with a virtually unknown and largely inexperienced US oil company, the Environmental Remediation Holding Corporation (ERHC), which promised to deliver STP's offshore oil. In return for a fee of US$5 million, ESRC gained preferential access to oil concessions; it also promised to initiate scientific assessments of the country's oil prospects and to attract additional foreign investors with the necessary know-how and capital. The deal has been widely decried as imbalanced and decidedly unfavourable for the country (Shaxson, 2007). In addition, Nigeria questioned STP's claim to an exclusive economic zone, resulting in the creation of a joint development zone straddling the two countries' maritime territory and shared at a ratio of 40:60 (STP : Nigeria). International observers have consistently interpreted such occurrences, including the attempted *coup d'état* in 2003, as indicators of an incipient resource curse (Weszkalnys, 2011). For them, these were early warning signs of a disaster yet to come.

The disastrous capacity of Santomean oil has partly been explained in terms of geopolitics. São Tomé and Príncipe denote two points in the chain of volcanic islands running diagonally south-westwards from Mount Cameroon through the Gulf of Guinea. The region's tumultuous geology, a long history of exploration, and more recent significant finds have made it one of Africa's most prominent oil frontiers. But Gulf of Guinea oil has also been marked out as particularly problematic. Most, if not all, of the oil-producing countries straddling the Gulf of Guinea coast – from Nigeria to Angola – have been diagnosed with one or another version of the resource curse (Shaxson, 2007; Soares de Oliveira, 2007). These specific and deeply localized disastrous situations can be expressed in the economist's universalizing script of statistical correlations, and be compared and contrasted with similar phenomena elsewhere. At the same time, the resource curse's range of impact is clearly presumed to be global. This is echoed in the contributions to *Escaping the Resource Curse*, a volume that is intended as a compendium for policy and decision makers in resource-rich countries and that draws directly on the advisory work some of the contributing authors carried out in the future oil state of São Tomé and Príncipe. As the editors write:

> [T]he 'resource curse' afflicts not just host country governments and their populations; it also affects the operations of major international corporations, their home governments, and those in consuming nations. We believe that reforms that bring an end to the resource curse are also in the interests of the oil companies and consumer states. (Humphreys *et al.*, 2007b: 322)

Across the globe, efforts to avoid a curse now abound. For example, the World Bank, keen to harness the power of natural resources for 'sustainable' development, has made resource governance a central policy issue. Global campaigns such as the Extractive Industries Transparency Initiative (EITI), announced by British Prime Minister Tony Blair at the World Summit on Sustainable Development in Johannesburg in 2002, constitute another effort to create transparency in the natural resource sector by bringing national governments, companies, and civil society to one table with open books. There is also the Resource Charter, a set of principles and suggestions for policy-makers in resource-rich countries, written by an eclectic group of scholars and practitioners, such as economist Paul Collier and Peter Eigen, the founder of the Berlin-based anti-corruption watchdog Transparency International.[10] In addition, there are numerous non-governmental organizations, including Global Witness, Revenue Watch, and Transparency International that have made the link between natural resources and corruption, war and similar economic and political disaster their cause. These organizations, their programmes and activities partake, without completely exhausting, what Andrew Barry (2006) has called a technological zone of qualification typical of the contemporary oil industry. Within this zone, issues of transparency and ethical conduct have become subject to new kinds of evaluation, standard judgements, and regulation.

Taking this observation further, I want to connect the techno-political governance of oil to the proliferating regimes of anticipation identified by Adams *et al.* (2009). Indeed, some scholars suggest that notions of disaster have become characteristic of the contemporary condition. In this view, we all live and act always with the worst-case scenario in mind (Adams *et al.*, 2009; Beck, 1992; Sarat and Lezaun, 2009). It could be argued that the resource curse can be considered a disaster not primarily because it *is* a disaster like a flood or an earthquake, but because the activities designed to prevent a curse, such as those implemented in STP, are akin to what people have done elsewhere to prepare themselves for disaster. Oil, especially potentially disastrous oil, thus receives a temporal framing, which I refer to as the 'not yet' of disaster. My notion of the 'not yet' of disaster has much in common with anthropologist Jane Guyer's account of the *near future* (Guyer, 2007). In Guyer's somewhat disheartening sketch, an overly dominant emphasis on what macroeconomists refer to as the long term has led to a gradual evacuation of the near future. She invites us to explore what has come to fill the near future at this time as a kind of ethical project for the here and now. Indeed, I argue that the 'not yet' of disaster is filled with busy activity. Charters, policies, and campaigns are aimed at transforming potentially 'bad' into 'good' oil. However, I do not think that they therefore contain a disavowal of the economists' long term; rather they are about a reordering and recalibration of energies and affects, and the means with which to achieve such ends.

In other words, STP's potentially disastrous oil has produced a temporal politics of anticipation that is animated by a variety of programmes, plans, and measures. The disaster-yet-to-come is politically productive not just because, as a moment of breakdown and social, political, and economic exposure, it is a test to human-made systems and legal and political infrastructures (Sarat and Lezaun, 2009). Its capacity for politics rests also not simply in the ways in which it can become politically expedient, instrumentalized in neoliberal policy-making in order to push through different kinds of policies that prescribe austerity and free market mechanisms, and take away health care and other welfare provisions, leading to even greater calamity for the poor (Klein, 2007). Rather, potentially 'bad' oil has mapped out its own political space, framed by notions of scientific, technological, and economic management, and by contestation, moral evaluation, and ethical concerns (Barry, 2001; Braun and Whatmore, 2010). It is this process to which I now turn.

The Sociological Review, 62:S1, pp. 211–235 (2014), DOI: 10.1111/1467-954X.12130
© 2014 The Author. Editorial organisation © 2014 The Editorial Board of the Sociological Review

'Bad' oil politics

'There is no oil yet. But we need to *prepare*', noted the head of STP's parliamentary commission for oil matters in our interview. Preparations in STP have been comprehensive, aimed at realizing oil's generative potential and creating resilience in the face of its negative impacts. Scientific expeditions have been sent out to establish petroleum prospects through seismic research. The government successfully, if not without dispute, applied for recognition of its maritime boundaries with the United Nations Law of the Sea Commission. Several licensing rounds have been held to allocate exploration rights to multinational consortia of oil companies who bid millions of dollars and promise much technological and human resource investment. At the same time, legislative guidelines for the collection, distribution, and use of oil revenues have been passed, including the so-called Abuja declaration, a document signed by STP and Nigeria that promises the publication of contracts, revenues, and expenditures in relation to the two country's joint development zone. In addition, dedicated entities – from a ministry for natural resources to a parliamentary commission and a national petroleum agency – have been set up to manage the new national asset.

STP's oil emerges as a kind of technical cum political 'gathering' (Latour, 2004) whose multiple contours are visualized by seismic measurements, delineated by maritime boundaries, inscribed in the contracts signed with international partners and investors, and regulated nationally and in the global domain by laws and agreements. Even the IMF economists I talked to, who monitored the country's economic performance, did not apprehend future oil purely as an economic category. As I show in the following, oil's potentially disastrous consequences are dispersed across an array of institutions, technical devices, regulations, and administrative, commercial, and political practices, where this potential gets stabilized, albeit momentarily, in specific ways.

The oil sector has become, without a doubt, one of the most developed parts of STP's public administration today. Let's take STP's National Petroleum Agency as an example.[11] In a sense, the Agency has anticipation as its *modus operandi* and is key to the country's project of becoming an exemplary oil state in the context of the ill-fated Gulf of Guinea. Funded by a World Bank infrastructure and capacity-building programme (which since 2003 has focused on the improvement of oil-related infrastructures in STP), the Agency has been in charge of overseeing government policy in the sector. It embodies a notion of 'good governance'[12] that has become central to the World Bank's efforts to defend its support for natural resource extraction as a source of 'sustainable development', in the face of multiplying reports about their negative social, environmental, and economic effects (cf. Liebenthal *et al.*, 2005). Institutional and regulatory failure is branded as the primary cause of countries' inability to turn resource wealth into economic prosperity. Consequently, notions of good governance and transparency have been the preferred instruments with which to

The Sociological Review, 62:S1, pp. 211–235 (2014), DOI: 10.1111/1467-954X.12130

effect transformation. This resonates with a broader policy shift within the Bank. Specifically in sub-Saharan Africa, the World Bank began in the late 1980s to pursue a project of so-called political renewal in order to 'reconstruct the state, its personnel, the institutional structure necessary to sustain a market economy, and the nature of society itself' (Williams, 2008: 49). Indeed, World Bank policy would seem increasingly hybrid, reconnecting abstract economic ideals with political expediency (Williams, 2008).

The multiple facets of oil as a new 'matter of concern' (Latour, 2004) are built into the Agency's structure – comprised of a technical, an environmental, an economic, and a legal department. Staff asserted the Agency's explicit, if precarious, a-political function.[13] They claimed to hold a merely technical an advisory role. Discussions about revenues and transparency, I was informed, were being led elsewhere. This self-consciously technocratic spirit guided individual and collective performance, as did the strategy papers, annual training plans, production sharing contracts, forms of accounting, seminars run by international consultants, and training trips abroad. Staff were learning about oil geology, prospectivity, and economic modelling, at the same time that they were improving their negotiating and English-language skills. Personal performance, in this context, was improved not only by the much-cherished capacity building aimed at enhancing individual talent but also by standardizing skills and behaviour.

In this way, the Agency constitutes one of STP's many prospective infrastructures, seeking to achieve procedural and behavioural change to ensure transparent and objective conduct, based on balanced information and best practice, emulating similar institutions in countries such as Norway and Brazil.[14] In some sense, the Agency is a locally inflected imitation of scripts and devices that pass through the global circuits of the international financial institutions, think tanks, and other centres of expertise. Far from being merely technical or auxiliary this type of infrastructure is arranged to prevent a future resource disaster. It is to deliver particular goods associated with oil – or, more precisely, to assure that the oil delivered will be good.

It would be wrong, however, to see the stabilization of oil's disastrous potential as the outcome of World Bank policy alone. Some institutions and individuals may quite clearly hold more 'powers of definition'; but even those who do not do so to the same extent may be compliant with their terms or be required to instantiate them in their actions (Simmons, 2003). For example, STP's state-of-the-art oil management legislation I referred to earlier was the result of unrelated but convergent advisory initiatives. While it was developed partly in cooperation with a five-member expert team hired by the World Bank and led by Alaska's former governor Steve Cowper (Seibert, 2008), there was also a group of high-powered US lawyers working *pro bono* for the Columbia University team. The latter collaborated with local lawyers in designing a made-to-measure oil law, drawing on best practices and worst experiences encountered elsewhere. Some of the participating Santomean lawyers I spoke to described this process not as an imposition but as a careful negotiation of different possible models

(US, Norwegian, etc.) from which they picked whatever elements seemed most appropriate to them.

The resource-revenue law is often invoked as the prime mechanism that will help STP avoid the rent seeking, inflation, and corruption that trouble other oil-rich developing countries. A final draft was passed by the Santomean parliament in 2004. The law now sets out how oil revenues are to be spent; that a part should be saved in a future-generations fund with the US Federal Reserves;[15] that a committee of people has to approve any withdrawals to be made from this account; and that there should be an oversight commission controlling how the money is used. The Santomean legislation is now held up as a model case for other African countries (Bell and Maurea Faria, 2007), superior even to that governing the Chad-Cameroon pipeline, which did not seem to withhold the pressure of national politics (Massey and May, 2005; Pegg, 2005).

In a much-cited book, the anthropologist James Ferguson (1990) speaks of development as an 'anti-politics machine', unresponsive to the politics that shape a country's society and economy. The National Petroleum Agency and the resource revenue management law may similarly be seen to be the kind of evacuation of politics by managerialism, which Ferguson notes. Politics, in the self-consciously technocratic replies of my Agency interlocutors, was happening elsewhere. It could be ignored or, preferably, displaced by technical solutions. Though not inaccurate, this formulation presumes a rather limited scope of where politics happens and how (Barry, 2001).

Entities such as STP's Petroleum Agency embody new lines of accountability and types of relevant expertise, technical capacities and ethical comportment, which are also penned into the national resource revenue management law. In some sense, uncertainty about a future with oil has led the technical and the political to intersect in such governmental structures. At the same time, politicized discussion about STP's oil continues. For example, doubt has remained as to the effectiveness of certain governance initiatives, including the oil agency and the legislation, even as many people thoroughly welcome their existence. Questions about who should have a say in decision-making processes related to oil, about the accountability of those involved, or about the ways in which oil money will be spent, have persisted (or perhaps gained even more salience) and are widely discussed in Santomean restaurants, offices, banks, newspapers, and online forums. They include procedural, managerial, or administrative questions that also raise assessments of right and wrong. Beyond these specific questions thus looms a larger issue. As I discuss in the following section, what is being scrutinized is, quite simply, how people should orient themselves towards a future with oil.

Temporal dispositions

The proliferation of anticipation strategies in relation to new types of technology and scientific knowledge has been commented on by sociologists and anthropologists, particularly in situations where potentials and implications are unclear and perhaps hardly predictable (Adams *et al.*, 2009). More specifically, security measures and preparedness apparatuses aim to bring disaster to life in order to detect, and enable us to get ready for, what is to come (Cooper, 2006; Lakoff, 2008; Samimiam-Darash, 2013). Shelters, ostensibly built in response to risk, are concretizations and transformations of that from which they are to protect (Deville *et al.*, this volume). These studies have broadened the scope of anticipation to include not just discourses about the future but practices, technologies, and material devices that, it is hoped, will allow people to encounter, act on and shape the future in specific ways. In doing so, anticipation brings unknown or uncertain futures into the present. Similarly, the programmes, laws and institutions implemented in anticipation of STP's oil – from the National Petroleum Agency to the mobilization of civil society discussed below – are, in a sense, effects of disaster that is yet to come. They are anticipatory strategies designed to enhance the robustness of state and societal institutions and to allow them to cope with any economic vagaries that might come their way. In this sense, anticipation (en)acts disaster in advance.

In examining how the prerequisite for anticipation is articulated, I draw attention to the ways that anticipation guides a collective and individual temporal reorientation vis-à-vis the disastrous matter of STP's oil. Anticipation desires to displace other modes of engaging the future, which are deemed somewhat deficient. I want to highlight the specificity of anticipation as an affective state briefly, by way of contrast.[16] The contrast is between anticipation and other types of future orientation, namely speculating and waiting. In my conversations with Santomeans and foreign commentators and observers, waiting and speculating were recurrently identified as two prevalent modes of engaging a future with oil. And both of them were considered problematic.[17]

Speculation is said to be the temporal disposition from which Santomean oil has sprung, ever since the signing of first contracts between ERHC and the Santomean government in 1997. Particularly foreign investors, local politicians and members of the Santomean elite have been considered prone to engaging in speculations of all kinds. They are accused of conjuring riches out of thin air without taking any visible steps towards getting oil out of the ground. Their speculating seems to have kept oil in a state of indeterminacy and, by creating unwarranted expectations at home and abroad, risks contributing to future resource disaster. Waiting is quite different. International agency staff and Santomeans themselves tended to describe waiting to me as the first reaction to the announcement of oil among the population at large. Waiting has been equated with a passive leaning back, a disengagement from all productive activity in expectation of large sums of oil money. This attitude of alleged inactivity was considered detrimental to the country's development, and could similarly be seen as exacerbating the effects of the resource curse. By contrast, to anticipate is to substitute fresh certainties and uncertainties about what oil might bring for those produced by speculation and waiting. It generates a sense of urgency and need for action. In doing so, it cultivates a dynamic, responsible sense of self –

a self that relates to oil in a rational, informed, and non-selfish manner. Anticipating is also to grasp the implications of individual actions for the attainment
(or non-attainment) of 'long-term' futures (cf. Guyer, 2007).

I suggest that an ability to differentiate between these types of temporal
orientation implied by waiting, speculation and anticipation, is central to the
politics of disaster yet to come. I want to illustrate this process by exploring the
work carried out by NGOs campaigning for transparency in the resource sector.
Specifically I look at the mobilization of civil society, which has been key to this
project. As the entity that would be capable of demanding disclosure and the fair
distribution of resource revenues, civil society has been attributed a vital role
as counter-force to corrupt governments and powerful industry players. As
Humphreys *et al.* put it, for example:

> If we are to make progress in dealing with the resource curse, governments in both
> consuming and producing countries will have to change what they do; the interna-
> tional community will have to act in concert. Corporations will have to take an active
> role. And so too will civil society. We can ask corporations to act more ethically, in a
> more 'socially responsible way,' but they are more likely to do so when pressure is
> brought to bear. We cannot rely on goodwill alone. (Humphreys *et al.*, 2007b: 323)

Civil society is projected as an entity held together not just by shared discourses
of transparency and accountability, but also by shared ways of knowing and
worrying about the future, which provoke collective attachments. It moreover
implicates a particular kind of subject constituting herself knowledgeably and
responsibly in relation to potentially disastrous oil.

In October 2007, the NGO Publish What You Pay (PWYP) and the
London-based NGO International Alert convened a 'National Discussion of
Oil-Revenue Management' in STP. While PWYP provides a global network
for civil society groups campaigning for transparency and accountability in the
natural resource sector, International Alert specializes in conflict resolution
and peace building. For some years, International Alert had been running a
local office in STP implementing a diverse set of projects, including several
oil-related training sessions for civil society activists and parliamentarians, a
centre for local journalists, and two independent community radio stations.
The 2007 National Discussion received further support from United Nations
Development Programme (UNDP) and UNICEF and a range of organizations
that have been leading in this field of activism, among them Global Witness,
Revenue Watch, the Open Society Institute, and the Norwegian Agency for
Development Cooperation (Norad). It was opened by STP's president,
Fradique de Menezes, and included staff of the National Petroleum Agency,
the local representative of Chevron Texaco, the president of STP's federation
of NGOs (FONG), as well as a founding member of Webeto, a Santomean
NGO operating out of the Portuguese diaspora, which had called for increasing transparency in STP's oil sector already since 2003.[18] Among the participants were activists from other Lusophone African countries as well as Nigeria
(with which STP shares a joint development zone).

As members of Santomean civil society were invited to exchange their experiences, and staff at the National Petroleum Agency explained how much oil STP might have and how it was governed, and the representatives of International Alert, Global Witness, and the World Bank outlined the benefits of joining a regulatory initiative, such as the EITI, they were tracing the outlines of STP's resource disaster in a number of ways.

First, with its international audience and the aim to multiply networks across the region, the National Discussion performed the disaster as a problem with global reach. Importantly, this was not the first and not the last event of this kind in STP. A previous workshop entitled 'Living with Oil' had been held in 2005, and another followed in 2010. A lively interchange of ideas, tools, documents, and experiences linked past and present events, and some of the people there would have also participated in one or another meeting held in Cameroon, South Africa, Germany, or Norway. This afforded multiple connections around a common cause. When a few weeks later I visited Ana, an energetic and outspoken woman in her thirties from Príncipe (the smaller of the two islands) and one of the participants in the National Discussion, she told me enthusiastically about the email exchanges that had followed: not only with the leaders of other Santomean NGOs, but also Matteo from Revenue Watch in Gabon, Elias from the Open Society Institute in Angola, and Carla from Webeto in Portugal. For her, these exchanges were hugely important in organizing her own NGO that she had founded to take up the cause of oil. These people, she surmised, living and working outside the country could provide her with better access to information.

Second, the National Discussion revealed a lack of transparency and thus reinforced the need to disseminate 'best practices' and 'share lessons'. In other words, it exposed vulnerabilities that would then justify certain interventions (Lakoff, 2008). The event reminded people of the uncomfortable truth of oil in STP. As José – an experienced civil society activist, participant of many meetings in Gabon, Cameroon and South Africa, and a some time representative of PWYP in STP – summed it up in a subsequent conversation: Oil was prone to bring conflict because the flow of money deriving from oil, just like oil itself, was so easily channelled, diverted or blocked. Similarly, in his opening speech, President de Menezes did not hesitate to spell out the difficulties that had been encountered due to what he described as a lack of experience and capacity. The report summarizing the event's results highlighted the 'nebulousness' surrounding oil in STP, the 'confusion' among citizens, the 'lack of clarity', and the absence of detailed information from the website of the JDA, the authority that managed and, in theory, was obliged to report on issues pertaining to the joint development zone (International Alert *et al.*, 2007).[19] It was this obscurity on which participants in the event were to act.

Third, the National Discussion anticipated the existence of Santomean civil society itself, which paradoxically was claimed to be largely absent. In our conversations, local and international NGO staff lamented about the weakness and lack of commitment of the non-governmental sector in a small country like

STP. For many people, it was thought, NGO work was just another source of income rather than an expression of loyalty to the cause. More training and capacity-building would partly remedy this situation; another strategy was to learn from other countries. This sentiment was reflected in what Carlos, a young journalist from Príncipe, told me about an educational trip to Norway in which he had participated. Organized by International Alert, the trip had been intended to give members of Santomean civil society – including journalists, business leaders, and NGO activists – an opportunity to get to know, first hand a model oil state and a country that has benefited from its oil wealth while avoiding the resource curse.[20] Now, Carlos expressed his wholehearted admiration for what he had encountered: a strong and organized civil society that had a true presence in public debates about the distribution of oil revenues. 'There,' Carlos noted, 'civil society meets, discusses and has a forum where problems are discussed, where one can object, and that's crucial.'

Fourth, events such as the National Discussion and other training opportunities compelled a desire to do something. Being prepared, becoming active and holding the government to account (*responsibilizar*) were recurrent themes in my conversations with self-declared civil society members. It was about developing a certain consciousness, Ana explained to me in our conversation. As she put it, people would not be able to find the solution to life's perennial problems, from poverty and malnutrition to ill health, which they so desperately required, by simply waiting with folded arms for oil to arrive. The desire to implicate oneself in the future with oil is captured well in the online publications of Webeto, the diaspora NGO. Incidentally, the NGO's name is taken from *uê beto*, an expression in Santomean Creole, which translates as 'open eyes'. Indeed, Webeto sought to encourage people to open their eyes:

> If we want the possible exploitation of petroleum in our country to be a blessing and not to condemn the majority of citizens to extreme poverty, as has unfortunately been the case in many African countries that count oil among their natural riches, each one of us, as part of this civil society, has to assume their role as auditing agent, and thus contribute to the campaign for transparency in the management of this common patrimony.[21]

Becoming an auditing agent and campaigning for transparency: this was about how to develop a specific disposition towards a future with oil. A conversation I had with Mohamed, the West Africa manager of International Alert, was telling in this regard. He explained to me that while International Alert's work was founded on the premise that there was an indisputable link between natural resources (especially oil) and conflict, it was important to them that they had found this view reflected in Santomean people's assessments of the situation. There already seemed to exist local awareness of this connection. This was a type of consciousness that would be vital to their successful work. Not that Santomeans predicted imminent social conflict, Mohamed clarified, but they saw it *as a possibility*.

The Sociological Review, 62:S1, pp. 211–235 (2014), DOI: 10.1111/1467-954X.12130

These examples illustrate some of the methods for discernment between waiting, speculation, and anticipation, which were being nurtured in the 'not yet' of STP's resource disaster. People like Ana, José and Carlos found themselves addressed as potential exemplary subjects, cultivating an affective state from which to engage STP's potentially 'cursed' oil. The report on the 2007 National Discussion also contained some more concrete instructions. Seeking knowledge, demanding information, taking initiative, having a vision, uniting one's efforts, expecting to face obstacles, setting up an EITI committee, developing work plans, devising audits, and sticking to deadlines – those are the things that can be done in anticipation of a resource curse (International Alert *et al.*, 2007). Task lists of this kind index a complex temporality that 'punctuates' (Guyer, 2007) or makes more 'manageable' what might otherwise be seen as an ill-defined process of individual and collective transformation.

As Adams *et al.* (2009: 248) poignantly put it, anticipation occasions the sense that 'regardless of whether disasters actually come to pass, they have already had their impact on our present lives'. For the people addressed as Santomean civil society in the National Discussion, the parliamentarians instructed in proper conduct by international consultants, or the journalists who were taught reporting techniques in International Alert's journalist centre, this was indeed true. Instead of speculating on the arrival of oil, or simply waiting for something to happen, people were given the resources that would enable them to engage the 'not yet' of resource disaster. They would apprehend oil afresh, be suspicious of the unfounded promises made by their leaders, ask the right questions, critically reflect on the information offered to them, and also act as multipliers of this stance in their own communities. They would not just expect STP's double-edged future to arrive, but implicate themselves in the job of securing an adequate management of oil as potentially disastrous matter. They would thus contribute to the country's economic stability and ultimately to the prevention of the resource curse. In forming new temporal orientations towards, and attachments with, oil, they would start living in the 'not yet' of resource disaster to come.

Anticipation's excess

My analysis to this point may be taken to indicate that STP's future has been largely predetermined, leaving it poised between two extremes: prosperous oil state vs. a place shattered by the impact of resource disaster. I may have given the impression that this is a world where people transform themselves into anticipating automatons in order to avoid becoming either greedy rent-seekers or hopelessly impoverished and disenfranchised individuals. However, I want to suggest something further about the incompleteness of anticipation. This incompleteness stems only partly from the fact that new knowledge is constantly being produced, throwing into doubt the precarious certainties we have carved out of uncertain terrains (Samimiam-Darash, 2013: 5), though its effects are similar.

Going beyond this reading of uncertainty, I point instead to an excess of anticipation, not unlike the atmosphere of indagation described by Tironi (this
volume). That is, the emergence of all kinds of suspicions, which have as their
object anticipation itself and thus seem to place its full achievement always
slightly out of reach.

In a phone call made around the time that the 2007 National Discussion was
taking place in S.Tomé, the Santomean President put the following accusation
to one of the leading figures of NGO Webeto: Might not all that talk about oil
and about the need to manage supposedly large sums of revenues generate false
expectations among the Santomean population? The president's accusation thus
raised the paradoxical (and somewhat misplaced) question whether the well-
intended work of Webeto and other NGOs could inadvertently contribute to
creating conditions favourable to an oil curse. This suspicion might seem to echo
my own earlier interpretation of the NGO advocacy work as a performance of
yet-to-come resource disaster. However, it could also be seen as itself a result of
the politics of anticipation put in place in STP.

Although suspicion frequently invokes empirical underpinnings, it is not
simply caused by the failure or shortcomings of the objects to which it pertains.
For example, in 2005, International Alert found itself publicly accused of
embezzlement and undue profiteering as the result of a dispute with the
Santomean union of journalists. The union, which from the start had been one
of the primary beneficiaries of the journalists' centre funded by International
Alert, demanded that it be given exclusive access rights to the facility. Its leaders
claimed that the union was the rightful representative of all Santomean journalists and should, therefore, be in charge. While the suspicions about these alleged
misdemeanours were soon dispelled, they did temporarily upset International
Alert's relation with its local partners.

'Suspicions amongst thoughts, are like bats amongst birds, they ever fly by
twilight', wrote Francis Bacon in 1625. It might be suggested that suspicions
such as those levelled against International Alert were simply part of the fabric
of Santomean sociality where rumour and gossip abound. Anthropologist
Gerhard Seibert (2006), for example, explains the persistence of rumours that
are spread through anonymous political pamphlets in STP, particularly in the
1990s, in reference to the context of African societies, characterized by oral
traditions and a lack of literacy, and the limits on free speech during STP's
one-party regime lasting through the late 1970s and 1980s, as well as the
limited access to trustworthy news and information due to a lack of appropriate media. The flipside of this assumption would be that nagging suspicions could be made to disappear with greater knowledge, information, and
transparency.

However, suspicion is perhaps not so much external to transparency, or its
opposite, as implicated in it. The suspicion that power does not always operate
in the open is at the heart of discourses on transparency, such as those promoted
to prevent STP's resource disaster (cf. Sanders and West, 2003). More specifically, in his analysis of contemporary practices of transparency in the oil indus-

try, Andrew Barry (2013) has demonstrated how the production of information may lead to a change in the conceptual nature of that which is considered valuable and therefore to be kept secret. Paradoxically, proliferating information thus seems to increase rather than reduce the number of secrets that need to be revealed (see also Mair *et al.*, 2012).

Something similar to this process was hinted at by a member of staff of the Public Information Office (Gabinete de Registo de Informação Pública) set up to archive and publicize information about STP's oil. When we spoke not long after the Office's inauguration in 2008, this man voiced doubt about whether the Office team would be able to achieve the goal they had been set. The intention was that, in the future, citizens would be able to come to the Office, demand to see contracts or reports, and learn about the amount of money the country had received from signature bonuses and revenues. However, despite repeated enquiries and requests, he claimed, the Office still had not received all the relevant documents, for example those referring to the joint development zone with Nigeria, the country's most prominent zone of oil-related activity. These documents, he seemed to imply, were being held back on purpose.

However, consider the additional twist to this observation offered by António, a self-conscious member of Santomean civil society in a conversation we had in late 2012. I had told António about my earlier attempts to receive oil-related documents from the Public Information Office when I was informed that the scanner needed to make copies had broken down and that 'some missing part' had not yet been supplied. António was unsurprised and did not think that the scanner was just a feeble excuse. People working in the Office might simply not quite understand their own role, he explained; they did not feel the urgency to get all the information out. But then, António speculated that the Office's director might indeed have an interest in not revealing all available information. Information that is out there for everyone – that is public – doesn't give you any power, António explained. But hiding information, having information that others don't have, is what makes you powerful.

António's observations echo analyses of the conceptual contradictions of regimes of free information, such as those promoted in the US Securities and Exchange Commission (SEC) (Fortun and Fortun, 1999). While 'perfect information' may have come to be considered a key factor in creating perfect markets, promoters of transparency tend to romanticize information. They forget that information has become a commodity in itself, a limited and necessarily carefully guarded good. Yet, in some sense similar to the SEC bureaucrats, members of Santomean civil society continue to 'pursue the promise of information as a social good, knowing full well that the utopian desire to be "in the know" can never be fulfilled' (Fortun and Fortun, 1999: 190).

The suspicions voiced in the above examples do not simply occur *in the context of* STP's anticipatory activities; they have *as their object* the very forms and terms that are constitutive of anticipation – be that the alleged misappropriation of money by the advocacy NGO or the official's apparent disregard for legal requirements to provide the conditions for transparency (i.e. a functioning scanner). That is, they do not indicate a failure that could be explained by a lack of anticipation (in the sense discussed earlier) or by faulty procedure. Rather such suspicions are, in some sense, an important index of anticipation itself, which in its particular orientation to the future encourages a kind of questioning stance that it shares with suspicion. Both suspicion and anticipation partly rely on what people already know from experience and what seems likely to repeat itself in the future; but while anticipation is bound to rely on information or 'facts', suspicion makes do with perhaps less certain items of knowledge. (Of course, what confers factuality and what doesn't is also up for grabs.) Suspicion, in this sense, cannot readily be regulated away or eliminated through more numerous revelations. Rather, like Barry's secrets, suspicion occasionally appears to be multiplied by efforts to control it (Barry, 2013).

What are the implications of these anticipatory excesses that happen when efforts to anticipate become themselves suspect? I suggest they open up some of the faultlines of the anticipatory regime, of its conditions of possibility, of anticipation's ethics, which get readily overlooked. For who would object to the project of preventing disaster that is yet to come? A last example will suffice. The 2007 National Discussion had been surrounded by some disagreement regarding the implementation of another, or rather two other, Santomean anticipatory devices. The first device was a local committee for the Extractive Industries Transparency Initiative (EITI) mentioned earlier. The second was an Oversight Commission that, like the Public Information Office, was stipulated by STP's oil revenue management law. Although an independent campaign, the EITI has received much support from the World Bank in an effort to guarantee what is deemed good governance in the extractive industries sector. In STP, the process of setting up an EITI committee was run by the Ministry of Natural Resources; while the eleven members of the Oversight Commission were to be selected by the parliamentary committee in charge of oil matters.

While meetings were being held, candidates put forward, and work plans drafted, a convoluted discussion ensued, involving international NGO representatives and World Bank advisors, local civil society, and government. The focus of their disagreement was the appropriate relationship between the two entities. Would they be duplicating each other's work? Would the expense of having two bodies with similar functions be justified? Would one be better designed than the other to do the job at hand? Which would be more readily dominated by government interests? Which would better represent the will of civil society and the Santomean population at large? In contrast to the EITI committee, which would consist of civil society, government, and oil companies with equal representation and weight, the Oversight Commission was to be composed exclusively of local actors; three of them would be civil society and the remaining would be drawn from a range of government institutions, including parliament, tribunal and presidency. Although both entities were to have an auditing function, each was also conceived to have a distinctive remit: the Oversight Commission was to watch over government expenditure only while

The Sociological Review, 62:S1, pp. 211–235 (2014), DOI: 10.1111/1467-954X.12130

the EITI committee was to create accountability between all three stakeholder groups.

As a simple merger between the two bodies seemed out of the question (after all, this would violate Santomean state law), suspicions about the entities' real purposes and politics could be heard. While a home-grown oversight body might seem preferable, the EITI would be a better conduit for transparent external pressure. At the same time, the Oversight Commission was also readily manipulable by political interests and could become a mere front of transparency, and an EITI committee pushed by the World Bank as a mechanism for 'naming and shaming' could be something to which governments were inclined to sign up only tokenistically. In other words, both of them or neither could work as a mechanism to avoid a resource curse.

While these debates were being held about the modalities of STP's compliance to local and international transparency standards, and work on the EITI committee was well under way in 2007 and 2008, by 2010 this work had ground to an abrupt halt. The country was officially divested of its candidate status. The reason cited for the decision was a lack of progress, principally the failure to meet certain deadlines. Some observers readily saw this as signalling a lack of commitment to transparency on the part of the Santomean government. In other words, it could only be interpreted as a refusal to anticipate. Adherence to deadlines and dates that frame the process for EITI candidature becomes a measure for sincerity of a will to be transparent. Conversely, the failure to meet such deadlines can be read as defiance, and as yet another step towards an impending resource disaster. In the 'not yet' of resource disaster, the date (STP's unmet EITI deadline) became exemplary of what Jane Guyer appositely refers to as 'signal event moments in near-future time at which the whole world could change' (2007: 417).

Conclusion

The whole world did not change with STP's temporary expulsion from the EITI process. Two years later, the country had been readmitted and a new committee had been installed, now chaired by José who, when we talked in late 2012, was already projecting a possible future for himself in the international career structure of the EITI. While items on task lists and deadlines mark and break up the near future into small chunks, this process is interwoven with the cyclical time frames embedded in systems of global governance; and hopes for a personal long term may give new purpose by implicating oneself in the pursuing of the macroeconomic long term. The complex enfolding of multiple temporalities seems to me characteristic of, or even compulsory to, the 'not yet' of disaster as a project that posits both the existence of a desirable long term as well as its undesirable, disastrous alternative, and suggests steps on the way to prevent such disaster from happening. With the methods of anticipation, any strict distinctions between the present, the near and the long-term future collapse.

In exploring the 'not yet' of disaster as a temporality in which disaster has effects in the present, prior to – or rather in anticipation of – its occurrence, this article has thrown up some pertinent questions about when disasters start. We have seen that for resource curse theorists, disaster would seem to start with the hopes and expectations that people entertain some time before, or independently of, the start of commercial oil extraction. I am tempted to trace it back even further to other disastrous moments many million years ago. This was when, for reasons scientists today seek to reveal, oceans entered an extended state of oxygen starvation, or anoxia, while atmospheric and oceanic temperatures increased rather noticeably for the numerous organisms that were extinguished as a consequence. Intrusions of molten rock into older organic-rich shales likely released the greenhouse gases that triggered what geologists now call Oceanic Anoxic Events (OAEs), notably the Toarcian OAE nearly 200 million years ago and the Cenomanian Turonian OAE about a hundred million years later. Layer upon layer of phytoplanktonic organic matter began to accumulate on a scale much greater than usual, squashed, intensely heated up, and transformed first into a waxy substance, and then into liquid and gaseous hydrocarbons.

I offer this juxtaposition of possible, though as such also fictive, starting moments of resource disaster partly as a reminder of a question I posed earlier in this article. Do we think of disasters as natural or social events, as hybrid, or as in fact generative of precisely those kinds of distinctions? How can we, as social scientists, conceptualize and describe the possible 'ontological impact of volatile earth processes' (Clark 2011: 84)? Explanations of the seemingly detrimental effects of natural resources on their 'host' countries, as we have seen, have moved the focus to social and political factors, rather than assuming what has been criticized as resource determinism. In this article, I have tried to make explicit the methods entailed in this process, as well as the important ontological conversions involved: for example, from oil as a substance that is itself the product of geological disaster into a fungible commodity and a money equivalent circulating on multiple scales. Resource economics, as Tim Mitchell (2009) notes, has almost exclusively preoccupied itself with the latter, thereby overlooking its very material framings and political effects. By contrast, what I have sought to show here is how oil that is potentially disastrous is also politically productive. It becomes a new matter of concern with its own specific temporal framing.

This article has aimed to sketch how anticipation prompts a disaster yet to come. It trailed the emergence of a particular temporal politics in the expectation of future oil in São Tomé and Príncipe – two islands that, in the eyes of many observers, seem destined by their geographic, cultural, and political connections to experience both the best and the worst of what resource wealth can bring. The assumption that natural resource development, especially where hydrocarbons are involved, can have potentially disastrous consequences for its host nations has had remarkable effects not just in STP, but indeed worldwide. Sociologists and anthropologists studying science and technology have now for some time drawn attention to the ways in which certain epistemic practices –

The Sociological Review, 62:S1, pp. 211–235 (2014), DOI: 10.1111/1467-954X.12130
© 2014 The Author. Editorial organisation © 2014 The Editorial Board of the Sociological Review

including those of economists, political scientists, and international policy makers as well as their own – are co-constitutive of the phenomena they purport to describe. Here, I have focused less on scientific knowledge production *per se* than on its extensions within intermediary (and not so intermediary) global agencies and organizations. Indeed, I would argue that such bodies are particularly instrumental in effecting articulations of economic, social, or political knowledge within specific locales.

The anticipation of yet-to-come resource disaster is thus not a unitary or predetermined project. In my analysis, it involves broader logics and the micromanagement of individual practices, long-term perspectives, and short-term goals. It involves individuals and institutions who, for a wide variety of reasons, both readily embrace and occasionally eschew what anticipation has to offer them as an affective state oriented towards a possibly dangerous and disastrous future. Anticipation is entangled, on the one hand, with the logics of what Barry (2006) calls a technological zone that seeks to encompass the contemporary oil industry, and that is itself an assemblage of technical devices, standards, practices, personnel, and so on. On the other hand, as Barry also points out, it is capable of bringing with it its own limitations and apparent failures that may not be fully recognized by those who foster its implementation and expansion. This suggests a somewhat different perspective on governance and disaster management, a perspective that directs our attention to what I have described as questions of incompleteness and excess.

The elaborate anticipatory apparatus implemented in STP with the aim of keeping potentially cursed matter under control and preventing future resource disaster has itself generated a series of effects in the present. These include not only the multiple entities charged with managing oil but also fresh suspicions and uncertainties regarding the operations of anticipation itself. I discussed the emergence of new types of contestations and of concerns about anticipation's form and functions, including the worry that if anticipation is not carried out properly, it may itself introduce uncertainties that contribute to the resource curse. The question is how this type of uncertainty, generated in the context of prevention or preparation, can itself be managed. Suspicion is thus not the flipside of anticipation or its target in any simplistic way. Suspicion is something that is implicated in the diverse practices of anticipation and it may even call the project into doubt, thus redirecting anticipation against itself.

Acknowledgements

This article is based on fieldwork funded by the British Academy and the John Fell OUP Research Fund. A Leverhulme Research Fellowship (2012–13) provided time for further reflection and writing. Versions of this paper were presented at the 2012 4S/EASST conference in Copenhagen and at the National Research Center for Integrated Natural Disasters Management (CIGIDEN) in Santiago de Chile. Manuel Tironi, Israel Rodríguez-Giralt, and Michael

Guggenheim provided helpful editorial guidance. I am grateful to Eeva Berglund, Steve Hesselbo, Javier Lezaun, and three anonymous reviewers for their invaluable comments and suggestions. I am particularly indebted to the many people in STP who allowed my questions to interrupt their lives and who patiently shared their knowledge and insight. Special thanks go to the Earth Institute and International Alert teams for providing me with access to their work. Some names have been changed.

Notes

1 IMF Country Report 12/216, August 2012, www.imf.org/external/pubs/ft/scr/2012/cr12216.pdf
2 I will use the terms 'resource curse' and 'oil curse' interchangeably.
3 Not all disasters are sudden or unforeseen. Toxic pollution is a case in point (eg Simmons, 2003; Auyero, 2012).
4 A growing literature now questions the existence of the resource curse phenomenon (eg Brunnschweiler and Bulte, 2008; Haber and Menaldo, 2010).
5 My aims in developing the 'not yet' as a critical ethnographic concept are quite different from those of philosopher Ernst Bloch who deploys the term in his philosophical project to connote a 'forward-looking temporality' directed toward what is feared or hoped for (in Crapanzano, 2004: 111).
6 The details of this project are discussed in Weszkalnys (2011).
7 Earth Institute, 'Popular Information Bulletin', www.earth.columbia.edu/cgsd/stp/documents/ bulletin_english_3.1.pdf (emphasis added) (accessed 12 August 2013).
8 In an attempt to reduce disaster to a common denominator (eg 'the disruption of important societal routines') some scholars have opened up space for including into the category the effects of economic processes as well; though ultimately they have recommended the dissolution of 'disaster' as a conceptual focus of social scientific analysis (Stallings, 1998: 129).
9 On the notion of the Anthropocene, see Clark (this volume).
10 See http://naturalresourcecharter.org
11 A separate institution, the Joint Development Authority, manages the STP-Nigeria joint development zone.
12 The World Bank defines governance as 'the manner in which power is exercised in the management of a country's economic and social resources for development' (World Bank, 1992, cited in Williams 2008: 77).
13 Critics always suspected that staff of the National Petroleum Agency was implicated in local politics. This suspicion was highlighted in December 2007 when the Minister for Natural Resources decided to fire the Agency's entire team of technical directors with immediate effect. The news was even run by RTP Africa, the international TV station for lusophone Africa, showing individual 'mug shots' of each of the directors. There are conflicting opinions about whether the dismissal was justified and followed correct procedure. The form it took, however, was rumoured to have been motivated, in particular, by political differences between the Minister and the Agency's directors. Within two months, most of the newly redundant staff, except for the executive director, had vacated their positions with hardly any provisions for passing on their carefully acquired technical knowledge and standardized forms of conduct.
14 STP also set up a national oil company similar to those of Norway, Brazil or Angola, which would function as owner, operator and manager of natural resources. However, due to a lack of regulations as well as technical capacity and financial resources, the company is currently not operating.
15 This is under revision.

The Sociological Review, 62:S1, pp. 211–235 (2014), DOI: 10.1111/1467-954X.12130

16 I depart here from Adams *et al.*'s (2009) analysis that subsumes a variety of affect states or what I call temporal dispositions, including speculation and hope, under the more generic category of anticipation.

17 My comments on 'waiting' and 'speculation' refer exclusively to how they were problematized in contemporary STP. A growing literature in the social sciences has analysed, for example, speculation as a form of knowing rather than not knowing (Walsh, 2004), and waiting as a temporal process of political subordination (Auyero, 2012).

18 Because it was operating out of Portugal, Webeto was seen to be in a better position to criticize Santomean government policies and actions. However, its diaspora status also led some people to doubt the NGO's authenticity.

19 In this context, a comment by the local representative of Chevron seemed poignant. He suggested that STP's limited oil revenues to date could readily be summed up on a sheet of paper, without a need for expensive audits. Of course, he assured his audience, this did not mean that the company wasn't committed to transparency.

20 The Norwegian government organized a similar trip for Santomean members of parliament.

21 Webeto, *A Coisa Publica IV*, May 2006, author's translation. See www.webeto.org.

References

Adams, V., Murphy, M. and Clarke, A. E., (2009), 'Anticipation: technoscience, life, affect, temporality', *Subjectivity*, 28: 246–265.

Agamben, G., (1999), 'On potentiality', *Potentialities: Collected Essays in Philosophy*, 177–184, Stanford, CA: Stanford University Press.

Auty, R., (1993), *Sustaining Development in Mineral Economies: The Resource Curse Thesis*, London: Routledge.

Auyero, J., (2012), *Patients of the State: The Politics of Waiting in Argentina*, Durham, NC: Duke University Press.

Barry, A., (2001), *Political Machines: Governing a Technological Society*, London and New York: Athlone Press.

Barry, A., (2006), 'Technological zones', *European Journal of Social Theory*, 9 (2): 239–253.

Barry, A., (2013), *Material Politics: Disputes along the Pipeline*, Oxford: Wiley-Blackwell.

Beck, U., (1992), *Risk Society: Towards a New Modernity*, London: Sage.

Bell, J. C. and Maurea Faria, T., (2007), 'Critical issues for a revenue management law', in M. Humphreys, J. D. Sachs and J. E. Stiglitz (eds), *Escaping the Resource Curse*, 286–321, New York: Columbia University Press.

Braun, B. and Whatmore, S. J., (2010), 'The stuff of politics: an introduction', in B. Braun and S. J. Whatmore (eds), *Political Matter: Technoscience, Democracy, and Public Life*, ix–xl, Minneapolis: University of Minnesota Press.

Brunnschweiler, C. N. and Bulte, E. H., (2008), 'Linking natural resources to slow growth and more conflict', *Science*, 320: 616–617.

Clark, N., (2011), *Inhuman Nature: Sociable Life on a Dynamic Planet*, London: Sage.

Clark, N., (2012), 'Rock, life, fire: speculative geophysics and the anthropocene', *Oxford Literary Review*, 34 (2): 259–276.

Collier, P. and Hoeffler, A., (2000), 'Greed and grievance in civil war', World Bank Policy Research Working Paper.

Cooper, M., (2006), 'Pre-empting emergence: the biological turn in the war on terror', *Theory, Culture and Society*, 23 (4): 113–135.

Crapanzano, V., (2004), *Imaginative Horizons: An Essay in Literary-Philosophical Anthropology*, Chicago: University of Chicago Press.

Ferguson, J., (1990), *The Anti-Politics Machine: 'Development', Depoliticization, and Bureaucratic Power in Lesotho*, Cambridge: Cambridge University Press.

Ferry, E. E. and Limbert, M. E., (2008), 'Introduction', in E. E. Ferry and M. E. Limbert (eds), *Timely Assets: The Politics of Resources and Their Temporalities*, 3–24, Santa Fe: School for Advanced Research Press.

Fortun, K. and Fortun, M., (1999), 'Due diligence and the pursuit of transparency: the Securities and Exchange Commission, 1996', in G. E. Marcus (ed.), *Paranoia within Reason: A Casebook on Conspiracy as Explanation*, 157–192, Chicago and London: University of Chicago Press.

Guyer, J., (2007), 'Prophecy and the near future: thoughts on macroeconomic, evangelical, and punctuated time', *American Ethnologist*, 34 (3): 409–421.

Haber, S. and Menaldo, V., (2010), 'Do natural resources fuel authoritarianism? A reappraisal of the resource curse', *American Political Science Review*, 105 (1): 1–24.

Hoffman, S. M. and Oliver-Smith, A., (1999), 'Anthropology and the angry earth: an overview', in A. Oliver-Smith and S. M. Hoffman (eds), *The Angry Earth: Disaster in Anthropological Perspective*, 1–16, New York and London: Routledge.

Humphreys, M., Sachs, J. D. and Stiglitz, J. (eds), (2007a), *Escaping the Resource Curse*, New York: Columbia University Press.

Humphreys, M., Sachs, J. D. and Stiglitz, J. E., (2007b), 'Future directions for the management of natural resources', in M. Humphreys, J. D. Sachs and J. E. Stiglitz (eds), *Escaping the Resource Curse*, 322–336, New York: Columbia University Press.

International Alert, Publish What You Pay, and UNDP, (2007), 'National discussion on oil revenue management in São Tomé and Príncipe, and regional coordination meeting of civil society from Portuguese-speaking countries in Africa', unpublished report, São Tomé.

Karl, T. L., (1997), *The Paradox of Plenty: Oil Booms and Petro States*, Berkeley, CA: University of California Press.

Klein, N., (2007), *The Shock Doctrine*, New York: Penguin Books.

Labban, M., (2008), *Space, Oil and Capital*, London: Routledge.

Lakoff, A., (2008), 'The generic biothreat, or, how we became unprepared', *Cultural Anthropology*, 23 (3): 399–423.

Lakoff, A., (2010), 'Introduction', in A. Lakoff (ed.), *Disaster and the Politics of Intervention*, 1–13, New York: Columbia University Press.

Latour, B., (2004), 'Why has critique run out of steam? From matters of fact to matters of concern', *Critiqual Inquiry*, 30: 225–248.

Liebenthal, A., Michelitsch, R. and Tarazona, E., (2005), 'Extractive industries and sustainable development: an evaluation of World Bank group experience', Washington, DC: The International Bank for Reconstruction and Development / World Bank.

Mair, J., Kelly, A. H. and High, C., (2012), 'Introduction: making ignorance an ethnographic object', in C. High, A. H. Kelly and J. Mair (eds), *The Anthropology of Ignorance: An Ethnographic Approach*, 1–32, New York: Palgrave Macmillan.

Massey, S. and May, R., (2005), 'Dallas to Doba: oil and Chad, external controls and internal politics', *Journal of Contemporary African Studies*, 23 (2): 253–276.

McGuire, T. and Austin, D., (2013), 'Beyond the horizon: oil and gas along the Gulf of Mexico', in S. Strauss, S. Rupp and T. Love (eds), *Culture of Energy: Power, Practices, Technologies*, 298–311, Walnut Creek, CA: Left Coast Press.

Mitchell, T., (2009), 'Carbon democracy', *Economy and Society*, 38 (3): 399–432.

Oliver-Smith, A. and Hoffman, S. M., (2002), 'Introduction: why anthropologists should study disasters', in S. M. Hoffman and A. Oliver-Smith (eds), *Catastrophe and Culture: The Anthropology of Disaster*, 3–22, Santa Fe: School of American Research Press.

Pegg, S., (2005), 'Can policy intervention beat the resource curse? Evidence from the Chad-Cameroon pipeline project', *African Affairs*, 105 (418): 1–25.

Quarantelli, E. L. (ed.), (1998), *What Is a Disaster? Perspectives on the Question*, London and New York: Routledge.

Ross, M. L., (2012), *The Oil Curse: How Petroleum Wealth Shapes the Development of Nations*, Princeton, NJ: Princeton University Press.

The Sociological Review, 62:S1, pp. 211–235 (2014), DOI: 10.1111/1467-954X.12130

Sachs, J. and Warner, A., (2001), 'The curse of natural resources', *European Economic Review*, 45: 827–838.

Samimiam-Darash, L., (2013), 'Governing future potential biothreats: toward an anthropology of uncertainty', *Current Anthropology*, 54 (1): 1–22.

Sanders, T. and West, H. G., (2003), 'Power revealed and concealed in the New World order', in H. G. West and T. Sanders (eds), *Transparency and Conspiracy: Ethnographies of Suspicion in the New World Order*, 1–37, Durham, NC: Duke University Press.

Sarat, A. and Lezaun, J., (2009), 'Introduction: the challenge of crisis and catastrophe in law and politics', in A. Sarat and J. Lezaun (eds), *Catastrophe: Law, Politics, and the Humanitarian Impulse*, Amherst and Boston: University of Massachusetts Press.

Seibert, G., (2006), *Comrades, Clients and Cousins: Colonialism, Socialism and Democratization in São Tomé e Príncipe*, Leiden and Boston: Brill.

Seibert, G., (2008), 'São Tomé and Príncipe: the troubles of oil in an aid-dependent micro-state', in K. Omeje (ed.), *Extractive Economies and Conflicts in the Global South: Multi-Regional Perspectives on Rentier Politics*, 119–134, Aldershot: Ashgate.

Shaxson, N., (2007), *Poisoned Wells: The Dirty Politics of African Oil*, New York and Basingstoke: Palgrave Macmillan.

Simmons, P., (2003), 'Performing safety in faulty environments', *The Sociological Review*, 51 (s2): 78–93.

Sims, B., (2007), 'Things fall apart: disaster, infrastructure, and risk', *Social Studies of Science*, 37 (1): 93–95.

Soares de Oliveira, R., (2007), *Oil and Politics in the Gulf of Guinea*, London: Hurst & Co.

Stallings, R. A., (1998), 'Disaster and the theory of social order', in E. L. Quarantelli (ed.), *What Is a Disaster? Perspectives on the Question*, 237–274, London and New York: Routledge.

Walsh, A., (2004), 'In the wake of things: speculating in and about sapphires in northern Madagascar', *American Anthropologist*, 106 (2): 225–237.

Watts, M., (2004), 'Resource curse? Governmentality, oil and power in the Niger Delta, Nigeria', *Geopolitics*, 9 (1): 50–80.

Weszkalnys, G., (2011), 'Cursed resources, or articulations of economic theory in the Gulf of Guinea', *Economy and Society*, 40 (3): 345–372.

Weszkalnys, G., (2013), 'Oil's magic: contestation and materiality', in S. Strauss, S. Rupp and T. Love (eds), *Cultures of Energy: Anthropological Perspectives on Powering the Planet*, Walnut Creek, CA: Left Coast Press.

Williams, D., (2008), *The World Bank and Social Transformation in International Politics*, London and New York: Routledge.

Afterword: on the topologies and temporalities of disaster

Mike Michael

Introduction

In Tracy Moffat's 2007 video montage 'Doomed', we are presented with a sequence of clips of disaster drawn from the movies. The earth cracks open, fire incinerates, waves overwhelm, and the wild wind lashes. And people are consumed by flame, swallowed up by the earth, crushed under debris, washed away by the ocean, and plucked toward the eye of the storm. As part of a series of works that include 'Revolution' (2008) and 'Other' (2009), Moffat and Gary Hillberg, her editor collaborator, bring together and ironically juxtapose a range of scenes from particular genres such as the disaster film. Thus terror registers in a victim's face, but it is at the impending calamity in a scene taken from a different film. One after another, people stumble, scrabble and fall into the rent earth, and though the pounding soundtrack suggests that all this mayhem is part of the same event, the differences in clothes, buildings, film stock, even the body techniques of dramatic dying, indicate that these victims come from different eras and belong to separate tragedies. Yet, the point of the artwork is, of course, that they also don't: at the same time, for all this difference, these disasters belong to the same cinematic tradition, and inhabit the same apocalyptic aesthetic conventions.

Can we apply a similar sensibility to the variety of disasters and complexity of analytic treatment evidenced in this volume, and in the social scientific literature on disasters more generally? Is it feasible to derive commonalities across the disparate analyses of divergent disasters? In this Afterword, I will focus on one such possible conventionalized framing, namely the apparent analytic structuring of disaster around a particular version of temporality. However, I will also look to these analyses for clues of an alternative model. If, at one level, reading within and across the articles, one can trace a shared linear temporality in operation, it is also possible to detect topological elements in these accounts. The aim of the Afterword is thus to attempt to push this topological dimension – to ask what analytic advantages emerge with a topological analysis and what are the politics that might become available?

The Sociological Review, 62:S1, pp. 236–245 (2014), DOI: 10.1111/1467-954X.12131

Linearities

In brief, and in contrast both to the organization of the articles in this book, and to Michael Guggenheim's excellent Introduction, one could have structured the collection in terms of points on a timeline – a before, a during and an after the disaster. In some ways, this should come as no surprise given the continued predominance of clock time, and the common idea of disasters as a punctuation in the flow of normality. On this latter score, Easthope and Mort (this volume) provide an example of this linear temporal motif in the official narratives of disaster which are structured around a beginning, a middle and an end. We also find this linearity in the early sociological work on disasters. For instance, Prince (1920) periodizes disasters into three segments: the preparatory or preliminary phase, the actual occurrence of the catastrophe, and a period of reorganization and readjustment. This is developed in subsequent work. Thus Carr (1932) advances a typology which classifies disasters according to the combination of the disaster's temporal form (whether it is instantaneous or progressive) and its aftermath (whether it results in social disarray, or leaves social organization by and large intact). And Moore's (1956) refinements point to consecutive periods of disbelief, bewilderment, and an inability to acknowledge the reality of the disaster, followed by a rescue period marked by confusion, then a descent into fatigue, aggression and disillusion as the enormity of the disaster becomes apparent, before a period in which the community pulls together to reorganize and rehabilitate.

We can also detect this linear temporality informing even the more sophisticated contemporary treatments of disasters: thus in Anderson's (2010) very useful analysis of anticipatory action and future geographies, there is a reworking of present normality as a time of precaution, pre-emption and preparedness. These anticipatory actions are oriented toward futures that are demarcated, respectively, as named possible future, potential 'high impact, low probability' future, and generic 'as if' future (2010: 792).

In any case, in this present collection, some articles deal primarily with the 'before' of a possible disaster, some with the 'during' of a disaster, and some with the 'after' of a disaster.

In the 'before the disaster' category, we might place: Gisa Weszkalnys' insightful article on the ironies of developing an anticipatory politics around the potential costs and benefits of oil for São Tomé and Príncipe – ironies that include involutions of transparency and suspicion; Joe Deville, Michael Guggenheim and Zuzana Hrdličková's comparative analysis of concrete shelters as 'materialized forms of preparedness' toward future disasters (such as cyclones or nuclear assault) that reflected and mediated the distinctive and emerging relationships between states and their publics; and, at an altogether grander scale, Nigel Clark's provocative meditation on the implications of the Anthropocene for a future geo-politics of disaster that entails 'a complex entanglement – of both cultural political and material negotiations' (one might even say, that here is a sort of cosmopolitics under the sign of panic – Stengers, 2005a).

Under the rubric of 'during the disaster', we might gather: Rodríguez-Giralt and Tirado's nuanced account of the ways in which birds came to be both 'objects' and 'things' in relation to the 1998 toxic spill disaster at Doñana (minimally victims and vectors), in the process differentially affecting the politics of dealing with the disaster; Ignacio Farías's subtle study of the systemic failure to identify and provide appropriate warnings about 2010 tsunamis in Chile – a failure that, grounded in an ethos of certainty and a logic of sacrifice, reflects the marginalization of the moral recognition of the uncertainty and liveliness of nature; and Katrina Petersen's investigations into the complex role of contrasting mapping systems – official maps that are oriented toward imminent action in the field on the basis of experience and knowledge that reflect institutional divisions and unofficial maps that are concerned with the immediacy of representation that draws in hybrid information from multiple sources – in the 2007 wildfire disasters in San Diego.

Finally, the following articles relate to the 'after the disaster' period: Manuel Tironi carefully excavates how the responses to the 2010 Chilean earthquake entailed two contrasting versions in the city of Talca allied with particular forms of political subjectivization in which local residents were either enacted as seeking direction from experts or, in contrast, as engaged citizens impatient to participate in the process of rebuilding; Ryan Ellis charts the selective reconfiguration of the US postal network after the 2001 anthrax attacks, showing how the newly installed biosecurity measures favoured the economic interests of large-volume mailers and postal management's efforts to casualize labour; and Lucy Easthope and Maggie Mort focus on what they call 'the technologies of recovery' after the devastating 2007 floods in South Yorkshire in the UK, demonstrating the ways in which the official narrative and narrativization of the floods could both disempower residents but also be appropriated and put locally to use by those same residents.

To be sure, summarizing and reordering these articles barely does justice to the empirical richness and conceptual sophistication that marks each of them. Nevertheless, in arranging the articles in this way, we can at least acknowledge how they can be arrayed along a linear timeline. Moreover, we begin to see how the articles in themselves organize their subject matter and their analysis around the occasion of a disaster, whether actualized or virtual.

And yet, these accounts are also doing something much more. They are tying up futures, pasts and presents in complex knots – a disaster is, in Haraway's all too apt phrase, a 'black hole' in which 'the mythic, textual, political, organic and economic dimensions implode. That is, they collapse into each other in a knot of extraordinary density that constitutes the objects themselves' (1994: 63). Here, past, present and future compact in dense 'involutions'. Current plans for future disasters draw on past examples and plans. Practices for dealing with ongoing disasters are shaped by, on the one hand, the past tools and skills inherited by professions and, on the other, imperatives to identify, and prepare for, emerging

The Sociological Review, 62:S1, pp. 236–245 (2014), DOI: 10.1111/1467-954X.12131

impacts. Attempts to respond to disasters after the event are rooted in pre-existing interests and prior models of political subjectivity and practical competence which point to particular organizational and social futures.

Time and topology

It has long been argued that our contemporary linear models of temporality are historically situated, superseding, in some measure, older models such as time as cyclical or pre-destined. Authors such as Macnaghten and Urry (1998) and Adam (1998) amongst others have shown how linear temporality is grounded in such sociotechnical conditions as early modern industrialization, the emergence of clock-time, and the processes of individualization. However, this linearity is not simple. For instance, the future toward which we are moving seems to reside in the present, the future's motion toward us has accelerated. According to Nowotny (1994: 52) we now inhabit an 'extended present' typified by 'the mounting pressure that solutions to impending, recognizable problems have to be found now'. Is it we who move more or less proactively toward the future, or are we passively drawn toward the future (Kern, 2003)? Do we seek in the future the right time – the 'kairos' – to act (Brown, 2000) or do we 'make' the right time (Michael, 2006). And in any case who is this 'we' that is transported from present to future – is it the individual, the group, society, the planet and how is it being heterogeneously constructed (Michael, 2000)? It is not difficult to find echoes of these questions in the articles above.

Notice however that, ironically, this temporal linearity seems to apply to its own emergence: in the past there was cyclical time in which diurnal and seasonal rhythms shaped our sense of time passing; by contrast, in the present, partly shaped by technoscience, we have linear time (in its various guises). According to the philosopher Michel Serres, this linear version of time, while it has its uses, is analytically limiting. He says:

> [Time] is not laminar (flowing smoothly). The usual theory supposes time to be always and everywhere laminar. With geometrically rigid and measurable distances – at least constant . . . . No, time flows in a turbulent and chaotic manner; it percolates . . . this time can be schematized by a kind of crumpling, a multiple, foldable diversity. (Serres and Latour, 1995: 59)

He continues:

> If you take a handkerchief and spread it out in order to iron it, you can see certain fixed distances and proximities. If you sketch a circle in one area, you can mark out nearby points and far-off distances. Then take the same handkerchief and crumple it by putting it in your pocket. Two distant points suddenly are close, even superimposed. If, further, you tear it in certain places, two points that were close can become very distant. The science of nearness and rifts is called topology, and the science of stable and well-defined distances is called metrical geometry . . . Admittedly, we need the latter for measurements, but why extrapolate from it a general theory of time.

People usually confuse time and the measurement of time which is a metrical reading on a straight line. (1995: 60)

So, we have a model of time characterized topologically by a 'foldable diversity'. Recently, topology has been making inroads into the social sciences (eg DeLanda, 2002; Mol and Law, 1994; Lash and Lury, 2007; Lury *et al.*, 2012), and though some circumspection is warranted (eg Marres, 2012; Michael and Rosengarten, 2012), it can nevertheless help to shed light on the complexities of sociomaterial process in general, and on how we trace the temporalities of disasters in particular. Of especial relevance is the topology that space and time do not comprise external dimensions. Accordingly, the temporal foldable diversity of a disaster is not located within (and should not be assessed against), parameters that lie outside of its eventuation. Rather what is to count as (the measure of) temporality can be regarded as emergent from *within* the event of a disaster (for a different topological perspective on disaster – specifically on spatialization and zoonoses – see Hinchliffe *et al.*, in press).

We have already been witness to this local emergence of external parameters in many of the present articles. While not directly addressed to temporality, there has been a concern with external parameters as embodied in 'proper procedures' such as those entailed in the 'professionally accredited' assessment of risk or mapping of threat, or the 'politically appropriate' process of engaging with publics to rebuild after a disaster, or in 'technically correct' institution of measures of preparedness. Again and again we have seen how these external criteria of 'good conduct' are compromised, challenged, reworked and rearticulated in the process of their local implementation (see Bowker and Star, 1999). We shall return to this process of emergence below, when we consider the complexities of these external parameters as they enter into but, additionally, disparately affect the concrete unfolding of disaster events.

Crucially, this process of emergence also reflects the indeterminacy at play in the specific eventuation of temporality. The ways in which pasts, presents and futures combine within the event of a disaster, or rather, the ways in which entities and occasions, discourses and practices, humans and non-humans, in Whitehead's (1929) terms, 'concresce' can be treated as open, immanent. As, to some extent, we have already seen across the contributions to the present volume, the seemingly disparate, divergent and distanciated elements of a disaster intra-relate with (Barad, 2007), and become-with (Fraser, 2010), one another. In the process, what a public is, what a measure of risk is, what expertise is, what the mapping of an emerging threat is, what a mitigating intervention is (along with myriad other elements of a disaster) mutually shift and change in intra-relation to one another. The result is that what the 'event of disaster is' – its 'meaning' (in the heterogeneous sense of practical and material as well semiotic order-making – see Akrich and Latour, 1992) – also transforms. The challenge now is to find a way of tracing how in this process of co-becoming and shifting 'meanings', new temporalities are eventuated and the sorts of politics to which these point.

The Sociological Review, 62:S1, pp. 236–245 (2014), DOI: 10.1111/1467-954X.12131

Disaster, event and abstraction

In essence, the point I want to make is that what a disaster 'is' – and the temporalities that are associated with it – emerges in the concreteness of the particular disastrous event. For Whitehead (1929), any event (or actual occasion) is heterogeneously composed (concresced) of various social and material elements (prehensions). Thus, an event is marked by its concrete specificity. As such, an event of disaster does not exist in the abstract. There is no abstracted disaster that sits on an abstracted linear timeline. The timelines of past-present-future (for instance, in the form of preparation-disaster-recovery) are actively abstracted in the particular by this institutional body or that. Nevertheless, disasters are indeed abstracted – there are institutions, plans and infrastructures that, as several articles here show, share assumptions and are designed to apply across disasters. Disasters are thus situated within existing frames of reference or in relation to generic 'abstractions' (what above were called external parameters).

We can approach the conjoint specificity and generality of abstraction through Whitehead's notion of 'eternal objects' (for an extended discussion see Halewood and Michael, 2008). Whitehead uses this term in order to express the fact that objects and events have a potentiality, but that this potentiality is limited. Further, this is not exhausted insofar as other objects and events can partake of it. In this way, Whitehead accesses both the potentiality present in the concrete specificity of a particular object or event, and the way that such a potentiality is actualized across numerous objects and events. Thus a black cab can actualize the particular potentiality of blackness (Whitehead uses colour as an example of the eternal object) but blackness can also enter into the actualization of other sorts of vehicles, or objects.

In part, in order to avoid the connotation of universality that can attach to the notion of 'eternal object', here I use the term 'abstraction' (see Michael and Rosengarten, 2013). More crucially, the application of Whitehead is itself an event that entails a becoming-with in which we might need to rethink our conceptual and methodological approaches, to engage with, as Stengers (2005b: 45) puts it, 'the very possibility of changing the problem'. 'Abstraction' is thus a heuristic term that allows us to explore this interplay of potentiality in its generality and specificity. The particular abstraction I focus on is the linear temporality mentioned above: this 'enters' into many disaster events but is eventuated in its concrete specificity in different ways across disasters.

These aspects of the role of abstraction in eventuation can be further disaggregated. First, an abstraction can serve as a state toward which a class of events is inclined. In other words, an abstraction can be regarded as an attractor – a sociomaterial 'aspiration' or potential – toward which an event of a particular sort is moving. However, secondly, such abstractions are also enacted in their specificity within an event. An abstraction is thus a practical component in the concrete emergence of that event. Not least, the event can be enunciated –

accounted for – along the lines of that abstraction and such enunciation will affect what the event can be. Thirdly, within an event's complex specificity, an abstraction is, additionally, itself in the process of emerging. That is to say, an abstraction 'becomes' in relation to the particular contingencies that characterize a given event. Fourthly, an abstraction can also be understood as an 'anti-attractor' – ironically, it can serve as a lure for other abstractions that re-orient the unfolding that is typical of a class events. In summary, an abstraction at once (i) specifies what a class of events can move toward, what they can be, (ii) is a reproducible component within a specific event, (iii) emerges and becomes through the specific event, and (iv) engenders other abstractions that differ from, or counter, it and opens up other possibilities of becoming for that class of events.

We see echoes of this heuristic schema in the analytic sensibilities of the articles of this book. Let us briefly consider three examples. First, in Deville *et al.*'s piece, the abstracted, standardized design of (and the accompanying regulations for) shelters in Switzerland at once 'attracts' the meaning (see above) of those shelters, 'anti-attracts' other 'meanings' (such as the 'end of the cold war'), is realized in the concrete and local process of partially practically maintaining those shelters, and is rearticulated in the locally contingent ways by which the functions of shelters are reconfigured (eg as storage space). Second, in Petersen's essay, the county wildfire map is at once the abstracted 'ideal' that applies to any wildfire disaster, is reasserted as such in the local accounting of its implementation, is compromised in its concrete enactment, for instance, through the use of informal channels, and anti-attracts an alternative Google-based map that serves linked but tangential ends and that likewise can be applied to any wildfire event. Finally, in Easthope and Mort's article, the technologies of recovery constitute an abstraction that simultaneously generically characterizes the events of a disaster and the process of recovery. These technologies are instantiated in locally implemented procedures (such as those of a limited 'consultation') that contribute to 'recovery'. They are also reconfigured through a local practical transformation of protocols, and they serve as an anti-attractor, perhaps something like a collaborative 'communitas' that encompasses local people, whether they be residents or responders, and that begins to redefine 'recovery'.

This schema – tentative as it is – can also be applied to the ways in which temporality is eventuated. Abstractions that entail procedural standardization typically will also entail a particular sort of temporality. We have seen this already in Easthope and Mort's analysis of technologies of recovery. Another illustration can be found in Farías's case study of the misrecognition of the 2010 Chilean tsunami. The abstraction here entails the procedures by which tsunamis would be identified – procedures marked by smooth linear temporality with a prescribed tempo of informational movement from the local to the global (and which might include sacrifice for the sake of subsequent escape). Even after the tragedy, though still within the event of the disaster, this temporal abstraction was practically reasserted, for instance, when the Minister of National Defence blamed human errors, rather than the systemic fractures that Farías identifies.

However, through Farías's account we glimpse how this abstraction was practically reconfigured during the disaster: instead of a smooth linear temporality, practical time was at once compressed and distended, marked by turbulence and chaos, as information moved swiftly but meaning decelerated once data was caught up in eddies of certainty and ossified decision-making. The anti-attractor to this smooth procedural temporality is Farías's own brilliant advocacy of a cosmopolitical openness that is allied to an ethos of uncertainty. Accordingly (at least along the lines of the present formulation), to be cosmopolitically sensitive to the heterogeneity and complexity entailed in decision-making is also to be practically attuned to the turbulent and chaotic flows of time. At certain moments, action needs to slow down, at others acceleration is required; sometimes past and future (eg data and intervention) seem very distant, at other points, they are all too close.

Concluding remarks

Farías's use of Isabelle Stengers' (2005a) notion of cosmopolitics usefully points the way to further unpacking what it is that the four-fold schema of the event presented here affords. In Stengers' article 'Introductory notes on an ecology of practices' she hints at a certain dissatisfaction with how the notion of cosmopolitics has been appropriated (2005c: 192). 'Ecology of practices' does similar work insofar as it tries to address the construction of 'new practical identities for practices, that is, new possibilities for them to be present, or in other words to connect. It thus does not approach practices as they are . . . but as they may become' (2005c: 186). So in engaging with an event, we need to be attuned to the ways in which different practices emerge. At the same time, Stengers is fully aware that such practices also reflect belonging and attachment – of professionals to their protocols, their skills, their experience, the objects and events with which they are charged and to which they are obligated. This does not simply make such practices inertial, but also allows for certain lines of becoming. The idea of an abstraction as an attractor and anti-attractor is meant to address just these dynamics.

Further, read through the four-fold schema outlined here, the disaster becomes a topological event. Disaster is not seen in terms of the failures or limitations in the practices of a particular set of professionals – whether these practices concern anticipatory regulation, anticipatory design, risk assessment, and damage limitation, public engagement, biosecurity measures or recovery procedures. Such would entail a focus on, and critique of, the supposedly standard temporalities and smooth tempos embodied in these (more or less standardized) practices. Rather, the disaster event is topologically expanded to connect together professional and expert practices and those of various others not least publics of one sort or another (with their own abstractions, ie attachments to different objects and events, skills and experience). An ecology of practices thus topologically encompasses county maps *and* Google maps, birds as local *and* migratory, top-down *and* bottom-up political forms. Along the way, temporality can become turbulent and chaotic, as well as smooth and laminar as different futures (eg new procedures, potential disasters) and pasts (eg prior experience, standard models) are rendered both more proximal and more distal. One upshot is, of course, that the practices of the various actors involved themselves can change through this process: indeed, the 'meaning' of a disaster event – what orderings it can yield – can be transformed.

It is well known that one of the mantras – indeed abstractions – of cosmopolitics is that there is an urgent need to slow down the process of 'reaching a decision'. Accordingly, we should be wary of considering 'ourselves authorized to believe we possess the meaning of what we know' (Stengers, 2005a: 995). Put another way, and to paraphrase Latour (1993), it is important to decelerate the production of yet more potentially unruly 'hybrids'. By contrast, the present article provides a glimpse of how temporalities other than (the abstraction of) 'slowing down' might topologically emerge. To be sure such temporalities can be turbulent and chaotic, but within an event of disaster, potentially at least, they can be productively creative. The implication – and this is no bad thing in the heat of a disaster – is that there can also be acceleration in the processes of asking more inventive questions, of finding better meanings, and of enabling finer responses.

References

Adam, B., (1998), *Timescapes of Modernity*, London: Routledge.

Akrich, M. and Latour, B., (1992), 'A summary of a convenient vocabulary for the semiotics of human and nonhuman assemblies', in W. E. Bijker and J. Law (eds), *Shaping Technology/Building Society*, Cambridge, MA: MIT Press.

Anderson, B., (2010), 'Preemption, precaution, preparedness: anticipatory action and future geographies', *Progress in Human Geography*, 34: 777–798.

Barad, K., (2007), *Meeting the Universe Halfway: Quantum Physics and the Entanglement of Matter and Meaning*, Durham, NC: Duke University Press.

Bowker, G. C. and Star, S. L., (1999), *Sorting Things Out: Classification and its Consequences*, Cambridge, MA: MIT Press.

Brown, N., (2000), 'The breakthrough motif', in N. Brown, B. Rappert and A. Webster (eds), *Contested Futures*, Aldershot: Ashgate.

Carr, L. J., (1932), 'Disaster and the sequence-pattern concept of social change', *The American Journal of Sociology*, 38: 207–218.

DeLanda, M., (2002), *Intensive Science and Virtual Philosophy*, London: Continuum.

Fraser, M., (2010), 'Facts, ethics and event', in C. Bruun Jensen and K. Rödje (eds), *Deleuzian Intersections in Science, Technology and Anthropology*, 57–82, New York: Berghahn Press.

Halewood, M. and Michael, M., (2008), 'Being a sociologist and becoming a Whiteheadian: concrescing methodological tactics theory', *Culture and Society*, 25 (4): 31–56.

Haraway, D., (1994), 'A game of cat's cradle: science studies, feminist theory, cultural studies', *Configurations*, 2: 59–71.

Hinchliffe, S. J., Allen, J. R., Lavau, S., Bingham, N., Carter, S., (in press), 'Biosecurity and the topologies of infected life: from borderlines to borderlands', *Transactions of the Institute of British Geographers*.

Kern, S., (2003), *The Culture of Time and Space, 1880–1918*, Cambridge, MA: Harvard University Press.

The Sociological Review, 62:S1, pp. 236–245 (2014), DOI: 10.1111/1467-954X.12131

Lash, S. and Lury, C., (2007), *Global Culture Industry: The Mediation of Things*, Cambridge: Polity Press.

Latour, B., (1993), *We Have Never Been Modern*, Hemel Hempstead: Harvester Wheatsheaf.

Lury, C., Parisi, L. and Terranova, T., (2012), 'Introduction: the becoming topological of culture', *Theory, Culture and Society*, 29: 3–35.

Macnaghten, P. and Urry, J., (1998), *Contested Nature*, London: Sage.

Marres, N., (2012), 'On some uses and abuses of topology in the social analysis of technology (or the problem with smart meters)', *Theory, Culture and Society*, 29: 288–310.

Michael, M., (2000), 'Futures of the present: from performativity to prehension', in N. Brown, B. Rappert and A. Webster (eds), *Contested Futures*, 21–39, Aldershot: Ashgate.

Michael, M., (2006), *Technoscience and Everyday Life*, Maidenhead: Open University Press/ McGraw-Hill.

Michael, M. and Rosengarten, M., (2012), 'HIV, globalization and topology: of prepositions and propositions', *Theory, Culture and Society*, 29 (45): 93–115.

Michael, M. and Rosengarten, M., (2013), *Innovation and Biomedicine: Ethics, Evidence and Expectation in HIV*, Basingstoke: Palgrave.

Mol, A. and Law, J., (1994), 'Regions, networks and fluids: anaemia and social topology', *Social Studies of Science*, 24 (4): 641–671.

Moore, H., (1956), 'Toward a theory of disaster', *American Sociological Review*, 21: 733–737.

Nowotny, H., (1994), *Time: The Modern and Postmodern Experience*, Cambridge: Polity Press.

Prince, S., (1920), *Catastrophe and Social Change, Based upon a Sociological Study of the Halifax Disaster*, New York: Columbia University Press.

Serres, M. and Latour B., (1995), *Conversations on Science, Culture and Time*, Ann Arbor, MI: Michigan University Press.

Stengers, I., (2005a), 'The cosmopolitical proposal', in B. Latour and P. Webel (eds), *Making Things Public*, 994–1003, Cambridge, MA: MIT Press.

Stengers, I., (2005b), 'Whitehead's account of the sixth day', *Configurations*, 13: 35–55.

Stengers, I., (2005c), 'Introductory notes on an ecology of practices', *Cultural Studies Review*, 11: 183–196.

Whitehead, A. N., (1929), *Process and Reality: An Essay in Cosmology*, New York: The Free Press.

Notes on contributors

Nigel Clark is Chair in Social Sustainability at the Lancaster Environment Centre, Lancaster University. He is the author of *Inhuman Nature: Sociable Life on a Dynamic Planet* (Sage, 2011) and co-editor of *Material Geographies* (Sage, 2008), *Extending Hospitality* (Edinburgh University Press, 2009), and *Atlas: Geography, Architecture and Change in an Interdependent World* (Black Dog Publishing, 2012). He is currently working on an edited collection entitled *Capitalism and the Earth,* and exploring ideas about geologic politics, geo-social formations and speculative geophysics. e-mail: n.clark2@lancaster.ac.uk.

Joe Deville is a postdoctoral researcher at the Centre for the Study of Invention and Social Process at Goldsmiths, University of London. He works on the sociologies of disaster and economic life and is currently writing a book about consumer credit default and the debt collection industry. e-mail: j.deville@gold.ac.uk.

Lucy Easthope is a Senior Lecturer in Life Sciences at the University of Lincoln, UK and an experienced disaster responder. She is also an associate Teaching Fellow at the Centre for Death and Society, University of Bath, an associate course director at the Cabinet Office Emergency Planning College and a research affiliate at the Joint Centre for Disaster Research, Massey University, New Zealand. She teaches and supervises in disaster studies, forensic science, risk management and legal issues. She has published widely on issues relating to disaster management and is currently working on the application of science and technologies studies to the tools and technologies of Disaster Victim Identification. e-mail: LEasthope@lincoln.ac.uk.

Ryan Ellis is a postdoctoral fellow at the Harvard Kennedy School's Belfer Center for Science and International Affairs. Dr Ellis writes and researches on topics related to cybersecurity, infrastructure politics, homeland security, and communication law and policy. He holds a PhD in communication from the University of California, San Diego. e-mail: Ryan_Ellis@hks.harvard.edu.

Ignacio Farías is senior researcher at the research unit 'Cultural Sources of Newness' of WZB Berlin Social Science Center and associate researcher of ICSO

The Sociological Review, 62:S1, pp. 246–248 (2014), DOI: 10.1111/1467-954X.12133
Editorial organisation © 2014 The Editorial Board of the Sociological Review. Published by John Wiley & Sons Ltd, 9600 Garsington Road, Oxford OX4 2DQ, UK and 350 Main Street, Malden, MA 02148, USA

at Universidad Diego Portales in Chile. His main research involvements are in cultural sociology, urban studies and STS. He has published on mobilities and tourist practices, creative industries and studio processes, and urban disasters and reconstruction planning, as well as contributed to current urban theory discussions on assemblage thinking. His work has appeared in the *European Journal of Social Theory*, *CITY, Space and Culture*, and *Mobilities*. He co-edited with Thomas Bender *Urban Assemblages: How Actor-Network Theory Changes Urban Studies* (Routledge, 2009), as well as two volumes tracing heterodox receptions of Luhmann's social systems theory in Latin America. e-mail: farias@wzb.eu.

Michael Guggenheim is a senior lecturer at the Department of Sociology at Goldsmiths, University of London. He is currently directing a research project entitled 'Organising Disaster: Civil Protection and the Population' and has previously studied environmental experts and change of use of buildings. e-mail: m.guggenheim@gold.ac.uk.

Zuzana Hrdličková is a social anthropologist with interest in development, disaster, conflict and gender. She did research on the relationship between gender and war in her PhD ('The Impact of Sri Lankan Conflict on the Status of Sri Lankan Tamil Women', Charles University in Prague, 2009) and she worked in humanitarian organizations in post-disaster recovery and in conflict context. She is currently working on a post-doctoral research project 'Organizing Disaster: Civil Protection and Population'. e-mail: z.hrdlickova@gold.ac.uk.

Mike Michael is Professor of Sociology and Social Policy in the School of Social and Political Sciences, University of Sydney. His interests include the relation of everyday life to technoscience, biotechnological and biomedical innovation and culture, and process methodology. Current research projects include the inter-disciplinary exploration of energy consumption (with Bill Gaver and Jennifer Gabrys) and the role of digital media in epidemiological responses (with Deborah Lupton). Recent publications include *Innovation and Biomedicine: Ethics, Evidence and Expectation in HIV* (co-authored with Marsha Rosengarten, Palgrave, 2013) and *Accumulation: The Material Politics of Plastic* (co-edited with Jennifer Gabrys and Gay Hawkins, Routledge, 2013). e-mail: mike.michael@sydney.edu.au.

Maggie Mort is Reader in the Sociology of Science, Technology and Medicine at Lancaster University, UK. She recently coordinated the EC FP7 Science in Society project, Ethical Frameworks for Telecare Technologies for older people at home (EFORTT). She teaches and supervises in disaster studies, health policy and practice, patient safety and medical uncertainty. She has published widely on technological change in healthcare, most recently: 'Ageing with telecare: care or coercion in austerity?' (2013) in *Sociology of Health & Illness* and 'Calling for care, "disembodied" work, teleoperators and older people living at home' (with Celia Roberts), *Sociology*. e-mail: m.mort@lancaster.ac.uk.

Katrina Petersen is a PhD candidate at University of California, San Diego in the Communication Department and Science Studies Program. Her research explores how knowledge of the environment is bound to the material practices, from everyday interactions with physical landscapes to the introduction of new technological infrastructures, involved in visually representing it. e-mail: katrinkja@gmail.com.

Israel Rodríguez-Giralt is a Lecturer of Social Psychology at the Open University of Catalonia. His research aims at connecting the Study of Social Movements and Science and Technology Studies. He has contributed to rethink social movements as actor-networks as well as to the study of the material politics of public controversies and ecological crisis. His more recent research focuses on the practices of protest and public involvement of social care activists in an age of austerity. His work has appeared in several international journals and edited volumes. He was visiting research fellow at Goldsmiths College, Department of Sociology, from 2010 to 2012. e-mail: irra.rg@gmail.com.

Francisco Tirado Francisco Tirado holds a PhD in social psychology. He is a Senior Lecturer in the Social Psychology Department of the Universitat Autònoma de Barcelona and full member of the Group for Social Studies of Science and Technology (GESCIT). His main research interests are power relations in socio-technical contexts, biopolitics, technology and biomedicine and biosecurity. e-mail: franciscojavier.tirado@uab.es.

Manuel Tironi is Assistant Professor in the Instituto de Sociología at Pontificia Universidad Católica de Chile. He is also associate researcher at the National Research Center for Integrated Natural Disasters Management (CIGIDEN) and the Center for Urban Sustainability (CEDEUS), both in Santiago de Chile. He is currently a visiting research fellow at the Centre for the Study of Innovation and Social Process at Goldsmiths College, University of London, where he is investigating the articulation of political experiments in contexts of radical uncertainty. e-mail: metironi@uc.cl.

Gisa Weszkalnys is Assistant Professor in anthropology at the London School of Economics. She is author of *Berlin, Alexanderplatz: Transforming Place in a Unified Germany* (Berghahn, 2010) and co-editor of *Elusive Promises: Planning in the Contemporary World* (Berghahn, 2013). Her current research deals with speculation, potentiality and absence in the context of an emerging West African oil economy. e-mail: g.weszkalnys@lse.ac.uk.

The Sociological Review, 62:S1, pp. 246–248 (2014), DOI: 10.1111/1467-954X.12133
Editorial organisation © 2014 The Editorial Board of the Sociological Review

Index

The Sociological Review, 62:S1, pp. 249–252 (2014), DOI: 10.1111/1467-954X.12150
Editorial organisation © 2014 The Editorial Board of the Sociological Review

The Sociological Review, 62:S1, pp. 249–252 (2014), DOI: 10.1111/1467-954X.12150
Editorial organisation © 2014 The Editorial Board of the Sociological Review